CAMBI

SOPHOCLES

OEDIPUS REX

EDITED BY

R. D. DAWE

Fellow of Trinity College, Cambridge

CAMBRIDGE UNIVERSITY PRESS
Cambridge, New York, Melbourne, Madrid, Cape Town, Singapore, São Paulo,
Delhi, Mexico City

Cambridge University Press
The Edinburgh Building, Cambridge CB2 8RU, UK

Published in the United States of America by Cambridge University Press, New York

www.cambridge.org
Information on this title: www.cambridge.org/9780521617352

First edition published 1982
Reprinted 1992, 1995, 1997, 1999, 2000, 2002, 2003
Revised edition published 2006
7th printing 2013

Printed and bound in the United Kingdom by the MPG Books Group

A catalogue record for this publication is available from the British Library

ISBN 978-0-521-85177-0 Hardback
ISBN 978-0-521-61735-2 Paperback

CONTENTS

PREFACE

As this little by-product of more austere researches goes out into the world, it carries with it acknowledgements of three different kinds. There was the advice I received from the Editors of the series and from Miss Pauline Hire of the University Press. There were those trenchantly phrased and instantly convincing criticisms from Dr James Diggle, for which I shall hope to forgive him in time. Then there were the comments of my own pupils who used a draft of this commentary for some classes on *Oedipus Rex* given in my College in the Michaelmas Term 1980. That Eleanor Cranmer, Clive Galliver, Claire Lobel, Peter Singer and Jeremy Spencer (alphabetical order, τί μήν;) should be so tolerant of their supervisor's little ways that they continued coming week after week (well, almost) to something entirely voluntary is a tribute to the stamina of their characters. To them in particular, and to those like them everywhere, this book is dedicated.

Trinity College   **R. D. Dawe**
April 1982

PREFACE TO SECOND EDITION

The need for a second edition of this play was brought home to me when, under the stimulus of an article by C. W. Mueller (*Rheinisches Museum* 139 (1996) 193–224), I took a more intensive look at the closing scenes, which had for many years been, in certain quarters, under an ill-defined cloud of suspicion. It seemed to me that the suspicion was justified, but that there was a need for greater precision in deploying the arguments which had led some scholars in the past to scent interpolation, and a need too – a harder one to fill, this – to define more exactly what it was that had been interpolated, and what, if anything, had survived of the authentic ending. An editor cannot conscientiously send out a commentary purporting to be on Sophocles if he is convinced that some of his notes relate to an entirely different author. But once one has recognized that the end of the play is spurious, other doubts begin to assail one, and at a late stage I began to wonder whether the children of Oedipus, who figure prominently in the spurious portion, should be receiving any mention at all in the earlier, authentic part of the play. One cannot tamper with *prima facie* evidence in the interests of supporting an argument, and I have not marked all the relevant lines as spurious (261, 425, 1247–50, 1375–7); but I have felt justified in writing notes on those lines which should be enough to cause intelligent brows to furrow. Apart from those major considerations, there was a host of places where there was room for improvement, and I have taken the opportunity, perhaps not often enough, to do just that.

The massive book by Michael Lurje entitled *The search for guilt* (or *The quest for responsibility*): *Sophocles' Oedipus Rex, Aristotle's Poetics and the understanding of tragedy in recent times*[1] quotes from Dr Johnson: 'The chief desire of him that comments an authour, is to shew how much other commentators have corrupted and obscured him. The opinions prevalent in one age, as truths above the reach of controversy, are confuted and rejected in another, and rise again to reception in remoter time. Thus the human mind is kept in motion without progress.' Lurje's book, with its confirmatory evidence, makes salutary reading, and I commend it to the reader. The present edition strives to be an exception to the Johnsonian law, but if it fails, there is always the comfort that it is better to keep the human mind in motion than to let it ossify completely.

One mind that has been very much in motion is that of Mr Nicholas Lane, a London solicitor who volunteered to read the proofs. Mr Lane is plainly not the man to subscribe to his profession's insouciant motto, *de minimis non curat lex*, and for his corrections, which went well beyond *minima*, everyone who uses this book has cause to be grateful.

Finally I should like to express my regrets to the reader for the involuntary discourtesy of compelling him to keep moving from the text to that section of the book known to generations of schoolboys as 'the back'. I would much have preferred the format favoured by most earlier editions, with text and commentary on the same page. But the requirements of the series apparently rule out such dangerous regressions to convenience.

---

[1] *Die Suche nach der Schuld*. Beiträge zur Altertumskunde Band 209 (Leipzig 2004).

ABBREVIATIONS

Denniston, *GP*²	J. D. Denniston, *The Greek particles*, Oxford 1954
FGE	D. L. Page, *Further Greek epigrams*, Cambridge 1981
GAI	L. Threatte, *The grammar of Attic inscriptions*, Berlin and New York 1980
GVI	W. Peek, *Griechische Vers-Inschriften*, Berlin 1955
HE	A. S. F. Gow and D. L. Page, *Hellenistic epigrams*, Cambridge 1965
ITAS	S. L. Schein, *The iambic trimeter in Aeschylus and Sophocles*, Leiden 1979
K–G	Kühner's *Ausführliche Grammatik der griechischen Sprache*, 3rd ed. Part ii, rev. B. Gerth, Hannover and Leipzig 1898–1904
LSJ	*A Greek-English Lexicon* compiled by H. G. Liddell and R. Scott, new edition rev. by H. S. Jones, Oxford 1940 (with numerous corrected reprints since)
STE	J. Diggle, *Studies on the text of Euripides*, Oxford 1981
Studies	R. D. Dawe, *Studies on the text of Sophocles*, Leiden, i and ii 1973, iii 1978
VUS	J. Wackernagel, *Vorlesungen über Syntax*, Basel 1926

In citing fragments the following works are taken as standard: for comedy *Poetae Comici Graeci* (PCG), ed. R. Kassel et C. Austin, Berlin and New York 1983–.

For tragedy *Tragicorum Graecorum Fragmenta* (TrGF): adespota in vol. 2, ed. R. Kannicht and B. Snell, Göttingen 1981; Aeschylus in vol. 3, ed. S. Radt 1977; Sophocles in vol. 4, ed. S. Radt 1999²; Euripides in vols. 5.1 and 5.2, ed. R. Kannicht 2004.

INTRODUCTION*

1. THE CONTENT AND STRUCTURE OF THE PLAY

When Homer (*Od.* 11.271ff.), in a piece of undistinguished poetry, alludes to the Oedipus story, he does so in these words:

> I (sc. Odysseus in the underworld) saw the mother of Oedipus, the fair Epicaste, who committed an enormity (ἣ μέγα ἔργον ἔρεξεν) in ignorance, marrying her son. He married her after killing his father. But in time the gods made matters known to men. He ruled the Cadmean people in lovely Thebes in sorrow, through the dreadful will of the gods, and she went to strong-gated Hades, after stringing a high noose from the top of a room, gripped by her own misery, leaving behind for him many causes of pain, and all the things that the avenging spirits of a mother bring about.

Incest, parricide and suicide by hanging are the only themes that this, our earliest, account has in common with Sophocles' version of the story. In particular the bland statement that the gods made matters known to men contrasts in emphasis as sharply as possible with the Sophoclean version, in which it was Oedipus himself who made matters known (but see 1213); and the dismal continuation of Oedipus' rule in Thebes after the suicide of his wife/mother has no counterpart in our play. The facts of the tale in Homer are horrendous, but in its telling no religious or moral judgement is passed, and the poet, beyond a few perfunctory remarks about pain, seems no more excited over the wholly abnormal tale he is telling than if he were entering marriages and deaths in a parish register. The brief remarks about Oedipus who 'crashed to his tomb' (δεδουπότος Οἰδιπόδαο ἐς τάφον *Il.* 23.679f.) in the *Iliad* are even less illuminating.

The emotions of Aristotle (*Poet.* 1453b3–7) were more deeply stirred. 'A plot should be so constituted that even without seeing a performance the person who hears the events that take place shivers and feels pity at what happens – as anyone would do who heard the story of Oedipus.'

Clearly between the time of Homer and the time of Aristotle a huge change of feeling has taken place. What caused that change? In a word, Sophocles, who, in a play that won only the second prize (possibly because of the eccentricities of the voting system),** created a masterpiece that in the eyes of posterity has overshadowed every other achievement in the field of ancient drama. In it he played on certain latent terrors that are part of man's nature in all kinds of societies and at all epochs; terrors

---

* A helpful guide through the maze of literary criticism on this play is the article 'Oedipus and Jonah' by D. A. Hester, in *Proc. Camb. Phil. Soc.* n.s. 23 (1977) 32–61.

** See C. W. Marshall and S. van Willigenburg in *J. H. S.* 124 (2004) 90–107 for a detailed investigation of the voting procedures. The failure of Sophocles to win the first prize excited the indignation of the rhetor Aristides in the second century A.D., oration 46, 256, 11.

whose influence may pervade our lives in ways we scarcely guess; and if we are aware of them at all, it is because our eyes have been opened by Sigmund Freud, upon whom this play made such a profound impression. The following quotation comes from his *Introductory lectures on psycho-analysis* (transl. J. Riviere, ed. 2 (1929) 278).

The Attic poet's work portrays the gradual discovery of the deed of Oedipus, long since accomplished, and brings it slowly to light by skilfully prolonged enquiry, constantly fed by new evidence; it has thus a certain resemblance to the course of a psycho-analysis. In the dialogue the deluded mother-wife, Jocasta, resists the continuation of the enquiry; she points out that many people in their dreams have mated with their mothers, but that dreams are of no account. To us dreams are of much account, especially typical dreams which occur in many people; we have no doubt that the dream Jocasta speaks of is intimately related to the shocking and terrible story of the myth.

It is surprising that Sophocles' tragedy does not call forth indignant remonstrance in its audience . . . For at bottom it is an immoral play; it sets aside the individual's responsibility to social law, and displays divine forces ordaining the crime and rendering powerless the moral instincts of the human being which would guard him against the crime. It would be easy to believe that an accusation against destiny and the gods was intended in the story of the myth; in the hands of the critical Euripides, at variance with the gods, it would probably have become such an accusation. But with the reverent Sophocles there is no question of such an intention; the pious subtlety which declares it the highest morality to bow to the will of the gods, even when they ordain a crime, helps him out of the difficulty. I do not believe that this moral is one of the virtues of the drama, but neither does it detract from its effect; it leaves the hearer indifferent; he does not react to this, but to the secret meaning and content of the myth itself. He reacts as though by self-analysis he had detected the Oedipus complex in himself, and had recognized the will of the gods and the oracle as glorified disguises of his own unconscious; as though he remembered in himself the wish to do away with his father and in his place to wed his mother, and must abhor the thought. The poet's words seem to him to mean: 'In vain do you deny that you are accountable, in vain do you proclaim how you have striven against these evil designs. You are guilty, nevertheless; for you could not stifle them; they still survive unconsciously in you.' And psychological truth is contained in this; even though man has repressed his evil desires into his Unconscious and would then gladly say to himself that he is no longer answerable for them, he is yet compelled to feel his responsibility in the form of a sense of guilt for which he can discern no foundation.

Many critics would sweep aside most of what Freud has to say here. Yet there must be some reason why this play has exercised such a powerful and long-lasting fascination on the human mind. It is not as though its story had an immediate and obvious relevance to the lives of most of us. We do not expect to meet Sphinxes, kill fathers, marry mothers, blind ourselves, etc. We are entitled to argue that we have enough to do in establishing contact with Sophocles' conscious mind without embarking on the attempt to understand his unconscious, or the way in which he is toying with ours. We may justifiably dismiss with impatience the lurid fantasies of those who see sexual symbolism lurking in every line. On the other hand it would be carrying impatience too far to treat the branching road as a mere geographical detail, for the imagery is common enough, representing a point where a crucial decision has to be made (see 716n., Theognis 911–12, Pindar, *Pyth.* 11.38f., Hdt. 1.11 (δύο ὁδοί, with a queen and her realm as the prize), Plato, *Laws* 799c, etc.), and that the structure of the play itself offers more than adequate justification for its mention. *Oedipus Rex*, we may insist, is a play about the legendary Oedipus, King of Thebes, written by Sophocles, and adhering to the curiously rigid conventions of Greek tragedy. It is not Man's Quest for his own Identity. It has managed perfectly well for two millennia, we may conclude belligerently, without any help from Viennese psychiatrists. It is right and good that we should say these things. But one who pursues the pedestrian trade of an editor and commentator is not well placed to deny that a poet may have a private vision that looks far beyond the confines of the art that he has inherited.

The one part of Freud's remarks with which almost everyone agrees is precisely the part over which the present commentator feels most hesitation. Freud dismisses the idea that Sophocles could be accusing destiny and the gods, and he speaks of the 'reverent Sophocles' and his 'pious subtlety'. Now Antiquity has many tales to tell of the easy-going Sophocles. We are told how this paragon of piety kept a holy snake in his house. What more natural than to ascribe to such a person the orthodox outlook of a country parson with a taste for the good life? The contrast with the brooding Aeschylus, and the protesting Euripides, affords the literary critic a peculiar satisfaction. Sophocles, it appears, was a genial old soul, with a knack of writing timeless dramatic masterpieces.

But is conventional piety manifest in *Oedipus Rex*? The question is not one to be solved one way or the other by selectively accumulating quotations with which to bolster one's case. But there is one prime piece of evidence, which even if it comes from a later play, does at least come from the author himself, writing about the same hero. It cannot be left unheard (*Oed. Col.* 962ff.):

(The killing and the marriage and all my misfortunes) were things I had to endure, alas, against my will. It was the way the gods wanted it, angry perhaps with my family from times past. So far as I myself am concerned, you could not find any offence to reproach me with that led me to do these deeds against my self and my kin. Tell me this: if a divine oracle was given to my father, to the effect that he was to die at his son's hand, how can you properly make that into any fault of mine, seeing that my father had as yet done nothing to give me birth, nor my mother either? At the time I was *unborn*. And if later my ruin became manifest, as it did, and I fought with and killed my father, not knowing what it was that I was doing, and who I was doing it to – how can you reasonably blame me for this act, which was nothing that I intended?

Oedipus goes on to point out that marriage with Jocasta was again something done in total ignorance, on both sides, of the reality of the situation.

Now it is certainly true that a speech for the Defence, from Oedipus himself, and from a different play, need not constitute the total objective truth. Yet if we examine the myth as told in *Oedipus Rex* and measure it against the speech just quoted, we have to concede that every word uttered corresponds precisely with the facts. Even in Aristophanes (*Frogs* 1182–5) we find the same evaluation, with the identical repeated stress on 'before being born'. When, at 828 of our play, Oedipus asks if a man would not be entirely justified in passing the verdict of cruelty on the *daemon* who had visited him with such a fate, we may feel his rhetorical question can admit of only one answer. Outright condemnation of fate or the gods is not something to be expected of a playwright competing in a religious festival. But Sophocles' Chorus and characters are notably silent when it comes to any actual defence, or even explanation ('angry perhaps with my family from times past' – but *why*?) of the workings of fate or heaven. The horror and sympathy they express for the human victim must imply a compensatory, if unspoken, verdict against those forces that permit, or cause, such things to happen. The Olympians are as they are: their help against plagues must be implored, for who else of more than mortal power can help us? Of course it is important that oracles should come true, for if they do not, how are we to orient ourselves in our lives? Suppose we all lived, all the time, εἰκῆ, as Jocasta recommends at a moment of great stress, and as Oedipus sees himself when fate seems to be tightening her grip on him? Weak, and ultimately alone, men pursue their course from the cradle to the grave against an imperfectly understood background. The benefactors of whole cities suffer physical outrage as soon as they are born, and end as blind beggars. But what is this to a Bacchus, as he romps over mountains in pursuit of dark-eyed Nymphs (1105–9)? If this is conventional piety, what price conventional piety? If Sophocles is, as Wilamowitz (*Hermes* 34 (1899) 57) said, 'the most distinguished representative of the established religion of the Athenians', what are we to think of that religion?

And even if one were to imagine that a court composed of gods or men had acquitted Oedipus of all guilt, like Orestes in Aeschylus, it would still not help him in the least; for what meaning would such an acquittal have in the face of the contradiction between what he has imagined he is, and what he is? Nor would the opposite verdict of 'guilty' add anything to his state. Orestes *can* be acquitted, by himself and by others, but Oedipus *cannot* be released from what he has recognised as the truth about himself. The question of responsibility for what has happened, wherever it is raised and in whatever form, whether this responsibility lies with men, with gods or with the laws of nature, and whether the answer is yes or no – this question, without which the greatest tragedies of Euripides and Aeschylus are unthinkable, just does not arise in Sophocles. So there is no decision here about justice and atonement – nothing would be more misguided than to regard Oedipus' blinding as an atonement – or about freedom and necessity. What we have had to consider is illusion and truth as the opposing forces between which man is bound, in which he is entangled, and in whose shackles, as he strives towards the highest he can hope for, he is worn down and destroyed. (K. Reinhardt, *Sophocles,* Engl. transl. H. Harvey and D. Harvey (Oxford 1979) 134)

Reinhardt's verdict is eloquent and perceptive. But who forged those shackles? Freedom and Necessity. But, as we have seen, there is no Freedom, only Necessity. Why is it then that notwithstanding the underlying logic of the play, we are left at the end of it with emotions much more complex than those which would be engendered by the mere spectacle of a great hero being sandbagged by Fate, a story of oracles coming true? Why is it that we feel, as the play progresses, that we are watching a hero exercising free will to a degree not easily paralleled from any other Greek tragedy? To answer these questions we must keep separate in our minds what Sophocles has fused in his play: content, the data of the story, the most vital parts of which were determined at a time long before the play opens, and technique, the way the story is told before our eyes and ears from the opening of the play to its conclusion. We have already looked briefly at some aspects of content. It is now to technique that we turn, to learn how the play is actually put together in such a way that the illusion of free will is preserved against a certain background of necessity.

Artistically speaking structural analysis of *Oedipus Rex* is an act of vandalism; at least it is if after stripping it down we persuade ourselves that we have been victims of a confidence trick, that we have been wrong all these years to regard it as a masterpiece of construction, and that now, having penetrated into the poet's workshop, we know better. We must understand that what we are doing is, in effect, examining from a distance of a few centimetres the exact placing of paint on a canvas that enables an Impressionist to convey a ripple on the surface of water, or Rembrandt the glint of armour in a dim light. What we think we see as we look at the picture from an intended distance, and what is actually there when we get very close, may differ in ways that catch us totally by surprise. If the art of Sophocles turns out, on close inspection, to have more in common with the painter than with the watchmaker, that is no good reason to depreciate the quality of his skill.

Sophocles has severe technical problems to surmount. In the person of Oedipus there intersect two separate themes. He is the killer of the previous king of Thebes. He is also the man who has committed parricide and incest. When Aeschylus wrote his play about Eteocles, the son of Oedipus, he was also faced with a dual theme: for Eteocles was the captain of a beleaguered city, assailed by an army as Oedipus' city is assailed by a plague; and he was secondly the son of a family under a curse which finds fulfilment just as the oracles find fulfilment with Oedipus. Aeschylus' method of solving the problem was, not to put too fine a point on it, to treat the first theme up to 653, and then concentrate on the other. Sophocles is much more skilful, but there is still a limit to what he can do. The conventions of the medium in which he works will not allow him to use more than three actors, and there is much else in the way of inherited convention which restricts his movements. He has therefore to exploit to the utmost a technique which he has developed over the years, a technique which at times defies the laws of natural logic or probability, and the laws of dramaturgy also – the latter a particularly venial offence, for Aristotle has not yet invented them. The principal casualties will be consistency of plot and consistency of character. But consistency is the virtue of tiny minds.

First impressions are of the highest importance. Aristotle (*Politics* 1336b 28ff.) tells us of an actor Theodorus* who would not allow even minor characters to appear on stage before him, since in this way he could best enlist the audience's sympathies. Sophocles seems to agree, for at the very beginning of his play he establishes in a handful of lines the leading characteristics of his hero. They are characteristics which an Athenian audience of the fifth century B.C. would admire as an embodiment of all that they believed was best in their own corporate life.

An aged priest describes to Oedipus the plight of the city in a speech of some 44 lines. At the end of it the audience in the theatre of Dionysus are much better informed. As for Oedipus himself, he hardly needed to be told. 'Known to me and not unknown' he replies in measured tones, 'are your motives in coming.' He has already taken steps to meet the menace, by sending Creon to ask the advice of the Delphic oracle. The happy coincidence, to which the priest himself draws attention (78), whereby Creon arrives dead on cue, is again perfectly legitimate stagecraft, a kind of dramatic shorthand for events which would in real life hardly work out so neatly. Just as Sophocles anticipated our unvoiced objection that it was unlikely that Oedipus would know nothing of the plague – particularly as he is supposed to be suffering from it himself, if we take 60 at its face value – by using the words 'known to me and not unknown', so here the arrival of Creon is prepared by having Oedipus say that he is surprised he is not here already. We are disarmed by the transparent honesty with which Sophocles avails himself of accepted stage convention to overcome certain improbabilities. If we were not so disarmed, we might fret over the sequence of improbabilities that follows. To put the audience in full possession of the facts Sophocles makes Creon tell Oedipus a number of things which Oedipus must have known already. 'We had a king once called Laius' says Creon (103). 'I've heard of him. Never actually saw him of course' replies Oedipus. Dramatic irony certainly, but at a price. When Aristotle (*Poet.* 1460a30; cf. 1454b7) writes that a play should for preference contain nothing improbable, but that if it does, the improbability should lie outside the tale, not in the play itself, and gives as an example ὥσπερ Οἰδίπους τὸ μὴ εἰδέναι πῶς ὁ Λάϊος ἀπέθανεν, we have to reply to him that though the death of Laius may not be ἐν τῶι δράματι, τὸ μὴ εἰδέναι certainly is, and it is ἄλογον. The blanket of ignorance extends over the expository conversation that follows. Oedipus has been king of Thebes for a number of years, yet he knows nothing of his predecessor except his name. But his lack of curiosity does not prevent him from asking Creon

---

* See P. Ghiron-Bistagne, *Recherches sur les acteurs dans la Grèce antique* (Paris 1976), esp. 160f., 329.

some sharp questions about why the circumstances surrounding Laius' death were not more vigorously investigated.

In reply to one of these questions, Creon says (118) that when Laius made his last and fatal journey, all his retainers were killed except one. This sole survivor was unable to provide any reliable information except on a single point. 'What point?' asks Oedipus, adding that any clue, however tenuous, might enable them to find out a lot. 'He said', replies Creon, 'that Laius was killed not by the strength of one man, but many hands were raised against him.' The survivor was not telling the truth. If he had told the truth, the plot of *Oedipus Rex* as Sophocles conceives it would not work. Now we may say that the survivor was exaggerating from fear, or shame at his own conduct at a moment of physical danger. But that is an explanation invented by us, not one given by Sophocles, and it breaks down the moment we look at the wording of Oedipus' reply: what then made the brigand (singular) so bold? And this, just after he has been told with the utmost emphasis that there were a number of brigands. Is this a Freudian slip? It is not. When Creon reports the oracle at 107 he uses a plural, and so does Oedipus at 108. The Chorus use plurals at 292, though Oedipus again responds with a singular at 293 – which does not prevent him from using a plural at 308. Oedipus uses the singular here at 124, and again at 139, 225, 230, 236, but at 246–7 he says 'I curse the doer of this deed, whether he be one or acting with several others.' At 277 the Chorus use the singular, and at 715ff. Jocasta uses the plural.

It could hardly be more confusing. And it was meant to be. The simple mathematical proposition of 845 'one cannot be equal to many' must be present to our minds, but kept out of focus, for as long as possible. It is not for nothing that at 290 Sophocles describes the point at issue as κωφὰ καὶ παλαί' ἔπη. The technique of blurring the prehistory of a play is one that Sophocles uses elsewhere, but nowhere else is it a matter of such urgency.

Voltaire was among those who noted another important difficulty over these lines. The obvious thing to do on hearing that there was a survivor was to send for him at once. Why does Oedipus not do so? This is the man whose intelligence so far exceeded all other men's that he was able to answer the Sphinx's question. This is the man with enough foresight to send Creon to the Delphic oracle. This is the man who has a moment ago said that no clue, however slight, must be overlooked; and said it, moreover, in connection with the survivor. This is the man who reviews censoriously the lack of energy exhibited by others in finding the killer, who promises that he himself will strain every nerve to find the guilty man. But in spite of all this, he fails to send for this one surviving eye-witness. Why? Because of the conflicting demands of the two themes that we noticed above. What Sophocles most wants to uncover is not the killer of the last king of Thebes, but the man who killed his father and married his mother. If Oedipus sent for the eye-witness now, we would have a very short play about the discovery of the killer of the king of Thebes, whose presence in the city was causing pollution and hence the plague. Sophocles has rather more ambitious plans in mind.

In the first choral song we continue with the theme of the plague. But when the song is over, it fades rapidly and soon vanishes almost entirely (allusions at 636, 665). It was simply a device to set the play in motion; when its object is achieved, we hear no more of it. Just as well, perhaps, for it would not do to enquire too closely into the reasons why the gods had allowed years to elapse between the death of Laius and the sending of the plague.

After the long curse speech which follows this choral song, packed with the kind of irony for which the play is famous, the plot receives its next nudge forward. The Chorus suggest that Teiresias be sent for. But Oedipus has anticipated them. Just as Creon had been sent to the Delphic oracle, so also someone has been sent to fetch Teiresias. Just as Oedipus expressed unease because Creon's return was overdue, so now he admits to surprise that Teiresias has not already turned up. After a moment of conversation with the Chorus, the sole purpose of which is to confuse still further the question of whether there was one brigand or more – except that the brigands may now have suddenly become merely 'wayfarers' (but see 292n.), Teiresias arrives, and is greeted in terms of extreme reverence. Oedipus, the most brilliant of men, greets the prophet with humility and trust.

Teiresias' first words are not encouraging: φεῦ φεῦ. 'What a terrible thing it is', he continues, 'to possess knowledge where knowledge can do no good to the one who has it. I knew this well enough, but I forgot it, otherwise I wouldn't have come.' Oedipus replies either with genuine concern, or if with humour, then humour of an even gentler kind than that with which he had greeted Creon's equally gnomic initial remarks (89–90). 'What is the matter? You look quite despondent.' – 'Let me go home' . . . and so the scene continues, with Teiresias refusing to give the information which alone can save the city. Relations between the two men deteriorate until at 362 Teiresias explicitly denounces Oedipus as the murderer of Laius. At 366 he hints at incest.

Now to accuse of causing the present plague the very man who had once liberated Thebes from a comparable scourge, the Sphinx (a thing which Teiresias himself had conspicuously failed to do (391 ff.)), is nonsense. Oedipus had never even seen Laius (105). To hint at incest is no less ridiculous, for Oedipus had taken the most extravagant precautions to keep far away from his parents, as he supposes them to be, Polybus and Merope. Oedipus saves till later (562–4, 568; see below) the really devastating question: if Teiresias was so knowledgeable about the murder of Laius, why did he keep silent so long? If he was determined to keep silent, why did he answer Oedipus' summons at all? Because he *forgot* (318) the validity of a gnomic reflection? Oedipus' anger on behalf of the city has every justification, and on his own behalf every *apparent* justification. The audience would have felt much sympathy with his attitude. It is likely that at the time the play was produced they had themselves just lived through a great plague, and were disillusioned with prophets (Thuc. 2.47.4).

The allegations of Teiresias become clearer and clearer until at 447–62 he delivers a speech which has caused the more conscientious students of Sophocles much worry.

I have said what I came to say, and now I am going home, unmoved by fear in your presence. You cannot hurt me, and I will tell you why. The man that you have been looking for all this time, with all your threats and proclamations about the murder of Laius, that man is here. He is supposed to be a stranger living in our midst, but in time he will be found to be a native Theban, a turn of events that will give him no pleasure. He who once had vision will be blind; no longer wealthy, he will be a mendicant, feeling the ground before him with his staff as he traverses a foreign land. And every one will know that he is both the brother and the father of his own children, the son and husband of the woman that gave him birth, the man who killed his father and climbed into the empty bed. Now go and think about that for a while, and if you find that I have spoken false, then consider that I know nothing of prophecy.

There is no way round this speech. It is useless to say (G. M. Kirkwood, *A study of Sophoclean drama* (Ithaca, N.Y. 1958) 129) 'Oedipus . . . flies into a terrible rage . . . Teiresias can shout aloud the whole truth without any chance of Oedipus' discovering it.' Line 747 affords one refutation, and the Chorus afford another, for with the echoes of the prophet's denunciation still ringing through the theatre of Dionysus, they begin their song with the artless words 'Who is it that the Delphic oracle spoke of?' and at 483 they say 'The sage observer of birds has made some extremely disturbing remarks, which I can neither approve of nor reject, and I simply don't know what to say' – though they do in fact carry on for another 25 lines. The technique which Sophocles is using here is one very familiar to us from all his extant plays, but some critics feel that here, at any rate, the technique has been pushed beyond acceptable limits. The essence of the matter is this: the apparent failure of the highly intelligent Oedipus to grasp what has been said to him is unconvincing; and the structure of the plot suffers from premature disclosure.

To the second point we can make two answers: (*a*) that *Oedipus Rex* is not concerned with gradual disclosure of the story to the audience, but with gradual disclosure to Oedipus, and it is important that every member of the audience shall be fully apprised, at an early stage, of just what there is to disclose. We shall accuse of exaggeration the comic poet Antiphanes (frg. 189 Kassel–Austin) when he says that you have only to say the word 'Oedipus' and everyone knows all the rest – his father Laius, his mother Jocasta, his daughters, his (male) children, what will happen to him and what he did. But even as we point out to Antiphanes that some of the younger members of the audience may be unfamiliar with the story, and that anyway there are to all intents and purposes no male children in *Oedipus Rex*, we shall be conscious of scoring cheap debating points rather than voicing deep and essential truths. We do better to employ argument (*b*): whatever one may think about Teiresias' speech in its relation to the play as a whole, it affords a moment of tense theatrical horror. The blind, feeble, sullen priest is right, and we know that he is right. If only he were wrong.

As for the first point, the apparent failure of Oedipus at the time to grasp what is being said to him, we can do no more than admit that it is so, adding that Greek tragedy at large teems with examples of inconsistency of character, and that actors of great professional skill can get away with almost anything. But some of those who have studied this play would not rest content with the application of these general considerations to this particular point.

Whatever misgivings we may have, we are given little time to develop them. The immediately following choral song takes our minds along a different path, and when it is over, religious considerations take second place as we watch a political argument between Creon and Oedipus, a secular counterpart of the Teiresias scene we have just been witnessing. The charge of collusion which Oedipus brings against Creon is natural enough. Creon would (and does) succeed to the throne if anything happened to Oedipus. If the argument '*cui bono?*' has any validity, it points to Creon, and it was Creon who had made the original suggestion, which led to so much unpleasantness, that Teiresias should be sent for. At least it seems to be agreed on all sides that Creon gave this advice (288, 555), though in fact he has had no opportunity to do so, at any time since his return from Delphi, without our knowing about it; and we have heard no such advice given. But this is not a point we have time to notice as the play unfolds, and it makes a very useful opening gambit in the cross-examination that begins at 555.

> – Did you or did you not persuade me that I had to send someone to fetch the holy prophet?
> – I did, and I stand by my advice now.
> (A sudden new tack, apparently not connected with the first question.)
> – How long is it now since Laius . . .
> – Did what? I don't know.
> – . . . perished in the fatal attack?
> – It would be far back in the past.
> (Again another apparently irrelevant question.)
> – Was the prophet in practice at that time?
> – Yes, as skilled as now, and held in no less honour.
> – Did he ever make any mention of me at that time?
> – Not at any time that I was around.
> – Well, didn't you hold an investigation to find the killer?
> – We did, of course, and heard all sorts of things.
> – So how was it that this clever prophet of yours never said anything at the time on the matter?
> – I don't know, and on matters that I do not understand I like to keep silent.

It is a good, crisp law-court scene, and it shows us how reasonable it was for Oedipus to suspect Creon and Teiresias. But if we have leisure to reflect, we shall see that Sophocles has put into the mouth of his hero questions which ruthlessly expose certain weak features in the foundation on which his own play has been built. If Sophocles had anachronistically heard of Aristotelian canons about construction according to probability or necessity, he could in his own defence have exploited the loophole (see above, p. 6) about ἄλογα lying outside the drama itself. If, that is, he did not feel himself above such pedantic restrictions altogether.

It is possible to divine good reasons for most of the inconsistencies of plot or character which we detect in this play. But once or twice we may have to admit that if the poet has a purpose, it eludes us. One whole nexus of confusions arises over the question of exile or death. At 100 exile or death was the choice for the killer of Laius. Similarly, in reverse order, at 308–9. At 622–3 Creon is threatened with death, and exile is ruled out as an alternative – i.e. he is threatened with the more severe of the two penalties for the murder of Laius. But although Oedipus had accused Teiresias (346–9) of being the murderer of Laius in intent, he has never explicitly accused Creon of that crime; what he has done is to call Creon (534) the murderer of 'this man', i.e. 'myself, Oedipus'. Then at 640–1 Creon speaks again of exile or death, as if 623 had never been uttered. At 659 and 669–70 Oedipus regards Creon's treason as threatening himself with death or exile. We may feel that Sophocles has been guilty of carelessness, or over-use, in his treatment of the death and/or exile theme; that besides the flat contradiction between 640–1 and 622–3 some essential stages in the argument have been omitted, as he applies, indiscriminately it seems, the same proposed penalties to the unknown murderer, to Creon and to Oedipus.

But it is deliberate technique, not carelessness, that lies behind the next ἄλογον we have to consider, perhaps the least obtrusive and at the same time most important in the whole play. At 698–700 Jocasta asks the king why he and Creon have been quarrelling. Oedipus replies: 'He says that I am the murderer of Laius.' Now this statement is totally untrue, even though, as we have just seen with the death/exile theme, affairs seem at times to be conducted as if Oedipus were accusing Creon, and Creon accusing Oedipus, of precisely that crime. If the quarrel took place in real life we might now expect from Jocasta one of two types of response: either a question, 'Did you really say that, Creon?' or an outraged comment, 'What a preposterous idea!' The one thing that we would never expect is the very thing that we actually get: 'Is this a matter of his own knowledge, or did he learn of it from someone else?' The question would appear less remarkable to an ancient audience than it does to us, since, to quote from our commentary on 6 'the contrast between receiving reports at second hand and having first-hand knowledge is a commonplace in tragedy'. (See also 705n.)

What has Sophocles gained by putting this standard antithesis to such novel use? What we have been concerned with hitherto is the alleged corruption of Creon. What Jocasta goes on to discuss is the alleged reliability of oracles and prophets. This one question of hers, and the backtracking that is done in 705, which itself does not squarely meet her question, provides the bridge between the two themes. Up to now there has been no suggestion that Oedipus has even contemplated the possibility that Teiresias might have been speaking the truth. In the preceding choral song Teiresias' version of events has been all but rejected. Even Creon himself (526) seemed to take it for granted that Teiresias' words must be false. But now the tenor of Jocasta's speech – don't worry about prophecies, they don't always come true – makes sense only if everybody, especially Oedipus, has been taking Teiresias seriously. To give an example of a prophecy which did not come true, Jocasta relates the case of her former husband Laius. An oracle, or at any rate an oracle's spokesman, had said that he would die at the hands of his son. Actually he was killed by brigands at a place where a road branched into two. As for the child that was supposed to kill him, he was exposed at birth with his feet pierced.

Now Oedipus had received a prophecy that he was to kill his father (though Sophocles deliberately holds back this item of information until 793). Laius had received a prophecy that he was to be killed by his son. The child of Laius had been exposed with pierced feet. Oedipus has pierced feet. (See however the note on 1031 ff.) We are not therefore surprised when he tells Jocasta that her words have caused him grave concern. Why is that? asks the queen. Oedipus surprisingly fastens not upon the startling coincidences involved, but on the mention of the place where a road divided. If we are candid, we will admit that the real reason why he does so is because Sophocles cannot allow the onward drive of the play to degenerate into a headlong rush; at this point suspicions must be nascent, not confirmed – at any rate so far as parricide and incest are concerned. A resemblance between Oedipus and Laius is then established, but an outward rather than a family resemblance. Remarkably enough it is now for the first time that Oedipus learns of when the killing took place and how many retainers there were with Laius.

It is this numerical agreement – numbers are important in this play – which prompts Oedipus to cry (754) that 'this is now clear'. But what does he mean by 'this'? And is it absolutely clear? By 'this' Oedipus means regicide. Lines 825–7 make it certain that Oedipus is thinking only in terms of regicide at this stage in the play; his acknowledgement therefore that Teiresias 'had sight' (747) excludes the more sinister things that Teiresias had included in his denunciation. As for whether the circumstances surrounding the death of Laius are indeed absolutely clear, two possible loopholes still remain: (a) Oedipus thinks he killed the whole of the party that met him on the road (813), whereas he has been told that one member of Laius' entourage escaped; hence the party he met was not the party of Laius. This is an avenue of thought which Sophocles does not explore at all. (b) The prevailing story spoke (715–16) of a plurality of brigands, not of one man alone. It is on this that Sophocles now concentrates.

How is it that Jocasta is in a position, at this late stage in their married life, to impart all this information about the death of Laius to her husband? Because the sole survivor had told her. And what happened to him? This is another question which will have to be answered in a way which defies the logic and probabilities of real life. After killing Laius, Oedipus had the Sphinx to deal with. He also married the widowed queen – after a decent interval, we must charitably suppose – and he became king of Thebes. (Sophocles does not expressly say so, but it would be reasonable to assume that these two last events were synchronous.) All these things take time. And yet the sole survivor, running for his life, does not arrive at Thebes until Oedipus is already established as king. The telescoping of time is of course perfectly familiar in

Greek tragedy, but there are no other places where temporal relativity receives such arbitrary treatment. More serious perhaps than the offence against real-life logic is the offence against dramatic likelihood. When this survivor reached Thebes, he took one look at Oedipus (if we may slightly parody 759), prostrated himself before the queen and asked to be removed to some quiet spot in the country. Strange behaviour in a footman, one might think, but Jocasta never gives it a second thought. This account of the survivor's flight from the scene of Laius' murder is also hard to reconcile with an unprejudiced reading of 118ff. In that version he tells his tale, at Thebes one must assume, before, or at best at the same time as, the episode of the Sphinx. His rôle at 122–3 was to speak of multiple brigands, but at 759 it is the sight of the one man Oedipus that causes him to opt for the health-giving properties of the countryside.

Now at last (765, 860) the order which we might reasonably have expected to hear as far back as 120 is actually given. Well over 600 lines have been spent in building up atmosphere. We are now half-way through the play, and the switch is at last thrown which will set the fatal machinery in motion. But between 765 and 860 Sophocles imparts yet more background information to the audience, information which can only be put into the mouth of the king himself. 'My father was Polybus of Corinth, and my mother the Dorian Merope.' Strange words for a man to address to the lady who has been his wife for so many years, but dramatic necessity is paramount. It is now that we are told of the oracle that he was to kill his father and marry his mother. Sophocles has taken care not to remind us of this too soon, for otherwise the preceding passage about the forking road and what happened there would have had its true significance shown up in too glaring a light. Now, however, it suits his purpose to show us just how extreme the coincidences are, and we learn of the death of Laius, or rather of some nameless man in a carriage, from none other than the king himself. He had left Corinth, to avoid fulfilling the oracle. But the gods, showing noticeably greater speed than they did when they sent the plague, arranged that he should meet Laius on the road. Laius, with all the superiority of the motorist over the pedestrian, tries to force Oedipus off the road, and aims a lethal blow at his head. But our hero kills the lot. The story is told with a vividness that is almost cinematic (ὅτι μάλιστα πρὸ ὀμμάτων τιθέμενον Arist. *Poet.* 1455a23). The emotions of the man who tells it are blended with the detachment of a third-party witness. παίω δι' ὀργῆς says Oedipus, crisply stating facts. οὐ μὴν ἴσην γ' ἔτεισεν he adds with relish. Modern critics who feel that odds of five to one against should provoke from the victim of an assault on a lonely road no more than a well-phrased remonstrance suck in their breath as Oedipus unwittingly makes this damning admission.

Sophocles has led us to believe that all now hangs on the survivor's story. Did he say one brigand, or more than one? At 848 Jocasta takes up this point, and, just as she did at 704, switches the course of the play onto a new set of rails. The question to which she gives prominence now is not, did Oedipus kill Laius, but rather, was the oracle fulfilled? 'Even if he deviates from his previous story, he will never, O King, show that the death of Laius turned out properly (ὀρθόν), who Apollo said had to die by the hand of my son.' Jocasta's complacent acceptance of the idea that her second husband may very well have killed her first is not to worry us. The question that Sophocles wants us to think about now is, who is Oedipus, and has he in fact committed parricide and incest? The ground is now laid for the following scene, where the splendid prospect of the throne of Corinth is virtually disregarded, so that attention may instead be focused on the thought that the death of Polybus has, to all appearance, refuted the oracle.

The relevance of the ensuing choral ode is much less of a problem than it used to be, now that even respectable figures of the literary Establishment have steeled themselves to follow in the wake of that textual critic of a hundred years ago who wished to eliminate from our texts the absurdity of 'Hybris begets the tyrant.' We are now much better placed to see how this once highly contentious choral ode takes the action of the play and freezes it for a moment or two, so that we may dwell briefly on the religious and philosophical issues that are at stake. (See the note on 872.) Is there any point in maintaining religious practices?

The only person who has been casting doubt on religion is Jocasta, but it is she, none other, who approaches Apollo's altar immediately the choral song is over. Oedipus is still within the palace, in a high state of nervous agitation. Jocasta asks Apollo for a λύσις, by a curious coincidence using the word which Aristotle, that great admirer of *Oedipus Rex*, was to use a century later as his technical term for the dénouement of a tragedy (*Poetics* 1455b24, 1456a9). The answer to her prayer, and not the answer she would wish, arrives in an unlikely form. With Creon, Teiresias, and later with the herdsman, much care is taken to prepare us for the arrival of a fresh character on stage. But now, unannounced, there appears, by a piece of shameless dramaturgy that has attracted the displeasure of, *inter alios*, Pierre Corneille, an aged Corinthian, with, as he supposes, good news; news of a kind that with any luck should bless both him that gives and him that takes. Polybus has died, and Oedipus is to be king not only of Thebes but of Corinth too. But, as we have said, this theme is allowed to drop at once, and Jocasta with deceptive rapidity performs her by now familiar rôle of channelling all our thoughts in the direction that her creator, Sophocles, wishes us to take. It is to the apparent falsification of the oracles that our minds are turned. When Oedipus comes and learns the news, his relief is so great that he goes almost hysterical with joy.

He has heard that his father Polybus is dead, but what of his mother? This is a question which, for all his hysteria, he does not overlook (976). It is at this point that the messenger chips in, and in the hope of setting Oedipus' mind at rest makes the fatal disclosure that Polybus and Merope were not in fact his parents. It is the high season for coincidences: this very messenger, it seems, had once been given the infant Oedipus by another herdsman. And who was that herdsman? Why, it was 'none other than', as the Chorus ingenuously put it (1052), our elusive friend, the sole survivor. Four men are thus neatly reduced to two.

We must not over-react to these two coincidences. In theory it would have been possible for Sophocles to have created four different rôles: Corinthian messenger, receiver of baby, giver of baby and sole survivor. But the three-actor convention would have made it impossible to deal with all these persons without a severe loss in tautness of composition. We must accept this piece of dramatic shorthand for what it is, pausing only to note that Sophocles does not take any unfair advantage of it, e.g. by stressing how to the gods no coincidences are too extreme. Nothing is to be gained by asking ourselves, e.g., why a country shepherd of many years ago abandoned his rural pursuits in order to serve as part of Laius' escort of heralds, drivers and λοχῖται. (On this, as with all matters Sophoclean, we do well to bear in mind the dictum of Aristarchus, who, says the scholion D on *Il.* 5.385, ἀξιοῖ τὰ φραζόμενα ὑπὸ τοῦ ποιητοῦ μυθικώτερον ἐκδέχεσθαι κατὰ τὴν ποιητικὴν ἐξουσίαν, μηδὲν ἔξω τῶν φραζομένων ὑπὸ τοῦ ποιητοῦ περιεργαζομένους.)

In establishing the identity of Oedipus with the infant exposed on Mt Cithaeron the messenger refers to the child's injured feet. Oedipus had ignored Jocasta's reference to the mutilation of the feet of her exposed child at 718. But here, at 1031, Oedipus' question 'What injury was I suffering from when you took me in your arms?' makes it clear that he knew the cause of his injury. Oedipus knows what Sophocles wants him to know, and at the time that Sophocles wants him to know it.

Jocasta realizes the whole truth, and urges Oedipus not to pursue his enquiries any further. Sophocles does not give us time to consider the alternatives: divorce or the continuation of incest. Dramatically the sole reason why Jocasta tells Oedipus not to go any further is so that he may disobey her. When she sees that his purpose cannot be deflected, she leaves, never to be seen again. The Chorus comment that her departure looks ominous. But the poet still wishes us to cling to the illusion that there is a glimmer of hope left. Hence the extraordinary speech put into the mouth of Oedipus at 1076ff. in which he makes some unconvincing speculations about his parentage. To make this glimmer seem brighter Sophocles changes the mood of his Chorus from the foreboding of 1075 to the hopefulness of 1086ff. Perhaps Oedipus will turn out to be the love-child of some errant deity.

No, he will not. The Theban herdsman is at hand to put an end to our brief excursion into the realms of picturesque mythology. This is the man for whom we have been sending ever since the plot returned to the point first made about 118. But we sent for him in his capacity as the sole survivor of Laius' entourage, to solve the problem of who killed the last king of Thebes. We were intensely interested to find out whether he would stick to his story that there was a plurality of brigands. This enticing possibility has been dangled before our eyes for hundreds of lines, but now it is quite forgotten. All that matters now is the identity of Oedipus. Brigands are no longer germane to the issue, so we interrogate this man not in his capacity as sole survivor, but in his capacity as a herdsman in the employ of King Laius, the exposer of children.

It was said, a page or two ago, that Sophocles took no unfair advantage of the conflation of rôles. Nor does he, explicitly. But when we have said that the Theban herdsman is two characters rolled into one, we have not exhausted the matter, and we may feel much sympathy with these words of Alister Cameron in his book *The identity of Oedipus the King* (New York & London 1968), 22: 'This Theban is the man who took the infant Oedipus to "trackless Cithaeron", who witnessed the murder in the pass, who saw Oedipus in Thebes married to Jocasta. In other words, astonishingly, wildly improbably, he has been keeping company with Oedipus all Oedipus' life – hidden company.'

At the end of the interview Oedipus cries aloud that everything is now clear. We have already seen how he had used similar language as far back as 754, though our horizons were there, somewhat artificially, limited to regicide. Now, at 1182, parricide and incest are included.

Does this mean that it is not until 1182 that Oedipus realizes the truth? If earlier, when? It is characteristic of the art of Sophocles that though we may ask a straight question, we cannot get a straight answer. At 1170 it is evident that Oedipus has grasped the truth, and is only waiting for the formality of oral confirmation. Presumably we are not meant to think that he knew the whole truth a hundred lines earlier, and yet, as far back as 1076, when Oedipus was proclaiming himself the child of Fortune, he was in fact in possession of the following items of information:

(a)   He was virtually certain that he had killed Laius, the former king of Thebes.
(b)   He knew of the oracle that Laius would be killed by his son.
(c)   He knew that he was himself destined to kill his father.
(d)   He knew that Polybus and Merope were not his parents.
(e)   He knew that Laius and Jocasta had exposed a baby with mutilated feet.
(f)   He knew that he himself as a baby had mutilated feet. (See 1031 n.)
(g)   Independently of all the above he had been told all the vital truths not long since by the hitherto infallible prophet Teiresias.

The fact that he knows that Jocasta is old enough to be his mother is not relevant. The disparity in age may have provided grist to the mill of Aristophanes (*Frogs* 1193), but for Sophocles, and hence for us, this disparity is neither here nor there. The considerations (a) to (g) above should have led even the least gifted intelligence to the right conclusion, let alone a man whose intuitive brilliance had solved the riddle of the Sphinx. But Sophocles does not throw away the thrill of discovery in a few brief seconds when he has it in his power to bring his audience to a peak of excitement for an appreciably longer time.

In the choral ode that follows, sorrow and compassion prevail. With Oedipus' example before us there is nothing in the life of men over which we can feel any secure happiness. The plot has by now run its course in the sense that all the oracles are seen to have been fulfilled. There remains only the prediction of blindness, wrung much earlier from an angered Teiresias. Now someone emerges from the palace to tell us that Jocasta has hanged herself, and Oedipus, who began life with two pierced feet, is to end it with two pierced eyeballs. 'Something which is peculiar to Attic tragedy as a whole, the habit of luxuriating in horror, of investing terror with a kind of voluptuousness, has in this play more than any other extended into the attitude of the tragic hero' (Reinhardt, English translation, 130). As the blinded Oedipus reels across the stage he tells the Chorus that all that has happened is the work of Apollo. The most far-sighted of men accuses the most far-sighted of gods, the Apollo of Delphi, the Apollo at whose altar Jocasta was vainly sacrificing just before the messenger from Corinth arrived.

The ending of the play as we have it today is not the work of Sophocles, though snatches of Sophocles may surface in the last hundred lines or so from time to time; detailed examination of what is authentic and what is spurious is offered in the commentary. But though we may not know what Sophocles would have wished to leave us with as a conclusion, and though it is wrong to interpret one play in the light of another, and wrong to speak of a 'Theban trilogy', if we add together all the components of *Antigone* and the two *Oedipus* plays, to assess what the author thought of the human condition, we shall find a picture of regicide, parricide, suicide, fratricide, laced with pestilence, immurement and incest. Such is the fall of the house of Agenor. The lady who adversely compared *Hamlet* with the home life of our own dear Queen, never, we must hope, had her attention drawn to the excesses inherent in Sophocles' treatment of Theban legend. Conventional piety has much to answer for.

It is time to repeat what we said at the outset, that the numerous offences against dramatic or real-life logic which we have traced in this Introduction are not a condemnation of Sophoclean technique. That his art should differ from the expertise of an engineer matching gearwheels with sub-millimetre precision is a conclusion from which we need not recoil. ὅ τ' ἀπατήσας δικαιότερος τοῦ μὴ ἀπατήσαντος καὶ ὁ ἀπατηθεὶς σοφώτερος τοῦ μὴ ἀπατηθέντος (Gorgias *ap.* Plutarch *de glor. Ath.* 5, 348c). Let us remember the reply which Goethe gave Napoleon, who had censured him for some improbability in *Werther* (Goethe, Hamburger Ausgabe, vol. VI, p. 532).

(I replied that I found the criticism) quite correct, and admitted that it was possible to show that there was something not quite right in this place. But, I added, an author ought perhaps to be forgiven if he availed himself of an artistic device not easily detectable, in order to achieve certain effects which he could not have brought about in a simple and natural way.

"Der Kaiser", Goethe concluded, "seemed content with that."

2. THE TEXT

When Mr Tom Stoppard lectured in Cambridge in 1980 on the relationship between a dramatist and his text, he drew attention to the great number of alterations which may take place between the time of composition of a play and its first performance on stage. He described how the reception accorded to the play by the public might lead to further, and in some cases drastic, revision of the original words; and he mentioned that the text printed in book form after the stage production was over might again be at variance with the words actually spoken by the actors on stage. Most dispiriting of all, to the practising textual critic, he made it clear that the question 'Which of all these various evolving versions do you regard as your own *authentic* text?' is one that had no meaning for him.

Liberties taken with the text of Shakespeare over the centuries suggest that there is nothing new in the theatrical practice described by Mr Stoppard. Laurence Olivier in his *Confessions of an actor* complained over something he called 'gibberish' in the text of Hamlet: 'Why does your researcher always apply to a professor rather than to a practitioner?' His own explanation was that on one occasion an actor missed his cue, 'and the wretched Hamlet had to gag, filling in with whatever nonsensical words came into his mouth – all faithfully taken down by the shorthand plagiarist present at this performance. In *Richard III*, when I had played it too long and too often for the memory to be faithfully retentive, I had to do the same . . . the audience will stand for quite a few lines of such stuff; provided you keep in rhythm they'll accept that it's an abstruse bit of Shakespeare.' An editor of Greek tragedy is not permitted to take refuge in such explanations of difficult passages, but it is certainly the case that when it comes to the relationship between the text first written by Sophocles and the words spoken by the actors at the first or any subsequent performance, we know nothing. What we do know is that about a century after the first production of *Oedipus Rex* an official version of the texts of the tragic poets was made, and actors were told to adhere to it (Plutarch, *Life of Lycurgus* 15). We are not told what sources were used for establishing that official text. The fact that it was necessary to bring in such a measure at all, and the undoubted presence of actors' interpolations in our manuscripts notwithstanding this measure, are alike causes for concern.

This official copy of the text, Galen tells us, was acquired by some sharp practice for the great library of Alexandria, but this would not have been in time to be of help to Alexander the Aetolian, who 'corrected' the tragedians. It may however have been available to the greater scholar Aristophanes of Byzantium, who is known to have occupied himself with the texts of Sophocles and Euripides, and whose particular interest in establishing colometry for lyric poems, previously written out as prose, should have helped greatly in reducing the speed with which the lyric sections of drama underwent corruption. Then later the famous Homeric scholar Aristarchus may have written a commentary on Sophocles (Pfeiffer, *History of Classical scholarship* 1 (Oxford 1968) 223): no great labour perhaps for a man able 'to recite the whole of tragedy by heart' (*loc. cit.* 224). If so, this commentary will have been among the sources used by the compiler Didymus, active at the time of Cicero. Didymus' name is mentioned nine times in the scholia to Sophocles which we find in the medieval manuscripts still extant today, and we are thus the heirs of a tradition of scholarly comment reaching back to a time only a century or two later than the time of Sophocles himself. But so far as the texts of the plays themselves are concerned, we know much less about their transmission than we do about commentaries or special studies on tragic diction, etc. All we can do is work back from the materials at hand, and try to reconstruct the older text from which they all derive.

The numerous quotations from Sophocles preserved in ancient authors or Byzantine works of reference are of remarkably little help to us in our task, except perhaps in bolstering our uncertain confidence that even if our own texts are not a secure record of what Sophocles wrote, they are none the less not inferior to the sort of text that might have been in the library of, let us say, a Maecenas. As for our exiguous fragments from the era of papyrus, these may contain one or two mild surprises, but nothing has yet been found to suggest that our texts of Sophocles today are *worse* than an ordinary text circulating in later antiquity. But even our best endeavours cannot bridge that fatal gap between the time of Sophocles himself and the first official transcript. We do not even know how close or distant the common ancestor of all our manuscripts stood to the Alexandrian editions.

The modern textual critic then may be straining at gnats and swallowing camels. But if one is to swallow a camel, one may as well do so in a gnat-free atmosphere. To change the metaphor, the Venus of Melos may be deficient in that she lacks the customary number of limbs, but that is no good reason for allowing the surface of her body to become encrusted with grime.

About 200 manuscripts of *Oedipus Rex* exist, of which only one-tenth have been fully collated. There is no absolute guarantee that good readings may not lurk in the uncollated manuscripts – one or two good things do surface from time to time – but specimen probes driven into this material incline us to believe that we have a fairly accurate idea of the total picture, and that new information will put additional flesh on to the skeletal body we have reconstructed rather than reshape the skeleton itself. Our oldest manuscript is L, written about A.D. 950. Under its other symbol M it is of the highest importance for Aeschylus too. (M is for Mediceus, as L is for Laurentianus, the manuscript being in the Florence library attached to the Church of San Lorenzo; this library benefited much from the Medici collections when it was founded in 1571.) A textual twin of L, though of only half its size in format, called Λ, is at Leiden. It is for most practical purposes unusable, since in almost all parts the original text has been erased so as to provide a surface for religious tracts. Since Dindorf's edition of 1832 L has been widely regarded as 'the best' manuscript of Sophocles. Certainly its correctness on small matters of orthography encourages a belief in its trustworthiness which is not entirely dispelled even by the highly suspicious variants put before us by the so-called 'corrector' – the same man who added the full and valuable marginal commentary (scholia).

The manuscripts most different from L are AUY, which in textual content are almost identical triplets, and a host of congeners. In this edition the manuscripts used from this numerous and tightly disciplined family are ADXrXs, with which Zr often agrees. The symbol α is used to denote the common reading of ADXrXs when they all agree. A itself is usually treated as the prime representative of the group, though U is in fact of similar age and authority (early fourteenth century). The very first printed edition of Sophocles, the Aldine of 1502, was based on a member of the α group, Y. Fifty years later the influential edition of de Tournebou (Turnebus) made T the principal authority for the text. T is a copy of the handwritten edition of the great Byzantine scholar and metrician Demetrius Triclinius, active in the early fourteenth century. In 1786 Brunck's edition reinstated the α family, being largely based on A. Then, as we have seen, in 1832, the lead passed to L. Indeed the importance of L was so far exaggerated that for a time, incredibly, L was declared to be the sole authority for the text; scholars attributed more importance than they should to the gap of three centuries or more which separate L from all our other MSS.

In more recent times the text of Sophocles has been thought of as something to be fought out between L and A, with various *recentiores* acting as a sort of destroyer escort to the two great opposing battleships. More recently still it has been fashionable to elevate the status of GR, whether retaining or excising A from the list of authorities. Some of the attendant scholarly discussion has shown classical scholarship in its worst possible light. All that was required was an application of the scientist's routine experimental method, i.e. to collate a number of manuscripts thoroughly, and to frame a theory in the light of the observed facts. This has now been done, with a result confirming the dictum that the truth is never pure and rarely simple. Even the highly abbreviated *apparatus criticus* printed in this edition will suffice to show how confusingly the various manuscripts can shift their affiliations, and how valuable old readings can filter down to us in only one or two manuscripts. There is thus no mechanical way of constituting the text of Sophocles; guesswork has still a large rôle to play, and that editor will guess best who has immersed himself for a long time in his author's style, and who has built up by constant study a kind of intuition into the behaviour of the various manuscripts on which his text is based. It is not so much a question of tabling variants, and choosing one, or emending where none is satisfactory, but rather of continually asking oneself the question 'What is it that all of these scribes are trying to tell me?' and on the basis of the answer striving to get as close as possible to the poetic mind of Sophocles. Total success is far beyond our grasp, but in the words of Plato – and indeed of Sherborne Girls School – καλὸν τὸ ἆθλον, καὶ ἡ ἐλπὶς μεγάλη.

MANUSCRIPT SYMBOLS

A	Par. gr. 2712
D	Neapol. II. F. 9
Xr	Vindob. phil. gr. 161 (A.D. 1412)
Xs	Vindob. phil. suppl. gr. 71

α (bracketing A, D, Xr, Xs)

Zr	Ven. gr. 616
L	Flor. Laur. 32.9
Zc	Vatic. gr. 1333
C	Par. gr. 2735
F	Flor. Laur. 28.25
H	Flor. Laur. 32.40
N	Matrit. 4677
O	Lugd. Voss. gr. Q 6
P	Heidelberg Palat. gr. 40
Pa	Vatic. gr. 904
V	Ven. gr. 468
G	Flor. Laur. conv. soppr. 152 (A.D. 1282)
R	Vatic. gr. 2291
T	Par. gr. 2711

Apart from L (ca. A.D. 950) and RXrXsZr (fifteenth century) all the above manuscripts belong to the fourteenth century or the last part of the thirteenth century.

B^{ac}	The reading of B before correction
B^{pc}	The reading of B after correction
B^c	The corrected reading of B when B^{ac} cannot be read
B^1	The original scribe of B's poetic text
B^{1pc}	The reading of B after correction by B^1
B^2	Any scribe other than B^1
B^{2pc}	The reading of B after correction by B^2
B^s	The scribe of the scholia or the regular writer of glosses
$B^{\gamma\rho}$	A variant in B introduced by γράφεται or some such formula as εὕρηται δὲ ἔν τισι
B^{gl}	A gloss in B, or a variant written as a gloss without γράφεται or any such formula
B in lin.	The reading of B in the line, as opposed to B s.l.
B s.l.	The reading of B above the line
Σ	Scholia
*	An erasure occupying the space of one letter

rell.   The reading of all other of our 18 manuscripts. On rare occasions trivial
            slips in one or two manuscripts (not more) may be disregarded
fere rell. Similar to rell., but with a wider disregard for errors of no critical signifi-
            cance
rec.   The reading of one or more manuscripts not collated for this edition
< >   Something supplied by an editor
[ ]   Something an editor wishes to delete

The *apparatus criticus* in this edition is intended to provide the information necessary
for the reader to follow any textual discussion in the commentary – and the reader
should bear in mind that the commentary makes no attempt to cover systematically
every textual difficulty; to indicate where the text is dependent on conjecture and not
on manuscript testimony at all; and to offer a selection of further readings to give
some idea of how manuscripts actually behave, and how they relate to each other and
(occasionally) to papyrus fragments or quotations in other authors. It will be noticed
how precariously the true reading has survived in a number of places.

ΟΙΔΙΠΟΥΣ ΤΥΡΑΝΝΟΣ

ΤΑ ΤΟΥ ΔΡΑΜΑΤΟΣ ΠΡΟΣΩΠΑ

ΟΙΔΙΠΟΥΣ	ΙΟΚΑΣΤΗ
ΙΕΡΕΥΣ	ΑΓΓΕΛΟΣ
ΚΡΕΩΝ	ΘΕΡΑΠΩΝ ΛΑΙΟΥ
ΧΟΡΟΣ	ΕΞΑΓΓΕΛΟΣ
ΤΕΙΡΕΣΙΑΣ	

ΟΙΔΙΠΟΥΣ ΤΥΡΑΝΝΟΣ

ΟΙΔΙΠΟΥΣ

Ὦ τέκνα Κάδμου τοῦ πάλαι νέα τροφή,
τίνας ποθ᾽ ἕδρας τάσδε μοι θοάζετε
ἱκτηρίοις κλάδοισιν ἐξεστεμμένοι;
πόλις δ᾽ ὁμοῦ μὲν θυμιαμάτων γέμει,
ὁμοῦ δὲ παιάνων τε καὶ στεναγμάτων·   5
ἀγὼ δικαιῶν μὴ παρ᾽ ἀγγέλων, τέκνα,
ἄλλων ἀκούειν αὐτὸς ὧδ᾽ ἐλήλυθα,
ὁ πᾶσι κλεινὸς Οἰδίπους καλούμενος.
    ἀλλ᾽, ὦ γεραιέ, φράζ᾽, ἐπεὶ πρέπων ἔφυς
πρὸ τῶνδε φωνεῖν· τίνι τρόπωι καθέστατε,   10
δείσαντες ἢ στέργοντες; ὡς θέλοντος ἂν
ἐμοῦ προσαρκεῖν πᾶν· δυσάλγητος γὰρ ἂν
εἴην τοιάνδε μὴ οὐ κατοικτίρων ἕδραν.

ΙΕΡΕΥΣ

ἀλλ᾽, ὦ κρατύνων Οἰδίπους χώρας ἐμῆς,
ὁρᾶις μὲν ἡμᾶς ἡλίκοι προσήμεθα   15
βωμοῖσι τοῖς σοῖς, οἱ μὲν οὐδέπω μακρὰν
πτέσθαι σθένοντες, οἱ δὲ σὺν γήραι βαρεῖς·
ἱερεὺς ἐγώ εἰμι Ζηνός, οἵδε τ᾽ ἠιθέων
λεκτοί· τὸ δ᾽ ἄλλο φῦλον ἐξεστεμμένον
ἀγοραῖσι θακεῖ, πρός τε Παλλάδος διπλοῖς   20
ναοῖς, ἐπ᾽ Ἰσμηνοῦ τε μαντείαι σποδῶι.
πόλις γάρ, ὥσπερ καὐτὸς εἰσορᾶις, ἄγαν
ἤδη σαλεύει, κἀνακουφίσαι κάρα
βυθῶν ἔτ᾽ οὐχ οἵα τε φοινίου σάλου,
φθίνουσα μὲν κάλυξιν ἐγκάρποις χθονός,   25
φθίνουσα δ᾽ ἀγέλαις βουνόμοις τόκοισί τε
ἀγόνοις γυναικῶν· ἐν δ᾽ ὁ πυρφόρος θεὸς
σκήψας ἐλαύνει, λοιμὸς ἔχθιστος, πόλιν,
ὑφ᾽ οὗ κενοῦται δῶμα Καδμεῖον, μέλας
δ᾽ Ἅιδης στεναγμοῖς καὶ γόοις πλουτίζεται.   30

---

11 στέργοντες Dawe: στέξαντες αZrZcT: στέρξαντες rell.   18 ἱερεὺς ἐγώ εἰμι Herwerden:
ἱερεῖς ἐγὼ μὲν codd.

θεοῖσι μέν νυν οὐκ ἰσούμενός σ' ἐγώ
οὐδ' οἵδε παῖδες ἑζόμεσθ' ἐφέστιοι,
ἀνδρῶν δὲ πρῶτον ἔν τε συμφοραῖς βίου
κρίνοντες ἔν τε δαιμόνων συναλλαγαῖς·
ὅς γ' ἐξέλυσας ἄστυ Καδμεῖον μολών   35
σκληρᾶς ἀοιδοῦ δασμὸν ὃν παρείχομεν,
καὶ ταῦθ' ὑφ' ἡμῶν οὐδὲν ἐξειδὼς πλέον
οὐδ' ἐκδιδαχθείς, ἀλλὰ προσθήκηι θεοῦ
λέγηι νομίζηι θ' ἡμὶν ὀρθῶσαι βίον.
νῦν τ', ὦ κράτιστον πᾶσιν Οἰδίπου κάρα,   40
ἱκετεύομέν σε πάντες οἵδε πρόστροποι
ἀλκήν τιν' εὑρεῖν ἡμίν, εἴτε του θεῶν
φήμην ἀκούσας, εἴτ' ἀπ' ἀνδρὸς οἶσθά που·
ὡς τοῖσιν ἐμπείροισι καὶ τὰς ξυμφορὰς
<............................>
ζώσας ὁρῶ μάλιστα τῶν βουλευμάτων.   45
ἴθ', ὦ βροτῶν ἄριστ', ἀνόρθωσον πόλιν·
ἴθ', εὐλαβήθηθ'· ὡς σὲ νῦν μὲν ἥδε γῆ
σωτῆρα κλήιζει <'κ> τῆς πάρος προθυμίας·
ἀρχῆς δὲ τῆς σῆς μηδαμῶς μεμνώμεθα
στάντες τ' ἐς ὀρθὸν καὶ πεσόντες ὕστερον·   50
[ἀλλ' ἀσφαλείαι τήνδ' ἀνόρθωσον πόλιν.]
ὄρνιθι γὰρ καὶ τὴν τότ' αἰσίωι τύχην
παρέσχες ἡμῖν, καὶ τανῦν ἴσος γενοῦ·
ὡς εἴπερ ἄρξεις τῆσδε γῆς ὥσπερ κρατεῖς,
ξὺν ἀνδράσιν κάλλιον ἢ κενῆς κρατεῖν·   55
ὡς οὐδέν ἐστιν οὔτε πύργος οὔτε ναῦς
ἔρημος ἀνδρῶν μὴ ξυνοικούντων ἔσω.
ΟΙ. ὦ παῖδες οἰκτροί, γνωτὰ κοὐκ ἄγνωτά μοι
προσήλθεθ' ἱμείροντες· εὖ γὰρ οἶδ' ὅτι
νοσεῖτε πάντες, καὶ νοσοῦντες ὡς ἐγὼ   60
οὐκ ἔστιν ὑμῶν ὅστις ἐξ ἴσου νοσεῖ.
τὸ μὲν γὰρ ὑμῶν ἄλγος εἰς ἕν' ἔρχεται
μόνον καθ' αὑτὸν κοὐδέν' ἄλλον, ἡ δ' ἐμὴ
ψυχὴ πόλιν τε κἀμὲ καί σ' ὁμοῦ στένει.
ὥστ' οὐχ ὕπνωι γ' εὕδοντά μ' ἐξεγείρετε·   65

31 ἰσούμενός Stanley: -μενόν codd.   40 νῦν δ' GR   42 εὑρεῖν ἡμίν FaT: ἡμῖν εὑρεῖν rell.
43 που HVG^{ac}αZcT: του rell.   44–45 lacunam indicavit Dawe   48 <'κ> Dawe | πάλαι
L in lin., CNO   50 τ' α: γ' T: om. rell.   51 del. Ritter   54 κρατεῖς vix sanum

ἀλλ' ἴστε πολλὰ μέν με δακρύσαντα δή,
πολλὰς δ' ὁδοὺς ἐλθόντα φροντίδος πλάνοις·
ἣν δ' εὖ σκοπῶν ηὕρισκον ἴασιν μόνην,
ταύτην ἔπραξα· παῖδα γὰρ Μενοικέως,
Κρέοντ', ἐμαυτοῦ γαμβρόν, ἐς τὰ Πυθικὰ 70
ἔπεμψα Φοίβου δώμαθ', ὡς πύθοιθ' ὅ τι
δρῶν ἢ τί φωνῶν τήνδ' ἐρυσαίμην πόλιν.
καὶ μ' ἦμαρ ἤδη ξυμμετρούμενον χρόνωι
λυπεῖ τί πράσσει· τοῦ γὰρ εἰκότος πέρα
ἄπεστι, πλείω τοῦ καθήκοντος χρόνου. 75
ὅταν δ' ἵκηται, τηνικαῦτ' ἐγὼ κακὸς
μὴ δρῶν ἂν εἴην πάνθ' ὅσ' ἂν δηλοῖ θεός.
ΙΕ. ἀλλ' εἰς καλὸν σύ τ' εἶπας, οἵδε τ' ἀρτίως
Κρέοντα προσστείχοντα σημαίνουσί μοι.
ΟΙ. ὦναξ Ἄπολλον, εἰ γὰρ ἐν τύχηι γέ τωι 80
σωτῆρι βαίη λαμπρὸς ὥσπερ ὄμματι.
ΙΕ. ἀλλ' εἰκάσαι μέν, ἡδύς· οὐ γὰρ ἂν κάρα
πολυστεφὴς ὧδ' εἷρπε παγκάρπου δάφνης.
ΟΙ. τάχ' εἰσόμεσθα· ξύμμετρος γὰρ ὡς κλύειν.
ἄναξ, ἐμὸν κήδευμα, παῖ Μενοικέως, 85
τίν' ἡμὶν ἥκεις τοῦ θεοῦ φήμην φέρων;

ΚΡΕΩΝ

ἐσθλήν· λέγω γὰρ καὶ τὰ δύσφορ', εἰ τύχοι
κατ' ὀρθὸν ἐξιόντα, πάντ' ἂν εὐτυχεῖν.
ΟΙ. ἔστιν δὲ ποῖον τοὔπος; οὔτε γὰρ θρασὺς
οὔτ' οὖν προδείσας εἰμὶ τῶι γε νῦν λόγωι. 90
ΚΡ. εἰ τῶνδε χρήιζεις πλησιαζόντων κλύειν,
ἕτοιμος εἰπεῖν, εἴτε καὶ στείχειν ἔσω.
ΟΙ. ἐς πάντας αὔδα· τῶνδε γὰρ πλέον φέρω
τὸ πένθος ἢ καὶ τῆς ἐμῆς ψυχῆς πέρι.
ΚΡ. λέγοιμ' ἂν οἷ' ἤκουσα τοῦ θεοῦ πάρα. 95
ἄνωγεν ἡμᾶς Φοῖβος ἐμφανῶς ἄναξ
μίασμα χώρας ὡς τεθραμμένον χθονὶ
ἐν τῆιδ' ἐλαύνειν μηδ' ἀνήκεστον τρέφειν.
ΟΙ. ποίωι καθαρμῶι; τίς ὁ πόρος τῆς ξυμφορᾶς;

---

66 διακρούσαντα Naber   67 πλάναις L^acHN^2pcα, s.l. PT   72 τήνδ' ἐρ- LPa^acV: τήνδε
ρ- Pa^2pc rell.   75 χρόνον V   77 ὅσ' ἂν CaT: ὅσα rell.   88 ἐξιόντα Suda: ἐξελθόντα
codd.   99 πόρος F. W. Schmidt: τρόπος codd.

ΚΡ. ἀνδρηλατοῦντας, ἢ φόνωι φόνον πάλιν   100
     λύοντας, ὡς τόδ᾽ αἷμα χειμάζον πόλιν.
ΟΙ. ποίου γὰρ ἀνδρὸς τήνδε μηνύει τύχην;
ΚΡ. ἦν ἡμίν, ὦναξ, Λάιός ποθ᾽ ἡγεμὼν
     γῆς τῆσδε, πρὶν σὲ τήνδ᾽ ἀπευθύνειν πόλιν.
ΟΙ. ἔξοιδ᾽ ἀκούων· οὐ γὰρ εἰσεῖδόν γέ πω.   105
ΚΡ. τούτου θανόντος νῦν ἐπιστέλλει σαφῶς
     τοὺς αὐτοέντας χερὶ τιμωρεῖν †τινας†.
ΟΙ. οἱ δ᾽ εἰσὶ ποῦ γῆς; ποῦ τόδ᾽ εὑρεθήσεται
     ἴχνος παλαιᾶς δυστέκμαρτον αἰτίας;
ΚΡ. ἐν τῆιδ᾽ ἔφασκε γῆι· τὸ δὲ ζητούμενον   110
     ἁλωτόν, ἐκφεύγει δὲ τἀμελούμενον.
ΟΙ. πότερα δ᾽ ἐν οἴκοις, ἢ ᾽ν ἀγροῖς ὁ Λάιος
     ἢ γῆς ἐπ᾽ ἄλλης τῶιδε συμπίπτει φόνωι;
ΚΡ. θεωρός, ὡς ἔφασκον, ἐκδημῶν πάλιν
     πρὸς οἶκον οὐκέθ᾽ ἵκεθ᾽ ὡς ἀπεστάλη.   115
ΟΙ. οὐδ᾽ ἄγγελός τις οὐδὲ συμπράκτωρ ὁδοῦ
     κατεῖδ᾽, ὅτωι τις ἐκμαθὼν ἐχρήσατ᾽ ἄν;
ΚΡ. θνήισκουσι γάρ, πλὴν εἷς τις, ὃς φόβωι φυγὼν
     ὧν εἶδε πλὴν ἓν οὐδὲν εἶχ᾽ εἰδὼς φράσαι.
ΟΙ. τὸ ποῖον; ἓν γὰρ πόλλ᾽ ἂν ἐξεύροι μαθεῖν,   120
     ἀρχὴν βραχεῖαν εἰ λάβοιμεν ἐλπίδος.
ΚΡ. ληιστὰς ἔφασκε συντυχόντας οὐ μιᾶι
     ῥώμηι κτανεῖν νιν, ἀλλὰ σὺν πλήθει χερῶν.
ΟΙ. πῶς οὖν ὁ ληιστής, εἴ τι μὴ ξὺν ἀργύρωι
     ἐπράσσετ᾽ ἐνθένδ᾽, ἐς τόδ᾽ ἂν τόλμης ἔβη;   125
ΚΡ. δοκοῦντα ταῦτ᾽ ἦν· Λαΐου δ᾽ ὀλωλότος
     οὐδεὶς ἀρωγὸς ἐν κακοῖς ἐγίγνετο.
ΟΙ. κακὸν δὲ ποῖον ἐμποδών, τυραννίδος
     οὕτω πεσούσης, εἶργε τοῦτ᾽ ἐξειδέναι;
ΚΡ. ἡ ποικιλωιδὸς Σφὶγξ τὸ πρὸς ποσὶ σκοπεῖν   130
     μεθέντας ἡμᾶς τἀφανῆ προσήγετο.
ΟΙ. ἀλλ᾽ ἐξ ὑπαρχῆς αὖθις αὔτ᾽ ἐγὼ φανῶ·
     ἐπαξίως γὰρ Φοῖβος, ἀξίως δὲ σὺ
     πρὸ τοῦ θανόντος τήνδ᾽ ἔθεσθ᾽ ἐπιστροφήν·
     ὥστ᾽ ἐνδίκως ὄψεσθε κἀμὲ σύμμαχον,   135

101 χειμάζει CF²ᵖᶜHNOR, s.l. LP²Xr   104 πόλιν] χθόνα rec.   107 τινα ut vid.
LPᶜAᵖᶜ: τίται Dawe   108 τόδ᾽] ποθ᾽ Meineke   111 ἐκφεύγειν Valckenaer   114
ἔφασκον Kousis: ἔφασκεν codd.   117 κατεῖδ᾽ αZrT: κατεῖδεν rell. | ὅτωι Seager: ὅτου codd.
127 οὐχ εἷς Lange   130 τὰ HaZr

γῆι τῆιδε τιμωροῦντα τῶι θεῶι θ' ἅμα.
ὑπὲρ γὰρ οὐχὶ τῶν ἀπωτέρω φίλων,
ἀλλ' αὐτὸς αὑτοῦ τοῦτ' ἀποσκεδῶ μύσος.
ὅστις γὰρ ἦν ἐκεῖνον ὁ κτανὼν τάχ' ἂν
κἄμ' ἂν τοιαύτηι χειρὶ τιμωρεῖν θέλοι.
κείνωι προσαρκῶν οὖν ἐμαυτὸν ὠφελῶ.   140
   ἀλλ' ὡς τάχιστα, παῖδες, ὑμεῖς μὲν βάθρων
ἵστασθε, τούσδ' ἄραντες ἱκτῆρας κλάδους,
ἄλλος δὲ Κάδμου λαὸν ὧδ' ἀθροιζέτω,
ὡς πᾶν ἐμοῦ δράσοντος· ἢ γὰρ εὐτυχεῖς   145
σὺν τῶι θεῶι φανούμεθ', ἢ πεπτωκότες.
ΙΕ.   ὦ παῖδες, ἱστώμεσθα· τῶνδε γὰρ χάριν
καὶ δεῦρ' ἔβημεν ὧν ὅδ' ἐξαγγέλλεται.
Φοῖβος δ' ὁ πέμψας τάσδε μαντείας ἅμα
σωτήρ θ' ἵκοιτο καὶ νόσου παυστήριος.   150

ΧΟΡΟΣ

ὦ Διὸς ἁδυεπὲς Φάτι, τίς ποτε   στρ.α
   τᾶς πολυχρύσου
Πυθῶνος ἀγλαὰς ἔβας
Θήβας; ἐκτέταμαι φοβερὰν φρένα
   δείματι πάλλων,
ἰήιε Δάλιε Παιάν,
ἀμφὶ σοὶ ἁζόμενος· τί μοι ἢ νέον   155
   ἢ περιτελλομέναις ὥραις πάλιν
ἐξανύσεις χρέος;
   εἰπέ μοι, ὦ χρυσέας τέκνον Ἐλπίδος,
   ἄμβροτε Φήμα.

πρῶτα σὲ κεκλόμενος, θύγατερ Διός,   ἀντ.α
   ἄμβροτ' Ἀθάνα,
γαιάοχόν τ' ἀδελφεὰν   160
Ἄρτεμιν, ἃ κυκλόεντ' ἀγορᾶς θρόνον
   εὐκλέα θάσσει,
καὶ Φοῖβον ἑκαβόλον, ἰὼ
τρισσοὶ ἀλεξίμοροι προφάνητέ μοι·
   εἴ ποτε καὶ προτέρας ἄτας ὕπερ

139 ἐκεῖνος LFNOPZc   158 Φήμα P: Φάμα rell.   159 -μένωι PaᵖᶜDXsZr, s.l. AXr
161 ἀγοραῖς V

ὀρνυμένας πόλει   165
ἠνύσατ᾽ ἐκτοπίαν φλόγα πήματος,
ἔλθετε καὶ νῦν.

ὦ πόποι, ἀνάριθμα γὰρ φέρω   στρ. β
πήματα· νοσεῖ δέ μοι πρόπας
στόλος, οὐδ᾽ ἔνι φροντίδος ἔγχος   170
ὧι τις ἀλέξεται· οὔτε γὰρ ἔκγονα
κλυτᾶς χθονὸς αὔξεται οὔτε τόκοισιν
ἰηίων καμάτων ἀνέχουσι γυναῖκες·
ἄλλον δ᾽ ἂν ἄλλαι προσίδοις ἅπερ εὔπτερον ὄρνιν   175
κρεῖσσον ἀμαιμακέτου πυρὸς ὄρμενον
ἀκτὰν πρὸς ἑσπέρου θεοῦ·

ὧν πόλις ἀνάριθμος ὄλλυται·   ἀντ. β
νηλέα δὲ γένεθλα πρὸς πέδωι   180
θαναταφόρα κεῖται ἀνοίκτως·
ἐν δ᾽ ἄλοχοι πολιαί τ᾽ ἔπι ματέρες
ἀκτὰν παρὰ βώμιον ἄλλοθεν ἄλλαι
λυγρῶν πόνων ἱκετῆρες ἐπιστενάχουσι·   185
παιὼν δὲ λάμπει στονόεσσά τε γῆρυς ὅμαυλος·
τῶν ὕπερ, ὦ χρυσέα θύγατερ Διός,
εὐῶπα πέμψον ἀλκάν.

Λύκει᾽ ἄναξ, τά τε σὰ χρυ-   ἀντ. γ
σοστρόφων ἀπ᾽ ἀγκυλᾶν
βέλεα θέλοιμ᾽ ἂν ἀδάματ᾽ ἐνδατεῖσθαι   205
ἀρωγὰ προσταθέντα, τάς τε πυρφόρους
Ἀρτέμιδος αἴγλας, ξὺν αἷς
Λύκι᾽ ὄρεα διάισσει·
τὸν χρυσομίτραν τε κικλήσκω,
τᾶσδ᾽ ἐπώνυμον γᾶς,   210
οἰνῶπα Βάκχον, εὔιον
Μαινάδων ὁμόστολον,
πελασθῆναι φλέγοντ᾽
ἀγλαῶπι ‹– ‿ – ›
πεύκαι ᾽πὶ τὸν ἀπότιμον ἐν θεοῖς θεόν·   215

---

165 ὑπερορνυμένας Musgrave   175 ἄλλαι Dobree: ἄλλωι codd.   185 ἱκετῆρες O: ἱκτῆρες rell.   186 παιὼν pap. L^ac T et lemma schol. in LNO: παιὰν rell.   187 τῶν Kennedy et ut vid. pap.: ὧν codd.   212 ὁμόστολον L^syp PaXs, fort. Zc^ac: μονόστολον Pa²ypZc^c rell.   214 ‹σύμμαχον› G. Wolff

Ἄρεά τε τὸν μαλερόν, ὃς   στρ. γ
νῦν ἄχαλκος ἀσπίδων   191
φλέγει με περιβόητος ἀντιάζων,
παλίσσυτον δράμημα νωτίσαι πάτρας
ἄπουρον, εἴτ᾽ ἐς μέγαν
    θάλαμον Ἀμφιτρίτας,   195
εἴτ᾽ ἐς τὸν ἀπόξενον ὅρμων
Θρήικιον κλύδωνα·
τέλει γάρ, εἴ τι νὺξ ἀφῆι,
τοῦτ᾽ ἐπ᾽ ἦμαρ ἔρχεται·
    τόν, ὦ τᾶν πυρφόρων   200
ἀστραπᾶν κράτη νέμων,
ὦ Ζεῦ πάτερ, ὑπὸ σῶι φθίσον κεραυνῶι.

ΟΙ. αἰτεῖς· ἃ δ᾽ αἰτεῖς, τἄμ᾽ ἐὰν θέληις ἔπη
    κλύων δέχεσθαι τῆι νόσωι θ᾽ ὑπηρετεῖν,
    ἀλκὴν λάβοις ἂν κἀνακούφισιν κακῶν·
    ἁγὼ ξένος μὲν τοῦ λόγου τοῦδ᾽ ἐξερῶ,
    ξένος δὲ τοῦ πραχθέντος· οὐ γὰρ ἂν μακρὰν   220
    ἴχνευον αὐτός, μὴ οὐκ ἔχων τι σύμβολον.
    νῦν δ᾽, ὕστερος γὰρ ἀστὸς εἰς ἀστοὺς τελῶ,
    ὑμῖν προφωνῶ πᾶσι Καδμείοις τάδε·
    ὅστις ποθ᾽ ὑμῶν Λάιον τὸν Λαβδάκου
    κάτοιδεν ἀνδρὸς ἐκ τίνος διώλετο,   225
    τοῦτον κελεύω πάντα σημαίνειν ἐμοί.
    κεἰ μὲν φοβεῖται τοὐπίκλημ᾽ ὑπεξελὼν
    < . . . . >
    αὐτὸς καθ᾽ αὑτοῦ· πείσεται γὰρ ἄλλο μὲν
    ἀστεργὲς οὐδέν, γῆς δ᾽ ἄπεισιν ἀσφαλής.
    εἰ δ᾽ αὖ τις ἄλλον οἶδεν ἐξ ἄλλης χθονὸς   230
    τὸν αὐτόχειρα, μὴ σιωπάτω· τὸ γὰρ
    κέρδος τελῶ 'γὼ χἠ χάρις προσκείσεται.
    εἰ δ᾽ αὖ σιωπήσεσθε, καί τις ἢ φίλου
    δείσας ἀπώσει τοὔπος ἢ χαὑτοῦ τόδε,
    ἃκ τῶνδε δράσω, ταῦτα χρὴ κλύειν ἐμοῦ·   235
    τὸν ἄνδρ᾽ ἀπαυδῶ τοῦτον, ὅστις ἐστί, γῆς

190 sqq. 190–202 post 215 traiecit Haase   192 περιφόβητος ἀντιάζειν Dawe   196 ὅρμων
Doederlein: ὅρμον codd.   221 αὐτό LF^{pc}N^{ac}OPPa^{ac}VG^{γp}Zc: αὐτῶ H | ἔχειν Blaydes
222 ὕστερον Zr | αὐτὸς F²^{pc}OXr^{syp}Zr | τελῶν C^{ac}FHNOPZc   227–278 lacunam indi-
cavit Schwabe   229 ἀσφαλής LCPPaGRZc: ἀβλαβής rell.

τῆσδ', ἧς ἐγὼ κράτη τε καὶ θρόνους νέμω,
μήτ' εἰσδέχεσθαι μήτε προσφωνεῖν τινα,
μήτ' ἐν θεῶν εὐχαῖσι μήτε θύμασιν
κοινὸν ποεῖσθαι, μήτε χέρνιβος νέμειν·   240
ὠθεῖν δ' ἀπ' οἴκων πάντας, ὡς μιάσματος
τοῦδ' ἡμὶν ὄντος, ὡς τὸ Πυθικὸν θεοῦ
μαντεῖον ἐξέφηνεν ἀρτίως ἐμοί.
καὶ ταῦτα τοῖς μὴ δρῶσιν εὔχομαι θεοὺς   269
μήτ' ἀροτὸν αὐτοῖς γῆς ἀνιέναι τινὰ   270
μήτ' οὖν γυναικῶν παῖδας, ἀλλὰ τῶι πότμωι   271
τῶι νῦν φθερεῖσθαι κἄτι τοῦδ' ἐχθίονι.   272
ὑμῖν δὲ ταῦτα πάντ' ἐπισκήπτω τελεῖν   252
ὑπέρ τ' ἐμαυτοῦ, τοῦ θεοῦ τε, τῆσδέ τε   253
γῆς ὧδ' ἀκάρπως κἀθέως ἐφθαρμένης.   254
    οὐδ' εἰ γὰρ ἦν τὸ πρᾶγμα μὴ θεήλατον,   255
ἀκάθαρτον ὑμᾶς εἰκὸς ἦν οὕτως ἐᾶν,
ἀνδρός γ' ἀρίστου βασιλέως τ' ὀλωλότος,
ἀλλ' ἐξερευνᾶν· νῦν δ' ἐπεὶ κυρῶ τ' ἐγὼ
ἔχων μὲν ἀρχὰς ἃς ἐκεῖνος εἶχε πρίν,
ἔχων δὲ λέκτρα καὶ γυναῖχ' ὁμόσπορον,   260
κοινῶν τε παίδων κοίν' ἄν, εἰ κείνωι γένος
μὴ δυστύχησεν, ἦν ἂν ἐκπεφυκότα –
νῦν δ' ἐς τὸ κείνου κρᾶτ' ἐνήλαθ' ἡ τύχη·
ἀνθ' ὧν ἐγὼ τάδ', ὡσπερεὶ τοὐμοῦ πατρός,
ὑπερμαχοῦμαι, κἀπὶ πάντ' ἀφίξομαι,   265
ζητῶν τὸν αὐτόχειρα τοῦ φόνου λαβεῖν,
τῶι Λαβδακείωι παιδὶ Πολυδώρου τε καὶ
τοῦ πρόσθε Κάδμου τοῦ πάλαι τ' Ἀγήνορος.   268
    ἐγὼ μὲν οὖν τοιόσδε τῶι τε δαίμονι   244
τῶι τ' ἀνδρὶ τῶι θανόντι σύμμαχος πέλω·   245
κατεύχομαι δὲ τὸν δεδρακότ', εἴτε τις
εἷς ὢν λέληθεν εἴτε πλειόνων μέτα,
κακὸν κακῶς νιν ἄμορον ἐκτρῖψαι βίον·
ἐπεύχομαι δ', οἴκοισιν εἰ ξυνέστιος
ἐν τοῖς ἐμοῖς γένοιτ' ἐμοῦ ξυνειδότος,   250
παθεῖν ἅπερ τοῖσδ' ἀρτίως ἠρασάμην.   251

---

239 μήτε] μήτ' ἐν CFNOZr: μηδὲ Elmsley   240 χέρνιβος LN: -ους P: -ας rell.   270
ἀροτὸν P^{ac}Zc: ἄροτον P^{pc} rell. | γῆς Vauvilliers: γῆν codd.   244–251 et 269–272 invicem
traiecit Dawe   258 ἐπεὶ κυρῶ rec.: ἐπικυρῶ vel sim. rell.   248 ἄμορον Porson: ἄμοιρον
codd.   250 γένοιτ' L^{pc}α: γένοιτ' ἂν L^{ac} rell.

ὑμῖν δὲ τοῖς ἄλλοισι Καδμείοις, ὅσοις 273
τάδ᾽ ἔστ᾽ ἀρέσκονθ᾽, ἥ τε σύμμαχος Δίκη 274
χοἰ πάντες εὖ ξυνεῖεν εἰσαεὶ θεοί. 275

ΧΟ. ὥσπερ μ᾽ ἀραῖον ἔλαβες, ὧδ᾽, ἄναξ, ἐρῶ·
οὔτ᾽ ἔκτανον γὰρ οὔτε τὸν κτανόντ᾽ ἔχω
δεῖξαι. τὸ δὲ ζήτημα τοῦ πέμψαντος ἦν
Φοίβου τόδ᾽ εἰπεῖν, ὅστις εἴργασταί ποτε.

ΟΙ. δίκαι᾽ ἔλεξας· ἀλλ᾽ ἀναγκάσαι θεοὺς 280
ἂν μὴ θέλωσιν οὐδ᾽ ἂν εἷς δύναιτ᾽ ἀνήρ.

ΧΟ. τὰ δεύτερ᾽ ἐκ τῶνδ᾽ ἂν λέγοιμ᾽ ἅ μοι δοκεῖ.

ΟΙ. εἰ καὶ τρίτ᾽ ἐστί, μὴ παρῇς τὸ μὴ οὐ φράσαι.

ΧΟ. ἄνακτ᾽ ἄνακτι ταῦθ᾽ ὁρῶντ᾽ ἐπίσταμαι
μάλιστα Φοίβωι Τειρεσίαν, παρ᾽ οὗ τις ἂν 285
σκοπῶν τάδ᾽, ὦναξ, ἐκμάθοι σαφέστατα.

ΟΙ. ἀλλ᾽ οὐκ ἐν ἀργοῖς οὐδὲ τοῦτ᾽ ἐπραξάμην·
ἔπεμψα γὰρ Κρέοντος εἰπόντος διπλοῦς
πομπούς· πάλαι δὲ μὴ παρὼν θαυμάζεται.

ΧΟ. καὶ μὴν τά γ᾽ ἄλλα κωφὰ καὶ παλαί᾽ ἔπη. 290

ΟΙ. τὰ ποῖα ταῦτα; πάντα γὰρ σκοπῶ λόγον.

ΧΟ. θανεῖν ἐλέχθη πρός τινων ὁδοιπόρων.

ΟΙ. ἤκουσα κἀγώ· τὸν δὲ δρῶντ᾽ οὐδεὶς ὁρᾷ.

ΧΟ. ἀλλ᾽ εἴ τι μὲν δὴ δείματός γ᾽ ἔχει μέρος,
τὰς σὰς ἀκούων οὐ μενεῖ τοιάσδ᾽ ἀράς. 295

ΟΙ. ὧι μή ᾽στι δρῶντι τάρβος, οὐδ᾽ ἔπος φοβεῖ.

ΧΟ. ἀλλ᾽ οὑξελέγξων αὐτὸν ἔστιν· οἵδε γὰρ
τὸν θεῖον ἤδη μάντιν ὧδ᾽ ἄγουσιν, ὧι
τἀληθὲς ἐμπέφυκεν ἀνθρώπων μόνωι.

ΟΙ. ὦ πάντα νωμῶν Τειρεσία, διδακτά τε 300
ἄρρητά τ᾽, οὐράνιά τε καὶ χθονοστιβῆ,
πόλιν μέν, εἰ καὶ μὴ βλέπεις, φρονεῖς δ᾽ ὅμως
οἵαι νόσωι σύνεστιν· ἧς σὲ προστάτην
σωτῆρά τ᾽, ὦναξ, μοῦνον ἐξευρίσκομεν.
Φοῖβος γάρ, εἰ καὶ μὴ κλύεις τῶν ἀγγέλων, 305
πέμψασιν ἡμῖν ἀντέπεμψεν ἔκλυσιν
μόνην ἂν ἐλθεῖν τοῦδε τοῦ νοσήματος,
εἰ τοὺς κτανόντας Λάιον μαθόντες εὖ

273 ἡμῖν LFHNOPaVGZc   276 εἷλες Eustathius 1809.14   281 οὐδ᾽ ἂν εἷς rec.: οὐδεὶς HV: οὐδὲ εἷς rell.   284 ταῦτα Xrˢʸᵖ: ταῦθ᾽ rell.   287 ἐταξάμην Weckl   293 δὲ δρῶντ᾽ anon.: δ᾽ ἰδόντ᾽ codd.   294 γ᾽ rec.: om. PaD: τ᾽ rell. | τρέφει Wunder   295 σάς δ᾽ H: σάς δ᾽ GR   297 -ξων pap. Oxy. 2180, Lˢ s.l., αΖrΖc: -χων rell. | εἴσιν Wecklein: ἔστιν codd.   305 καὶ] τι L. Étienne

κτείναιμεν ἢ γῆς φυγάδας ἐκπεμψαίμεθα.
σὺ δ᾽ οὖν φθονήσας μήτ᾽ ἀπ᾽ οἰωνῶν φάτιν,　　　　310
μήτ᾽ εἴ τιν᾽ ἄλλην μαντικῆς ἔχεις ὁδόν,
ῥῦσαι σεαυτὸν καὶ πόλιν, ῥῦσαι δ᾽ ἐμέ,
ῥῦσαι δὲ πᾶν μίασμα τοῦ τεθνηκότος·
ἐν σοὶ γὰρ ἐσμέν· ἄνδρα δ᾽ ὠφελεῖν ἀφ᾽ ὧν
ἔχοι τε καὶ δύναιτο κάλλιστος πόνων.　　　　315

ΤΕΙΡΕΣΙΑΣ

　　　 φεῦ φεῦ· φρονεῖν ὡς δεινὸν ἔνθα μὴ τέλη
　　　 λύηι φρονοῦντι· ταῦτα γὰρ καλῶς ἐγὼ
　　　 εἰδὼς διώλεσ᾽· οὐ γὰρ ἂν δεῦρ᾽ ἱκόμην.
ΟΙ.　 τί δ᾽ ἔστιν; ὡς ἄθυμος εἰσελήλυθας.
ΤΕ.　 ἄφες μ᾽ ἐς οἴκους· ῥᾷστα γὰρ τὸ σόν τε σὺ　　　　320
　　　 κἀγὼ διοίσω τοὐμόν, ἢν ἐμοὶ πίθηι.
ΟΙ.　 οὔτ᾽ ἔννομ᾽ εἶπας οὔτε προσφιλῆ πόλει
　　　 τῆιδ᾽ ἥ σ᾽ ἔθρεψε, τήνδ᾽ ἀποστερῶν φάτιν.
ΤΕ.　 ὁρῶ γὰρ οὐδὲ σοὶ τὸ σὸν φώνημ᾽ ἰὸν
　　　 πρὸς καιρόν· ὡς οὖν μηδ᾽ ἐγὼ ταὐτὸν πάθω.　　　　325
ΟΙ.　 μή, πρὸς θεῶν, φρονῶν γ᾽ ἀποστραφῆις, ἐπεὶ
　　　 πάντες σε προσκυνοῦμεν οἵδ᾽ ἱκτήριοι.
ΤΕ.　 πάντες γὰρ οὐ φρονεῖτ᾽· ἐγὼ δ᾽ οὐ μή ποτε
　　　 τὰ λῶιστά γ᾽ εἴπω, μὴ τὰ σ᾽ ἐκφήνω κακά.
ΟΙ.　 τί φήις; ξυνειδὼς οὐ φράσεις, ἀλλ᾽ ἐννοεῖς　　　　330
　　　 ἡμᾶς προδοῦναι καὶ καταφθεῖραι πόλιν;
ΤΕ.　 ἐγὼ οὔτ᾽ ἐμαυτὸν οὔτε σ᾽ ἀλγυνῶ· τί ταῦτ᾽
　　　 ἄλλως ἐλέγχεις; οὐ γὰρ ἂν πύθοιό μου.
ΟΙ.　 οὐκ, ὦ κακῶν κάκιστε – καὶ γὰρ ἂν πέτρου
　　　 φύσιν σύ γ᾽ ὀργάνειας – ἐξερεῖς ποτε,　　　　335
　　　 ἀλλ᾽ ὧδ᾽ ἄτεγκτος †κἀτελεύτητος† φανῆι;
ΤΕ.　 ὀργὴν ἐμέμψω τὴν ἐμήν, τὴν σὴν δ᾽ ὁμοῦ
　　　 ναίουσαν οὐ κατεῖδες, ἀλλ᾽ ἐμὲ ψέγεις.
ΟΙ.　 τίς γὰρ τοιαῦτ᾽ ἂν οὐκ ἂν ὀργίζοιτ᾽ ἔπη
　　　 κλύων ἃ νῦν σὺ τήνδ᾽ ἀτιμάζεις πόλιν;　　　　340
ΤΕ.　 ἥξει γὰρ αὐτά, κἂν ἐγὼ σιγῆι στέγω.
ΟΙ.　 οὔκουν ἅ γ᾽ ἥξει καὶ σὲ χρὴ λέγειν ἐμοί;

315 πόνων Hᵃᶜ PaAXr, et s.l. Lᵃᶜ NOVD: πόνος rell.　　322 ἔννομ᾽ α: ἔννομον fere rell. | προσ-
φιλῆ LPZc: -ὲς L s.l., rell.　　324 φρόνημ᾽ Cᵃᶜ GR　　325 sunt qui πάθω ... malint　　329
τὰ λῶιστά γ᾽ Dawe: τἀμ᾽ ὡς ἂν codd.　　336 κἀπαραίτητος Sehrwald

ΤΕ. οὐκ ἂν πέρα φράσαιμι· πρὸς τάδ᾽, εἰ θέλεις,
     θυμοῦ δι᾽ ὀργῆς ἥτις ἀγριωτάτη.

ΟΙ. καὶ μὴν παρήσω γ᾽ οὐδέν, ὡς ὀργῆς ἔχω,   345
     ἅπερ ξυνίημ᾽· ἴσθι γὰρ δοκῶν ἐμοὶ
     καὶ ξυμφυτεῦσαι τοὔργον, εἰργάσθαι θ᾽, ὅσον
     μὴ χερσὶ καίνων· εἰ δ᾽ ἐτύγχανες βλέπων,
     καὶ τοὔργον ἂν σοῦ τοῦτ᾽ ἔφην εἶναι μόνου.

ΤΕ. ἄληθες; ἐννέπω σε τῶι κηρύγματι   350
     ὧιπερ προεῖπας ἐμμένειν, κἀφ᾽ ἡμέρας
     τῆς νῦν προσαυδᾶν μήτε τούσδε μήτ᾽ ἐμέ,
     ὡς ὄντι γῆς τῆσδ᾽ ἀνοσίωι μιάστορι.

ΟΙ. οὕτως ἀναιδῶς ἐξεκίνησας τόδε
     τὸ ῥῆμα; καὶ ποῦ τοῦτο φεύξεσθαι δοκεῖς;   355

ΤΕ. πέφευγα· τἀληθὲς γὰρ ἰσχῦον τρέφω.

ΟΙ. πρὸς τοῦ διδαχθείς; οὐ γὰρ ἔκ γε τῆς τέχνης.

ΤΕ. πρὸς σοῦ· σὺ γάρ μ᾽ ἄκοντα προυτρέψω λέγειν.

ΟΙ. ποῖον λόγον; λέγ᾽ αὖθις, ὡς μᾶλλον μάθω.

ΤΕ. οὐχὶ ξυνῆκας πρόσθεν, ἢ ᾽κπειρᾶι λέγων;   360

ΟΙ. οὐχ ὥστε γ᾽ εἰπεῖν γνωστόν· ἀλλ᾽ αὖθις φράσον.

ΤΕ. φονέα σέ φημι τἀνδρὸς οὗ ζητεῖς δίκας.

ΟΙ. ἀλλ᾽ οὔ τι χαίρων δίς γε πημονὰς ἐρεῖς.

ΤΕ. εἴπω τι δῆτα κἄλλ᾽, ἵν᾽ ὀργίζηι πλέον;

ΟΙ. ὅσον γε χρήιζεις· ὡς μάτην εἰρήσεται.   365

ΤΕ. λεληθέναι σέ φημι σὺν τοῖς φιλτάτοις
     αἴσχισθ᾽ ὁμιλοῦντ᾽ οὐδ᾽ ὁρᾶν ἵν᾽ εἶ κακοῦ.

ΟΙ. ἦ καὶ γεγηθὼς ταῦτ᾽ ἀεὶ λέξειν δοκεῖς;

ΤΕ. εἴπερ τί γ᾽ ἐστὶ τῆς ἀληθείας σθένος.

ΟΙ. ἀλλ᾽ ἔστι, πλὴν σοί· σοὶ δὲ τοῦτ᾽ οὐκ ἔστ᾽, ἐπεὶ   370
     τυφλὸς τά τ᾽ ὦτα τόν τε νοῦν τά τ᾽ ὄμματ᾽ εἶ.

ΤΕ. σὺ δ᾽ ἄθλιός γε ταῦτ᾽ ὀνειδίζων, ἃ σοὶ
     οὐδεὶς ὃς οὐχὶ τῶνδ᾽ ὀνειδιεῖ τάχα.

ΟΙ. μιᾶς τρέφηι πρὸς νυκτός, ὥστε μήτ᾽ ἐμὲ
     μήτ᾽ ἄλλον, ὅστις φῶς ὁρᾶι, βλάψαι ποτ᾽ ἄν.   375

ΤΕ. οὐ γάρ σε μοῖρα πρός γ᾽ ἐμοῦ πεσεῖν, ἐπεὶ
     ἱκανὸς Ἀπόλλων, ὧι τάδ᾽ ἐκπρᾶξαι μέλει.

ΟΙ. Κρέοντος ἢ τοῦ ταῦτα τἀξευρήματα;

---

349 εἶναι om. LPPaZc   351 προεῖπας Brunck: προσεῖπας codd.   355 καί που Brunck
360 λέγων Heath: λέγειν codd.: μ᾽ ἑλεῖν Arndt   362 δίκας seu δίκην Dawe: κυρεῖν codd.
375 βλέψαι pap. Oxy. 22 CPa^{ac}VR, in lin. GD, fort. L^{ac}   376 με . . . γε σοῦ pap. et codd.:
corr. Brunck   378 τοῦ] του pap.^{ac}: σοῦ rell.

ΤΕ. Κρέων γέ σοι πῆμ᾽ οὐδέν, ἀλλ᾽ αὐτὸς σὺ σοί.

ΟΙ. ὦ πλοῦτε καὶ τυραννὶ καὶ τέχνη τέχνης   380
      ὑπερφέρουσα τῶι πολυζήλωι βίωι,
      ὅσος παρ᾽ ὑμῖν ὁ φθόνος φυλάσσεται,
      εἰ τῆσδέ γ᾽ ἀρχῆς οὕνεχ᾽, ἣν ἐμοὶ πόλις
      δωρητόν, οὐκ αἰτητόν, εἰσεχείρισεν,
      ταύτης Κρέων ὁ πιστός, οὕξ ἀρχῆς φίλος,   385
      λάθραι μ᾽ ὑπελθὼν ἐκβαλεῖν ἱμείρεται,
      ὑφεὶς μάγον τοιόνδε μηχανορράφον,
      δόλιον ἀγύρτην, ὅστις ἐν τοῖς κέρδεσιν
      μόνον δέδορκε, τὴν τέχνην δ᾽ ἔφυ τυφλός.
      ἐπεί, φέρ᾽ εἰπέ, ποῦ σὺ μάντις εἶ σαφής;   390
      πῶς οὐχ, ὅθ᾽ ἡ ῥαψωιδὸς ἐνθάδ᾽ ἦν κύων,
      ηὔδας τι τοῖσδ᾽ ἀστοῖσιν ἐκλυτήριον;
      καίτοι τό γ᾽ αἴνιγμ᾽ οὐχὶ τοὐπιόντος ἦν
      ἀνδρὸς διειπεῖν, ἀλλὰ μαντείας ἔδει·
      ἣν οὔτ᾽ ἀπ᾽ οἰωνῶν σὺ προυφάνης ἔχων   395
      οὔτ᾽ ἐκ θεῶν του γνωτόν· ἀλλ᾽ ἐγὼ μολών,
      ὁ μηδὲν εἰδὼς Οἰδίπους, ἔπαυσά νιν,
      γνώμηι κυρήσας, οὐδ᾽ ἀπ᾽ οἰωνῶν μαθών·
      ὃν δὴ σὺ πειρᾶις ἐκβαλεῖν, δοκῶν θρόνοις
      παραστατήσειν τοῖς Κρεοντείοις πέλας.   400
      κλαίων δοκεῖς μοι καὶ σὺ χὠ συνθεὶς τάδε
      ἀγηλατήσειν· εἰ δὲ μὴ δόκεις γέρων
      εἶναι, παθὼν ἔγνως ἂν οἷά περ φρονεῖς.

ΧΟ. ἡμῖν μὲν εἰκάζουσι καὶ τὰ τοῦδ᾽ ἔπη
      ὀργῆι λελέχθαι καὶ τὰ σ᾽, Οἰδίπου, δοκεῖ.   405
      δεῖ δ᾽ οὐ τοιούτων, ἀλλ᾽ ὅπως τὰ τοῦ θεοῦ
      μαντεῖ᾽ ἄριστα λύσομεν, τόδε σκοπεῖν.

ΤΕ. εἰ καὶ τυραννεῖς, ἐξισωτέον τὸ γοῦν
      ἴσ᾽ ἀντιλέξαι· τοῦδε γὰρ κἀγὼ κρατῶ·
      οὐ γάρ τι σοὶ ζῶ δοῦλος, ἀλλὰ Λοξίαι,   410
      ὥστ᾽ οὐ Κρέοντος προστάτου γεγράψομαι.
      λέγω δ᾽, ἐπειδὴ καὶ τυφλόν μ᾽ ὠνείδισας·
      σὺ καὶ δεδορκὼς οὐ βλέπεις ἵν᾽ εἶ κακοῦ,
      οὐδ᾽ ἔνθα ναίεις οὐδ᾽ ὅτων οἰκεῖς μέτα.
      ἆρ᾽ οἶσθ᾽ ἀφ᾽ ὧν εἶ; καὶ λέληθας ἐχθρὸς ὤν   415

379 γέ Brunck: δέ codd. (δή D)   389 μόνος Groeneboom   398 γνώμης L^{ac}CHNOPa,
P²s.l.   404–7 post 428 trai. Enger   405 Οἰδίπους Elmsley, cf. 646   413 δέδορκας κού
codd.: corr. Reiske

τοῖς σοῖσιν αὐτοῦ νέρθε κἀπὶ γῆς ἄνω;

< . . . . >

καί σ᾽ ἀμφιπλὴξ μητρός τε καὶ τοῦ σοῦ πατρὸς

ἐλᾶι ποτ᾽ ἐκ γῆς τῆσδε δεινόπους ἀρά,

βλέποντα νῦν μὲν ὄρθ᾽, ἔπειτα δὲ σκότον.

βοῆς δὲ τῆς σῆς ποῖος οὐκ ἔσται λιμήν,   420

ποῖος; Κιθαιρὼν οὐχὶ σύμφωνος τάχα,

ὅταν καταίσθηι τὸν ὑμέναιον ὃν δόμοις

< . . . . >

ἄνορμον εἰσέπλευσας εὐπλοίας τυχών;

ἄλλων δὲ πλῆθος οὐκ ἐπαισθάνηι κακῶν

ἅ σ᾽ ἐξισώσει σῶι τοκεῖ καὶ σοῖς τέκνοις.   425

    πρὸς ταῦτα καὶ Κρέοντα καὶ τοὐμὸν στόμα

    προπηλάκιζε· σοῦ γὰρ οὐκ ἔστιν βροτῶν

    κάκιον ὅστις ἐκτριβήσεταί ποτε.

ΟΙ.   ἦ ταῦτα δῆτ᾽ ἀνεκτὰ πρὸς τούτου κλύειν;

    οὐκ εἰς ὄλεθρον; οὐχὶ θᾶσσον αὖ πάλιν   430

    ἄψορρος οἴκων τῶνδ᾽ ἀποστραφεὶς ἄπει;

ΤΕ.   οὐδ᾽ ἱκόμην ἔγωγ᾽ ἄν, εἰ σὺ μὴ ᾽κάλεις.

ΟΙ.   οὐ γάρ τί σ᾽ ἤιδη μῶρα φωνήσοντ᾽, ἐπεὶ

    σχολῆι γ᾽ ἂν οἴκους τοὺς ἐμοὺς <σ᾽> ἐστειλάμην.

ΤΕ.   ἡμεῖς τοιοίδ᾽ ἔφυμεν, ὡς μὲν σοὶ δοκεῖ   435

    μῶροι, γονεῦσι δ᾽, οἵ σ᾽ ἔφυσαν, ἔμφρονες.

ΟΙ.   ποίοισι; μεῖνον· τίς δέ μ᾽ ἐκφύει βροτῶν;

ΤΕ.   ἥδ᾽ ἡμέρα φύσει σε καὶ διαφθερεῖ.

ΟΙ.   ὡς πάντ᾽ ἄγαν αἰνικτὰ κἀσαφῆ λέγεις.

ΤΕ.   οὔκουν σὺ ταῦτ᾽ ἄριστος εὑρίσκειν ἔφυς;   440

ΟΙ.   τοιαῦτ᾽ ὀνείδιζ᾽ οἷς ἔμ᾽ εὑρήσεις μέγαν.

ΤΕ.   αὕτη γε μέντοι σ᾽ ἡ τέχνη διώλεσεν.

ΟΙ.   ἀλλ᾽ εἰ πόλιν τήνδ᾽ ἐξέσωσ᾽, οὔ μοι μέλει.

ΤΕ.   ἄπειμι τοίνυν· καὶ σύ, παῖ, κόμιζέ με.

ΟΙ.   κομιζέτω δῆθ᾽· ὡς παρὼν σύ γ᾽ ἐμποδὼν   445

    ὀχλεῖς, συθείς τ᾽ ἂν οὐκ ἂν ἀλγύναις πλέον.

ΤΕ.   εἰπὼν ἄπειμ᾽ ὧν οὕνεκ᾽ ἦλθον, οὐ τὸ σὸν

    δείσας πρόσωπον· οὐ γὰρ ἔσθ᾽ ὅπου μ᾽ ὀλεῖς.

416–417 lacunam indicavit Dawe   421 ποῖος; Dawe: ποῖος codd.   422–423 lacunam indicavit Dawe   425 σοί τε καὶ τοῖς σοῖς codd.: corr. Nauck   430 αὖ pap. Oxy. 22 in lin.: οὐ idem s.l., pap. Oxy. 2180, codd.   433 ἤιδη pap. Oxy. 2180 i.m.: ἤιδει LPa: ἤιδειν rell. 434 σχολῆι γ᾽ H, lemma Sudae eiusdemque codex G: σχολησγ᾽ pap. Oxy. 22 a.c.: σχολῆι σ᾽ volunt rell. | <σ᾽> Porson   442 τέχνη Bentley: τύχη codd.   446 ἀλγύνοις N

λέγω δέ σοι· τὸν ἄνδρα τοῦτον, ὃν πάλαι
ζητεῖς ἀπειλῶν κἀνακηρύσσων φόνον   450
τὸν Λαΐειον, οὗτός ἐστιν ἐνθάδε,
ξένος λόγωι μέτοικος, εἶτα δ' ἐγγενὴς
φανήσεται Θηβαῖος, οὐδ' ἡσθήσεται
τῆι ξυμφορᾶι· τυφλὸς γὰρ ἐκ δεδορκότος,
καὶ πτωχὸς ἀντὶ πλουσίου, ξένην ἔπι   455
σκήπτρωι προδεικνὺς γαῖαν ἐμπορεύσεται.
φανήσεται δὲ παισὶ τοῖς αὑτοῦ ξυνὼν
ἀδελφὸς αὑτὸς καὶ πατήρ, κἀξ ἧς ἔφυ
γυναικὸς υἱὸς καὶ πόσις, καὶ τοῦ πατρὸς
ὁμόσπορός τε καὶ φονεύς. καὶ ταῦτ' ἰὼν   460
εἴσω λογίζου· κἂν λάβηις μ' ἐψευσμένον,
φάσκειν ἔμ' ἤδη μαντικῆι μηδὲν φρονεῖν.

ΧΟ. τίς ὅντιν' ἁ θεσπιέπει-   στρ. α
     α Δελφὶς ἦιδε πέτρα
     ἄρρητ' ἀρρήτων τελέσαν-   465
     τα φοινίαισι χερσίν;
     ὥρα νιν ἀελλάδων
     ἵππων σθεναρώτερον
       φυγᾶι πόδα νωμᾶν·
     ἔνοπλος γὰρ ἐπ' αὐτὸν ἐπενθρώισκει
     πυρὶ καὶ στεροπαῖς ὁ Διὸς γενέτας,   470
     δειναὶ δ' ἅμ' ἕπονται
     Κῆρες ἀναπλάκητοι.

     ἔλαμψε γὰρ τοῦ νιφόεν-   ἀντ. α
     τος ἀρτίως φανεῖσα
     φήμα Παρνασοῦ τὸν ἄδη-   475
     λον ἄνδρα πάντ' ἰχνεύειν.
     φοιτᾶι γὰρ ὑπ' ἀγρίαν
     ὕλαν ἀνά τ' ἄντρα καὶ
       πετραῖος ὁ ταῦρος,
     μέλεος μελέωι ποδὶ χηρεύων,
     τὰ μεσόμφαλα γᾶς ἀπονοσφίζων   480
     μαντεῖα· τὰ δ' ἀεὶ
     ζῶντα περιποτᾶται.

458 αὑτὸς Xsᶜ: αὐτὸς rell.   461 μ' om. L.   464 ἦιδε J. E. Powell: εἶδε G in lin., novit ΣL: εἶπε rell. (in ras. scr. L²)   467 ἀελλάδων Hesychius: ἀελλοπόδων codd.   478 fort. πετραῖος ὁ Lᵃᶜ: πέτραις ὡς FNPaG: πετραῖος ὡς VRZc: πέτρας ὡς rell.

δεινὰ μὲν οὖν δεινὰ ταράσσει σοφὸς οἰωνοθέτας   στρ.β
οὔτε δοκοῦντ᾽ οὔτ᾽ ἀποφάσκονθ᾽, ὅ τι λέξω δ᾽ ἀπορῶ·   485
πέτομαι δ᾽ ἐλπίσιν οὔτ᾽ ἐνθάδ᾽ ὁρῶν οὔτ᾽ ὀπίσω.
τί γὰρ ἢ Λαβδακίδαις
ἢ τῶι Πολύβου νεῖᶜ   490
  κος ἔκειτ᾽ οὔτε πάροιθέν ποτ᾽ ἔγωγ᾽ οὔτε τανῦν πω
ἔμαθον, πρὸς ὅτου δὴ
  βασάνωι < – ⏑ ⏑ – >
ἐπὶ τὰν ἐπίδαμον   495
φάτιν εἶμ᾽ Οἰδιπόδα, Λαβδακίδαις
ἐπίκουρος ἀδήλων θανάτων.

ἀλλ᾽ ὁ μὲν οὖν Ζεὺς ὅ τ᾽ Ἀπόλλων ξυνετοὶ καὶ τὰ βροτῶν   ἀντ.β
εἰδότες· ἀνδρῶν δ᾽ ὅτι μάντις πλέον ἢ ᾽γω φέρεται,   500
κρίσις οὐκ ἔστιν ἀληθής· σοφίαι δ᾽ ἂν σοφίαν
παραμείψειεν ἀνήρ·
ἀλλ᾽ οὔποτ᾽ ἔγωγ᾽ ἄν,
  πρὶν ἴδοιμ᾽ ὀρθὸν ἔπος, μεμφομένων ἂν καταφαίην.   505
φανερὰ γὰρ ἐπ᾽ αὐτῶι
  πτερόεσσ᾽ ἦλθε κόρα
ποτέ, καὶ σοφὸς ὤφθη
βασάνωι θ᾽ ἡδύπολις· τῶι πρὸς ἐμᾶς   510
φρενὸς οὔποτ᾽ ὀφλήσει κακίαν.

ΚΡ.   ἄνδρες πολῖται, δείν᾽ ἔπη πεπυσμένος
κατηγορεῖν μου τὸν τύραννον Οἰδίπουν,
πάρειμ᾽ ἀτλητῶν. εἰ γὰρ ἐν ταῖς ξυμφοραῖς
ταῖς νῦν νομίζει πρός τί μου πεπονθέναι   515
λόγοισιν εἴτ᾽ ἔργοισιν εἰς βλάβην φέρον,
οὔτοι βίου μοι τοῦ μακραίωνος πόθος,
φέροντι τήνδε βάξιν. οὐ γὰρ εἰς ἁπλοῦν
ἡ ζημία μοι τοῦ λόγου τούτου φέρει,
ἀλλ᾽ ἐς μέγιστον, εἰ κακὸς μὲν ἐν πόλει,   520
κακὸς δὲ πρός του καὶ φίλων κεκλήσομαι.
ΧΟ.   ἀλλ᾽ ἦλθε μὲν δὴ τοῦτο τοὔνειδος τάχ᾽ ἂν
ὀργῆι βιασθὲν μᾶλλον ἢ γνώμηι φρενῶν.

499 τὰν βροτοῖς FVGRZc   500 δ᾽ om. LᵃᶜPa Dᵃᶜ·   510 δ᾽ Lᵃᶜ FHNOGR | των pap. Oxy. 2180 | πρὸς Elmsley: ἀπ᾽ codd.   516 τί μου Hartung: τι τ᾽ ἐμοῦ O (τι T s.l., et gl. in L²AD): γ᾽ ἐμοῦ HPPaXrT, fort. Lᵃᶜ: τ᾽ἐμοῦ L²ᶜ rell.: τ legitur in pap. Oxy. 2180   522 πρός του Kvičala: πρὸς σοῦ codd.

ΚΡ.   τοῦπος δ' ἐφάνθη ταῖς ἐμαῖς γνώμαις ὅτι   525
        πεισθεὶς ὁ μάντις τοὺς λόγους ψευδεῖς λέγοι;
ΧΟ.   ηὐδᾶτο μὲν τάδ', οἶδα δ' οὐ γνώμηι τίνι.
ΚΡ.   ἐξ ὀμμάτων δ' ὀρθῶν τε κἀξ ὀρθῆς φρενὸς
        κατηγορεῖτο τοὐπίκλημα τοῦτό μου;
ΧΟ.   οὐκ οἶδ'· ἃ γὰρ δρῶσ' οἱ κρατοῦντες οὐχ ὁρῶ.   530
        αὐτὸς δ' ὅδ' ἤδη δωμάτων ἔξω περᾶι.
ΟΙ.   οὗτος σύ, πῶς δεῦρ' ἦλθες; ἦ τοσόνδ' ἔχεις
        τόλμης πρόσωπον ὥστε τὰς ἐμὰς στέγας
        ἵκου, φονεὺς ὢν τοῦδε τἀνδρὸς ἐμφανῶς
        λῃστής τ' ἐναργὴς τῆς ἐμῆς τυραννίδος;   535
        φέρ' εἰπὲ πρὸς θεῶν, δειλίαν ἢ μωρίαν
        ἰδών τιν' ἐν ἐμοὶ ταῦτ' ἐβουλεύσω ποεῖν;
        ἢ τοὔργον ὡς οὐ γνωριοῖμί σου τόδε
        δόλωι προσέρπον κοὐκ ἀλεξοίμην μαθών;
        ἆρ' οὐχὶ μῶρόν ἐστι τοὐγχείρημά σου,   540
        ἄνευ τε πλούτου καὶ φίλων τυραννίδα
        θηρᾶν, ὃ πλήθει χρήμασίν θ' ἁλίσκεται;
ΚΡ.   οἶσθ' ὡς πόησον· ἀντὶ τῶν εἰρημένων
        ἴσ' ἀντάκουσον, κᾆτα κρῖν' αὐτὸς μαθών.
ΟΙ.   λέγειν σὺ δεινός, μανθάνειν δ' ἐγὼ κακὸς   545
        σοῦ· δυσμενῆ γὰρ καὶ βαρύν σ' ηὕρηκ' ἐμοί.
ΚΡ.   τοῦτ' αὐτό νυν μου πρῶτ' ἄκουσον ὡς ἐρῶ.
ΟΙ.   τοῦτ' αὐτὸ μή μοι φράζ, ὅπως οὐκ εἶ κακός.
ΚΡ.   εἴ τοι νομίζεις κτῆμα τὴν αὐθαδίαν
        εἶναί τι τοῦ νοῦ χωρίς, οὐκ ὀρθῶς φρονεῖς.   550
ΟΙ.   εἴ τοι νομίζεις ἄνδρα συγγενῆ κακῶς
        δρῶν οὐχ ὑφέξειν τὴν δίκην, οὐκ εὖ φρονεῖς.
ΚΡ.   ξύμφημί σοι ταῦτ' ἔνδικ' εἰρῆσθαι· τὸ δὲ
        πάθημ' ὁποῖον φὴις παθεῖν δίδασκέ με.
ΟΙ.   ἔπειθες ἢ οὐκ ἔπειθες ὡς χρείη μ' ἐπὶ   555
        τὸν σεμνόμαντιν ἄνδρα πέμψασθαί τινα;
ΚΡ.   καὶ νῦν ἔθ' αὑτός εἰμι τῶι βουλεύματι.
ΟΙ.   πόσον τιν' ἤδη δῆθ' ὁ Λάιος χρόνον . . .
ΚΡ.   δέδρακε ποῖον ἔργον; οὐ γὰρ ἐννοῶ.

525 τοῦπος GR pap. Oxy. 2180 τοῦ πρὸς LCFHNOPV: πρὸς τοῦ Pa^c αZrT: πρὸς ●ῦ πρός
Zc^c   528 δ' CHNOGR, pap. Oxy. 2180, Suda: om. rell | τε LPaZrT: γε C: om. HD: δὲ rell.
531 versum om. pap. Oxy. 2180   538 γνωρίσοιμι codd., corr. Elmsley   539 ἢ οὐκ A.
Spengel   541 πλούτου anon.: πλήθους codd.   547 νυν Blaydes: νῦν codd.   549 τὴν
αZrZcT, Suda: τήνδ' rell.   556 τινάς Elmsley

ΟΙ. ἄφαντος ἔρρει θανασίμωι χειρώματι; 560
ΚΡ. μακροὶ παλαιοί τ' ἂν μετρηθεῖεν χρόνοι.
ΟΙ. τότ' οὖν ὁ μάντις οὗτος ἦν ἐν τῆι τέχνηι;
ΚΡ. σοφός γ' ὁμοίως κἀξ ἴσου τιμώμενος.
ΟΙ. ἐμνήσατ' οὖν ἐμοῦ τι τῶι τότ' ἐν χρόνωι;
ΚΡ. οὔκουν ἐμοῦ γ' ἑστῶτος οὐδαμοῦ πέλας. 565
ΟΙ. ἀλλ' οὐκ ἔρευναν τοῦ κτανόντος ἔσχετε;
ΚΡ. παρέσχομεν, πῶς δ' οὔ; τί δ' οὐκ ἠκούσαμεν;
ΟΙ. πῶς οὖν τόθ' οὗτος ὁ σοφὸς οὐκ ηὔδα τάδε;
ΚΡ. οὐκ οἶδ'· ἐφ' οἷς γὰρ μὴ φρονῶ σιγᾶν φιλῶ.
ΟΙ. τοσόνδε γ' οἶσθα καὶ λέγοις ἂν εὖ φρονῶν . . . 570
ΚΡ. ποῖον τόδ'; εἰ γὰρ οἶδά γ', οὐκ ἀρνήσομαι.
ΟΙ. ὁθούνεκ', εἰ μὴ σοὶ ξυνῆλθε, τὰς ἐμὰς
οὐκ ἄν ποτ' εἶπε Λαΐου διαφθοράς.
ΚΡ. εἰ μὲν λέγει τάδ', αὐτὸς οἶσθ'· ἐγὼ δὲ σοῦ
μαθεῖν δικαιῶ ταῦθ' ἅπερ κἀμοῦ σὺ νῦν. 575
ΟΙ. ἐκμάνθαν'· οὐ γὰρ δὴ φονεύς γ' ἁλώσομαι.
ΚΡ. τί δῆτ'; ἀδελφὴν τὴν ἐμὴν γήμας ἔχεις;
ΟΙ. ἄρνησις οὐκ ἔνεστιν ὧν ἀνιστορεῖς.
ΚΡ. ἄρχεις δ' ἐκείνηι ταὐτὰ γῆς ἴσον νέμων;
ΟΙ. ἂν ἦι θέλουσα πάντ' ἐμοῦ κομίζεται. 580
ΚΡ. οὔκουν ἰσοῦμαι σφῶιν ἐγὼ δυοῖν τρίτος;
ΟΙ. ἐνταῦθα γὰρ δὴ καὶ κακὸς φαίνηι φίλος.
ΚΡ. οὔκ, εἰ διδοίης γ' ὡς ἐγὼ σαυτῶι λόγον.
σκέψαι δὲ τοῦτο πρῶτον, εἴ τιν' ἂν δοκεῖς
ἄρχειν ἑλέσθαι ξὺν φόβοισι μᾶλλον ἢ 585
ἄτρεστον εὕδοντ', εἰ τά γ' αὔθ' ἕξει κράτη.
ἐγὼ μὲν οὖν οὔτ' αὐτὸς ἱμείρων ἔφυν
τύραννος εἶναι μᾶλλον ἢ τύραννα δρᾶν,
οὔτ' ἄλλος ὅστις σωφρονεῖν ἐπίσταται.
νῦν μὲν γὰρ ἐκ σοῦ πάντ' ἄνευ φθόνου φέρω, 590
εἰ δ' αὐτὸς ἦρχον, πολλὰ κἂν ἄκων ἔδρων.
πῶς δῆτ' ἐμοὶ τυραννὶς ἡδίων ἔχειν
ἀρχῆς ἀλύπου καὶ δυναστείας ἔφυ;
οὔπω τοσοῦτον ἠπατημένος κυρῶ

566 θανόντος codd.: corr. Meineke   567 οὔ; τί δ' οὐκ Dawe: οὐχὶ κοὐκ codd.   568 τόθ' post οὗτος collocant LPa, post σοφός C   570 τὸ σὸν δέ γ' L^{ac}V: τὸ σόν δέ γ' L^{pc}F^{pc}P: τὸ σόν γε δ' Pa   572 τάσδ' Doederlein   575 ταῦθ' codd., corr. Brunck   576 γ' Blaydes: om. codd.   590 φθόνου Blaydes: φόβου codd.

ὥστ' ἄλλα χρήιζειν ἢ τὰ σὺν κέρδει καλά.   595
νῦν πᾶσι χαίρω, νῦν με πᾶς ἀσπάζεται,
νῦν οἱ σέθεν χρήιζοντες ἐκκαλοῦσ' ἐμέ·
τὸ γὰρ τυχεῖν αὐτοῖσι πᾶν ἐνταῦθ' ἔνι.
πῶς δῆτ' ἐγὼ κεῖν' ἂν λάβοιμ', ἀφεὶς τάδε;
[οὐκ ἂν γένοιτο νοῦς κακὸς καλῶς φρονῶν.]   600
ἀλλ' οὔτ' ἐραστὴς τῆσδε τῆς γνώμης ἔφυν,
οὔτ' ἂν μετ' ἄλλου δρῶντος ἂν τλαίην ποτέ.
καὶ τῶνδ' ἔλεγχον, τοῦτο μὲν Πυθώδ' ἰών,
πεύθου τὰ χρησθέντ' εἰ σαφῶς ἤγγειλά σοι·
τοῦτ' ἄλλ', ἐάν με τῶι τερασκόπωι λάβηις   605
κοινῆι τι βουλεύσαντα, μή μ' ἁπλῆι κτάνηις
ψήφωι, διπλῆι δέ, τῆι τ' ἐμῆι καὶ σῆι, λαβών·
γνώμηι δ' ἀδήλωι μή με χωρὶς αἰτιῶ.
οὐ γὰρ δίκαιον οὔτε τοὺς κακοὺς μάτην
χρηστοὺς νομίζειν οὔτε τοὺς χρηστοὺς κακούς.   610
φίλον γὰρ ἐσθλὸν ἐκβαλεῖν ἴσον λέγω
καὶ τὸν παρ' αὑτῶι βίοτον, ὃν πλεῖστον φιλεῖ.
ἀλλ' ἐν χρόνωι γνώσηι τάδ' ἀσφαλῶς, ἐπεὶ
χρόνος δίκαιον ἄνδρα δείκνυσιν μόνος,
κακὸν δὲ κἂν ἐν ἡμέραι γνοίης μιᾶι.   615
ΧΟ. καλῶς ἔλεξεν, εὐλαβουμένωι πεσεῖν,
ἄναξ· φρονεῖν γὰρ οἱ ταχεῖς οὐκ ἀσφαλεῖς.
ΟΙ. ὅταν ταχύς τις οὑπιβουλεύων λάθραι
χωρῆι, ταχὺν δεῖ κἀμὲ βουλεύειν πάλιν.
εἰ δ' ἡσυχάζων προσμενῶ, τὰ τοῦδε μὲν   620
πεπραγμέν' ἔσται, τἀμὰ δ' ἡμαρτημένα.
ΚΡ. τί δῆτα χρήιζεις; ἦ με γῆς ἔξω βαλεῖν;
ΟΙ. ἥκιστα· θνήισκειν, οὐ φυγεῖν σε βούλομαι.
ΚΡ. <.......................>
ΟΙ. ὅταν προδείξηις οἷόν ἐστι τὸ φθονεῖν.
ΚΡ. ὡς οὐχ ὑπείξων οὐδὲ πιστεύσων λέγεις.   625
ΟΙ. <.......................>
ΚΡ. οὐ γὰρ φρονοῦντά σ' εὖ βλέπω.
ΟΙ.   τὸ γοῦν ἐμόν.

---

597 -οῦσί με codd.: corr. Meineke   598 αὐτοῖσι GR: om. O: αὐτοὺς LᵃᶜCPPaZr: αὐτοῖς rell | πᾶν GRC: ἅπαν LF²ᶜNOP: ἅπαντ' rell.   600 versum eiecit G. Wolff   618 οὑπιβουλεύσων volunt FOVZrXr₁ˢʸᵖ, T s.l.   623-4 lacunam nescio quis primus statuerit   624 Creonti, 625 Oedipodi trib. codd., corr. Haase, qui tamen vv. invicem traiecit   προδείξηις γ' Meineke   625-6 lacunam indicavit Jebb

ΚΡ. ἀλλ' ἐξ ἴσου δεῖ κἀμόν.
ΟΙ.   ἀλλ' ἔφυς κακός.
ΚΡ. εἰ δὲ ξυνίης μηδέν;
ΟΙ.   ἀρκτέον γ' ὅμως.
ΚΡ. οὔτοι κακῶς γ' ἄρχοντος.
ΟΙ.   ὦ πόλις, πόλις.
ΚΡ. κἀμοὶ πόλεως μέτεστιν, οὐχὶ σοὶ μόνωι.   630
ΧΟ. παύσασθ', ἄνακτες· καιρίαν δ' ὑμῖν ὁρῶ
     τήνδ' ἐκ δόμων στείχουσαν Ἰοκάστην, μεθ' ἧς
     τὸ νῦν παρεστὸς νεῖκος εὖ θέσθαι χρεών.

ΙΟΚΑΣΤΗ
     τί τήνδ' ἄβουλον, ὦ ταλαίπωροι, στάσιν
     γλώσσης ἐπήρασθ' οὐδ' ἐπαισχύνεσθε γῆς   635
     οὕτω νοσούσης ἴδια κινοῦντες κακά;
     οὐκ εἶ σύ τ' οἴκους σύ τε, Κρέον, κατὰ στέγας,
     καὶ μὴ τὸ μηδὲν ἄλγος εἰς μέγ' οἴσετε;
ΚΡ. ὅμαιμε, δεινά μ' Οἰδίπους, ὁ σὸς πόσις,
     δρᾶσαι δικαιοῖ, δυοῖν ἀποκρίνας κακοῖν,   640
     ἢ γῆς ἀπῶσαι πατρίδος, ἢ κτεῖναι λαβών.
ΟΙ. ξύμφημι· δρῶντα γάρ νιν, ὦ γύναι, κακῶς
     εἴληφα τοὐμὸν σῶμα σὺν τέχνηι κακῆι.
ΚΡ. μὴ νῦν ὀναίμην, ἀλλ' ἀραῖος, εἴ σέ τι
     δέδρακ', ὀλοίμην, ὧν ἐπαιτιᾶι με δρᾶν.   645
ΙΟ. ὦ πρὸς θεῶν πίστευσον, Οἰδίπους, τάδε,
     μάλιστα μὲν τόνδ' ὅρκον αἰδεσθεὶς θεῶν,
     ἔπειτα κἀμὲ τούσδε θ' οἳ πάρεισί σοι.

ΧΟ. πιθοῦ θελήσας φρονήσας τ', ἄναξ, λίσσομαι.   στρ.
ΟΙ. τί σοι θέλεις δῆτ' εἰκάθω;   650
ΧΟ. τὸν οὔτε πρὶν νήπιον
     νῦν τ' ἐν ὅρκωι μέγαν καταίδεσαι.
ΟΙ. οἶσθ' οὖν ἃ χρήιζεις;
ΧΟ.   οἶδα.
ΟΙ.   φράζε δὴ τί φήις.   655
ΧΟ. τὸν ἐναγῆ φίλον μήποτ' ἐν αἰτίαι

628 ξυνίης CPaXrZrT: ξυνίεις rell., et Xr s.l.   630 μέτεστιν T: μέτεστι τῆσδ' fere rell.
631 καιρίαν ADXsZrZc²ʸᵖ T, fort. Lᵃᶜ: κυρίαν L²ᶜXr rell. | ἡμῖν NOPPa VXrT, C s.l.   634
τήνδ' Doederlein: τὴν codd.   637 σύ τ' α: σύ τ' εἰς ZrT: σύ τ' ἐς rell. | Κρέον CᵖᶜFXr, Vs.l.:
Κρέων rell. | κατὰ om. ZrT, del. Paᵖᶜ   646 Οἰδίπου Pa: cf. 405

σὺν ἀφανεῖ λόγωι σ' ἄτιμον βαλεῖν.

ΟΙ. εὖ νῦν ἐπίστω, ταῦθ' ὅταν ζητῇς, ἐμοὶ
ζητῶν ὄλεθρον ἢ φυγὴν ἐκ τῆσδε γῆς.

ΧΟ. οὐ τὸν πάντων θεῶν θεὸν πρόμον   660
Ἅλιον· ἐπεὶ ἄθεος ἄφιλος ὅ τι πύματον
ὀλοίμαν, φρόνησιν εἰ τάνδ' ἔχω.
ἀλλά μοι δυσμόρωι γᾷ φθίνου-   665
σα τρύχει †ψυχὰν καί† τὰ δ' εἰ κακοῖς κακὰ
προσάψει τοῖς πάλαι τὰ πρὸς σφῷν.

ΟΙ. ὁ δ' οὖν ἴτω, κεἰ χρή με παντελῶς θανεῖν
ἢ γῆς ἄτιμον τῆσδ' ἀπωσθῆναι βίαι.   670
τὸ γὰρ σόν, οὐ τὸ τοῦδ', ἐποικτίρω στόμα
ἐλεινόν· οὗτος δ' ἔνθ' ἂν ἦι στυγήσεται.

ΚΡ. στυγνὸς μὲν εἴκων δῆλος εἶ, βαρὺς δ' ὅταν
θυμοῦ περάσῃς· αἱ δὲ τοιαῦται φύσεις
αὑταῖς δικαίως εἰσὶν ἄλγισται φέρειν.   675

ΟΙ. οὔκουν μ' ἐάσεις κἀκτός εἶ;

ΚΡ.   πορεύσομαι,
σοῦ μὲν τυχὼν ἀγνῶτος, ἐν δὲ τοῖσδ' ἴσος.

ΧΟ. γύναι, τί μέλλεις κομίζειν δόμων τόνδ' ἔσω;   ἀντ.

ΙΟ. μαθοῦσά γ' ἥτις ἡ τύχη.   680

ΧΟ. δόκησις ἀγνὼς λόγων
ἦλθε, δάπτει δὲ καὶ τὸ μὴ 'νδικον.

ΙΟ. ἀμφοῖν ἀπ' αὐτοῖν;

ΧΟ.   ναίχι.

ΙΟ.   καὶ τίς ἦν λόγος;

ΧΟ. ἅλις ἔμοιγ' ἅλις, γᾶς προπονουμένας,   685
φαίνεται, ἔνθ' ἔληξεν, αὐτοῦ μένειν.

ΟΙ. ὁρᾶις ἵν' ἥκεις, ἀγαθὸς ὢν γνώμην ἀνήρ,
τοὐμὸν παριεὶς καὶ καταμβλύνων κέαρ;

ΧΟ. ὦναξ, εἶπον μὲν οὐχ ἅπαξ μόνον,
ἴσθι δὲ παραφρόνιμον ἄπορον ἐπὶ φρόνιμα   690
πεφάνθαι μ' ἄν, εἴ σε νοσφίζομαι,

657 λόγωι σ' Hermann: λόγον L: λόγων CFPVGR: rell.: λόγωι γ' Blaydes (γ post
σύν habet T) | βαλεῖν T, Suda: ἐκβαλεῖν rell.   658 χρήζης R: χρήζεις G   659 φυγὴν
L²ᶜCPADXsZrT, Xr s.l.: φυγεῖν Xr in lin., rell.   666 ψυχάν] κέαρ Arndt: κῆρ malit Page |
καὶ eiecit Hermann: cf. 695 | τὰ δ' Kennedy: τάδ' codd.   672 ἐλεινόν codd.   677 ἴσως
HVGRAXr, post quod lacunam statuit J. E. Powell: ἴσοις Cᵃᶜ Pᵃᶜ: ἴσων Blaydes   685
προνοουμένωι V: προπονουμένωι CHG, R in lin.   689 ὦναξ T: ἄναξ rell., sed ὦ G i.m.
692 σ' ἐνοσφιζόμαν Hermann

ὅς γ' ἐμὰν γᾶν φίλαν ἐν πόνοις
ἀλύουσαν κατ' ὀρθὸν οὔρισας.   695
τανῦν δ' εὔπομπος †εἰ δύναιο γενοῦ†.

ΙΟ.   πρὸς θεῶν δίδαξον κἄμ', ἄναξ, ὅτου ποτὲ
μῆνιν τοσήνδε πράγματος στήσας ἔχεις.
ΟΙ.   ἐρῶ — σὲ γὰρ τῶνδ' ἐς πλέον, γύναι, σέβω —   700
Κρέοντος, οἷά μοι βεβουλευκὼς ἔχει.
ΙΟ.   λέγ', εἰ σαφῶς τὸ νεῖκος ἐγκαλῶν ἐρεῖς.
ΟΙ.   φονέα μέ φησι Λαΐου καθεστάναι.
ΙΟ.   αὐτὸς ξυνειδὼς ἢ μαθὼν ἄλλου πάρα;
ΟΙ.   μάντιν μὲν οὖν κακοῦργον εἰσπέμψας, ἐπεὶ   705
τό γ' εἰς ἑαυτὸν πᾶν ἐλευθεροῖ στόμα.
ΟΙ.   σὺ νῦν ἀφεὶς σεαυτὸν ὧν λέγεις πέρι
ἐμοῦ 'πάκουσον, καὶ μάθ' οὕνεκ' ἐστί σοι
βρότειον οὐδὲν μαντικῆς †ἔχον† τέχνης.
φανῶ δέ σοι σημεῖα τῶνδε σύντομα·   710
χρησμὸς γὰρ ἦλθε Λαΐωι ποτ', οὐκ ἐρῶ
Φοίβου γ' ἀπ' αὐτοῦ, τῶν δ' ὑπηρετῶν ἄπο,
ὡς αὐτὸν ἥξοι μοῖρα πρὸς παιδὸς θανεῖν,
ὅστις γένοιτ' ἐμοῦ τε κἀκείνου πάρα.
καὶ τὸν μέν, ὥσπερ γ' ἡ φάτις, ξένοι ποτὲ   715
λῃσταὶ φονεύουσ' ἐν τριπλαῖς ἁμαξιτοῖς·
παιδὸς δὲ βλάστας οὐ διέσχον ἡμέραι
τρεῖς, καί νιν ἄρθρα κεῖνος ἐνζεύξας ποδοῖν
ἔρριψεν ἄλλων χερσὶν εἰς ἄβατον ὄρος.
κἀνταῦθ' Ἀπόλλων οὔτ' ἐκεῖνον ἤνυσεν   720
φονέα γενέσθαι πατρός, οὔτε Λάιον
τὸ δεινὸν οὐφοβεῖτο πρὸς παιδὸς παθεῖν.
τοιαῦτα φῆμαι μαντικαὶ διώρισαν,
ὧν ἐντρέπου σὺ μηδέν· ἣν γὰρ ἂν θεὸς
χρείαν ἐρευνᾶι ῥαιδίως αὐτὸς φανεῖ.   725
ΟΙ.   οἷόν μ' ἀκούσαντ' ἀρτίως ἔχει, γύναι,
ψυχῆς πλάνημα κἀνακίνησις φρενῶν.
ΙΟ.   ποίας μερίμνης τοῦθ' ὑποστραφεὶς λέγεις;
ΟΙ.   ἔδοξ' ἀκοῦσαί σου τόδ', ὡς ὁ Λάιος

694 ὅς γ' OPa: ὅς τ' rell.   695 cf. 666   σαλεύουσαν Dobree: ἀλύουσαν <αὖ> Dawe |
οὔρισας GR, pap. Oxy. 1369, Eustathius: οὔρησας rell.   697 ἂν γένοιο Blaydes: εἰ γένοιο
Bergk   713 ἥξοι LFPV: ἥξειοι C: ἥξει rell.   716 διπλαῖς RDXsᶜZrT   719 ἄβατον εἰς
ὄρος Musgrave   722 παθεῖν Xr, et γρ. L²C²A²D²: θανεῖν rell.   724 ἣν Brunck, Musgrave: ὧν codd.

κατασφαγείη πρὸς τριπλαῖς ἁμαξιτοῖς.　730
ΙΟ.　ηὐδᾶτο γὰρ ταῦτ' οὐδέ πω λήξαντ' ἔχει.
ΟΙ.　καὶ ποῦ 'σθ' ὁ χῶρος οὗτος, οὗ τόδ' ἦν πάθος;
ΙΟ.　Φωκὶς μέν ἡ γῆ κλῄζεται, σχιστὴ δ' ὁδὸς
ἐς ταὐτὸ Δελφῶν κἀπὸ Δαυλίας ἄγει.
ΟΙ.　καὶ τίς χρόνος τοῖσδ' ἐστὶν οὑξεληλυθώς;　735
ΙΟ.　σχεδόν τι πρόσθεν ἢ σὺ τῆσδ' ἔχων χθονὸς
ἀρχὴν ἐφαίνου τοῦτ' ἐκηρύχθη πόλει.
ΟΙ.　ὦ Ζεῦ, τί μου δρᾶσαι βεβούλευσαι πέρι;
ΙΟ.　τί δ' ἐστί σοι τοῦτ', Οἰδίπους, ἐνθύμιον;
ΟΙ.　μήπω μ' ἐρώτα· τὸν δὲ Λάιον, φύσιν　740
τίν' εἶχε, φράζε, τίνα δ' ἀκμὴν ἥβης ἔχων.
ΙΟ.　μέλας, χνοάζων ἄρτι λευκανθὲς κάρα,
μορφῆς δὲ τῆς σῆς οὐκ ἀπεστάτει πολύ.
ΟΙ.　οἴμοι τάλας· ἔοικ' ἐμαυτὸν εἰς ἀρὰς
δεινὰς προβάλλων ἀρτίως οὐκ εἰδέναι.　745
ΙΟ.　πῶς φῄς; ὀκνῶ τοι πρός σ' ἀποσκοποῦσ', ἄναξ.
ΟΙ.　δεινῶς ἀθυμῶ μὴ βλέπων ὁ μάντις ἦι·
δείξεις δὲ μᾶλλον, ἢν ἓν ἐξείπῃς ἔτι.
ΙΟ.　καὶ μὴν ὀκνῶ μέν, ἃ δ' ἂν ἔρῃ μαθοῦσ' ἐρῶ.
ΟΙ.　πότερον ἐχώρει βαιός, ἢ πολλοὺς ἔχων　750
ἄνδρας λοχίτας, οἷ' ἀνὴρ ἀρχηγέτης;
ΙΟ.　πέντ' ἦσαν οἱ ξύμπαντες, ἐν δ' αὐτοῖσιν ἦν
κῆρυξ· ἀπήνη δ' ἦγε Λάιον μία.
ΟΙ.　αἰαῖ, τάδ' ἤδη διαφανῆ· τίς ἦν ποτε
ὁ τούσδε λέξας τοὺς λόγους ὑμῖν, γύναι;　755
ΙΟ.　οἰκεύς τις, ὅσπερ ἵκετ' ἐκσωθεὶς μόνος.
ΟΙ.　ἦ κἀν δόμοισι τυγχάνει τανῦν παρών;
ΙΟ.　οὐ δῆτ'· ἀφ' οὗ γὰρ κεῖθεν ἦλθε καὶ κράτη
σέ τ' εἶδ' ἔχοντα Λάιόν τ' ὀλωλότα
ἐξικέτευσε τῆς ἐμῆς χειρὸς θιγὼν　760
ἀγρούς σφε πέμψαι κἀπὶ ποιμνίων νομάς,
ὡς πλεῖστον εἴη τοῦδ' ἄποπτος ἄστεως.
κἄπεμψ' ἐγώ νιν· ἄξιος γάρ, οἷ' ἀνὴρ
δοῦλος, φέρειν ἦν τῆσδε καὶ μείζω χάριν.

730 τριπλαῖς HOPPaᶜAXr, T in lin., C² s.l.: διπλαῖς rell.　734 κἀπὶ FHNPPa　741 εἶχε] ἔτυχε Hartung　742 μέλας HNOPVᶜGR, fort. Cᵃᶜ: μέγας rell.　747 ἦν Campe　752 ἐν δ' αὐτοῖσιν PaᶜαZrT: ἐν αὐτοῖσι δ' LCFPVGR: ἐν αὐτοῖς δ' HNOZc: ἐν δὲ τοῖσιν Blaydes 762 ἄστεως L: ἄστεος rell.　763 οἷ' Hermann: ὅ γ' LPPaᵃᶜAᶜ: ὅδε γε DXrXsT: ὥδ' O: ὅδ' Aᶜ s.l., Paᵖᶜ, rell.

ΟΙ. πῶς ἂν μόλοι δῆθ᾽ ἡμὶν ἐν τάχει πάλιν; 765
ΙΟ. πάρεστιν. ἀλλὰ πρὸς τί τοῦτ᾽ ἐφίεσαι;
ΟΙ. δέδοικ᾽ ἐμαυτόν, ὦ γύναι, μὴ πόλλ᾽ ἄγαν
εἰρημέν᾽ ἦι μοι, δι᾽ ἃ νιν εἰσιδεῖν θέλω.
ΙΟ. ἀλλ᾽ ἵξεται μέν· ἀξία δέ που μαθεῖν
κἀγὼ τά γ᾽ ἐν σοὶ δυσφόρως ἔχοντ᾽, ἄναξ. 770
ΟΙ. κοὐ μὴ στερηθῆις γ᾽ ἐς τοσοῦτον ἐλπίδων
ἐμοῦ βεβῶτος· τῶι γὰρ ἂν κἀμείνονι
λέξαιμ᾽ ἂν ἢ σοί, διὰ τύχης τοιᾶσδ᾽ ἰών;
ἐμοὶ πατὴρ μὲν Πόλυβος ἦν Κορίνθιος,
μήτηρ δὲ Μερόπη Δωρίς. ἡγόμην δ᾽ ἀνὴρ 775
ἀστῶν μέγιστος τῶν ἐκεῖ, πρίν μοι τύχη
τοιάδ᾽ ἐπέστη, θαυμάσαι μὲν ἀξία,
σπουδῆς γε μέντοι τῆς ἐμῆς οὐκ ἀξία·
ἀνὴρ γὰρ ἐν δείπνοις μ᾽ ὑπερπλησθεὶς μέθης
καλεῖ παρ᾽ οἴνωι πλαστὸς ὡς εἴην πατρί. 780
κἀγὼ βαρυνθεὶς τὴν μὲν οὖσαν ἡμέραν
μόλις κατέσχον, θἀτέραι δ᾽ ἰὼν πέλας
μητρὸς πατρός τ᾽ ἤλεγχον· οἱ δὲ δυσφόρως
τοὔνειδος ἦγον τῶι μεθέντι τὸν λόγον.
κἀγὼ τὰ μὲν κείνοιν ἐτερπόμην, ὅμως 785
δ᾽ ἔκνιζέ μ᾽ αἰεὶ τοῦθ᾽· ὑφεῖρπε γὰρ πολύ.
λάθραι δὲ μητρὸς καὶ πατρὸς πορεύομαι
Πυθώδε, καί μ᾽ ὁ Φοῖβος ὧν μὲν ἱκόμην
ἄτιμον ἐξέπεμψεν, ἄλλα δ᾽ ἀθλίωι
καὶ δεινὰ καὶ δύστηνα προυφάνη λέγων, 790
ὡς μητρὶ μὲν χρείη με μειχθῆναι, γένος
δ᾽ ἄτλητον ἀνθρώποισι δηλώσοιμ᾽ ὁρᾶν,
φονεὺς δ᾽ ἐσοίμην τοῦ φυτεύσαντος πατρός.
κἀγὼ 'πακούσας ταῦτα, τὴν Κορινθίαν
ἄστροις τὸ λοιπὸν τεκμαρούμενος χθόνα 795
ἔφευγον, ἔνθα μήποτ᾽ ὀψοίμην κακῶν
χρησμῶν ὀνείδη τῶν ἐμῶν τελούμενα.
στείχων δ᾽ ἱκνοῦμαι τούσδε τοὺς χώρους ἐν οἷς
σὺ τὸν τύραννον τοῦτον ὄλλυσθαι λέγεις.

766 τοῦδ᾽ V^{pc} 772 κἀμείνονι Richards: καὶ μείζονι codd.   774 ἐμοὶ πατὴρ ἦν Πόλυβος
Arist. Rhet. 1415a20   779 μέθηι LCFN^{ac} VGR: καὶ μέθης H: non leg. OPa   780 παροινῶν
Heimsoeth   789 ἀθλίωι ut vid. L^{ac}: ἄθλια rell.   790 δύσφημα Heimsoeth | προύφηνεν
Hermann   795 ἐκμετρούμενος codd.: corr. Nauck   797 χρησμῶν γ᾽ FHNOVRAXr

καί σοι, γύναι, τἀληθὲς ἐξερῶ· τριπλῆς   800
ὅτ' ἦ κελεύθου τῆσδ' ὁδοιπορῶν πέλας,
ἐνταῦθά μοι κῆρύξ τε κἀπὶ πωλικῆς
ἀνὴρ ἀπήνης ἐμβεβώς, οἷον σὺ φῄς,
ξυνηντίαζον, κἀξ ὁδοῦ μ' ὅ θ' ἡγεμὼν
αὐτός θ' ὁ πρέσβυς πρὸς βίαν ἠλαυνέτην.   805
κἀγὼ τὸν ἐκτρέποντα, τὸν τροχηλάτην,
παίω δι' ὀργῆς· καί μ' ὁ πρέσβυς, ὡς ὁρᾶι,
ὄχους παραστείχοντα τηρήσας, μέσον
κάρα διπλοῖς κέντροισί μου καθίκετο.
οὐ μὴν ἴσην γ' ἔτεισεν, ἀλλὰ συντόμως   810
σκήπτρωι τυπεὶς ἐκ τῆσδε χειρὸς ὕπτιος
μέσης ἀπήνης εὐθὺς ἐκκυλίνδεται·
κτείνω δὲ τοὺς ξύμπαντας. εἰ δὲ τῶι ξένωι
τούτωι προσήκει Λαΐωι τι συγγενές,
[τίς τοῦδέ γ' ἀνδρός ἐστιν ἀθλιώτερος;]   815
τίς ἐχθροδαίμων μᾶλλον ἂν γένοιτ' ἀνήρ·
ὧι μὴ ξένων ἔξεστι μηδ' ἀστῶν τινα
δόμοις δέχεσθαι, μηδὲ προσφωνεῖν τινα,
ὠθεῖν δ' ἀπ' οἴκων; καὶ τάδ' οὔτις ἄλλος ἦν
ἢ 'γὼ 'π' ἐμαυτῶι τάσδ' ἀρὰς ὁ προστιθείς.   820
λέχη δὲ τοῦ θανόντος ἐν χεροῖν ἐμαῖν
χραίνω, δι' αἷνπερ ὤλετ'. ἆρ' ἔφυν κακός;
ἆρ' οὐχὶ πᾶς ἄναγνος; εἴ με χρὴ φυγεῖν
καί μοι φυγόντι μῆστι τοὺς ἐμοὺς ἰδεῖν
μηδ' ἐμβατεύειν πατρίδος, ἢ γάμοις με δεῖ   825
μητρὸς ζυγῆναι καὶ πατέρα κατακτανεῖν,
Πόλυβον, ὃς ἐξέθρεψε κἀξέφυσέ με.
ἆρ' οὐκ ἀπ' ὠμοῦ ταῦτα δαίμονός τις ἂν
κρίνων ἐπ' ἀνδρὶ τῶιδ' ἂν ὀρθοίη λόγον;
μὴ δῆτα, μὴ δῆτ', ὦ θεῶν ἁγνὸν σέβας,   830
ἴδοιμι ταύτην ἡμέραν, ἀλλ' ἐκ βροτῶν
βαίην ἄφαντος πρόσθεν ἢ τοιάνδ' ἰδεῖν

---

800 versum om. L^ac, vide comm.   801 ἦν codd.   808 ὄχους Doederlein: ὄχου codd.:
ὄχον Schaefer   810 συντόνως Dobree, cf. Trach. 923   815 versum eiecit Dindorf | ἐστιν
αZrT: ἐστ' L^pc O: νῦν ἐστ' L^ac rell.   817 ὄν . . . τινα Schaefer: ὄν . . . τινι Dindorf   822
αἷνπερ C: ηνπερ pap. Oxy. 1369 in lin.: ὧνπερ pap. s.l., rell.   824 μῆστι volunt LGRT^γρ: μή
'τι Zc: μή με F: μὴ δόμους V: μήτε rell., etiam ut vid. pap. Oxy. 1369   825 μηδ' Dindorf: μή
μ' CF^ac PR: μή με G: μήτ' L^2c rell. | ἐμβατεύειν] - ευσαι pap. Oxy. 1369 (ἐπιβῆναι L^sgl ante corr.)
827 Πόλυβον] Λάιον H | ἐξέθρεψε κἀξέφυσε pap. Oxy. 1369, HNOVZr: ἐξέφυσε κἀξέθρεψε
rell. | versum del. Wunder

κηλῖδ᾽ ἐμαυτῶι συμφορᾶς ἀφιγμένην.
ΧΟ. ἡμῖν μέν, ὦναξ, ταῦτ᾽ ὀκνήρ᾽ ἕως δ᾽ ἂν οὖν
πρὸς τοῦ παρόντος ἐκμάθηις, ἔχ᾽ ἐλπίδα. 835
ΟΙ. καὶ μὴν τοσοῦτόν γ᾽ ἐστί μοι τῆς ἐλπίδος,
τὸν ἄνδρα, τὸν βοτῆρα, προσμεῖναι μόνον.
ΙΟ. πεφασμένου δὲ τίς ποθ᾽ ἡ προθυμία;
ΟΙ. ἐγὼ διδάξω σ᾽· ἢν γὰρ εὑρεθῆι λέγων
σοὶ ταῦτ᾽, ἔγωγ᾽ ἂν ἐκπεφευγοίην πάθος. 840
ΙΟ. ποῖον δέ μου περισσὸν ἤκουσας λόγον;
ΟΙ. ληιστὰς ἔφασκες αὐτὸν ἄνδρας ἐννέπειν
ὥς νιν κατακτείνειαν· εἰ μὲν οὖν ἔτι
λέξει τὸν αὐτὸν ἀριθμόν, οὐκ ἐγὼ 'κτανον·
οὐ γὰρ γένοιτ᾽ ἂν εἷς γε τοῖς πολλοῖς ἴσος. 845
εἰ δ᾽ ἄνδρ᾽ ἕν᾽ οἰόζωνον αὐδήσει σαφῶς,
τοῦτ᾽ ἐστὶν ἤδη τοὖργον εἰς ἐμὲ ῥέπον.
ΙΟ. ἀλλ᾽ ὡς φανέν γε τοὖπος ὧδ᾽ ἐπίστασο,
κοὐκ ἔστιν αὐτῶι τοῦτό γ᾽ ἐκβαλεῖν πάλιν·
πόλις γὰρ ἤκουσ᾽, οὐκ ἐγὼ μόνη, τάδε. 850
εἰ δ᾽ οὖν τι κἀκτρέποιτο τοῦ πρόσθεν λόγου,
οὔτοι ποτ᾽, ὦναξ, τόν γε Λαΐου φόνον
φανεῖ δικαίως ὀρθόν, ὅν γε Λοξίας
διεῖπε χρῆναι παιδὸς ἐξ ἐμοῦ θανεῖν.
καίτοι νιν οὐ κεῖνός γ᾽ ὁ δύστηνός ποτε 855
κατέκταν᾽, ἀλλ᾽ αὐτὸς πάροιθεν ὤλετο·
ὥστ᾽ οὐχὶ μαντείας γ᾽ ἂν οὔτε τῆιδ᾽ ἐγὼ
βλέψαιμ᾽ ἂν οὕνεκ᾽ οὔτε τῆιδ᾽ ἂν ὕστερον.
ΟΙ. καλῶς νομίζεις· ἀλλ᾽ ὅμως τὸν ἐργάτην
πέμψον τινὰ στελοῦντα, μηδὲ τοῦτ᾽ ἀφῆις. 860
ΙΟ. πέμψω ταχύνασ᾽· ἀλλ᾽ ἴωμεν ἐς δόμους·
οὐδὲν γὰρ ἂν πράξαιμ᾽ ἂν ὧν οὔ σοι φίλον.

ΧΟ. εἴ μοι ξυνείη φέροντι μοῖρα τὰν   στρ.α
εὔσεπτον ἁγνείαν λόγων
ἔργων τε πάντων, ὧν νόμοι πρόκεινται 865
ὑψίποδες, †οὐρανίαν
δι᾽ αἰθέρα† τεκνωθέντες, ὧν Ὄλυμπος
πατὴρ μόνος, οὐδέ νιν
θνατὰ φύσις ἀνέρων

836 γ᾽ om. LCPPaGRZc: τ᾽ V   840 ἄγος Arndt   843 -ειαν NOPaZrT: -αιεν L²ᶜFVRα: -ειεν CHP, G in lin.: -ειν Zc: -κτάναιεν G. s.l.   845 τοῖς] τις Brunck   852 σόν γε Bothe, cf. 573   863 τρέφοντι Soutendam   867 οὐρανίαι ᾽ν αἰθέρι Enger

ἔτικτεν, οὐδὲ μήποτε λάθα κατακοιμάσηι.   870
μέγας ἐν τούτοις θεός, οὐδὲ γηράσκει.

ὕβριν φυτεύει τυραννίς· ὕβρις εἰ   ἀντ.α
  πολλῶν ὑπερπλησθῆι μάταν
ἃ μὴ ʼπίκαιρα μηδὲ συμφέροντα,   875
ἀκρότατα γεῖσ' ἀναβᾶσ'
  ἀπότομον ὤρουσεν εἰς ἀνάγκαν,
ἔνθ' οὐ ποδὶ χρησίμωι
χρῆται. τὸ καλῶς δ' ἔχον
πόλει πάλαισμα μήποτε λῦσαι θεὸν αἰτοῦμαι·   880
θεὸν οὐ λήξω ποτὲ προστάταν ἴσχων.

εἰ δέ τις ὑπέροπτα χερσὶν   στρ.β
  ἢ λόγωι πορεύεται,
Δίκας ἀφόβητος οὐδὲ   885
  δαιμόνων ἕδη σέβων,
κακά νιν ἕλοιτο μοῖρα,
  δυσπότμου χάριν χλιδᾶς,
εἰ μὴ τὸ κέρδος κερδανεῖ δικαίως
καὶ τῶν ἀσέπτων ἔρξεται   890
ἢ τῶν ἀθίκτων θίξεται ματάιζων.
τίς ἔτι ποτ' ἐν τοῖσδ' ἀνὴρ †θυμῶιτ† βέλη
†ἔρξεταιτ† ψυχᾶς ἀμύνειν;
εἰ γὰρ αἱ τοιαίδε πράξεις τίμιαι,   895
τί δεῖ με χορεύειν;

οὐκέτι τὸν ἄθικτον εἶμι   ἀντ.β
  γᾶς ἐπ' ὀμφαλὸν σέβων,
οὐδ' ἐς τὸν Ἀβαῖσι ναόν,
  οὐδὲ τὰν Ὀλυμπίαν,   900
εἰ μὴ τάδε χειρόδεικτα
  πᾶσιν ἁρμόσει βροτοῖς.
ἀλλ', ὦ κρατύνων, εἴπερ ὄρθ' ἀκούεις,
Ζεῦ, πάντ' ἀνάσσων, μὴ λάθοι
σὲ τάν τε σὰν ἀθάνατον αἰὲν ἀρχάν.   905
φθίνοντα γὰρ Λαΐου παλαίφατα

870 μήποτε Par. gr. 2884: μίν ποτε CGR: μήν ποτε rell.   873 ὕβρις φυτεύει τύραννον codd.: corr. Blaydes   876 ἀκρότατᾱν εἰσαναβᾶσ' fere codd.: corr. Wolff   883 ὑπέροπλα Cᵃᶜ fort. recte   891 θίξεται Blaydes: ἔξεται codd.   892 θυμοῦ NᵖᶜV, s.l.DXs: θεῶν Hermann   894 ἔξεται H: ἔρξεται vel ἔρξεται rell.: εὔξεται Musgrave: ἀρκέσει Enger   896 τί] ποῖ Dawe   906 Λαΐου παλαίφατα Hermann: Λαΐου παλαιὰ AXrXsZc: παλαιὰ Λαΐου HVDZr, Os.l.: πάλαι Λαΐου O, N in lin.: Λαΐου sine παλαιὰ LCFPGR: Pa non leg.

θέσφατ᾽ ἐξαιροῦσιν ἤδη,
κοὐδαμοῦ τιμαῖς Ἀπόλλων ἐμφανής·
ἔρρει δὲ τὰ θεῖα.   910

ΙΟ. χώρας ἄνακτες, δόξα μοι παρεστάθη
ναοὺς ἱκέσθαι δαιμόνων, τάδ᾽ ἐν χεροῖν
στέφη λαβούσηι κἀπιθυμιάματα.
ὑψοῦ γὰρ αἴρει θυμὸν Οἰδίπους ἄγαν
λύπαισι παντοίαισιν, οὐδ᾽ ὁποῖ᾽ ἀνὴρ   915
ἔννους τὰ καινὰ τοῖς πάλαι τεκμαίρεται,
ἀλλ᾽ ἔστι τοῦ λέγοντος, ἢν φόβους λέγηι.
ὅτ᾽ οὖν παραινοῦσ᾽ οὐδὲν ἐς πλέον ποιῶ,
πρὸς σ᾽, ὦ Λύκει᾽ Ἄπολλον, ἄγχιστος γὰρ εἶ,
ἱκέτις ἀφῖγμαι τοῖσδε σὺν κατάργμασιν,   920
ὅπως λύσιν τιν᾽ ἡμὶν εὐαγῆ πόρηις·
ὡς νῦν ὀκνοῦμεν πάντες ἐκπεπληγμένον
κεῖνον βλέποντες ὡς κυβερνήτην νεώς.

ΑΓΓΕΛΟΣ

ἆρ᾽ ἂν παρ᾽ ὑμῶν, ὦ ξένοι, μάθοιμ᾽ ὅπου
τὰ τοῦ τυράννου δώματ᾽ ἐστὶν Οἰδίπου;   925
μάλιστα δ᾽ αὐτὸν εἴπατ᾽, εἰ κάτισθ᾽ ὅπου.

ΧΟ. στέγαι μὲν αἵδε, καὐτὸς ἔνδον, ὦ ξένε·
γυνὴ δὲ μήτηρ θ᾽ ἥδε τῶν κείνου τέκνων.

ΑΓ. ἀλλ᾽ ὀλβία τε καὶ ξὺν ὀλβίοις ἀεὶ
γένοιτ᾽ ἐκείνου γ᾽ οὖσα παντελὴς δάμαρ.   930

ΙΟ. αὕτως δὲ καὶ σύ γ᾽, ὦ ξέν᾽· ἄξιος γὰρ εἶ
τῆς εὐεπείας οὕνεκ᾽. ἀλλὰ φράζ᾽ ὅτου
χρήιζων ἀφῖξαι χὤτι σημῆναι θέλων.

ΑΓ. ἀγαθὰ δόμοις τε καὶ πόσει τῶι σῶι, γύναι.

ΙΟ. τὰ ποῖα ταῦτα; πρὸς τίνος δ᾽ ἀφιγμένος;   935

ΑΓ. ἐκ τῆς Κορίνθου. τὸ δ᾽ ἔπος οὑξερῶ τάχα,
ἥδοιο μέν, πῶς δ᾽ οὐκ ἄν; ἀσχάλλοις δ᾽ ἴσως.

ΙΟ. τί δ᾽ ἔστι; ποίαν δύναμιν ὧδ᾽ ἔχει διπλῆν;

ΑΓ. τύραννον αὐτὸν οὑπιχώριοι χθονὸς
τῆς Ἰσθμίας στήσουσιν, ὡς ηὐδᾶτ᾽ ἐκεῖ.   940

ΙΟ. τί δ᾽; οὐχ ὁ πρέσβυς Πόλυβος ἐγκρατὴς ἔτι;

920 κατεύγμασιν codd.: corr. Wunder   928 μήτηρ θ᾽ Σ μήτηρ codd.   930 γένοι᾽
Wecklein   935 πρὸς aT: παρὰ rell.   938 ποῖον quasi e lapsu calami Earle

ΑΓ.   οὐ δῆτ᾽, ἐπεί νιν θάνατος ἐν τάφοις ἔχει.
ΙΟ.   πῶς εἶπας; ἦ τέθνηκε Πόλυβος, ὦ γέρον;
ΑΓ.   εἰ μὴ λέγω τἀληθές, ἀξιῶ θανεῖν.
ΙΟ.   ὦ πρόσπολ᾽, οὐχὶ δεσπότηι τάδ᾽ ὡς τάχος   945
      μολοῦσα λέξεις; ὦ θεῶν μαντεύματα,
      ἵν᾽ ἐστέ· τοῦτον Οἰδίπους πάλαι τρέμων
      τὸν ἄνδρ᾽ ἔφευγε μὴ κτάνοι, καὶ νῦν ὅδε
      πρὸς τῆς τύχης ὄλωλεν, οὐδὲ τοῦδ᾽ ὕπο.
ΟΙ.   ὦ φίλτατον γυναικὸς Ἰοκάστης κάρα,   950
      τί μ᾽ ἐξεπέμψω δεῦρο τῶνδε δωμάτων;
ΙΟ.   ἄκουε τἀνδρὸς τοῦδε, καὶ σκόπει κλύων
      τὰ σέμν᾽ ἵν᾽ ἥκει τοῦ θεοῦ μαντεύματα.
ΟΙ.   οὗτος δὲ τίς ποτ᾽ ἐστί, καὶ τί μοι λέγει;
ΙΟ.   ἥκει Κορίνθου, πατέρα τὸν σὸν ἀγγελῶν   955
      ὡς οὐκέτ᾽ ὄντα Πόλυβον, ἀλλ᾽ ὀλωλότα.
ΟΙ.   τί φήις, ξέν᾽; αὐτός μοι σὺ σημάντωρ γενοῦ.
ΑΓ.   εἰ τοῦτο πρῶτον δεῖ μ᾽ ἀπαγγεῖλαι σαφῶς,
      εὖ ἴσθ᾽ ἐκεῖνον θανάσιμον βεβηκότα.
ΟΙ.   πότερα δόλοισιν, ἦ νόσου ξυναλλαγῆι;   960
ΑΓ.   σμικρὰ παλαιὰ σώματ᾽ εὐνάζει ῥοπή.
ΟΙ.   νόσοις ὁ τλήμων, ὡς ἔοικεν, ἔφθιτο.
ΑΓ.   καὶ τῶι μακρῶι γε συμμετρούμενος χρόνωι.
ΟΙ.   φεῦ φεῦ· τί δῆτ᾽ ἄν, ὦ γύναι, σκοποῖτό τις
      τὴν Πυθόμαντιν ἑστίαν, ἢ τοὺς ἄνω   965
      κλάζοντας ὄρνις, ὧν ὑφ᾽ ἡγητῶν ἐγὼ
      κτενεῖν ἔμελλον πατέρα τὸν ἐμόν; ὁ δὲ θανὼν
      κεύθει κάτω δὴ γῆς, ἐγὼ δ᾽ ὅδ᾽ ἐνθάδε
      ἄψαυστος ἔγχους — εἴ τι μὴ τὠμῶι πόθωι
      κατέφθιθ᾽· οὕτω δ᾽ ἂν θανὼν εἴη ᾽ξ ἐμοῦ.   970
      τὰ δ᾽ οὖν παρόντα συλλαβὼν θεσπίσματα
      κεῖται παρ᾽ Ἅιδηι Πόλυβος ἄξι᾽ οὐδενός.
ΙΟ.   οὔκουν ἐγώ σοι ταῦτα προύλεγον πάλαι;
ΟΙ.   ηὔδας· ἐγὼ δὲ τῶι φόβωι παρηγόμην.
ΙΟ.   μὴ νῦν ἔτ᾽ αὐτῶν μηδὲν ἐς θυμὸν βάλης.   975

---

942 δόμοις Fᵃᶜ HN   943 τέθνηκε] τέθνηκέ που ZrT | ὦ γέρον Bothe: γέρων ZrT: om. rell.
ἦ τέθνηκεν Οἰδίπου πατήρ Nauck   944 μὴ GRZrT: δὲ μὴ rell.   λέγω GRZrT: λέγω ᾽γὼ
FHNV: λέγω ἐγὼ O: λέγω τ᾽ ἐγὼ Paᵃᶜ: λέγω γ᾽ ἐγὼ rell.   955 ἥκει seu ἥκει ᾽κ Dawe: ἐκ τῆς
codd.   957 σημήνας LPaGR, sed σημάντωρ Lˢʸᴾ Gˢʸᴾ: σημάνας Zc   966 ὑφ᾽ ἡγητῶν
HXrT: ὑφηγητῶν rell.   968 δὴ om. LᵃᶜCFHNOGRDXs, ante κάτω collocat Zr

ΟΙ. καὶ πῶς τὸ μητρὸς λέκτρον οὐκ ὀκνεῖν με δεῖ;
ΙΟ. τί δ᾽ ἂν φοβοῖτ᾽ ἄνθρωπος, ὧι τὰ τῆς τύχης
κρατεῖ, πρόνοια δ᾽ ἐστὶν οὐδενὸς σαφής;
εἰκῆι κράτιστον ζῆν, ὅπως δύναιτό τις.
σὺ δ᾽ εἰς τὰ μητρὸς μὴ φοβοῦ νυμφεύματα· 980
πολλοὶ γὰρ ἤδη κἀν ὀνείρασιν βροτῶν
μητρὶ ξυνηυνάσθησαν· ἀλλὰ ταῦθ᾽ ὅτωι
παρ᾽ οὐδέν ἐστι, ῥᾶιστα τὸν βίον φέρει.
ΟΙ. καλῶς ἅπαντα ταῦτ᾽ ἂν ἐξείρητό σοι,
εἰ μὴ 'κύρει ζῶσ᾽ ἡ τεκοῦσα· νῦν δ᾽, ἐπεὶ 985
ζῆι, πᾶσ᾽ ἀνάγκη, κεἰ καλῶς λέγεις, ὀκνεῖν.
ΙΟ. καὶ μὴν μέγας γ᾽ ὀφθαλμὸς οἱ πατρὸς τάφοι.
ΟΙ. μέγας, ξυνίημ᾽, ἀλλὰ τῆς ζώσης φόβος.
ΑΓ. ποίας δὲ καὶ γυναικὸς ἐκφοβεῖσθ᾽ ὕπερ;
ΟΙ. Μερόπης, γεραιέ, Πόλυβος ἧς ὤικει μέτα. 990
ΑΓ. τί δ᾽ ἔστ᾽ ἐκείνης ὑμὶν ἐς φόβον φέρον;
ΟΙ. θεήλατον μάντευμα δεινόν, ὦ ξένε.
ΑΓ. ἦ ῥητὸν ἢ οὐ θεμιστὸν ἄλλον εἰδέναι;
ΟΙ. μάλιστά γ᾽· εἶπε γάρ με Λοξίας ποτὲ
χρῆναι μιγῆναι μητρὶ τἠμαυτοῦ, τό τε 995
πατρῶιον αἷμα χερσὶ ταῖς ἐμαῖς ἑλεῖν.
ὧν οὕνεχ᾽ ἡ Κόρινθος ἐξ ἐμοῦ πάλαι
μακρὰν ἀπωικεῖτ᾽· εὐτυχῶς μέν, ἀλλ᾽ ὅμως
τὰ τῶν τεκόντων ὄμμαθ᾽ ἥδιστον βλέπειν.
ΑΓ. ἦ γὰρ τάδ᾽ ὀκνῶν κεῖθεν ἦσθ᾽ ἀπόπτολις; 1000
ΟΙ. πατρός γε χρήιζων μὴ φονεὺς εἶναι, γέρον.
ΑΓ. τί δῆτ᾽ ἐγὼ οὐχὶ τοῦδε τοῦ φόβου σ᾽, ἄναξ,
ἐπείπερ εὔνους ἦλθον, ἐξελυσάμην;
ΟΙ. καὶ μὴν χάριν γ᾽ ἂν ἀξίαν λάβοις ἐμοῦ.
ΑΓ. καὶ μὴν μάλιστα τοῦτ᾽ ἀφικόμην, ὅπως 1005
σοῦ πρὸς δόμους ἐλθόντος εὖ πράξαιμί τι.
ΟΙ. ἀλλ᾽ οὔποτ᾽ εἶμι τοῖς φυτεύσασίν γ᾽ ὁμοῦ.
ΑΓ. ὦ παῖ, καλῶς εἶ δῆλος οὐκ εἰδὼς τί δρᾶις.
ΟΙ. πῶς, ὦ γεραιέ; πρὸς θεῶν, δίδασκέ με.
ΑΓ. εἰ τῶνδε φεύγεις οὕνεκ᾽ εἰς οἴκους μολεῖν. 1010
ΟΙ. ταρβῶν γε μή μοι Φοῖβος ἐξέλθηι σαφής.

976 λέχος CPVGRZrZc, in lin. LPa   981 κἀν in ras. scr. L^c   987 μέγας γ᾽ anon.: μέγας
codd. | οἰωνὸς Blaydes   993 ἢ οὐχὶ Brunck | θεμιτὸν codd.: corr. Johnson   1001 γε CH,
fort. N: om. V· τε rell.   1002 ἐγὼ Lievens: ἐγωγ᾽ codd.   οὐ L^pc FDZrT   1011 ταρβῶν
Vind. phil. gr. 48, Ven. gr. 467: ταρβῶ codd. nostri | ἐξέλθηι FOαT: -οι rell.

ΑΓ. ἦ μὴ μίασμα τῶν φυτευσάντων λάβῃς;
ΟΙ. τοῦτ᾽ αὐτό, πρέσβυ, τοῦτό μ᾽ εἰσαεὶ φοβεῖ.
ΑΓ. ἆρ᾽ οἶσθα δῆτα πρὸς δίκης οὐδὲν τρέμων;
ΟΙ. πῶς δ᾽ οὐχί, παῖς γ᾽ εἰ τῶνδε γεννητῶν ἔφυν; 1015
ΑΓ. ὁθούνεκ᾽ ἦν σοι Πόλυβος οὐδὲν ἐν γένει.
ΟΙ. πῶς εἶπας; οὐ γὰρ Πόλυβος ἐξέφυσέ με;
ΑΓ. οὐ μᾶλλον οὐδὲν τοῦδε τἀνδρός, ἀλλ᾽ ἴσον.
ΟΙ. καὶ πῶς ὁ φύσας ἐξ ἴσου τῶι μηδενί;
ΑΓ. ἀλλ᾽ οὔ σ᾽ ἐγείνατ᾽ οὔτ᾽ ἐκεῖνος οὔτ᾽ ἐγώ. 1020
ΟΙ. ἀλλ᾽ ἀντὶ τοῦ δὴ παῖδά μ᾽ ὠνομάζετο;
ΑΓ. δῶρόν ποτ᾽, ἴσθι, τῶν ἐμῶν χειρῶν λαβών.
ΟΙ. κᾆθ᾽ ὧδ᾽ ἀπ᾽ ἄλλης χειρὸς ἔστερξεν μέγα;
ΑΓ. ἡ γὰρ πρὶν αὐτὸν ἐξέπεισ᾽ ἀπαιδία.
ΟΙ. σὺ δ᾽ ἐμπολήσας ἢ τυχών μ᾽ αὐτῶι δίδως; 1025
ΑΓ. εὑρὼν ναπαίαις ἐν Κιθαιρῶνος πτυχαῖς.
ΟΙ. ὡδοιπόρεις δὲ πρὸς τί τούσδε τοὺς τόπους;
ΑΓ. ἐνταῦθ᾽ ὀρείοις ποιμνίοις ἐπεστάτουν.
ΟΙ. ποιμὴν γὰρ ἦσθα κἀπὶ θητείαι πλάνης;
ΑΓ. σοῦ τ᾽, ὦ τέκνον, σωτήρ γε τῶι τότ᾽ ἐν χρόνωι. 1030
ΟΙ. τί δ᾽ ἄλγος ἴσχοντ᾽ ἐν χεροῖν με λαμβάνεις;
ΑΓ. ποδῶν ἂν ἄρθρα μαρτυρήσειεν τὰ σά.
ΟΙ. οἴμοι, τί τοῦτ᾽ ἀρχαῖον ἐννέπεις κακόν;
ΑΓ. λύω σ᾽ ἔχοντα διατόρους ποδοῖν ἀκμάς.
ΟΙ. δεινόν γ᾽ ὄνειδος σπαργάνων ἀνειλόμην. 1035
ΑΓ. ὥστ᾽ ὠνομάσθης ἐκ τύχης ταύτης ὃς εἶ.
ΟΙ. <.................>
ΑΓ. <.................>
ΟΙ. ὦ πρὸς θεῶν, πρὸς μητρὸς ἢ πατρός; φράσον.
ΑΓ. οὐκ οἶδ᾽· ὁ δοὺς δὲ ταῦτ᾽ ἐμοῦ λῶιον φρονεῖ.
ΟΙ. ἦ γὰρ παρ᾽ ἄλλου μ᾽ ἔλαβες οὐδ᾽ αὐτὸς τυχών;
ΑΓ. οὔκ, ἀλλὰ ποιμὴν ἄλλος ἐκδίδωσί μοι. 1040
ΟΙ. τίς οὗτος; ἦ κάτοισθα δηλῶσαι λόγωι;
ΑΓ. τῶν Λαΐου δήπου τις ὠνομάζετο.
ΟΙ. ἦ τοῦ τυράννου τῆσδε γῆς πάλαι ποτέ;
ΑΓ. μάλιστα· τούτου τἀνδρὸς οὗτος ἦν βοτήρ.
ΟΙ. ἦ κἄστ᾽ ἔτι ζῶν οὗτος, ὥστ᾽ ἰδεῖν ἐμέ; 1045
ΑΓ. ὑμεῖς γ᾽ ἄριστ᾽ εἰδεῖτ᾽ ἂν οὑπιχώριοι.

1025 τεκών codd.: corr. Bothe, Foertsch: κιχών Heimsoeth   1030 σοῦ τ᾽ Hermann: σοῦ δ᾽
G: σοῦ O: σοῦ γ᾽ rell. | πόνωι Hertel.   1031 χεροῖν F²ʸᴾ: καιροῖς LPZc: κακοῖς rell.   με
om. LHN   1036–7 lacunam notavit Herwerden   1046 γ᾽ α: om. T: γὰρ rell.

ΟΙ. ἔστιν τις ὑμῶν τῶν παρεστώτων πέλας
ὅστις κάτοιδε τὸν βοτῆρ᾽ ὃν ἐννέπει,
εἴτ᾽ οὖν ἐπ᾽ ἀγρῶν εἴτε κἀνθάδ᾽ εἰσιδών·
σημήναθ᾽, ὡς ὁ καιρὸς ηὑρῆσθαι τάδε.   1050
ΧΟ. οἶμαι μὲν οὐδέν᾽ ἄλλον ἢ τὸν ἐξ ἀγρῶν
ὃν κἀμάτευες πρόσθεν εἰσιδεῖν· ἀτὰρ
ἥδ᾽ ἂν τάδ᾽ οὐχ ἥκιστ᾽ ἂν Ἰοκάστη λέγοι.
ΟΙ. γύναι, νοεῖς ἐκεῖνον ὅντιν᾽ ἀρτίως
μολεῖν ἐφιέμεσθα; τόνδ᾽ οὗτος λέγει;   1055
ΙΟ. τί δ᾽ ὅντιν᾽ εἶπε; μηδὲν ἐντραπῇς· τὰ δὲ
ῥηθέντα βούλου μηδὲ μεμνῆσθαι μάτην.
ΟΙ. οὐκ ἂν γένοιτο τοῦθ᾽, ὅπως ἐγὼ λαβὼν
σημεῖα τοιαῦτ᾽ οὐ φανῶ τοὐμὸν γένος.
ΙΟ. μή, πρὸς θεῶν, εἴπερ τι τοῦ σαυτοῦ βίου   1060
κήδηι, ματεύσῃς τοῦθ᾽· ἅλις νοσοῦσ᾽ ἐγώ.
ΟΙ. θάρσει· σὺ μὲν γὰρ οὐδ᾽ ἐὰν τρίτης ἐγὼ
μητρὸς φανῶ τρίδουλος ἐκφανῇ κακή.
ΙΟ. ὅμως πιθοῦ μοι, λίσσομαι, μὴ δρᾶν τάδε.
ΟΙ. οὐκ ἂν πιθοίμην μὴ οὐ τάδ᾽ ἐκμαθεῖν σαφῶς.   1065
ΙΟ. καὶ μὴν φρονοῦσά γ᾽ εὖ τὰ λῷστά σοι λέγω.
ΟΙ. τὰ λῷστα τοίνυν ταῦτά μ᾽ ἀλγύνει πάλαι.
ΙΟ. ὦ δύσποτμ᾽, εἴθε μήποτε γνοίης ὃς εἶ.
ΟΙ. ἄξει τις ἐλθὼν δεῦρο τὸν βοτῆρά μοι;
ταύτην δ᾽ ἐᾶτε πλουσίωι χλίειν γένει.   1070
ΙΟ. ἰοὺ ἰού, δύστηνε· τοῦτο γάρ σ᾽ ἔχω
μόνον προσειπεῖν, ἄλλο δ᾽ οὔποθ᾽ ὕστερον.
ΧΟ. τί ποτε βέβηκεν, Οἰδίπους, ὑπ᾽ ἀγρίας
ἄιξασα λύπης ἡ γυνή; δέδοιχ᾽ ὅπως
μὴ ᾽κ τῆς σιωπῆς τῆσδ᾽ ἀναρρήξει κακά.   1075
ΟΙ. ὁποῖα χρῄζει ῥηγνύτω· τοὐμὸν δ᾽ ἐγώ,
κεἰ σμικρόν ἐστι, σπέρμ᾽ ἰδεῖν βουλήσομαι.
αὕτη δ᾽ ἴσως, φρονεῖ γὰρ ὡς γυνὴ μέγα,
τὴν δυσγένειαν τὴν ἐμήν γ᾽ αἰσχύνεται.
ἐγὼ δ᾽ ἐμαυτὸν παῖδα τῆς Τύχης νέμων   1080
τῆς εὖ διδούσης οὐκ ἀτιμασθήσομαι.

1053 τάδ᾽] τάχ᾽ G, sed τάδ᾽ G^{syp}   1054 νοεῖς εἰ κεῖνον A. Spengel   1055 τόνδ᾽ OPa: τόν
θ᾽ rell.   1061 ἐγώ PaGR, et ΣL: ἔχω R^{yp} rell.   1062 ἐὰν Hermann: ἂν ἐκ codd.   1064
δρᾶν αT: δρᾷ rell.   1070 χλίειν Subkoff: χαίρειν codd.   1074 λύσσης F. W. Schmidt
1078 αὕτη ΗΟ, fort. F: αὐτὴ rell.   1079 ἐμήν γ᾽ Dawe: ἐμήν δ᾽ FHPPa: ἐμὴν δ᾽ NZr: ἐμὴν∗
L^c: ἐμὴν rell.

τῆς γὰρ πέφυκα μητρός· οἱ δὲ συγγενεῖς
μῆνές με μικρὸν καὶ μέγαν διώρισαν.
τοιόσδε δ' ἐκφὺς οὐκ ἂν ἐξέλθοιμ' ἔτι
ποτ' ἄλλος, ὥστε μὴ 'κμαθεῖν τοὐμὸν γένος.   1085

ΧΟ. εἴπερ ἐγὼ μάντις εἰ-   στρ.
μὶ καὶ κατὰ γνώμαν ἴδρις,
οὐ τὸν Ὄλυμπον ἀπεί-
ρων, ὦ Κιθαιρών, οὐκ ἔσῃ τὰν αὔριον
πανσέληνον, μὴ οὐ σέ γε καὶ πατριώταν Οἰδίπουν   1090
καὶ τροφὸν καὶ ματέρ' αὔξειν,
καὶ χορεύεσθαι πρὸς ἡ-
μῶν ὡς ἐπίηρα φέρον-
τα τοῖς ἐμοῖς τυράννοις.   1095
ἰήιε Φοῖβε, σοὶ δὲ ταῦτ' ἀρέστ' εἴη.

τίς σε, τέκνον, τίς σ' ἔτι-   ἀντ.
κτε τᾶν μακραιώνων ἄρα,
Πανὸς ὀρεσσιβάτα   1100
πατρὸς πελασθεῖσ', ἢ σέ γ' εὐνάτειρά τις
Λοξίου; τῶι γὰρ πλάκες ἀγρόνομοι πᾶσαι φίλαι·
εἴθ' ὁ Κυλλάνας ἀνάσσων,
εἴθ' ὁ Βακχεῖος θεὸς   1105
ναίων ἐπ' ἄκρων ὀρέων
εὕρημα δέξατ' ἔκ του
Νυμφᾶν ἑλικωπίδων, αἷς πλεῖστα συμπαίζει.

ΟΙ. εἰ χρή τι κἀμὲ μὴ συναλλάξαντά πω,   1110
πρέσβυ, σταθμᾶσθαι, τὸν βοτῆρ' ὁρᾶν δοκῶ,
ὅνπερ πάλαι ζητοῦμεν· ἔν τε γὰρ μακρῶι
γήραι ξυνάιδει τῶιδε τἀνδρὶ σύμμετρος,
ἄλλως τε τοὺς ἄγοντας ὥσπερ οἰκέτας
ἔγνωκ' ἐμαυτοῦ· τῆι δ' ἐπιστήμηι σύ μου   1115
προύχοις τάχ' ἄν που, τὸν βοτῆρ' ἰδὼν πάρος.
ΧΟ. ἔγνωκα γάρ, σάφ' ἴσθι· Λαΐου γὰρ ἦν
εἴπερ τις ἄλλος πιστὸς ὡς νομεὺς ἀνήρ.
ΟΙ. σὲ πρῶτ' ἐρωτῶ, τὸν Κορίνθιον ξένον·

1084 τοιῶνδε fons codicum GR   1087 γνώμαν F, et ut vid O: γνώμην rell.   1091
Οἰδίπου codd., corr. Voelcker   1100 πατρὸς πελ. Lachmann: προσπελ- fere codd.   1101
σέ γ' εὐνάτειρά τις Arndt: σέ γε θυγάτηρ LHNOPaV: σέ γέ τις θυγάτηρ rell.   1103
ἀγρόνομοι ZrT: ἀγρόνομοι rell.   1108 ἑλικωπίδων Wilamowitz: Ἑλικωνίδων Aᵃᶜ: Ἑλικ-
ωνιάδων Aᵖᶜ rell.   1111 πρέσβυ PVXrᵃᶜ: -υν GRXrᵖᶜXsZr, in lin. DT, s.l. A: -ει LᵖᶜCNᵃᶜ,
A in lin., D s.l.: -εις FHZc, fort. Lᵃᶜ, T s.l.: ὦ πρέσβεις Pa: non leg. O

ἢ τόνδε φράζεις;
ΑΓ.   τοῦτον, ὅνπερ εἰσορᾶις.   1120
ΟΙ.   οὗτος σύ, πρέσβυ, δεῦρό μοι φώνει βλέπων
        ὅσ᾽ ἄν σ᾽ ἐρωτῶ. Λαΐου ποτ᾽ ἦσθα σύ;

ΘΕΡΑΠΩΝ

        ἦ, δοῦλος οὐκ ὠνητός, ἀλλ᾽ οἴκοι τραφείς.
ΟΙ.   ἔργον μεριμνῶν ποῖον, ἢ βίον τίνα;
ΘΕ.   ποίμναις τὰ πλεῖστα τοῦ βίου συνειπόμην.   1125
ΟΙ.   χώροις μάλιστα πρὸς τίσι ξύναυλος ὤν;
ΘΕ.   ἦν μὲν Κιθαιρών, ἦν δὲ πρόσχωρος τόπος.
ΟΙ.   τὸν ἄνδρα τόνδ᾽ οὖν οἶσθα τῆιδέ που μαθών;
ΘΕ.   τί χρῆμα δρῶντα; ποῖον ἄνδρα καὶ λέγεις;
ΟΙ.   τόνδ᾽ ὃς πάρεστιν. ἦ ξυνήλλαξάς τί πω;   1130
ΘΕ.   οὐχ ὥστε γ᾽ εἰπεῖν ἐν τάχει μνήμης ὕπο.
ΑΓ.   κοὐδέν γε θαῦμα, δέσποτ᾽· ἀλλ᾽ ἐγὼ σαφῶς
        ἀγνῶτ᾽ ἀναμνήσω νιν. εὖ γὰρ οἶδ᾽ ὅτι
        κάτοιδεν ἦμος τὸν Κιθαιρῶνος τόπον
        ὁ μὲν διπλοῖσι ποιμνίοις ἐγὼ δ᾽ ἑνὶ   1135
        <.............................>
        ἐπλησίαζον τῶιδε τἀνδρὶ τρεῖς ὅλους
        ἐξ ἦρος εἰς ἀρκτοῦρον ἐκμήνους χρόνους·
        χειμῶνα δ᾽ ἤδη τἀμά τ᾽ εἰς ἔπαυλ᾽ ἐγὼ
        ἤλαυνον, οὗτός τ᾽ εἰς τὰ Λαΐου σταθμά.
        λέγω τι τούτων ἢ οὐ λέγω πεπραγμένον;   1140
ΘΕ.   λέγεις ἀληθῆ, καίπερ ἐκ μακροῦ χρόνου.
ΑΓ.   φέρ᾽ εἰπέ νυν, τότ᾽ οἶσθα παῖδά μοί τινα
        δούς, ὡς ἐμαυτῶι θρέμμα θρεψαίμην ἐγώ;
ΘΕ.   τί δ᾽ ἔστι; πρὸς τί τοῦτο τοὔπος ἱστορεῖς;
ΑΓ.   ὅδ᾽ ἐστίν, ὦ τᾶν, κεῖνος, ὃς τότ᾽ ἦν νέος.   1145
ΘΕ.   οὐκ εἰς ὄλεθρον; οὐ σιωπήσας ἔσηι;
ΟΙ.   ἆ, μὴ κόλαζε, πρέσβυ, τόνδ᾽, ἐπεὶ τὰ σὰ
        δεῖται κολαστοῦ μᾶλλον ἢ τὰ τοῦδ᾽ ἔπη.
ΘΕ.   τί δ᾽, ὦ φέριστε δεσποτῶν, ἁμαρτάνω;
ΟΙ.   οὐκ ἐννέπων τὸν παῖδ᾽ ὃν οὗτος ἱστορεῖ.   1150

1123 ἦ Porphyrius ap. ΣΕ 533, θ 186: ἦν codd.   οἰκοτραφής Porph. ad E   1135–6 lacunam
indicavit Reiske   1137 ἐκμ- Porson: ἐκμ- rec.: ἔμμ- rell.: de χρόνος ἔκμηνος agit Eustathius
451.1   1138 χειμῶνα LNPaVZr, T s.l.: χειμῶν᾽, sine δ᾽, H: χειμῶνος G: χειμῶνι G i.m., T in
lin., rell.   1144 πρὸς τί τοὔπος ἱστορεῖς τόδε OGR

ΘΕ. λέγει γὰρ εἰδὼς οὐδέν, ἀλλ' ἄλλως πονεῖ.
ΟΙ. σὺ πρὸς χάριν μὲν οὐκ ἐρεῖς, κλαίων δ' ἐρεῖς.
ΘΕ. μὴ δῆτα, πρὸς θεῶν, τὸν γέροντά μ' αἰκίσῃ.
ΟΙ. οὐχ ὡς τάχος τις τοῦδ' ἀποστρέψει χέρας;
ΘΕ. δύστηνος, ἀντὶ τοῦ; τί προσχρῄζων μαθεῖν;   1155
ΟΙ. τὸν παῖδ' ἔδωκας τῷδ' ὃν οὗτος ἱστορεῖ;
ΘΕ. ἔδωκ', ὀλέσθαι δ' ὤφελον τῇδ' ἡμέραι.
ΟΙ. ἀλλ' εἰς τόδ' ἥξεις, μὴ λέγων γε τοὐνδικον.
ΘΕ. πολλῷ γε μᾶλλον, ἢν φράσω, διόλλυμαι.
ΟΙ. ἀνὴρ ὅδ', ὡς ἔοικεν, εἰς τριβὰς ἐλᾷ.   1160
ΘΕ. οὐ δῆτ' ἔγωγ', ἀλλ' εἶπον ὡς δοίην πάλαι.
ΟΙ. πόθεν λαβών; οἰκεῖον ἢ 'ξ ἄλλου τινός;
ΘΕ. ἐμὸν μὲν οὐκ ἔγωγ'· ἐδεξάμην δέ του.
ΟΙ. τίνος πολιτῶν τῶνδε κἀκ ποίας στέγης;
ΘΕ. μὴ πρὸς θεῶν, μή, δέσποθ', ἱστόρει πλέον.   1165
ΟΙ. ὄλωλας, εἴ σε ταῦτ' ἐρήσομαι πάλιν.
ΘΕ. τῶν Λαΐου τοίνυν τις ἦν γεννημάτων.
ΟΙ. ἦ δοῦλος, ἢ κείνου τις ἐγγενὴς γεγώς;
ΘΕ. οἴμοι, πρὸς αὐτῶι γ' εἰμὶ τῶι δεινῶι λέγειν.
ΟΙ. κἄγωγ' ἀκούειν· ἀλλ' ὅμως ἀκουστέον.   1170
ΘΕ. κείνου γέ τοι δὴ παῖς ἐκλῄζεθ'· ἡ δ' ἔσω
    κάλλιστ' ἂν εἴποι σὴ γυνὴ τάδ' ὡς ἔχει.
ΟΙ. ἦ γὰρ δίδωσιν ἥδε σοι;
ΘΕ.   μάλιστ', ἄναξ.
ΟΙ. ὡς πρὸς τί χρείας;
ΘΕ.   ὡς ἀναλώσαιμί νιν.
ΟΙ. τεκοῦσα τλήμων;
ΘΕ.   θεσφάτων γ' ὄκνωι κακῶν.   1175
ΟΙ. ποίων;
ΘΕ.   κτενεῖν νιν τοὺς τεκόντας ἦν λόγος.
ΟΙ. πῶς δῆτ' ἀφῆκας τῶι γέροντι τῶιδε σύ;
ΘΕ. κατοικτίσας, ὦ δέσποθ', ὡς ἄλλην χθόνα
    δοκῶν <σφ'> ἀποίσειν, αὐτὸς ἔνθεν ἦν· ὁ δὲ
    κἄκ' εἰς μέγιστ' ἔσωσεν· εἰ γὰρ αὐτὸς εἶ   1180
    ὅν φησιν οὗτος, ἴσθι δύσποτμος γεγώς.
ΟΙ. ἰοὺ ἰού· τὰ πάντ' ἂν ἐξήκοι σαφῆ.

1157 τῆιδ' ZrT: τῆιδ' ἐν rell.   1169 λέγων H   1170 ἀκούειν rec. et Plut. Mor. 522c et
1093b: ἀκούων (-σων H) codd. nostri, sed ὥστε ἀκούειν intelligit Σ Moschopuli   1179 <σφ'>
Blaydes ἔνθεν αὐτὸς O   1180 αὐτὸς Heimsoeth: ✳✳τος O: οὗτος rell.   1182 ἐξήκοι GXr:
ἐξίκοιτο OD: ἐξίκοι rell. (-κη Cᶜ)

ὢ φῶς, τελευταῖόν σε προσβλέψαιμι νῦν,
ὅστις πέφασμαι φύς τ᾿ ἀφ᾿ ὧν οὐ χρῆν, ξὺν οἷς
τ᾿ οὐ χρῆν ὁμιλῶν, οὕς τέ μ᾿ οὐκ ἔδει κτανών.   1185

XO. ἰὼ γενεαὶ βροτῶν,   στρ. α
ὡς ὑμᾶς ἴσα καὶ τὸ μη-
δὲν ζώσας ἐναριθμῶ.
τίς γάρ, τίς ἀνὴρ πλέον
τᾶς εὐδαιμονίας φέρει   1190
ἢ τοσοῦτον ὅσον δοκεῖν
καὶ δόξαν γ᾿ ἀποκλῖναι;
τὸν σόν τοι παράδειγμ᾿ ἔχων,
τὸν σὸν δαίμονα, τὸν σόν, ὦ
τλᾶμον Οἰδιπόδα, βροτῶν
οὐδὲν μακαρίζω.   1195

ὅστις καθ᾿ ὑπερβολὰν   ἀντ. α
τοξεύσας ἐκράτησας ἐς
πᾶν εὐδαίμονος ὄλβου,
ὦ Ζεῦ, κατὰ μὲν φθίσας
τὰν γαμψώνυχα παρθένον
χρησμῳδόν, θανάτων δ᾿ ἐμᾶι   1200
χώραι πύργος ἀνέστας.
ἐξ οὗ καὶ βασιλεὺς καλῆι
ἐμὸς καὶ τὰ μέγιστ᾿ ἐτι-
μάθης ταῖς μεγάλαισιν ἐν
Θήβαισιν ἀνάσσων.

τανῦν δ᾿ ἀκούειν τίς ἀθλιώτερος;   στρ. β
†τίς ἐν πόνοις, τίς ἄταις ἀγρίαισ†   1205
ξύνοικος ἀλλαγᾶι βίου;
ἰὼ κλεινὸν Οἰδίπου κάρα,
ὧι μέγας λιμὴν
αὑτὸς ἤρκεσεν
παιδὶ καὶ πατρὶ
θαλαμηπόλωι πεσεῖν.

1185 χρῆν μ᾿ α: χρῆν θ C   1192 δόξαν γ᾿ Dawe: δόξαντ᾿ codd.: δόξαν Stobaeus 5.836.10
1193 τὸν Kammermeister: τὸ codd.   1195 οὐδένα codd. (nisi οὐδὲν Cᵃᶜ): corr. Hermann
1197–1198 ἐκύρησε Heimsoeth | ἐς πᾶν Dawe, praeeunte Hermann: τοῦ πάντ᾿ codd.   1201
καλῆι τ᾿ Blaydes: ἐμὸς et καλῆι invicem traiecit Elmsley: κλύεις Heimsoeth   1203 Θήβαισιν
D: -αις rell.   1205 τίς ἄταις ἀγρίοισιν ἐν πόνοις Wilamowitz   1209 ᾿μπεσεῖν Hartung

πῶς ποτε πῶς ποθ᾽ αἱ πατρῷι-   1210
αί σ᾽ ἄλοκες φέρειν, τάλας,
σῖγ᾽ ἐδυνάθησαν ἐς τοσόνδε;

ἐφηῦρέ σ᾽ ἄκονθ᾽ ὁ πάνθ᾽ ὁρῶν χρόνος·   ἀντ.β
δικάζει τὸν ἄγαμον γάμον πάλαι
τεκνοῦντα καὶ τεκνούμενον.   1215
ἰὼ Λαΐειον ὦ τέκνον,
εἴθε σ᾽ εἴθε σε
μήποτ᾽ εἰδόμαν·
ὡς σ᾽ ὀδύρομαι
περίαλλ᾽ ἰὰν χέων
ἐκ στομάτων. τὸ δ᾽ ὀρθὸν εἰπεῖν, ἀνέπνευσά τ᾽ ἐκ σέθεν   1220
καὶ κατεκοίμησα τοὐμὸν ὄμμα.

ΕΞΑΓΓΕΛΟΣ

ὦ γῆς μέγιστα τῆσδ᾽ ἀεὶ τιμώμενοι,
οἷ᾽ ἔργ᾽ ἀκούσεσθ᾽, οἷα δ᾽ εἰσόψεσθ᾽, ὅσον
δ᾽ ἀρεῖσθε πένθος, εἴπερ εὐγενῶς ἔτι   1225
τῶν Λαβδακείων ἐντρέπεσθε δωμάτων.
οἶμαι γὰρ οὔτ᾽ ἂν Ἴστρον οὔτε Φᾶσιν ἂν
νίψαι καθαρμῶι τήνδε τὴν στέγην, ὅσα
κεύθει, τὰ δ᾽ αὐτίκ᾽ εἰς τὸ φῶς φανεῖ κακά,
ἑκόντα κοὐκ ἄκοντα· τῶν δὲ πημονῶν   1230
μάλιστα λυποῦσ᾽ αἳ φανῶσ᾽ αὐθαίρετοι.
ΧΟ. λείπει μὲν οὐδ᾽ ἃ πρόσθεν ᾔδεμεν τὸ μὴ οὐ
βαρύστον᾽ εἶναι· πρὸς δ᾽ ἐκείνοισιν τί φῄς;
ΕΞ. ὁ μὲν τάχιστος τῶν λόγων εἰπεῖν τε καὶ
μαθεῖν, τέθνηκε θεῖον Ἰοκάστης κάρα.   1235
ΧΟ. ὦ δυστάλαινα, πρὸς τίνος ποτ᾽ αἰτίας;
ΕΞ. αὐτὴ πρὸς αὑτῆς. τῶν δὲ πραχθέντων τὰ μὲν
ἄλγιστ᾽ ἄπεστιν· ἡ γὰρ ὄψις οὐ πάρα.
ὅμως δ᾽, ὅσον γε κἀν ἐμοὶ μνήμης ἔνι,

1210 ματρῶαι O   1212 -άθησαν Nᵖᶜ : -ήθησαν HVZr: -άσθησαν Nᵃᶜ rell.   1216 ὦ τέκνον Erfurdt: τέκνον codd.   1217 εἴθε σ᾽ εἴθε σε O: εἴθε σ᾽ εἴθε rell.   1218 εἰδόμαν T: ἰδόμαν VRαZr: ἰδοίμαν CFPGZc: ἰδοίμην HNOPa   1219 ὡς ὀδύρομαι Kamerbeek, σ᾽ add. Diggle: ὀδύρομαι γὰρ ὡς codd. | ἰὰν χέων Burges: ἰαχέων codd.:   1225 εὐγενῶς Hartung: ἐγγενῶς codd.: ἐμπέδως Hirzel   1232 ᾔδεμεν Zc in lin.: ᾔδημεν Zc s.l.: ᾔδει A: ᾔδειμεν rell. (εἰδ- O)

πεύσηι τὰ κείνης ἀθλίας παθήματα. 1240
ὅπως γὰρ ὀργῆι χρωμένη παρῆλθ᾽ ἔσω
θυρῶνος, ἵετ᾽ εὐθὺ πρὸς τὰ νυμφικὰ
λέχη, κόμην σπῶσ᾽ ἀμφιδεξίοις ἀκμαῖς.
πύλας δ᾽ ὅπως εἰσῆλθ᾽ ἐπιρράξασ᾽ ἔσω,
καλεῖ τὸν ἤδη Λάιον πάλαι νεκρόν, 1245
μνήμην παλαιῶν σπερμάτων ἔχουσ᾽, ὑφ᾽ ὧν
θάνοι μὲν αὐτός, τὴν δὲ τίκτουσαν λίποι
<.............................>
τοῖς οἷσιν αὐτοῦ δύστεκνον παιδουργίαν.
γοᾶτο δ᾽ εὐνάς, ἔνθα δύστηνος διπλῆι
ἐξ ἀνδρὸς ἄνδρα καὶ τέκν᾽ ἐκ τέκνων τέκοι· 1250
χὤπως μὲν ἐκ τῶνδ᾽ οὐκέτ᾽ οἶδ᾽ ἀπόλλυται.
βοῶν γὰρ εἰσέπαισεν Οἰδίπους, ὑφ᾽ οὗ
οὐκ ἦν τὸ κείνης ἐκθεάσασθαι κακόν,
ἀλλ᾽ εἰς ἐκεῖνον περιπολοῦντ᾽ ἐλεύσσομεν.
φοιτᾶι γὰρ ἡμᾶς ἔγχος ἐξαιτῶν πορεῖν, 1255
γυναῖκά τ᾽ οὐ γυναῖκα, μητρώιαν δ᾽ ὅπου
κίχοι διπλῆν ἄρουραν οὗ τε καὶ τέκνων.
λυσσῶντι δ᾽ αὐτῶι δαιμόνων δείκνυσί τις·
οὐδεὶς γὰρ ἀνδρῶν, οἳ παρῆμεν ἐγγύθεν.
δεινὸν δ᾽ ἀύσας, ὡς ὑφ᾽ ἡγητοῦ τινος, 1260
πύλαις διπλαῖς ἐνῆλατ᾽, ἐκ δὲ πυθμένων
ἔκλινε κοῖλα κλῆιθρα, κἀμπίπτει στέγηι·
οὗ δὴ κρεμαστὴν τὴν γυναῖκ᾽ ἐσείδομεν,
πλεκταῖς ἐώραις ἐμπεπλεγμένην· ὁ δέ,
ὅπως ὁρᾶι νιν, δεινὰ βρυχηθεὶς τάλας, 1265
χαλᾶι κρεμαστὴν ἀρτάνην· ἐπεὶ δὲ γῆι
ἔκειτο τλήμων, δεινά γ᾽ ἦν τἀνθένδ᾽ ὁρᾶν.
ἀποσπάσας γὰρ εἱμάτων χρυσηλάτους
περόνας ἀπ᾽ αὐτῆς, αἷσιν ἐξεστέλλετο,
ἄρας ἔπαισεν ἄρθρα τῶν αὐτοῦ κύκλων, 1270

1240 τὰ κείνης Xs: τἀκείνης rell. 1244 ἐπιρράξασ᾽ Lˢ s.l.: -ήξας rell. 1246 post hunc versum deficit F 1247–8 lacunam statuit Dawe 1249 διπλῆι P: διπλᾶ O s.l. διπλοῦς rell. 1252 εἰσέπαισεν AXrXsᶜZrT, fort. Hᵃᶜ: -έπεσεν rell. 1253 ἐνθεάσασθαι T in lin.: ἔτι θ-Blaydes 1255 φοίτα NO, v.l. in P 1260 ὑφ᾽ ἡγητοῦ LPGRXrXsT (vel Tᵖᶜ): ὑφηγητοῦ fere rell. 1262 κλῆιθρα VGR: κλεῖθρα rell.: cf. 1287 1264 ἐώραις LPaᵃᶜАᶜD, G in lin., fort. HᵃᶜN¹ s.l., Eustathius 389.42: ἐώραις RXs: αἰώραις Zr: αἰώραις Gs.l. Hᵖᶜ rell. 1264–5 πλεκταῖσιν αἰώραισιν (sic rec.) ἐμπεπλεγμένην. ὁ δ᾽ ὡς Blaydes 1265 ὅπως δ᾽ LPᶜVGRZc 1266 ἐπεὶ NαZrT: ἐπὶ rell. 1267 ἔκειτο L²ᶜ DXsᶜT: ἔκειθ᾽ ἡ N²ᵖᶜXrZc: ἔκειτ᾽ ἡ P: ἔκειθ᾽ ὁ rell. | γ᾽ D, Tˢ.l.: δ᾽ rell.

αὐδῶν τοιαῦθ', ὁθούνεκ' οὐκ ὀψοιντό νιν
οὔθ' οἷ' ἔπασχεν οὔθ' ὁποῖ' ἔδρα κακά,
ἀλλ' ἐν σκότωι τὸ λοιπὸν οὓς μὲν οὐκ ἔδει
ὀψοίαθ', οὓς δ' ἔχρηιζεν οὐ γνωσοίατο.
τοιαῦτ' ἐφυμνῶν πολλάκις τε κοὐχ ἅπαξ   1275
ἤρασσ' ἔπειρεν βλέφαρα, φοίνιαι δ' ὁμοῦ
γλῆναι γένει' ἔτεγγον, οὐδ' ἀνίεσαν
φόνου μυδώσας σταγόνας, ἀλλ' ὁμοῦ μέλας
ὄμβρος χαλάζης αἵματός †ἐτέγγετο†.
τάδ' ἐκ δυοῖν ἔρρωγεν οὐ μονούμενα,   1280
ἀλλ' ἀνδρὶ καὶ γυναικὶ συμμιγῆ κακά.
ὁ πρὶν παλαιὸς δ' ὄλβος ἦν πάροιθε μὲν
ὄλβος δικαίως· νῦν δὲ τῆιδε θἠμέραι
στεναγμός, ἄτη, θάνατος, αἰσχύνη, κακῶν
ὅσ' ἐστὶ πάντων ὀνόματ', οὐδέν ἐστ' ἀπόν.   1285
ΧΟ. νῦν δ' ἔσθ' ὁ τλήμων ἔν τινι σχολῆι κακοῦ;
ΕΞ. βοᾶι διοίγειν κλῆιθρα καὶ δηλοῦν τινα
τοῖς πᾶσι Καδμείοισι τὸν πατροκτόνον,
τὸν μητρός — αὐδῶν ἀνόσι' οὐδὲ ῥητά μοι,
ὡς ἐκ χθονὸς ῥίψων ἑαυτόν, οὐδ' ἔτι   1290
μενῶν δόμοις ἀραῖος ὡς ἠράσατο.
ῥώμης γε μέντοι καὶ προηγητοῦ τινος
δεῖται· τὸ γὰρ νόσημα μεῖζον ἢ φέρειν.
δείξει δὲ καὶ σοί· κλῆιθρα γὰρ πυλῶν τάδε
διοίγεται· θέαμα δ' εἰσόψει τάχα   1295
τοιοῦτον οἷον καὶ στυγοῦντ' ἐποικτίσαι.

ΧΟ. ὦ δεινὸν ἰδεῖν πάθος ἀνθρώποις,
ὦ δεινότατον πάντων ὅσ' ἐγὼ
προσέκυρσ' ἤδη· τίς σ', ὦ τλῆμον,
προσέβη μανία; τίς ὁ πηδήσας   1300
μείζονα δαίμων τῶν μακίστων
πρὸς σῆι δυσδαίμονι μοίραι;
φεῦ φεῦ, δύστην'· ἀλλ' οὐδ' ἐσιδεῖν
δύναμαί σε, θέλων πόλλ' ἀνερέσθαι,
πολλὰ πυθέσθαι, πολλὰ δ' ἀθρῆσαι·   1305

1276 ἤρασσ' ἐπαίρων fere codd.: corr. Page   1279 χαλαζῆς Bergk, praeeunte Hermann:
-άζης codd.   1280 μονούμενα Wilamowitz: μόνου κακά codd.   1287 κλῆιθρα LNDXs,
Ps.l.: κλεῖθρα rell., cf. 1262   1294 δόξει Xr (δείξει Xr^γρ)   1299 σ' AXrXsT: γ' C: om. rell.
1301 μακίστων L^pcA^cDZr: μηκ- T: κακίστων rell. (κακῶν Pa)   1303 δύσταν' T: δύστηνος
C: δύστανος rell.

τοίαν φρίκην παρέχεις μοι.
ΟΙ. αἰαῖ αἰαῖ δύστανος ἐγώ,
ποῖ γᾶς φέρομαι τλάμων; πᾶι μοι
φθογγὰ διαπωτᾶται φοράδαν;　　　　　　　1310
ἰὼ δαῖμον, ἵν' ἐξήλου.
ΧΟ. ἐς δεινόν, οὐκ ἀκουστὸν οὐδ' ἐπόψιμον.

ΟΙ. ἰὼ σκότου　　　　　　　　　　　　　　　στρ.α
νέφος ἐμὸν ἀπότροπον, ἐπιπλόμενον ἄφατον,
ἀδάματόν τε καὶ δυσούριστον <—>.　　　　1315
οἴμοι,
οἴμοι μάλ' αὖθις· οἶον εἰσέδυ μ' ἅμα
κέντρων τε τῶνδ' οἴστρημα καὶ μνήμη κακῶν.
ΧΟ. καὶ θαῦμά γ' οὐδὲν ἐν τοσοῖσδε πήμασιν
διπλᾶ σε πενθεῖν καὶ διπλᾶ φρονεῖν κακά.　　1320

ΟΙ. ἰὼ φίλος,　　　　　　　　　　　　　　　ἀντ.α
σὺ μὲν ἐμὸς ἐπίπολος ἔτι μόνιμος· ἔτι γὰρ
ὑπομένεις με τὸν τυφλὸν κηδεύων.
φεῦ φεῦ·
οὐ γάρ με λήθεις, ἀλλὰ γιγνώσκω σαφῶς,　　1325
καίπερ σκοτεινός, τήν γε σὴν αὐδὴν ὅμως.
ΧΟ. ὦ δεινὰ δράσας, πῶς ἔτλης τοιαῦτα σὰς
ὄψεις μαρᾶναι; τίς σ' ἐπῆρε δαιμόνων;

ΟΙ. Ἀπόλλων τάδ' ἦν, Ἀπόλλων, φίλοι,　　　στρ.β
ὁ κακὰ κακὰ τελῶν ἐμὰ τάδ' ἐμὰ πάθεα.　　1330
ἔπαισε δ' αὐτόχειρ νιν οὔ-
τις ἀλλ ἐγὼ τλάμων.
τί γὰρ ἔδει μ' ὁρᾶν,
ὅτωι γ' ὁρῶντι μηδὲν ἦν ἰδεῖν γλυκύ;　　　1335
ΧΟ. ἦν ταῦθ' ὅπωσπερ καὶ σὺ φήις.
ΟΙ. τί δῆτ' ἐμοὶ βλεπτὸν ἦν
στερκτόν, ἢ προσήγορον
ἔτ' ἔστ' ἀκούειν ἡδονᾶι, φίλοι;

1306 τοίαν NAXrXsZr, pap. Oxy. 1369: ὁποῖαν H: οἶαν GR: ποίαν A s.l., rell.　　1307 ante δύστανος (seu δύστηνος) φεῦ vel φεῦ φεῦ codd.: corr. Hermann　　1310 διαπωτᾶται vel -ποτᾶται pap. Oxy. 1369 p.c.: -πέταται LPPa²ᶜVADXsZr, Zc in lin., fort. pap.ᵃ·ᶜ·: -πέπταται CHNGRXrT, Zc² s.l.: -πέπαπται O | φοράδαν Page: φοράδην codd.　　1312 οὐκ NOGRZc: οὐδ' rell.　　1314 ἐπιπλόμενον NODZrZc: -πλώμενον fere rell.　　1315 ἀδάμαστον codd.: corr. Hermann | <όν> Hermann: -ούριστ' ἰόν Jebb: δυσεξούριστον Blaydes.　　1320 φρονεῖν XsXrˢʸᵖ: φέρειν CPa²ᵖᶜZrT: φορεῖν rell.　　1323 με τόν Erfurdt: τόν γε T: ἐμὲ τὸν rell.　　1336 ταῦθ' HNGRαZr: ταῦτα O: τάδ' rell.: ταῖδ' Nauck　　1337 ἦν Wilamowitz: ἢ codd.

ἀπάγετ᾽ ἐκτόπιον ὅτι τάχιστά με,   1340
ἀπάγετ᾽, ὦ φίλοι, τὸν μέγ᾽ ὀλέθριον,
τὸν καταρατότατον, ἔτι δὲ καὶ θεοῖς   1345
ἐχθρότατον βροτῶν.
ΧΟ. δείλαιε τοῦ νοῦ τῆς τε συμφορᾶς ἴσον,
ὥς σ᾽ ἠθέλησ᾽ ἂν μηδαμὰ γνῶναι τὸ πᾶν.

ΟΙ. ὄλοιθ᾽ ὅστις ἦν ὃς ἀγρίας πέδας   ἀντ.β
νομάδος ἐπὶ πόας λῦσέ μ᾽ ἀπό τε φόνου   1350
ἔρυτο κἀνέσωσεν, οὐ-
δὲν εἰς χάριν πράσσων.
τότε γὰρ ἂν θανὼν
οὐκ ἦ φίλοισιν οὐδ᾽ ἐμοὶ τοσόνδ᾽ ἄχος.   1355
ΧΟ. θέλοντι κἀμοὶ τοῦτ᾽ ἂν ἦν.
ΟΙ. οὔκουν πατρός γ᾽ ἂν φονεὺς
ἦλθον, οὐδὲ νυμφίος
βροτοῖς ἐκλήθην ὧν ἔφυν ἄπο.
νῦν δ᾽ ἄθεος μέν εἰμ᾽, ἀνοσίων δὲ παῖς,   1360
ὁμολεχὴς δ᾽ ἀφ᾽ ὧν αὐτὸς ἔφυν τάλας.
εἰ δέ τι πρεσβύτερον ἔτι κακοῦ κακόν,   1365
τοῦτ᾽ ἔλαχ᾽ Οἰδίπους.
ΧΟ. οὐκ οἶδ᾽ ὅπως σε φῶ βεβουλεῦσθαι καλῶς·
κρείσσων γὰρ ἦσθα μηκέτ᾽ ὢν ἢ ζῶν τυφλός.

ΟΙ. ὡς μὲν τάδ᾽ οὐχ ὧδ᾽ ἔστ᾽ ἄριστ᾽ εἰργασμένα,
μή μ᾽ ἐκδίδασκε, μηδὲ συμβούλευ᾽ ἔτι.   1370
ἐγὼ γὰρ οὐκ οἶδ᾽ ὄμμασιν ποίοις βλέπων
πατέρα ποτ᾽ ἂν προσεῖδον εἰς Ἅιδου μολών,
οὐδ᾽ αὖ τάλαιναν μητέρ᾽, οἷν ἐμοὶ δυοῖν
ἔργ᾽ ἐστὶ κρείσσον᾽ ἀγχόνης εἰργασμένα.
[ἀλλ᾽ ἡ τέκνων δῆτ᾽ ὄψις ἦν ἐφίμερος,   1375
βλαστοῦσ᾽ ὅπως ἔβλαστε, προσλεύσσειν ἐμοί;
οὐ δῆτα τοῖς γ᾽ ἐμοῖσιν ὀφθαλμοῖς ποτε·]
οὐδ᾽ ἄστυ γ᾽, οὐδὲ πύργος, οὐδὲ δαιμόνων
ἀγάλμαθ᾽ ἱερά, τῶν ὁ παντλήμων ἐγὼ

1343 τὸν ὀλέθριον μέγαν (μέγα PXrT) codd.: corr. Erfurdt: τὸν ὀλεθρόν με γᾶς Bergk   1348
ἠθέλησ᾽ ἂν Elmsley: ἠθέλησα codd. | μηδ᾽ ἀναγνῶναι codd.: corr. Dobree | τὸ πᾶν Dawe: ποτε
ADXrXs: ποτ᾽ ἂν rell.   1349 ἀγρίας T: ἐπ᾽ ἀγρίας O: ἀπ᾽ ἀγρίας rell.   1350 ἐπὶ πόας
Müller: ἐπιποδίας codd.   λῦσέ μ᾽ Bothe: ἔλυσεν L^{1pc}αZr: μ᾽ T: ἔλυσέ μ᾽ rell. praeter ἔλαβέ μ᾽ L^{ac}V:
ἔλαβ᾽ Elmsley   1355 ἦν codd.| ἄχος HVaT et fort. pap. Oxy. 1369: ἄχθος rell.   1360 ἄθεος
Erfurdt, Elmsley: ἄθλιος codd.   1362 ὁ μονογενὴς GDXs: ὁμογενὴς G^{syp} rell.: corr. Meineke
1365 ἔτι κακοῦ Hermann: ἔφυ (ἔφυι L) κακοῦ codd.   1375–7 eiecit Dawe

[κάλλιστ᾽ ἀνὴρ εἷς ἔν γε ταῖς Θήβαις τραφεὶς]   1380
ἀπεστέρησ᾽ ἐμαυτόν, αὐτὸς ἐννέπων
ὠθεῖν ἅπαντας τὸν ἀσεβῆ, τὸν ἐκ θεῶν
φανέντ᾽ ἄναγνον καὶ γένους τοῦ Λαΐου.
τοιάνδ᾽ ἐγὼ κηλῖδα μηνύσας ἐμὴν
ὀρθοῖς ἔμελλον ὄμμασιν τούτους ὁρᾶν;   1385
ἥκιστά γ᾽· ἀλλ᾽ εἰ τῆς ἀκουούσης ἔτ᾽ ἦν
πηγῆς δι᾽ ὤτων φαργμός, οὐκ ἂν ἐσχόμην
τὸ μὴ ἀποκλῆισαι τοὐμὸν ἄθλιον δέμας,
ἵν᾽ ἦ τυφλός τε καὶ κλύων μηδέν· τὸ γὰρ
τὴν φροντίδ᾽ ἔξω τῶν κακῶν οἰκεῖν γλυκύ.   1390
ἰὼ Κιθαιρών, τί μ᾽ ἐδέχου; τί μ᾽ οὐ λαβὼν
ἔκτεινας εὐθύς, ὡς ἔδειξα μήποτε
ἐμαυτὸν ἀνθρώποισιν ἔνθεν ἦ γεγώς;
ὦ Πόλυβε καὶ Κόρινθε καὶ τὰ πάτρια
λόγωι παλαιὰ δώμαθ᾽, οἷον ἄρά με   1395
κάλλος κακῶν ὕπουλον ἐξεθρέψατε·
νῦν γὰρ κακός τ᾽ ὢν κἀκ κακῶν εὑρίσκομαι.
ὦ τρεῖς κέλευθοι καὶ κεκρυμμένη νάπη,
δρυμός τε καὶ στενωπὸς ἐν τριπλαῖς ὁδοῖς,
αἳ τοὐμὸν αἷμα τῶν ἐμῶν χειρῶν ἄπο   1400
ἐπίετε πατρός, ἆρά μου μέμνησθ᾽ ἔτι,
οἷ᾽ ἔργα δράσας ὑμίν, εἶτα δεῦρ᾽ ἰὼν
ὁποῖ᾽ ἔπρασσον αὖθις; ὦ γάμοι, γάμοι,
ἐφύσαθ᾽ ἡμᾶς, καὶ φυτεύσαντες πάλιν
ἀνεῖτε ταὐτὸν σπέρμα, κἀπεδείξατε   1405
πατέρας, ἀδελφούς, παῖδας, αἷμ᾽ ἐμφύλιον,
νύμφας γυναῖκας μητέρας τε, χὠπόσα
αἴσχιστ᾽ ἐν ἀνθρώποισιν ἔργα γίγνεται.
ἀλλ᾽, οὐ γὰρ αὐδᾶν ἔσθ᾽ ἃ μηδὲ δρᾶν καλόν,
ὅπως τάχιστα, πρὸς θεῶν, ἔξω μέ που   1410
ἐκρίψατ᾽, ἢ φονεύσατ᾽, ἢ θαλάσσιον
καλύψατ᾽, ἔνθα μήποτ᾽ εἰσόψεσθ᾽ ἔτι.
ἴτ᾽, ἀξιώσατ᾽ ἀνδρὸς ἀθλίου θιγεῖν.
πίθεσθε, μὴ δείσητε· τἀμὰ γὰρ κακὰ
οὐδεὶς οἷός τε πλὴν ἐμοῦ φέρειν βροτῶν.   1415

1380 versum eiecit Deventer   1386 φραγμός codd.: corr. Dindorf   1388 ἀποκλεῖσαι
codd.: corr. Elmsley   1389 ἦ Dᵃᶜ: ἦν Dᵖᶜ rell.   1401 ἔτι Xsᵞᵖ Dᵍˡ: ὅταν Lˢᵞᵖ Gᵞᵖ R: ὅτι
rell.   1411–12 καλύψατ᾽ . . . ἐκρίψατ᾽ (-ύψατ᾽ HᵃᶜV) codd.: corr. Burges   1414 πίθεσθε
Elmsley: πείθ- codd.

ΧΟ. ἀλλ' ὧν ἐπαιτεῖς ἐς δέον πάρεσθ' ὅδε
Κρέων τὸ πράσσειν καὶ τὸ βουλεύειν, ἐπεὶ
χώρας λέλειπται μοῦνος ἀντὶ σοῦ φύλαξ.

ΟΙ. οἴμοι, τί δῆτα λέξομεν πρὸς τόνδ' ἔπος;
τίς μοι φανεῖται πίστις ἔνδικος; τὰ γὰρ   1420
πάρος πρὸς αὐτὸν πάντ' ἐφηύρημαι κακός.

ΚΡ. οὐχ ὡς γελαστής, Οἰδίπους, ἐλήλυθα,
οὐδ' ὡς ὀνειδιῶν τι τῶν πάρος κακῶν.

<.............................>
ἀλλ' εἰ τὰ θνητῶν μὴ καταισχύνεσθ' ἔτι
γένεθλα, τὴν γοῦν πάντα βόσκουσαν φλόγα   1425
αἰδεῖσθ' ἄνακτος Ἡλίου, τοιόνδ' ἄγος
ἀκάλυπτον οὕτω δεικνύναι, τὸ μήτε γῆ
μήτ' ὄμβρος ἱερὸς μήτε φῶς προσδέξεται.
ἀλλ' ὡς τάχιστ' ἐς οἶκον ἐσκομίζετε·
τοῖς ἐν γένει γὰρ τἀγγενῆ μάλισθ' ὁρᾶν   1430
μόνοις τ' ἀκούειν εὐσεβῶς ἔχει κακά.

ΟΙ. πρὸς θεῶν, ἐπείπερ ἐλπίδος μ' ἀπέσπασας,
ἄριστος ἐλθὼν πρὸς κάκιστον ἄνδρ' ἐμέ,
πιθοῦ τί μοι· πρὸς σοῦ γάρ, οὐδ' ἐμοῦ, φράσω.

ΚΡ. καὶ τοῦ με χρείας ὧδε λιπαρεῖς τυχεῖν;   1435

ΟΙ. ῥῖψόν με γῆς ἐκ τῆσδ' ὅσον τάχισθ', ὅπου
θνητῶν φανοῦμαι μηδενὸς προσήγορος.

ΚΡ. ἔδρασ' ἄν, εὖ τοῦτ' ἴσθ' ἄν, εἰ μὴ τοῦ θεοῦ
πρώτιστ' ἔχρῃζον ἐκμαθεῖν τί πρακτέον.

ΟΙ. ἀλλ' ἥ γ' ἐκείνου πᾶσ' ἐδηλώθη φάτις,   1440
τὸν πατροφόντην, τὸν ἀσεβῆ μ' ἀπολλύναι.

ΚΡ. οὕτως ἐλέχθη ταῦθ'· ὅμως δ' ἵν' ἕσταμεν
χρείας, ἄμεινον ἐκμαθεῖν τί δραστέον.

ΟΙ. οὕτως ἄρ' ἀνδρὸς ἀθλίου πεύσεσθ' ὕπερ;

ΚΡ. καὶ γὰρ σὺ νῦν τἂν τῷ θεῷ πίστιν φέροις.   1445

ΟΙ. <.............................>
καὶ σοί γ' ἐπισκήπτω τε καὶ προστρέψομαι·
τῆς μὲν κατ' οἴκους αὐτὸς ὃν θέλεις τάφον
θοῦ· καὶ γὰρ ὀρθῶς τῶν γε σῶν τελεῖς ὕπερ·
ἐμοῦ δὲ μήποτ' ἀξιωθήτω τόδε
πατρῷον ἄστυ ζῶντος οἰκητοῦ τυχεῖν,   1450
ἀλλ' ἔα με ναίειν ὄρεσιν, ἔνθα κλῄζεται
οὑμὸς Κιθαιρὼν οὗτος, ὃν μήτηρ τέ μοι

1422 οὐχ α: οὔτ' Lᵃᶜ: οὐ∗Lᵖᶜ: οὔθ' rell.   1423 οὐδ' α: οὔθ' rell.   1423–4 lacunam notavit
Schenkl   1445–1446 lacunam indicavit Wunder   1446 τε α: σε V: om. O: γε rell.

πατήρ τ' ἐθέσθην ζῶντι κύριον τάφον,
[ἵν' ἐξ ἐκείνων, οἵ μ' ἀπωλλύτην, θάνω.]
καίτοι τοσοῦτόν γ' οἶδα, μήτε μ' ἂν νόσον   1455
μήτ' ἄλλο πέρσαι μηδέν· οὐ γὰρ ἄν ποτε
θνήισκων ἐσώθην, μὴ 'πί τωι δεινῶι κακῶι.
ἀλλ' ἡ μὲν ἡμῶν μοῖρ' ὅπηιπερ εἶσ' ἴτω·
παίδων δὲ τῶν μὲν ἀρσένων μή μοι, Κρέον,
προσθῆι μέριμναν· ἄνδρες εἰσίν, ὥστε μὴ   1460
σπάνιν ποτὲ σχεῖν, ἔνθ' ἂν ὦσι, τοῦ βίου·
τοῖν δ' ἀθλίαιν οἰκτραῖν τε παρθένοιν ἐμαῖν,
οἷν οὔποθ' ἡμὴ χωρὶς ἐστάθη βορᾶς
τράπεζ' ἄνευ τοῦδ' ἀνδρός, ἀλλ' ὅσων ἐγὼ
ψαύοιμι, πάντων τῶνδ' ἀεὶ μετειχέτην·   1465
τοῖν μοι μέλεσθαι· καὶ μάλιστα μὲν χεροῖν
ψαῦσαί μ' ἔασον κἀποκλαύσασθαι κακά.
ἴθ', ὦναξ,
ἴθ', ὦ γονῆι γενναῖε· χερσί τὰν θιγὼν
δοκοῖμ' ἔχειν σφᾶς, ὥσπερ ἡνίκ' ἔβλεπον.   1470
τί φημί;
οὐ δὴ κλύω που, πρὸς θεῶν, τοῖν μοι φίλοιν
δακρυρροούντοιν, καί μ' ἐποικτίρας Κρέων
ἔπεμψέ μοι τὰ φίλτατ' ἐκγόνοιν ἐμοῖν;
λέγω τι;   1475
ΚΡ. λέγεις· ἐγὼ γάρ εἰμ' ὁ πορσύνας τάδε,
      γνοὺς τὴν παροῦσαν τέρψιν ἤ σ' ἔχει πάλαι.
ΟΙ. ἀλλ' εὐτυχοίης, καί σε τῆσδε τῆς ὁδοῦ
      δαίμων ἄμεινον ἢ 'μὲ φρουρήσας τύχοι.
      ὦ τέκνα, ποῦ ποτ' ἐστέ; δεῦρ' ἴτ', ἔλθετε   1480
ὡς τὰς ἀδελφὰς τάσδε τὰς ἐμὰς χέρας,
αἳ τοῦ φυτουργοῦ πατρὸς ὑμὶν ὧδ' ὁρᾶν
τὰ πρόσθε λαμπρὰ προυξένησαν ὄμματα,
ὃς ὑμίν, ὦ τέκν', οὔθ' ὁρῶν οὔθ' ἱστορῶν,
ἀροτὴρ ἐφάνθην ἔνθεν αὐτὸς ἠρόθην·   1485
καὶ σφὼ δακρύω, προσβλέπειν γὰρ οὐ σθένω,
νοούμενος τὰ πικρὰ τοῦ λοιποῦ βίου
οἷον βιῶναι σφὼ πρὸς ἀνθρώπων χρεών.
ποίας γὰρ ἀστῶν ἥξετ' εἰς ὁμιλίας,

1453 ζῶντι Pa: ζῶντε rell.   1454 ἀπωλλύτην aZrT: ἀπολλ- rell.   1454 eiecit Dawe
1462 τοῖν] ταῖν codd.   1465 τῷδ' Schneidewin   1466 τοῖν] ταῖν Zr: αἴν rell.   1474
ἐκγόνοιν rec.: ἐκγόνω <ν> G²ᵞᵖ: ἐγκ- Xr: ἐγγ- rell.   1477 ἤ σ' ἔχει rec.: ἤ σ' εἶχεν LᵃᶜT:
ἤν εἶχες LᵖᶜGRαZr: ἧς εἶχες H: ἤ σ' εἶχε rell.   1485 ἀροτὴρ Herwerden: πατὴρ codd.
1487 τὰ πικρὰ τοῦ λοιποῦ CHᵖᶜNOPa   τὰ λοιπὰ τοῦ πικροῦ rell: τὰ λ.τ. ****** Zc

ποίας δ' ἑορτάς, ἔνθεν οὐ κεκλαυμέναι   1490
πρὸς οἶκον ἵξεσθ' ἀντὶ τῆς θεωρίας;
ἀλλ' ἡνίκ' ἂν δὴ πρὸς γάμων ἥκητ' ἀκμάς,
τίς οὗτος ἔσται, τίς παρρρίψει, τέκνα,
τοιαῦτ' ὀνείδη λαμβάνων ἃ τοῖς †ἐμοῖς†
γονεῦσιν ἔσται σφῷν θ' ὁμοῦ δηλήματα;   1495
    τί γὰρ κακῶν ἄπεστι; τὸν πατέρα πατὴρ
ὑμῶν ἔπεφνε· τὴν τεκοῦσαν ἤροσεν,
ὅθεν περ αὐτὸς ἐσπάρη, κἀκ τῶν ἴσων
ἐκτήσαθ' ὑμᾶς ὧνπερ αὐτὸς ἐξέφυ.
τοιαῦτ' ὀνειδιεῖσθε· κᾆτα τίς γαμεῖ;   1500
οὐκ ἔστιν οὐδείς, ὦ τέκν', ἀλλὰ δηλαδὴ
χέρσους φθαρῆναι κἀγάμους ὑμᾶς χρεών.
    ὦ παῖ Μενοικέως, ἀλλ' ἐπεὶ μόνος πατὴρ
τούτοιν λέλειψαι, νὼ γάρ, ὣ 'φυτεύσαμεν,
ὀλώλαμεν δύ' ὄντε, μή σφε †παρίδῃς†   1505
πτωχὰς ἀνάνδρους †ἐγγενεῖς† ἀλωμένας,
μηδ' ἐξισώσῃς τάσδε τοῖς ἐμοῖς κακοῖς,
ἀλλ' οἴκτισόν σφας, ὧδε τηλικάσδ' ὁρῶν
πάντων ἐρήμους, πλὴν ὅσον τὸ σὸν μέρος.
ξύννευσον, ὦ γενναῖε, σῇ ψαύσας χερί.   1510
    σφῷν δ', ὦ τέκν', εἰ μὲν εἰχέτην ἤδη φρένας,
πόλλ' ἂν παρῄνουν· νῦν δὲ τοῦτ' εὔχεσθ' ἐμὲ
οὗ καιρὸς ἀεὶ ζῆν, βίου δὲ λῴονος
ὑμᾶς κυρῆσαι τοῦ φυτεύσαντος πατρός.
ΚΡ. ἅλις ἵν' ἐξήκεις δακρύων. ἀλλ' ἴθι στέγης ἔσω.   1515
ΟΙ. πειστέον, κεἰ μηδὲν ἡδύ;
ΚΡ.   πάντα γὰρ καιρῷ καλά.
ΟΙ. οἶσθ' ἐφ' οἷς οὖν εἶμι;
ΚΡ.   λέξεις, καὶ τότ' εἴσομαι κλύων.
ΟΙ. γῆς μ' ὅπως πέμψεις ἄποικον.
ΚΡ.   τοῦ θεοῦ μ' αἰτεῖς δόσιν.
ΟΙ. ἀλλὰ θεοῖς γ' ἔχθιστος ἥκω.
ΚΡ.   τοιγαροῦν τεύξῃ τάχα.
ΟΙ. φὴς τάδ' οὖν;
ΚΡ.   ἃ μὴ φρονῶ γὰρ οὐ φιλῶ λέγειν μάτην.   1520
ΟΙ. ἄπαγέ νύν μ' ἐντεῦθεν ἤδη.
ΚΡ.   στεῖχέ νυν, τέκνων δ' ἀφοῦ.

1494 λαμβάνειν Blaydes | ἃ τοῖσί τε Herwerden   1499 post hunc versum deficit N   1504
τούτοιν rec.: ταύταιν codd. nostri   1505 περίδῃς Dawes   1506 ἐγγενεῖς γ' Meineke:
ἐκστεγεῖς Schneidewin   1512 εὔχεσθ' ἐμὲ Deventer: εὔχεσθέ με DXr: εὔχεσθέ μοι fere rell.
1517 εἶμι Brunck: εἰμί codd.   1518 ἄποικον PaD^{sγρ}Xr^{sγρ}T: ἄποικος A^{γρ}: κἀπ' οἴκων O: τ'
ἀπ' οἴκων P: ἀπ' οἴκων rell.

ΟΙ.   μηδαμῶς ταύτας γ᾽ ἕληι μου.
ΚΡ.   πάντα μὴ βούλου κρατεῖν·
      καὶ γὰρ ἁκράτησας οὔ σοι τῶι βίωι ξυνέσπετο.

------------------------ ● ------------------------

ΧΟ.   ὦ πάτρας Θήβης ἔνοικοι, λεύσσετ᾽, Οἰδίπους ὅδε,
      ὃς τὰ κλείν᾽ αἰνίγματ᾽ ἤιδει καὶ κράτιστος ἦν ἀνήρ,   1525
      ὅστις οὐ ζήλωι πολιτῶν καὶ τύχαις ἐπιβλέπων,
      εἰς ὅσον κλύδωνα δεινῆς συμφορᾶς ἐλήλυθεν.
      ὥστε θνητὸν ὄντ᾽ ἐκείνην τὴν τελευταίαν ἰδεῖν
      ἡμέραν ἐπισκοποῦντα μηδέν᾽ ὀλβίζειν, πρὶν ἂν
      τέρμα τοῦ βίου περάσηι μηδὲν ἀλγεινὸν παθών.   1530

1523 post hunc versum deficit Pa   1524–30 eiecit Ritter

COMMENTARY

1 τέκνα: there are references to τέκνα again at 6, and to παῖδες at 32, 58, 142, 147. The rest of the citizen body (φῦλον 19, λαός 144) are elsewhere. The only adult person present besides Oedipus (and any possible attendants, who are not mentioned) is the old priest. In this way Sophocles shows Oedipus as a paternal and authoritative figure, upon whose shoulders alone (6off.) the weight of responsibility lies.

Κάδμου: in Greek poetry 'Cadmus' can mean either the legendary founder of Thebes, or, in certain contexts, the city itself: πόλιν ἐπώνυμον Κάδμου, as Aeschylus calls it (*Sept.* 135–6). Sometimes it is difficult to tell which of the two ideas predominates. The poets themselves move from phrases like Κάδμου πόλις 'city of Cadmus' to Κάδμου πολῖται 'citizens of Thebes' and thence to phrases like 'the gates of Cadmus', i.e. 'of Thebes' (Pindar, *Pyth.* 8.47; Eur. *Suppl.* 11–12, cf. *Herc.* 543). Here the addition of τοῦ πάλαι might make us think that only Cadmus himself was meant, but the contrast with νέα τροφή following suggests that we are meant to think primarily of the city.

νέα τροφή: the same words are used by Sophocles at *Ai.* 510f. and *Oed. Col.* 345f., referring to the care to be taken over, or enjoyed by, a child. The children are the *youthful charges* of the ancient city of Cadmus, and now the responsibility of Oedipus.

2 ἕδρας . . . θοάζετε: the ἕδρας are the positions symbolic of supplication which the children have taken up. For θοάζω the meaning 'sit' is assumed by Plutarch, *Mor.* 22e and the Byzantine dictionary called the *Etymologicum Magnum* (460.10), and appears in some scholiasts' notes on this passage. The same meaning is likely at Empedocles, frg. 3.7 DK[II], but there is a variant there, θαμίζειν. At Aesch. *Suppl.* 595 there is much surrounding corruption: 'sitting' is certainly mentioned there (597) but so too is speed in translating thought into action (σπεῦσαι 599). Now 'speed' is inherent in the transitive and intransitive uses of θοάζω, as derived from θοός, in the ten occurrences of the word in Euripides, and so some scholars have sought to give the meaning 'hasten to sit down as suppliants' to our present passage, but this view has not won much support. The etymological dictionaries of Boisacq, Frisk and Chantraine are willing to accept 'sit' as the meaning, the initial θο- being accounted for by Chantraine on the assumption that θοάζω, θῶκος and θᾶκος have their joint origin in a form θόϝακος or θώϝακος.

3 'Wreathed with suppliant branches' is what the text appears to say, but the meaning we require is either 'holding wreathed branches' (i.e. branches with wool entwined along them, as the custom was), or 'wreathed themselves, and holding wreathed branches too'. In the late thirteenth century the noted Greek scholar Manuel Moschopoulos, who composed a commentary carried by some of the α group of our manuscripts, favoured the first interpretation, and another scholar of the same era, Thomas Magister, the second. Neither is, strictly speaking, possible (but the first is less impossible than the second). Volgraff therefore suggested that ἱκτηρίοις κλάδοισιν

70

should be construed with ἕδρας θοάζετε, just as ἱκτῆρι θαλλῶι has to be construed with προσπίτνουσ' ἐμὸν γόνυ at Eur. *Suppl.* 10. 'Why do you sit there with suppliant branches?' ἐξεστεμμένοι then adds the separate idea, that the suppliants are themselves garlanded: cf. ἐξεστεμμένον at 19. The whole topic of supplication is discussed by J. Gould in *J.H.S.* 93 (1973) 74–103.

5 παιάνων: not the paean of victory, but the prayer to Παιάν, the healer: cf. 186.

6 μὴ παρ' ἀγγέλων: the contrast between receiving reports at second hand and having first-hand knowledge is a commonplace in tragedy, as we noted in the Introduction (p. 11), but here the idea is particularly helpful in establishing Oedipus' intellectual and personal character.

7 ἄλλων: 'other people, messengers'. This idiomatic use of ἄλλος is well established. A close parallel is Eur. *Or.* 532–3 τί μαρτύρων | ἄλλων ἀκούειν δεῖ μ' ἅ γ' εἰσορᾶν πάρα;

8 ὁ πᾶσι κλεινός: Homer's Odysseus put it more strongly: καί μευ κλέος οὐρανὸν ἵκει. Wunder and some others after him, who prefer their heroes to be more modest, have sought to remove this essential line. Sophocles has his hero identify himself to the audience in much the same way as Aeschylus does with Eteocles in *Sept.* 6. πᾶσι is probably masculine, 'in the eyes of all', not neuter, and the same is true of its occurrences at 40 (πᾶσι κράτιστον) and *Oed. Col.* 1446 (ἀνάξιαι γὰρ πᾶσίν ἐστε δυστυχεῖν). cf. πολλοῖσιν οἰκτρόν at *Trach.* 1071. As for κλεινός, this 'is a regular title of royalty' as Denniston notes on Eur. *El.* 327, comparing 776 of that play and *Or.* 17.

9 πρέπων ἔφυς: ἔφυς is especially appropriate, rather than πέλεις or κυρεῖς or any such alternative, since it is the age (i.e. part of the φύσις) of the priest, who has just been called γεραιέ, that makes him πρέπων; and πρέπων itself is appropriate in two ways: the priest's age makes him *stand out* from the rest, and it also makes him the *fitting person* to speak for the children. This latter sense is the one that predominates.

10 πρὸ τῶνδε continues the ambiguity of πρέπων: the priest stands out *in front of* the others, and is qualified to speak *for* them. The whole expression πρέπων ἔφυς πρὸ τῶνδε φωνεῖν is an unobtrusive example of Sophocles' ability to convey both primary and secondary meanings in the briefest phrase.

τίνι τρόπωι καθέστατε: the verb is ambiguously used either of the position taken up by the suppliants or simply of their mental attitude: 'In what frame of mind are you (here)?'

11 δείσαντες ἢ στέργοντες: one expects to find not two aorist participles (δείσαντες ἢ στέρξαντες MSS) but two present participles to describe the present τρόπος of the suppliants. However, for all its aorist appearance, δείσας both in verse and prose regularly means not 'having feared' or 'in a moment of fear' but simply 'in fear', as at 234, *Ant.* 459; cf. προδείσας at 90. So, e.g., at Homer *Od.* 9.377 and 396; 14.389; 17.577; Aesch. *Agam.* 933 (where 'in an hour of terror' – Fraenkel, and 'in a moment of terror' – Denniston and Page, both seem to be mistakenly attempting to account for the aorist); Eur. *Hec.* 6; *Ion* 1564; *El.* 22. The only problem then resides with the undoubtedly aorist participle στέρξαντες, and in determining what the object of the two participles is. In a context which is much concerned with establishing the nature of the relationship between the king and his people the opposed pair 'in fear of me or in loyal affection' is very much at home, and στέργειν is well chosen to convey exactly the sense we expect: cf. *Ant.* 292, Hdt. 9.113. But it will be necessary for us to change the tense from the aorist στέρξαντες to the present στέργοντες, assuming that it has been assimilated by scribal error to the tense of the aorist participle δείσαντες, for which no present participle exists. The variant στέξαντες will owe its popularity in one branch of the manuscript tradition to its use in post-classical Greek (e.g. *Christus Patiens* 698, 820, 1029) to mean 'endure'.

ὡς θέλοντος ἄν: the genitive absolute gives the reason why the attitude of στέργοντες would be more fitting than the attitude of δείσαντες, and is equivalent in sense to ὡς θελήσαιμι ἄν: 'for you should know that I would be willing . . .'.

12 προσαρκεῖν: see 141 n.

13 μὴ οὐ: δυσ-άλγητος is a virtual negative, and so μὴ οὐ, not just μή, is justified with the following participle. The tone is: 'I would be hard-hearted indeed if I did not feel pity.' If the infinitive κατοικτίρειν followed, the tone would be 'hard-hearted not to feel pity'. The construction recurs at 221, 1065, 1091, and τὸ μὴ οὐ at 283, 1232. μὴ οὐ are to be scanned as a single syllable, by synizesis, or synekphonesis.

16 'Your altars.' The possessive 'your' may be deliberately ambiguous, for the theme that Oedipus, though not a god, is the nearest thing to a god among Theban men will be developed in a moment (31, 38, 42–3). 'Your' is appropriate, however, for the altars are Oedipus' rather than the city's, which would be in the ἀγοραί where the rest of the citizenry is assembled.

17 σύν: weighed down *with* age. This use of σύν coupled with an adjective is rare, but is well paralleled by Aesch. *Agam.* 456 βαρεῖα δ' ἀστῶν φάτις σὺν κότωι, or *Oed. Col.* 1663–4 σὺν νόσοις ἀλγεινός. At Aesch. *Hik.* 186–7 in the phrase τεθηγμένος ὠμῆι ξὺν ὀργῆι it is uncertain whether ὠμῆι ξὺν ὀργῆι belongs primarily with τεθηγμένος or with the verb ἐπόρνυται. σύν phrases go with the verb at Aesch. *Pers.* 755, 775; *Sept.* 878, 884; Eur. *Bacch.* 886–7.

18 ἱερεὺς ἐγώ εἰμι: the mention of old men leads the priest by a natural progression to explain his own rôle in the proceedings. Contrary to what the manuscripts would have us believe, it is unlikely that there are other priests present. If they are, they are pointedly ignored at 9–10. They would be of more use in the ἀγοραί. The problem presented by the ἱερεῖς of the manuscript text was effectively solved by Herwerden. In his emendation the last syllable of ἐγώ and the first syllable of εἰμι are run together, as at *Phil.* 585, where the same corruption of εἰμί to μέν can be seen in some manuscripts. It is likely enough that ἐγώ εἰμ(ι) occurs also at *Phil.* 57, where the corruption in all manuscripts is to λέγειν. More familiar is the running together of syllables in ἐγὼ οὔτε and ἐγὼ οἶδα (= ἐγῶιδα).

ἠιθέων: an ἤιθεος is an unmarried youth. These acolytes of the priest are not to be confused with the young children just referred to.

20 ἀγοραῖσι: not necessarily poetic plural for singular: Thebes had two market places.

20–1 διπλοῖς | ναοῖς: the twin temples of Athena Onca (Phoenician name) and the other perhaps of Athena Καδμεία.

Ἰσμηνοῦ: one of the two famous rivers of Thebes, the other being Dirce. The correct spelling should be with a rough breathing as shown on Theban inscriptions and an Attic vase, but the literary sources preserve no trace of this. The 'oracular ash' may allude to the temple of Apollo σπόδιος, where there was an altar made from the ashes of sacrificial victims. 'There is here a regular system of divination by means of voices' writes Pausanias (9.11.7). Alternatively divination by burnt offering may be meant (Hdt. 8.134).

23–4 If it were not for κάρα, we would assume that σαλεύει … βυθῶν … σάλου was one more instance of the ship of state metaphor which goes back to Archilochus and remained a favourite of Greek poets: e.g. τὰ μὲν δὴ πόλεος … πολλῶι σάλωι σείσαντες Ant. 162–3. κάρα however suggests rather the image of a drowning man. One cannot argue that the σάλος metaphor rules out individual persons: cf. El. 1074 μόνα σαλεύει (of Electra): nor can one argue that βυθῶν 'from the depths' rules out ships. Cf. Ant. 337 περῶν ὑπ' οἴδμασιν, not 'travelling under the waves' but 'travelling through waves that tower over one'. Probably we have here, as Kamerbeek says, a metaphor within a metaphor.

26 ἀγέλαις βουνόμοις: ἀγέλαι βοῶν νεμομένων.

27 ἐν δ': an independent phrase with no further influence on the syntax of the sentence, used to introduce another item in a series: 'and what is more' rather over-translates it. It will recur in a similar context at 182. Cf. Ai. 675, Oed. Col. 55, and perhaps Trach. 208, though there only one other item precedes. Ant. 420 and El. 713 are different, for there ἐν is in tmesis with the verb μεστόω. It has been said that Homer and Herodotus are the only other authors to use the construction. In fact Homer does not use it at all (Od. 5.260 has ἐν in anticipation of ἐνέδησεν) and Herodotus uses only the forms ἐν δὲ καί or ἐν δὲ δὴ καί, where some case of ἄλλος, or rarely πᾶς or πολύς, precedes, and the author wishes to specify something in particular. Often the sense 'and among them' can be felt. Much closer parallels to Sophocles' usage can be found in Pindar, at Ol. 7.5, 10.73, and Dithyr. 2.10.

πυρφόρος θεός: one of the meanings of πῦρ is 'fever'. At Oed. Col. 55 in the identical phrase ἐν δ' ὁ πυρφόρος θεός the poet immediately explains whom he means: Τιτὰν Προμηθεύς. Here the god is not named: he is certainly not Prometheus, and we are probably not meant to think at this stage of any one specific deity; but at 192 the blame is assigned to Ares, and the word φλέγει used of him. Confusingly, however, at 206 Sophocles uses πυρφόρους of the αἴγλας of Artemis, sister of Apollo, the plague god of the *Iliad*, both of whom are jointly invoked as helpers; and of Zeus's lightning at 200.

30 The present edition places δ᾽ at the beginning of the line rather than at the end of the line before, because such is the practice of our manuscripts (see G. Zuntz, *An inquiry into the transmission of the plays of Euripides* (Cambridge 1965) 232). Sophocles places another such 'post-positive' word in this position, δῆτ᾽, at *Ai.* 986. Compare also σοι at 840 below and ποτ᾽ at 1085. Elided δ᾽ in the same place is found again at 786, 792, (τ᾽ at 1185), 1225, and at *El.* 1018, *Oed. Col.* 18. Aeschylus and Euripides do not share this practice. Sophocles evidently felt that there was no significant break at line end: he uses the definite article at the end of a line with its noun at the beginning of the next: *Ant.* 409, *El.* 879, *Phil.* 263, *Oed. Col.* 351. Very similar are *Trach.* 92, 383, 742; *Ant.* 67, 78, 238; *Phil.* 422, 674; *Oed. Col.* 265; frg. 28.2. At *Phil.* 312 τε καί ends a line, as it does in our play at 267, 1234. Most remarkable of all is ταῦτ᾽ | ἄλλως at 332–3.

Although the lines are so closely connected, Sophocles does not differ from the other poets in allowing short syllables to stand at the end of a line where a long is required by the metre, a practice normally justified by the evidently too facile explanation that the voice pauses there.

πλουτίζεται: opposed to κενοῦται. Hades is also Πλούτων.

31 It is most important that we should know at an early stage whether Oedipus is the kind of tyrant who might wish to be regarded as divine, or whether he keeps himself free from such impiety. The theme will be taken up later (872) at a critical point in the play. Oedipus is the sort of man who might reject extreme adulation with such words as οὐ τίς τοι θεός εἰμι· τί μ᾽ ἀθανάτοισιν ἐΐσκεις; like Odysseus, Hom. *Od.* 16.187; or λέγω κατ᾽ ἄνδρα, μὴ θεόν, σέβειν ἐμέ, like Agamemnon, Aesch. *Agam.* 925. The suppliants know this, and respect his wishes. They feel that he has some special relationship with the gods (38) but they carefully draw the vital distinction between gods (31) and men (33).

32 ἐφέστιοι: 'in arae gradibus' (F. Ellendt – H. Genthe, *Lexicon Sophocleum*, Berlin 1872); cf. 15–16.

34 συναλλαγαῖς: it is impossible to pin down Sophocles' exact meaning: 'dealings' with the gods, or a crisis caused by them, or even a reconciliation with them; all three meanings are well attested. 'Dealings' is perhaps the safest choice, to avoid duplication of συμφοραῖς, and to provide an introduction to 37–8.

35 ὅς γ᾽: used to introduce a reason, 'seeing that you ...'; ὅστις is often used in a similar way.

36 σκληρᾶς ἀοιδοῦ δασμόν· the tribute (men's lives) exacted by the Sphinx for failure to solve her riddle: see on 130 (also 464).

39 ἡμίν scanned as –◡ may be confined to Sophocles, but Page's edition of Aeschylus allows for this scansion at *Suppl.* 959 (Kirchhoff), and *Eum.* 349, where however Wilamowitz's conjecture, which would obviate the phenomenon, receives some kind of support from Tournier's at Soph. *El.* 85. The same scansion just below, 42, and again at 103, etc.

40 νῦν τ': one expects to see νῦν δ, which is what GR actually offer us. But the near unanimity of our MSS in resisting the obvious is impressive. If τ' is right, it will be intended to suggest that the chorus are asking for something similar to Oedipus' previous service to the state, and linking it closely to that service, rather than making a contrast between then and now.

43 οἶσθά που: the object of οἶσθα is ἀλκήν. The variant του (= τινός) may well be right, giving exact chiastic parallelism with του θεῶν. Cf. Hom. *Od.* 1.282–3

> ἤν τίς τοι εἴπηισι βροτῶν, ἢ ὄσσαν ἀκούσηις
> ἐκ Διός ἥ τε μάλιστα φέρει κλέος ἀνθρώποισι.

44 ξυμφοράς: no known meaning of this word will yield an acceptable sense if 44 is followed immediately by 45, with βουλευμάτων depending on ξυμφοράς. Hence the gap indicated in the text. But at 99 we may strongly suspect that once again ξυμφορᾶς is being used in a sense not otherwise known to us. Our difficulties are made worse by uncertainty over the meaning to be assigned to ζώσας, which can refer to either good things or bad things: metaphorical use again at 482.

46 ὦ βροτῶν ἄριστ': the same note is struck again: Oedipus is the best of men, of mortals, not a god, even if he is called by everyone a σωτήρ (48), an appellation used also of Zeus and other gods, as of Apollo at 150.

48 τῆς πάρος προθυμίας: the MSS have no <'κ>, and editors speak of the genitives as 'causal'. But the phrase falls far outside the categories copiously illustrated in K–G 1 388–94, and there is not much comfort to be drawn from the closest parallel, τῆσδε τῆς ὁδοῦ, at 1478, when we reflect that 1478 is in the spurious part of the play, and looks as though it may have been based on a misunderstanding of the same words at *Oed. Col.* 1506.

51 This verse adds very little to the sense, and has the same ending as 46. Similarly one may doubt whether at *Phil.* 906 and 913 Sophocles really wrote two lines ending with τοῦτ' ἀνιῶμαι πάλαι.

52 ὄρνιθι ... αἰσίωι: the 'favourable bird' is a good omen at Eur. *I.A.* 607 ὄρνιθα μὲν τόνδ' αἴσιον ποιούμεθα | τὸ σόν τε χρηστόν (your kind disposition) καὶ λόγων εὐφημίαν; Pindar, *Nem.* 9.18f. αἰσιᾶν οὐ κατ' ὀρνίχων ὁδόν, as we might say, changing the metaphor, 'an ill-starred expedition'. But here 'omen' does not exactly hit off the sense. It is rather that Oedipus' success was marked by divine favour; he made an auspicious beginning.

54 ἄρξεις ... ὥσπερ κρατεῖς: 'If you shall rule this land as you command it' – the sense is flabby, for the distinction, if any is intended, between ἄρχω and κρατῶ here is lost on us, and if stress is intended on the continuation in the future of a state existing now, then we miss a νῦν with κρατεῖς. With κρατεῖν immediately below suspicion is bound to focus on κρατεῖς.

56–7 There is a similar passage in Thucydides 7.77.7... καὶ οἱ Ἀθηναῖοι τὴν μεγάλην δύναμιν τῆς πόλεως καίπερ πεπτωκυῖαν ἐπανορθώσοντες· ἄνδρες γὰρ πόλις, καὶ οὐ τείχη, οὐδὲ νῆες ἀνδρῶν κεναί. See O. Longo, *Edipo e Nicia* (Padua 1975).

58–9 γνωτὰ κοὐκ ἄγνωτα: this cannot be called a typical example of polar expression. It is an extreme instance, for usually poets use a different word in the negative half of the expression from the word preceding in the positive half: e.g. πολλάκι καὶ οὐκὶ ἅπαξ in Hdt. (cf. 1275 below) or βάλεν οὐδ᾽ ἀφάμαρτεν or οὐκ ὄναρ ἀλλ᾽ ὕπαρ (Homer). An early collection of similar examples can be found in I. Bekker, *Homerische Blätter* II (Bonn 1872) 222–3. But an exact parallel occurs in ἑκόντα κοὐκ ἄκοντα below at 1230.

60 The sentence runs on naturally without strict regard for syntax. The logic can be improved, if that is our aim, by taking καί as equivalent to καίτοι, 'and yet', as at *Trach.* 1072, *El.* 597, Eur. *Herc.* 509. Further examples in Denniston, *GP*² 292 (9).

66 δακρύσαντα δή: Oedipus is more than just a man with a brilliant incisive intellect: he weeps over the fate of his city. Or does he? There is much to be said for Naber's διακρούσαντα, a metaphor from striking an object (as one might tap a crystal vase), to see if it rings εἴτε ὑγιὲς εἴτε σαθρόν, to quote the example given from Plato in LSJ *s.v.* This provides a better contrast with the 'asleep' of 65, and a better pairing with 68. Oedipus' spirit (64) στένει, but he is a man of action, trying everything and exploring every avenue of thought.

67 The language of politicians, 'exploring every avenue' (cf. ὁδόν 311), is clothed in poetic form. πλάνοις almost suggests a note of desperation, a mind 'wandering': cf. Eur. *Hipp.* 283. φροντίς is either just 'thought' or 'care', 'solicitude'. The decision which the experienced politician comes to after 'mature reflection' (εὖ σκοπῶν 68) is to have recourse to religion and oracles.

70–1 Πυθικὰ ... πύθοιθ᾽: it is very doubtful if Sophocles' audience would link these two words in their minds. Apart from anything else there is a difference in quantity between Πῡθικά and πῠθοιθ᾽. See, however, C. J. Ruijgh in *Mnemosyne* 30 (1977) 439, and 603–4 below.

74–5 τί πράσσει: not 'what he is doing' but 'how he is getting on', or 'what has happened to him'. 'The date now, measured against the time (that he has been away), makes me worried about how he is getting on. He has been away more than you would expect, a longer time than would be normal (for the journey).' Oedipus' style in the speech 58–77 is marked by a certain leisurely amplitude in the deployment of antithesis and repetition. As the tension in the play increases, so too does the tautness of his delivery. The reading of V, χρόνον, looks attractive and may be right. But cf. *El.* 1265–6 ὑπερτέραν (sc. χάριν) τᾶς πάρος ἔτι χάριτος.

78 εἰς καλὸν: this rare idiom recurs at Eur. *Herc.* 728–9, Plato, *Symp.* 174e, Menander, *Samia* 280, *Dysc.* 773, in all cases with a verb of motion or its equivalent (though παρόνθ is now read by Sandbach at *Sam.* 280 as in the Cairo MS). Thus in the Plato passage εἰς καλὸν ἥκεις ὅπως συνδειπνήσῃς means 'You're just in nice time to join us for dinner.' In our Sophocles passage the verb of motion is προσστείχοντα, and it is the opportune arrival of Creon that is the most important element in this sentence, notwithstanding its grammatical subordination. But the word order and the double τ' show that εἰς καλόν belongs formally to σὺ εἶπας and οἵδε σημαίνουσι. The precise nuance is elusive, perhaps something like: 'Well, your words and the arrival of Creon which these children have just this moment signalled to me are beautifully timed' – timed that is in the sense that they coincide with each other, and, more particularly, with the exigencies of the situation.

There are many coincidences in *Oedipus Rex*. This is the first, and one of the least important.

81 λαμπρός: Oedipus is plainly expressing the wish that Creon's return will be accompanied by some good fortune, corresponding with the cheerful look on his face, although the use of the word λαμπρός is not in itself proof of cheerfulness; it is used in connection with oracles at *Trach.* 1174, Aesch. *Agam.* 1180, *Eum.* 797, [Aesch.] *Prom. Vinct.* 833, with reference to their clarity or truth, which may be *un*pleasant.

ὄμματι: not 'to our eyes' but 'in his face'. Cf. *Oed. Col.* 319–20 φαιδρὰ γοῦν ἀπ' ὀμμάτων | σαίνει με προσστείχουσα.

The sequence of events is curious. At 79 the priest gets a signal that Creon has been sighted. At 81 Oedipus can see that Creon's face looks cheerful. At 82 the priest sees that Creon is wearing a laurel wreath, and at 84 Creon is within earshot. Unless there are long pauses in the actors' deliveries, we must assume some dramatically legitimate telescoping of time. But it remains awkward that Oedipus can discern the features of Creon's face *before* the priest mentions the larger and, one would think, more clearly visible sign of the laurel wreath, and that the priest should hazard a guess (εἰκάσαι μέν) based on a wreath when the much less ambiguous evidence of Creon's own face has already been spoken of. The parallel of *Oed. Col.* 319–20 just cited suggests that we should just accept the awkwardness rather than diagnose corruption in ὄμματι.

82 εἰκάσαι: 'at a guess'. The parenthetic infinitive is more usual with ὡς or ὅσον. Cf. *Trach.* 141, *Oed. Col.* 16 ὡς ἀπεικάσαι and *Trach.* 1220 ὡς ἀπεικάζειν. Other examples in K–G II 509. But for a use without ὡς or ὅσον cf. *El.* 410 δοκεῖν ἐμοί and K–G II 19.

ἡδύς: used of someone who brings pleasure to someone else, 'welcome'. Cf. *Ai.* 105, *El.* 929, *Phil.* 530, Eur. *Bacch.* 135.

γάρ: 'for otherwise'. A common usage.

83 πολυστεφής ... δάφνης: cf. *El.* 895–6 περιστεφῆ ... ἀνθέων. Further examples in Barrett on Eur. *Hipp.* 468–9.

84 ὡς: consecutive = ὥστε. At a fitting distance so as to hear, i.e. within earshot.

85 A solemn and formal address, appropriate to a man upon whose answer so much hangs, but useful too in obliquely reminding the audience that Creon is an important figure related to Oedipus by marriage. Compare the use of ἐμαυτοῦ, not ἐμόν, at 70 above.

88 πάντ᾿: a grammarian would correctly argue that πάντα does not agree with τὰ δύσφορα, but means 'in all respects'. In English we say 'will all work out happily' without being conscious of any grammatical ambiguities.

89–90 Creon has just delivered two lines of such bland and unhelpful superficiality that some scholars, stunned at what they see before them, have tried to emend the text and thereby do something to raise his intellectual stature by a notch or two. Oedipus' reaction is not far different: his ποῖον τοὖπος, and the γε in 90, are both implied criticisms, delivered with a touch of irony. Possibly however Creon is playing for time until he can be alone with Oedipus inside the palace (92).

90 οὔτ᾿ οὖν: οὖν can be used with either the first or the second member of an οὔτε ... οὔτε or εἴτε ... εἴτε phrase. See Denniston, *GP²* 418–20. οὖν does not stress προδείσας at the expense of θρασύς as a more likely alternative. The whole tone so far has been one of optimism. The nuance can be represented by something like 'What you have said so far does not engender confidence – or apprehension, come to that.' If Oedipus knew more, apprehension is exactly what he would feel.

91–4 Creon's suggestion is loaded in favour of (as καί shows) a confidential report inside the palace. Oedipus' democratic character is brought out by his repudiation of the idea. Discussion over the right composition of the audience of a messenger's report also at *Trach.* 342–4.

94 πέρι: when we reach this last word a slight anacolouthon becomes noticeable, for τῶνδε (93) is governed by τὸ πένθος, but τῆς ἐμῆς ψυχῆς by πέρι, and πένθος is not exactly the feeling that Oedipus would have for his own life. More than Aeschylus or Euripides, Sophocles likes to mirror in his own verse the imprecisions of real speech. 'The sorrow I feel for these people weighs more with me than where my own life is concerned.' In reality Oedipus' own life *is* concerned, and threatened by more than just the plague.

96 ἐμφανῶς: the oracle has given clear instructions. Cf. σαφῶς at 106, and see the notes on λαμπρός (81) and σαφῶς (846).

97 μίασμα: 'It is important to distinguish pollution clearly from the killed man's need to be avenged ... The pollution affects the whole state and all who come into contact with the killer ... It is not the case that pollution is the curse of the killed person which he removes only when he is avenged … for we hear of cases in which purification takes place after homicide although vengeance is obtained only later or not at all' (D. M. MacDowell, *Athenian homicide law* (Manchester 1963) 4). In Aesch. *Eum.* Orestes is purified long before the trial takes place.

But pollution of the kind MacDowell is talking about does not normally lead to plagues and blights. It is true that at 97, 101, 107, etc., we are told that these troubles stem from the presence in the land of the killer(s) of Laius, and that no one looks any deeper. But Sophocles has his own reasons for wanting to hold back the parricide and incest theme. It is also true that plagues and blights may affect cities ruled by unjust kings: see the parallels cited in M. L. West's note on Hesiod, *Works and Days* 225–47. But Oedipus is not in any conventional sense an unjust king: quite the reverse. In spite of the fact that Sophocles nowhere says so, it seems likely that in his own mind the evils in the land originated not so much from regicide as from parricide and incest. (Compare the unnatural family crimes and their punishment at Herodotus 6.139.) For a comprehensive account of pollution see R. Parker, *Miasma* (Oxford 1983).

'The latter taboo [sc. incest] is the great universal one, the most dreaded among all primitive societies and everywhere compounded with dire pollution. Patricide, while not so universal a taboo, was for the Greeks almost as culpable an offense, for in committing it one shed kindred blood. Thus these two taboos represented their life-and-death attitudes toward familial blood: it is sacred, and one must neither procreate with it nor destroy it … In the case of incest, "the fatal consequences are above all manifested in the fact that the plantations will no longer yield their produce … The scourge it lets loose will spare no one, for famine, epidemic, hurricane, earthquake are calamities that no one can escape. Hence the need for concerted action."' (T. P. Howe, *T.A.P.A.* 93 (1962) 124–43, quoting Lévy-Bruhl, *Primitives and the supernatural* (New York 1935).)

τεθραμμένον: it receives its τροφή in this land. We talk of nurturing vipers in bosoms, as did Aesch. *Cho.* 928, and, when properly emended, Theognis 602; and so too ἄτα (dual) is the object of τρέφω at *Ant.* 533, ἄταν at *Ai.* 643f. (cf. *Ai.* 503), μιάστορα *El.* 603, νόσον *Phil.* 795, ἄνδρας ἐκδίκους *Oed. Col.* 920. φόβον and δεῖμα are similarly fostered at *Trach.* 28 and 108. Sophocles does not scorn to repeat the same verb at the end of the next line, where it is unobtrusive because the stress falls on ἀνήκεστον.

98 **ἀνήκεστον:** either 'without curing it' or predicatively, 'so that it becomes incurable'.

99 **ὁ πόρος τῆς ξυμφορᾶς:** the point of the two definite articles is to give the sense: 'What is the way out (specified by the oracle) of the disaster (this one in which we find ourselves)?' For the use of πόρος here cf. Eur. *Alc.* 213 πόρος κακῶν. The MSS reading τρόπος can be dismissed, for Oedipus can hardly be asking for the characteristics of the misfortune, since everyone present knows them already.

100   The choice of exile or death, confirmed at 309, is one that will become curiously blurred in the Oedipus–Creon quarrel 622ff. See 622, 641, 659 and Introduction 11.

101   ὡς + acc. part. 'Knowing that.' Cf. *El.* 882, Eur. *Ion* 965, *Rh.* 145.

χειμάζον: an echo of the storm metaphor of 23–4, but also a medical term used, in the passive, of feverish patients: and so χειμῶνι is to be understood of the sick περθόμενοι δέμας at Pindar, *Pyth.* 3.50; cf. Soph. *Ai.* 206, *Phil.* 1459, and Pearson's note on *Ichn.* 267.

πόλιν: the same word ends 104, and πάλιν ends the line above, 100. At 104 one manuscript gives χθόνα. If χθόνα belongs anywhere, 101 would be the best place for it. The *country* is storm-tossed, but political direction is given to the *city*. For confusion, or rather synonym-substitution, of these two words, cf. Aesch. *Sept.* 1006 (Lc: cf. 1007), Soph. *Ant.* 187 (L^s), Eur. *Alc.* 479 (cf. 476).

105   γέ: Oedipus has heard of Laius. He never actually *saw* him. Or so he thinks.

πω: not 'yet' but 'at all', πω being used like πως, as often in Homer. The same use in οὔπω at 594. Further examples in R. D. Dawe, *Collation and investigation of MSS of Aeschylus* (Cambridge 1964) 122–3.

106   νῦν: not 'now' temporal but standing for νυν. Cf. LSJ *s.v.* νῦν II.

107   αὐτοέντας: this word can mean simply 'murderers', but its choice here would strike a particular chill into the audience, who would recognize its special associations with murders committed within the family. Etymology in Kretschmer, *Glotta* 3 (1912) 289ff.

†τινας†: this indefinite pronoun cannot be combined with τοὺς αὐτοέντας so as to mean 'the murderers, whoever they may be'. Such a usage is unknown. Equally strange is χειρί without further qualification: contrast the addition of τοιαύτηι at 140. It seems likely then that τινας is a corruption of an adjective to be construed with χειρί. τίται has been suggested, 'to punish them with an avenging hand'. The word is both poetic and legalistic, and so ideal for the context, but it is so rare that we can feel no confidence that it is right.

108   τόδ': ποθ was suggested by Meineke, since no ἴχνος has actually been referred to.

110   ἐν τῆιδ ... γῆι: not a helpful answer to Oedipus' question ποῦ γῆς (108) if the γῆ is in both cases the territory of Thebes. But the idiom 'where on earth?' is so common that the audience would not pause to reflect that γῆ two lines later was used in a different sense.

110–11   For the rhyming verses cf. *Ai.* 807–8, 1085–6, *Trach.* 1265–6, *Ant.* 272–3, *Phil.* 121–2 and in Euripides *Alc.* 782–5, *Hcld.* 541–2; *[Iph. Aul.]* 1442–3.

111   ἐκφεύγει: Valckenaer's suggestion ἐκφεύγειν makes Creon's sentence part of the oracle's remarks. The oracle will then be expressing in general terms a reproach over the Thebans' negligence, as Oedipus himself does at 255–8. The suggestion may well be right, but Creon's gift for stating the obvious on his own account (λέγω) has already appeared at 87–8. Valckenaer made a comparable suggestion of infinitive for finite verb at *Trach.* 66, where again there is some doubt whether the character is reporting the speech of others or not.

112 See Introduction 6.

113 συμπίπτει: the label 'vivid historic present' is too glibly attached to such usages. In Thucydides for example we can find many present tenses used alongside past tenses with no apparent differentiation. At *Ant.* 1174 in response to the statement τεθνᾶσιν the question is put καὶ τίς φονεύει, not ἐφόνευσεν. It may be worthwhile transcribing the introductory words of Kühner–Gerth in their standard Greek Grammar. 'The present is often used in the narration of past events, when the speaker transports himself back to the time in which the action took place (historic present). This kind of expression is common to all languages, and not merely as a form of lively and pictorial description, but also in the sober style of chronicles and genealogies, since the chronicler too transports himself back to the year whose events he is relating. So the Greek language too, indeed more often than the other related languages, employs the historic present in main and subordinate sentences both where there is particular liveliness in the description and where the tone is one of simple narrative.'

114 θεωρός: as at *Oed. Col.* 413 used of those on a mission to consult the Delphic oracle. In Eur. *Phoen.* 35–7 Laius' motive in going was to enquire if the child he had exposed was dead, while Oedipus, as in Sophocles, travelled there at the same time to learn about his parents.

ἔφασκον: Creon is passing on hearsay: 'People said.' At this stage in the play the more vagueness the better. The manuscripts here have ἔφασκεν, which would convey the unfortunate idea that Creon did not himself altogether believe Laius' story that he was going off to consult the oracle.

115 οὐκέθ: cf. Ar. *Lys.* 792: κοὐκέτι κατῆλθε πάλιν οἴκαδ᾽ ὑπὸ μίσους, 'he did not come back home any more, he hated them so much'. 'No longer' would be meaningless. We have before us an example of a still largely unrecognized idiom, which is best understood if the word is split into its component parts οὐκ and ἔτι. The underlying sense is 'not the further, and perhaps expected, step'. Thus at 1251 χὤπως μὲν ἐκ τῶνδ᾽ οὐκέτ᾽ οἶδ᾽ ἀπόλλυται the meaning cannot be 'and how after that she died I no longer know', but is 'and how after that she died, this is a further point on which I have no knowledge' (and so we are to understand ταῦτ᾽ οὐκέτ᾽ ἴδρις εἰμί in the Sophocles *Inachus* fragment, Pap. Oxy. 2369 col. 2, v. 3 = frg. 269a Radt, v. 31: left unexplained by R. Carden, *Sophocles: The papyrus fragments* (Berlin and New York 1974) 59, 62–3). At *El.* 610–11 ὁρῶ μένος πνέουσαν, εἰ δὲ σὺν Δίκηι | ξύνεστι τῆσδε φροντίς, οὐκέτ᾽ εἰσορῶ the meaning is 'I can see that she is furious, but whether she is on the same side as Justice, this is a further point that I cannot make out.' At Pindar, *Pyth.* 3.40 the sense 'no longer' will hardly do: a dead mother with a live baby within her is on the funeral pyre, and Apollo cries οὐκέτι | τλάσομαι ψυχᾶι γένος ἁμὸν ὀλέσσαι | οἰκτροτάτωι θανάτωι ματρὸς βαρείαι σὺν πάθαι, i.e. 'I will not take the further step of destroying my offspring by a pitiful death along with the fate of the mother.' Scholars have had better luck with 4. 243 ('that further trial' – Race). Similarly [Aesch.] *Prom. Vinct.* 520 τοῦτ' οὐκέτ' ἂν πύθοιο 'this is a further point on which I can give you no information'; Eur. *Tro.* 845f. τὸ μὲν οὖν Διὸς | οὐκέτ' ὄνειδος ἐρῶ 'I will not go on to mention the shame of Zeus'; *Anth. Pal.* 5. 177. 5 πατρὸς δ' οὐκέτ' ἔχω φράζειν τίνος. The usage is as old as Homer: *Il.* 1.406 οὐδ' ἔτ' ἔδησαν, 'they did not go on to tie him up', 9.598 τῶι δ' οὐκέτι δῶρ' ἐτέλεσσαν 'they did not go on to give him the gifts'. At *Od.* 9.95 it is said of any one who had eaten of the lotus plant that οὐκέτ' ἀπαγγεῖλαι πάλιν ἤθελεν οὐδὲ νέεσθαι. In the second half of the sentence 'he no longer wanted to return' is normal, but 'he no longer wanted to send a messenger back' is nonsense, and the meaning has to be that he was unwilling to take the additional step which one might reasonably expect, of notifying us. Further examples at *Od.* 12.223, 445; 17. 303, 460. (At Pind. *Ol.* 1.5 μηκέτι means 'Don't go on to take the further (and in this case *un*reasonable) step of looking for a warmer star in the sky than the sun.') The usage continues throughout Greek literature, in prose as well as poetry: examples can be found at Hdt. 1.31.3 (κατακοιμηθέντες ἐν αὐτῶι τῶι ἱρῶι οἱ νεάνιαι οὐκέτι ἀνέστησαν 'they did not <as you might have expected> get up again'), Plato *Lysis* 204 b, τοῦτο μὲν μηκέτι εἴπηις, Xenophon of Ephesus 1.13.6; 2.6.1; 4.2.1, and in fact, once one is alive to the idiom, examples seem to come flooding in. The idiom is discussed by J.R.Wilson, *Glotta* 65 (1987) 194–8 and by G. Giangrande in *Museum philologum londiniense* 7 (1987) 119–20.

   In the passage before us a full gloss of the sense would be: he did not take the further and expected step of returning in a way that would have matched his departure. ὡς = 'as' not 'when'.

116 οὐδ' ... οὐδέ: not in parallel, as if οὔτ' ... οὔτε, but 'And (*or* but) didn't any messenger come, or any one making the same journey either... ?'

117 κατεῖδ': the word has been (wrongly) emended because although a *traveller* might be an eye-witness, we do not expect this to be said of a messenger, whose function is not so much to see things as to report them. What we have before us cannot be properly called a zeugma, because the verb gives a fair meaning with only one of its two subjects which are not therefore 'yoked' together; we have to supply mentally a quite different verb to make sense of ἄγγελος. The idiom is commoner than one might expect: here are a few examples. Hom. *Il.* 17.385–7 καμάτωι δὲ καὶ ἱδρῶι νωλεμὲς αἰεὶ | γούνατά τε κνῆμαί τε πόδες θ' ὑπένερθεν ἑκάστου | χεῖρές τ' ὀφθαλμοί τε παλάσσετο μαρναμένοιιν (we may ignore the problem of the singular verb, and the dual in the last word). The parts of the body were flecked with sweat, but not with καμάτωι. *Od.* 20.312–13 μήλων σφαζομένων οἴνοιό τε πινομένοιο | καὶ σίτου, but σῖτος is neither slaughtered nor drunk. Pindar, *Pyth.* 6.9ff.: τὸν οὔτε χειμέριος ὄμβρος ἐπακτὸς ἐλθών, ἐριβρόμου νεφέλας | στρατὸς ἀμείλιχος, οὔτ' ἄνεμος ἐς μυχοὺς | ἁλὸς ἄξοισι παμφόρωι χεράδει τυπτόμενον. Winter rain and its thunderclouds are not responsible for stirring up the sea and shingle. *Pyth* 10.38f. παντᾶι δὲ χοροὶ παρθένων | λυρᾶν τε βοαὶ καναχαί τ' αὐλῶν δονέονται. The verb strictly fits only χοροί. In Sophocles there are a number of examples, of which two must suffice: *Trach.* 560–1 οὔτε πομπίμοις | κώπαις ἐρέσσων οὔτε λαίφεσιν νεώς where misplaced logic led Meineke to substitute πλέων for νεώς on the grounds that one does not row by sails. *El.* 435–6 ἀλλ' ἢ πνοαῖσιν ἢ βαθυσκαφεῖ κόνει | κρύψον νιν. κόνει fits κρύψον but πνοαῖσιν does not. Euripides has a remarkable instance at *Ion* 1064–5 ἢ θηκτὸν ξίφος ἢ λαιμῶν (Scaliger for δαίμων) ἐξάψει βρόχον ἀμφὶ δείραν, where clearly there is no thought of Creousa fastening a sharp sword around her neck, but of <driving into herself> a sharp sword, *or* hanging herself; *Herc.* 319–20 ἰδού, πάρεστιν ἥδε φασγάνωι δέρη | κεντεῖν, φονεύειν, ἰέναι πέτρας ἄπο. It is not particularly the *neck* that will be thrown from a rock. This peculiarity of language is not confined to Greek: Malory's *Morte d'Arthur* has the sentence 'Many a grym worde was there spokyn of aythir to othir, and many a deadly stroke' (ed. Vinaver, III p.1235).

ὅτωι: 'anything which a person, once he heard about it, could put to use'. Seager's correction of ὅτου gives ἐχρήσατ' ἄν something to govern. Without the correction we would have the incompleted sentence 'learning from whom a person might put to use'.

118 θνῄσκουσι: present tense, like συμπίπτει (113). However, θνῄσκω can mean 'be dead' as well as 'die', as at Pindar *Ol.* 9.35 and Aesch. *Cho.* 327. Hdt. 4.190 θάπτουσι τοὺς ἀποθνῄσκοντας οἱ νομάδες κατά περ οἱ Ἕλληνες, where nothing vile or macabre is implied, and the object is 'the dead' not 'the dying'. Thuc. 2.52 νεκροὶ ἐπ' ἀλλήλοις ἀποθνῄσκοντες ἔκειντο is more ambiguous.

γάρ: as often, conveying the meaning 'No, because...'

εἷς τις: on the solitary survivor, the confusion over the number of attackers, and the vital rôle that this has to play in the plot, see Introduction 7.

120–1 Oedipus speaks with the same eager confidence that he will display at 220–1. But the trail is cold, and the solitary eye-witness will be a long time appearing; and when he does appear it will be primarily in a different capacity: see 1051 ff.

124 εἴ τι regularly means 'if perhaps', but the sense here is not 'unless perhaps' but 'unless something'; i.e. τι is the subject of ἐπράσσετ'.

125 ἐπράσσετ': see LSJ *s.v.* III 6 b for the use of this verb in connection with political intrigues.

ἐνθένδ': 'from this end'. Oedipus is quick to scent palace intrigue and hired assassins. MacDowell in his note on Aristophanes *Wasps* 345 lists a number of passages to exemplify the tendency in Athens during the Peloponnesian War to make accusations of conspiracy with no justification. See also our Introduction 10.

126 Λαΐου δ' ὀλωλότος: genitive absolute (like τυραννίδος οὕτω πεσούσης just coming), and so not governed by ἀρωγός. With Laius dead no obvious ἀρωγός was there to help them in their troubles (the suspected conspiracy and the Sphinx). So at Aesch. *Cho.* 376 and Soph. *El.* 454 potential ἀρωγοί were dead.

127 οὐδείς: Lange's suggestion οὐχ εἷς will mean 'not one', i.e. 'many'. The question is, did the Thebans entirely fail to investigate the death of Laius, in spite of their suspicions (δοκοῦντα)? Or did they start an investigation, and then have to abandon it? Oedipus' reply 128–9 is compatible with either interpretation. 255–8 clearly imply, but do not absolutely prove, that no search was made. 566–7 state with absolute clarity that there was an investigation, but it was inconclusive. The experienced student of Sophocles will not attempt to force the meaning of any one individual passage to bring it into conformity with any other. *Studies* 1213–14 gives some arguments in favour of οὐχ εἷς. The present commentary favours the traditional οὐδείς.

128 κακὸν δὲ ποῖον: you speak of κακά, but what kind of κακόν could it have been that prevented you …? ποῖον conveys the same note of criticism that we saw in ποῖον τοὔπος (89).

129 ἐξειδέναι: εἰδέναι can mean 'find out' as well as 'know'. Here the compound with ἐξ- helps the sense, but in fact Sophocles is very liberal (and his scribes even more liberal) in using ἐκ- compounds which appear to be almost synonymous with the simple verb. Pearson in his note on frg. 524.4 refers to C. G. Cobet, *Collectanea critica* (Leiden 1878) 189 making exactly this point, with a long list of examples. See below on 827.

130 ποικιλῳδός: ποικίλος is used of an oracle at Aristoph. *Knights* 195–6 χρησμός … καὶ ποικίλως πως καὶ σοφῶς ᾐνιγμένος. Cf. Soph. *Trach.* 1121 οὐδὲν ξυνίημ' ὧν σὺ ποικίλλεις πάλαι. See LSJ *s.v.* ποικίλος III 3. The second part of the compound, from ᾠδή ~ ἀείδω, uses ἀείδω not in our sense of 'sing', but as with any solemn oracular or portentous utterance. Cf. ἀοιδοῦ (36), ῥαψωιδός (391), χρησμωιδόν (1200), all used of the Sphinx; and see 464n. For speculations on what the Sphinx's riddle might have been in the very distant past see W. Porzig, *Das Rätsel der Sphinx*, most conveniently to be found in R. Schmitt's *Indogermanische Dichtersprache* (Darmstadt 1968) 172–6.

Many of our MSS, and, curiously, most of our editions, have five undistinguished hexameters entitled τὸ αἴνιγμα τῆς Σφιγγός. And at least one MS has also the λύσις τοῦ αἰνίγματος, known also from other sources, which consists of six rather more ambitious hexameters. The 'enigma' was the identification of the animal that had one voice, but two, three, or four feet, being slowest on three. The answer was 'man', the third foot being a walking stick. Sophocles himself never alludes to the content of the enigma. It is left to the modern literary critic to dwell on the strange parallelism between the answer to the Sphinx, 'Man' (sc. such as I am), and the answer to the Plague, 'Me'. Nor does Sophocles make anything of the importance of all three stages in Oedipus' life: the exposed child on all fours, the king on two, and the beggar (456) on three. For a text and history of the riddle see Lloyd-Jones in *Dionysiaca* (Cambridge 1978) 60–1.

τὸ πρὸς ποσί: the tasteless possibility has presented itself to some minds that there is here some allusion to the 'foot' enigma, or, even worse, a connection with ἐμποδών

(128). In itself the phrase means 'our immediate concerns' or 'what lay before us' (lit. at our feet). Some of our manuscripts write τά, and τὰν ποσὶν κακά is the phrase used at *Ant.* 1327, while at Eur. *Alc.* 739 τοὐν ποσὶν ... κακόν is found. Pindar has τὸ πὰρ ποδός (*Pyth.* 3.60), τὸ πρὸ ποδός (*Isthm.* 8.12), and uses τὰν πὰρ ποδός to qualify φροντίδα at *Pyth.* 10.62. The plural τὰ δ᾽ ἐν ποσὶν ... κακά comes at Eur. *Andr.* 397–8 in a difficult and perhaps spurious passage. The weight of parallels supports what we might infer from the distribution of singular and plural in the scholia and MSS, namely that the singular is correct here.

131 προσήγετο 'induced': mild irony used as a defence in self-exculpation.

132 αὖθις: not 'again' in the sense of 'a second time' if we believe that no investigation ever took place the first time. Oedipus means that what became ἀφανής will now be rendered φανερός again.

133 ἀξίως, of Creon, looks like slightly less enthusiastic praise than the ἐπαξίως used of Phoebus, but it may be that the simple adverb follows the compound with no dilution of meaning, as often happens with verbs: see, e.g., Dodds on Eur. *Bacch.* 1064–5, K–G II 568, and J. Diggle, *STE* 18 with refs.

134 '...have you devoted all this energy on behalf of the dead man.' ἐπιστροφή, turning round to give something your attention. τίθεσθαι ἐπιστροφήν = ἐπιστρέφεσθαι, the verb used at *Phil.* 599. The reference is to the present and future enquiry, not to any steps taken when Laius was murdered, for Phoebus had, so far as we know, no rôle to play then.

135 ἐνδίκως: in fact with even greater justice than Oedipus realizes, if we judge by the standards of an Athenian audience. Failure by the appropriate blood relatives to take action against a killer was not only regarded as disgraceful, but could, under Attic law, lead to the blood-relatives themselves being prosecuted and convicted for neglect of duty.

κἀμέ: the καί implies some modesty, as if Oedipus were doing no more than joining the ranks of the others. In reality Oedipus has shown much more enterprise than Creon, and Phoebus has done no more than is to be expected of him. The σύμμαχος idea is taken up again at 245.

137 τῶν ἀπωτέρω φίλων: dramatic irony: see further the note on 258ff. for the importance of a personal relationship in initiating proceedings on behalf of someone deceased.

138 αὐτοῦ: when used for ἐμαυτοῦ or σεαυτοῦ some MSS and almost all editors use a rough breathing. There is no good reason for following the practice. Where αὐτοῦ stands for ἑαυτοῦ, third person, a rough breathing would of course be correct.

140 τιμωρεῖν: a strange word to use of action taken against an innocent party. Oedipus seems to be taking a vendetta against Laius and his family for granted. The scholia note: τὴν ἀλήθειαν αἰνίττεται τῶι θεάτρωι, ὅτι αὐτὸς δράσας τὸν φόνον ὁ Οἰδίπους καὶ ἑαυτὸν τιμωρήσεται.

141 προσαρκῶν: so the initial promise ὡς θέλοντος ἂν | ἐμοῦ προσαρκεῖν πᾶν (11–12) has become a reality. Oedipus will offer help for the dead man (134–5), the land of Thebes and the god (136), and finally himself (141). The word προσαρκεῖν is not common. One of its rare further appearances will be in *Oed. Col.* 72 of help extended *to* Oedipus, by Theseus. Both at 12 and here the word is followed by a monosyllable giving the unusual rhythm of word-end in the exact middle of the line. Since οὖν is a 'post-positive', and so metrically coheres with προσαρκῶν, the line lacks a normal caesura. See also 809n. According to M. Griffith, *The authenticity of Prometheus Bound* (Cambridge 1977) 85, Aesch. *Pers.* has nine such lines, *Suppl.* five, and the other plays of all three tragedians never more than three. See also Schein, *ITAS* 37–9.

145–6 Oedipus' concluding words are reminiscent of the end of his opening address to the priest, 11–12, and round off the exposition of the situation in which Thebes now finds itself as a result of the still unsolved mystery of the death of Laius.

148 καί coheres not with δεῦρο but with the verb: 'since that's what we *came* here for'. Similar displacement is possible at 772, 'to whom better *could* I talk?'
ὧν: attracted to the case of τῶνδε, and standing for ἅ.

149 ἅμα may do no more than link σωτήρ and παυστήριος (150) together, but it is tempting to assume that the link intended is between the sending of the oracle and the hoped-for cure.

151–215 The first chorus (parodos)

The optimistic tone which began (on insufficient grounds, many of us might think) with ἐσθλήν (87) has continued through to the end of the scene, and is taken up again now by the Chorus in their first ode (*parodos*) with the word ἀδυεπές. But within a line or two (153) they are voicing agitated apprehension. They call on Apollo, Athena and Artemis. In the second strophic pair they describe the horrors of the plague in the city, in this way retracing in lyric form some of the ground gone over in the iambics. This is a normal function of a Greek chorus, to give emotional depth to a situation where the factual details are already known to us. In the last two stanzas they pray again to Apollo, and to Artemis and Dionysus, and conclude, if we accept the transposition argued for below in the note on 190–205, by calling on father Zeus himself to annihilate Ares beneath a thunderbolt. In terms of choral technique for a *parodos* the nearest Sophoclean parallels would be *Trach.* and (even closer) *Ant.*, both comparatively early plays. For the metre of this and subsequent choruses see the metrical Appendix.

151 Διός: the oracle comes from a minister of Apollo (712) and Apollo is a minister of Zeus (Aesch. *Eum.* 19, 616–18, 713). Cf. 498–9.

τίς: what are you that have come from Pytho (Delphi) to Thebes: i.e. what exactly do you mean? A close parallel to this unusual kind of τίς occurs at Eur. *El.* 1303–4: τίς δ᾽ ἔμ᾽ Ἀπόλλων, ποῖοι χρησμοὶ | φονίαν ἔδοσαν μητρὶ γενέσθαι: 'What did Apollo mean by...?'

πολυχρύσου: the wealth of Delphi is often spoken of in Greek poetry. Pindar twice uses precisely this adjective of Apollo's temple (*Pyth.* 4.53) or νάπα (*Pyth.* 6.8) there.

153 Θήβας: to Thebes. Plain accusative after a verb of motion, common in poetry, cf. 434, 1178, and K–G I 311–12.

ἐκτέταμαι: not 'I am on the rack' (Jebb) but 'I am prostrate'.

φοβερὰν φρένα: accusative of respect, belonging equally to ἐκτέταμαι and δείματι πάλλων, 'quivering with fear'. πάλλων is intransitive, as at Eur. *El.* 435, 476; Ar. *Lys.* 1304.

154 Παιάν: this deity is known from the Mycenaean tablets, in which, up to now, no trace of the name of Apollo (or Athena or Aphrodite) has been found. Even in Sophocles παιών is not always used exclusively of Apollo, but here, with Δάλιε, the identification is certain. 'A paean is a hymn to Apollo sung for the stopping of plague but also for the stopping of war; and often too when danger is expected' (the scholia on Ar. *Plutus* 636, cited by R. W. B. Burton, *The chorus in Sophocles' tragedies* (Oxford 1980) 142).

155 ἀμφὶ σοί: Sophocles must intend some special nuance by writing the uncommon ἀμφὶ σοί where σε without ἀμφὶ would be obvious. So not simply 'in awe of you': the underlying thought must be something like 'in a state of awe and apprehension prompted by you'. Cf. [Aesch.] *Prom. Vinct.* 182 δέδια δ᾽ ἀμφὶ σαῖς τύχαις.

τί μοι ἢ νέον κ.τ.ἑ.: a difficult passage. In elucidating it the following points need to be borne in mind. (1) χρέος means primarily 'debt' – though it can also mean 'business', 'affair', 'matter'. In Hom. *Od.* 11.479 Τειρεσίαο κατὰ χρέος, it uniquely means 'oracle' or 'prophecy' – a meaning which looks promising for our present passage, but is probably a red herring. (2) ἐξανύσεις although not attested in this sense, probably could mean 'exact payment of', because ἐξάνυσις in an admittedly very late (*c.* VI A.D.) papyrus means 'exaction', and the range of meanings of ἀνύω is wide (cf., e.g., 166, 720) and largely overlaps with πράσσω, and πράσσω χρέος 'exact payment of a debt' is normal Greek. (3) πάλιν is to be construed with περιτελλομέναις, as is shown by the Homeric model ἂψ περιτελλομένου ἔτεος. (4) The dative, instead of the Homeric genitive absolute, may look strange, but the phrase is exactly paralleled by Ar. *Birds* 696. It is presumably some kind of 'dative of attendant circumstances' meaning 'with the passing of the years' (K–G I 435). Cf. κυλινδομέναις ἀμέραις Pindar, *Isthm.* 3.18.

What makes the balance of the sentence irregular is that such a dative must qualify the verb ἐξανύσεις, while νέον qualifies the noun χρέος. 'What is the debt that you will require me to pay? Is it a new one, or is it one you will be exacting as the year's seasons come round again?' (i.e. it falls due as the seasons go by and bring close the date for payment). The idea of time, whether the debt is new or old, is very relevant to the play: ἐφηῦρέ σ᾽ ἄκονθ᾽ ὁ πάνθ᾽ ὁρῶν χρόνος (1213), and the lapse in time between the offence and the present events is a matter raised in 558ff.

158 Φήμα: identical with Φάτις, who began the stanza. She is the child of Hope, because Hope is what causes people to consult oracles. None the less to call her the *child* of Hope is remarkable: much more so than, e.g., calling Πειθώ the child of Ἄτη (Aesch. *Agam*. 385–6). On the other hand to call Hope 'golden' smacks of the perfunctory, since there is no close link with πολυχρύσου (151). 'Golden' is applied without profound thought or discrimination to a wide range of persons and objects by, notoriously, Pindar. 'Bright' may be the idea uppermost in Sophocles' mind; at *Ant.* 103 he speaks of the sun's rays as the 'eye of golden day'. In a moment, at 187, the 'daughter of Zeus' will be golden (i.e. Athena: Homer uses the word of Aphrodite), and at 203 even Apollo's bow-strings will be woven with gold. Finally at 209 Dionysus will have a golden band on his hair: on which, however, see Dodds, Eur. *Bacch.* 553–5n.

159 κεκλόμενος: nominative, although προφάνητέ μοι is to follow. The change of construction is of a well-recognized type: see K–G II 105–7.

ἄμβροτ᾽: to use this word of Athena directly after using it of Φήμα is to modern taste inexcusable. But such repetitions are not rare in Sophoclean lyrics, as we have just seen with 'golden'. It would be quite mistaken to look in all such cases for thematic significance. A comprehensive treatment of repetition in Sophocles is given by A. Avezzù, *Bolletino dell' Istituto di Filologia Greca* I (1974) 54–69.

160 γαιάοχον: it is surprising to find this word used of Artemis, since it is so familiar as an epithet of Poseidon that Pindar (*Ol*. 13.81) can even use it as a noun synonym for him. Presumably the γαῖα meant here is not the world, but the land of Thebes.

161 ἀγορᾶς: one manuscript has ἀγοραῖς, which will fit θάσσει 'sit on a round throne *in* the market-place' just as ἀγοραῖσι suits θακεῖ at 20. If the genitive ἀγορᾶς is read, as editors prefer, the meaning is 'belonging to the market-place'. In spite of Eur. *Or*. 919 ἀγορᾶς (-αῖς three MSS!) κύκλον 'the round market-place' it is inconceivable that the genitive here could be constituent, i.e. the throne consisting of the market-place, as if the throne and the market-place were one and the same thing. Archaeology has yet to discover any such thing as a round market-place from the classical period.

162 εὐκλέα: since Artemis had the title Εὔκλεια in Boeotia, the adjective used here is not chosen at random. (See J. G. Frazer, *Pausanias* (repr. 1965) II 124; D. C. Braund, *J.H.S.* 100 (1980) 184–5.) Following the scholiast's lemma, Elmsley preferred actually to put Εὔκλεα into the text, θρόνον already having one epithet. But Εὔκλεα would not fit the metre, since it would scan not as –∪∪ but as ––∪ , appearances notwithstanding. We see this with the spelling εὐκλέαν for εὐκλείαν, found on an inscription dated to the first half of the fourth century B.C., where the metre proves that the quantity remained unaltered: κτώμενον εὔκλεαν δορὶ καὶ χερὶ τόνδε πρὸς ἀνδρὸς | ἐχθροῦ Ἀριστόκριτον ὤλεσε θοῦρος Ἄρης (Peek, *GVI* 1888 (p. 572) 3–4). K.

Meisterhans, *Grammatik der attischen Inschriften* (Berlin 1885) 40, notes that the spelling of women's names in –κλε(ι)α remained variable till Roman times. See L. Lupas, *Phonologie du grec antique* (The Hague and Paris 1972) 47ff., and Threatte, *GAI* I 211–12 and 319.

ἑκαβόλον: the etymological dictionaries of Boisacq, Frisk and Chantraine all prefer the derivation from ἑκών to the one from ἑκάς, though Chantraine points out that 'le rapprochement avec ἑκάς par etymologie populaire est probable' and that ἑκηβολίαι in Hom. *Il.* 5.54 must have been intended to mean 'coups tirés de loin'.

It is odd that the Chorus invoke Phoebus as the third of a trio of divinities as if they had not mentioned him in the first strophe. They take it for granted that Phoebus is not himself the sender of the plague, a traditional rôle for him. Why they should fasten on Ares as their prime enemy is something not easily to be explained from the play itself, for Ares was a god especially associated with Thebes, and not elsewhere associated with plague, not even at Aesch. *Suppl.* 664–6, 681–3. We must assume that the plague at Athens, brought about or made worse by conditions directly resulting from the Peloponnesian War, had forged a link in the mind of Sophocles and his audience between plague and the War God.

164 εἴ ποτε: the formula 'if ever you helped me/listened to me before, help/listen to me now' is common in invocations to deities: e.g. Hom. *Il.* 5.116, Sappho frg. 1.5, Pindar, *Isthm.* 6.42ff., Ar. *Knights* 594, *Thesm.* 1156ff.

ὕπερ: in Aesch. *Sept.* 111 an ἱκέσιον λόχον δουλοσύνας ὕπερ is a group of people making supplication 'over', i.e. to *avoid* slavery. So here the gods have in the past helped them 'over', i.e. to avoid, the ἄτα which faced them. See further 187n. and compare the same kind of thinking that lies behind a phrase like θυσαμένοις πρὸ τοῦ λοιμοῦ, Plato, *Symp.* 201 d 4. But Musgrave's ὑπερορνυμένας, although not attested, has much merit; the idea of some menace flying at speed over a city is one which occurs also at *Ant.* 113.

166 ἠνύσατ' ἐκτοπίαν: made it absent from the place, banished it. The same kind of phrase at 193–4. Although a compound adjective, ἐκτόπιος is given a separate feminine form, whereas ἔκτοπος, as expected, serves for both masc. and fem. See Pearson on frg. 394 and add to his references *Ant.* 339 and the present passage. The reverse also occurs, of non-compounded adjectives being given only two terminations. See 384n.

φλόγα: consonant with πυρφόρος at 27, and with φλέγει just coming at 192. See also 175–7n.

167 καὶ νῦν: as well as καὶ προτέρας. A severe critic might say that one of these two καί occurrences was redundant. But the same kind of duplication occurs at Pindar, *Nem.* 2, 1 and 3.

169–70 πρόπας | στόλος: πρόπας is almost confined to the lyric portions of tragedy. (Exceptions: Aesch. *Pers.* 434, *Eum.* 898, Eur. frg. 360.18.) It is an especial favourite when attached to words meaning 'house' or 'family' or 'land' when facing disaster or extinction. στόλος will be intended as a variant on στρατός, used in its sense of λεώς, λαός.

171 γάρ: explaining νοσεῖ, not ἀλέξεται.

172–3 The Chorus are clearly talking of sterility, still births, death in childbirth, or miscarriages (cf. 26–7), 'but as for the syntactical details, commentators and lexica alike seem to be at a loss' (H. Friis Johansen): we do not know for sure what kind of a dative τόκοισιν is, or what ἀνέχουσι means. τόκος can mean both 'child' and 'giving birth', and the two ideas may be fused here; but ἀνέχουσι remains intractable.

175 ἄλλοι δὲ ἄλληι τῆς πόλεως σποράδην (or-άδες) ἀπώλλυντο, Thuc. 2.4.

175–7 Very strange imagery. The 'western god' must be Hades, though this is not a normal description of him. The spirits of the dead flock to him like birds. ἄπερ is used like ἄτε or οἷα for ὡς. Their onward movement (ὄρμενον) is 'worse than irresistible (?) fire'. ἀμαιμάκετος is a Homeric word, of uncertain meaning, used again at *Oed. Col.* 127. It has been linked with words as diverse as αἷμα, μάχη, μῆκος and μαιμάω, and when used of the Chimaera or her πῦρ was glossed by φοβερός, χαλεπός, ἀκαταπόνητος and ἀπροσπέλατον. Chantraine calls it 'terme poétique traditionnel et expressif dont le sens originel est ignoré de ceux qui l'utilisent'. Sophocles has much to say about fire in connection with the plague (see 166n.), and the comparison of spirits to birds is easy enough: they are compared to bats in Hom. *Od.* 24.6–9. But the comparison with both birds and fire in the same sentence might tax the agility of some minds. As for κρεῖσσον, Eros is so described in *Anth. Plan.* 250 on breaking a thunderbolt: δεικνὺς ὡς κρεῖσσον πῦρ πυρός ἐστιν, Ἔρως, and at Eur. *Hec.* 607–8 a mutinous mob is called κρείσσων πυρός. See further 1374n., to dispel doubts whether 'worse' is a fit way to translate a Greek word that regularly means 'better'.

179 ὧν: the normal genitive with an alpha-privative adjective. The city wastes away, unable to count the number of its dead. The adjective is here active, not as in the strophe (167) 'countless'. The superficial parallelism ὧν πόλις ἀνάριθμος ∼ ὦ πόποι ἀνάριθμα is striking.

180 νηλέα: different from ἀνοίκτως only in so far as ἀνοίκτως may imply a formal lament, οἶκτος, for the dead: cf. *El.* 100.

181 θανατοφόρα: as the accent shows, an active adjective, 'death-bringing'. Even if the Greeks of Sophocles' time lived before the age of Pasteur, they must have been aware of the dangers of infection and contagion, otherwise Sophocles' one-word allusion to the ideas would not have been understood. Thucydides certainly recognized such dangers, as his description of the Great Plague shows: on which see the admirable article by J. C. F. Poole and A. J. Holladay in *C.Q.* n.s. 29 (1979) 282–300. Their concentration on Thucydides as an exceptional figure in this respect needs modification in the light of the present passage. The apparent failure of Hippocrates and the medical writers to understand the phenomenon of contagion is all the more remarkable.

182 ἐν δ': see 27n.

ἔπι: in addition.

184 ἀκτάν 'edge' here, 'shore' at 178. In view of the similarity of ἄλλοθεν here to ἄλλαι in 175 it is not impossible that Sophocles is somehow counterbalancing the widespread flight to Hades on the part of the dead with the confluence from all directions to the altars on the part of the living. But παρά + acc. is regular for 'alongside', and ἄλλοθεν may mean no more than that they are besieging the altar from every side.

185 πόνων ἱκετῆρες: suppliants about, over, and finally against. See 164n. above.

186 A restatement of 5 in lyric terms. ὅμαυλος, sharing the same αὐλή, corresponds with ὁμοῦ there. The preoccupation with old age (corrected in the Revised Supplement), flutes and concerts in LSJ *s.v.* ὅμαυλος should be disregarded.

In παιὼν λάμπει we find the same use of a visual verb with a noun of sound that will recur at 473–5 and 525. Such uses are not rare in poetry: e.g. Pind. *Ol.* 9.21–2, *Isthm.* 4.62, Bacchyl. frg. 4.80 (ὕμνοι φλέγονται), Aesch. *Pers.* 395, *Sept.* 286, Eur. *El.* 694–5. See further C. P. Segal, *Illinois Classical Studies* 2 (1977) 88–96. There is a constant problem over the spelling of παιών/παιάν which an examination of MSS and inscriptions leaves unresolved. So as not to tamper with the evidence, this edition leaves Παιάν untouched at 154 while following the oldest authorities in reading Παιών here.

187 τῶν: although τῶν could be interpreted as equivalent to ὧν (K–G 1 587 note that Sophocles has a penchant for such a usage), it is better taken a demonstrative, like τόν at 200 (K–G 1 583).

ὕπερ: perhaps identical with the kind of ὑπέρ discussed on 164, meaning 'against the λυγρῶν πόνων'. This will fit well with ἀλκάν, 'defence against'. But probably, since παιών and γῆρυς intervene, 'in the name of' or 'in return for', like λίσσομ' ὑπὲρ θυέων καὶ δαίμονος, Hom. *Od.* 15.261. See LSJ *s.v.* A II 4.

190–215 The text printed adopts a forgotten suggestion made by F. Haase in 1858, namely to alter the order given by the manuscripts by switching the strophe with the antistrophe. There is no other place in Sophocles where a plausible case has been made out for any such procedure, but there is one in Euripides and no less than five in Aeschylus (see *Eranos* 97 (1999) 24–44). The merits of the transposition are these: (1) It accounts for the τε in 190: on the traditional order δέ would be expected. (2) It brings 'Ares' directly next to the 'unhonoured god', the plain name resolving the more obscure allusion, a favourite technique of the tragedians. (3) The task of routing Ares is no longer to fall on the shoulders of 'the golden daughter of Zeus' (Athene) alone, but he will be subject to the combined firepower of Apollo, his archer sister Artemis, and Bacchus. (4) The ode is given a more decisive conclusion, not with a pictorial description of Bacchus and his entourage: instead Zeus, king of the gods, is to blast Ares beneath his thunderbolt.

203 Λύκει': the word is often associated with wolves, λύκοι, as at *El.* 6. It is also associated with light (*lux*), which would better fit the imagery of this ode. Apollo Λύκειος is invoked as a potential helper again at 919, and at *El.* 645, 655, 1379; in Aeschylus at *Sept.* 145, *Suppl.* 686, *Agam.* 1257. Not so in Euripides.

203–4 χρυσοστρόφων: cf. 158n.

ἀγκυλᾶν: Homer speaks of ἀγκύλα τόξα. The noun is used of anything bent or looped: πλεκτὰς ἀγκύλας are looped ropes at Eur. *I.T.* 1408. Here 'bowstrings'.

205 ἐνδατεῖσθαι: 'to be distributed', a curious choice of word, since there is only one target, Ares. But the Chorus are beginning to think pictorially, of a shower of arrows, of Artemis on the hills with her torches (what use would they be against Ares?) and of Dionysus with his maenads.

206 προστσθέντα: they are positioned before us, προ-στσθέντα, as our helpers, ἀρωγά. 'Positioned' seems hardly an ideal word for arrows, though in a differently constructed sentence προστσθέντα would do very well of the divinities themselves, standing forward as our champions.

208 *Lycian*, used of a region in Asia Minor, does not sound relevant to a specifically Theban problem, but Sophocles, when writing lyrics, is given to embroidery on a basic theme: e.g. at *Ant.* 1115–52, and more obviously still *Ant.* 944–87. A brief mention of Lycian mountains is a very restrained example. There is, in spite of appearances, no connection in sense with Λύκει' just above in 203.

209 '...both the god and his worshippers sometimes wear the μίτρα in vase-paintings from the middle of the fifth century onwards' (Dodds on Eur. *Bacch.* 831–3).

210 He is called with the same name as the land of Thebes, either taking his name from it, or giving his name to it: here the latter, cf. *Trach.* 510–11 βακχίας ... Θήβας.

211 οἰνῶπα: parallels in Dodds on Eur. *Bacch.* 236.
εὔιον: the adjective from the cry εὐοῖ (*Trach.* 219) as ἰήιος (154, 173, 1096) is from ἰή.

213–15 The idea is not one of fighting fire with fire (φλέγοντ' of Bacchus here, φλέγει of Ares 192). Sophocles is again thinking pictorially, as he was with Artemis, of certain standard attributes of these deities.

214 <σύμμαχον> will give excellent sense and balance to the sentence. It remains of course no more than a guess, with no particular arguments from palaeography in its favour.

215 τὸν ἀπότιμον ἐν θεοῖς θεόν: Not an unfounded theological speculation on the part of the chorus. In Homer (*Il.* 5.890) Zeus did not mince his words when addressing Ares: ἔχθιστος δέ μοι ἐσσι θεῶν οἳ Ὄλυμπον ἔχουσι.

190 The accusative and infinitive construction in prayers like this one is explained by the assumption that 'grant that' is to be mentally supplied. δός appears often enough in Homer in such phrases, and at, e.g., Aesch. *Cho.* 18–19 ὦ Ζεῦ, δός με τείσασθαι μόρον | πατρός. But Homer knows too the usage without δός, e.g. *Il.* 7.179 Ζεῦ πάτερ, ἢ Αἴαντα λαχεῖν ἢ Τυδέος υἱόν. If νωτίσαι could only be transitive, as the scholia take it, we could assume the construction to be carried on from κικλήσκω.

μαλερόν: in Homer always of fire, and so fitting the fire imagery of this chorus.

191 ἄχαλκος: another alpha-privative adjective with dependent genitive, like ἄσκευος ἀσπίδων at *El.* 36. 'Without (his usual) bronze shields', i.e. not in his capacity as War God. Ares is not elsewhere associated with plague.

192 περιβόητος ἀντιάζων: in battle Ares would oppose his enemies with cries of war resounding all round them. But now the cries which are all round are those of 186, the sounds of lamentation. However the phrase 'facing me with cries all round' seems difficult, since those uttering the cries are not the same as the one who is ἀντιάζων; though on reflection we may see that contagious victim and assailant plague are in a sense identical. But suspicions remain when we find that περιβόητος is predominantly a prose word, meaning 'famous' or 'notorious'. Possibly we should read περιφόβητος ἀντιάζειν, 'very terrible to encounter', like βαρὺς ἀντιάσαι in Pindar, *Nem.* 10.20. It is true that περιφόβητος (which appeared in a rewriting of the text by A. Y. Campbell) does not exist: but we could have said the same of φοβητός itself, did it not occur at *Phil.* 1154. The περι- is now intensificatory, 'very', as often in compound adjectives.

193 νωτίσαι: instead of facing us, may he turn his back in 'backward-speeding running' – internal accusatives.

193–4 πάτρας ἄπουρον: away from the ὅροι of our land. Sophocles uses the Ionic form -ουρος for -ορος again at *Phil.* 691. See also 1315n.

194 'Away from our land' would have been enough to serve the Chorus' purpose. Ares' ultimate destination is immaterial. But the Chorus helpfully suggest that the Atlantic or the Black Sea might be suitably remote places for him to go to. Such specific allusions, particularly on mythological topics, help to give Greek lyric poetry its distinctive character. By Alexandrian times, and in Roman poetry, the tail begins to wag the dog, and an irrelevant display of geographic or mythological learning all too often obscures or complicates the point being made.

195 'The great mansion of Amphitrite' must be the Atlantic. Amphitrite is only a minor goddess in Hesiod's system of mythology, until we reach *Theogony* 930, where, as for Pindar, she is the wife of Poseidon. In the *Odyssey* she is simply the Sea Goddess *par excellence*, and similarly at Eur. *I.T.* 425, the only certain passage in tragedy besides the present one to mention her name, frg. 673 being possibly from a satyr play.

196 ἀπόξενον: equivalent to an alpha-privative adjective (similarly ἀπότιμον 215), and so capable of governing the genitive ὅρμων: lit. 'unfriendly to anchorings'. So in *Phil.* 217 ναὸς ἄξενον ... ὅρμον. In the present passage ἀπόξενον reminds us of the remote sea later called 'Euxine': see LSJ *s.v.* ἄξενος II. At *Ant.* 970 Ares is expressly associated with the Thracian area. (For a suggestion that ἄξενος is a Greek corruption of an original Iranian epithet for the Black Sea meaning 'dark-coloured' see W. S. Allen, *C.Q.* 41 (1947) 86–8; also *C.Q.* 42 (1948) 59–60.) A comparable process has been suggested for ἁβροβάτης at Aesch. *Pers.* 1073 and Bacchyl. 3. 48; but for linguistic objections to this view see R. Schmitt in *Glotta* 53 (1975) 207–16.

198–9 This passage, consisting of simple enough words, and suffering from no obvious corruption, has never been satisfactorily explained. We have been hearing about Ares, and will hear of him again (τόν 200). What relevance 198–9 have to him is far from clear. Commentators look for the sense 'day brings to completion anything that night has let go', but quite apart from the question whether the Greek could mean that, there is the more important problem of how such a sense could be integrated into the Ares context. We can only suppose that the Chorus are saying something like 'he gives us no respite from our misfortunes by day or night'.

216–462 The first epeisodion

216 αἰτεῖς· ἃ δ αἰτεῖς: an arresting opening of unusual form to a speech which will address itself in a business-like manner to the problem in hand. 'You make a request; as to the terms of this request, if you . . .' The Pythian oracle at Hdt. 1. 66 is equally brisk: Ἀρκαδίην μ' αἰτεῖς; μέγα μ' αἰτεῖς.

217 τῆι νόσωι θ' ὑπηρετεῖν: 'minister to the disease'. At first right ὑπηρετεῖν seems to give the reverse of the sense required, but the text is sound. νόσοις ἐπικουρῆσαι is found at Xen. *Mem.* 1.4.13, and he has similar phrases elsewhere. Antiphon, *Tetral.* β δ 10 has μήτε αὐτοὶ ταῖς τούτων ἀτυχίαις βοηθοῦντες ἐναντία τοῦ δαίμονος γνῶτε; not 'helping their misfortunes' but 'being of help in their misfortunes'. So in English when we say that quinine is good for malaria, what we mean is that it is *bad* for malaria but *good* for the patient. The ambiguity is one which Thomas Mann makes some play with in *The magic mountain*. There is a distant analogy in the use of 'for' for 'against' discussed at 164n.

218 ἀλκήν: what the Chorus had been asking Athena for (188) and had asked Oedipus himself for at 42.

219 ἀγώ: ἅ = τἀμ ἔπη.

τοῦ λόγου τοῦδ: of vague reference. Oedipus means he was a stranger to the event at the time and everything said about it. The metre contains one peculiarity: τοῦδ ἐξερῶ does not obey the so-called Law of the Final Cretic, or Porson's Law, whereby a word ending before the final – ‿ ⏓ must end with a short syllable, or be a monosyllable. But Sophocles has exactly comparable elided disyllables at this point in the line at *Ant.* 910 εἰ τοῦδ ἤμπλακον, *Phil.* 1277 καὶ πέρα γ ἴσθ ἢ λέγω, and *Oed. Col.* 505 τοῦδ. ἢν δέ του. Further refinements and complications in P. Maas, *Greek metre* (Oxford 1962) §137; A. M. Devine and L. Stephens, *Classical Philology* 73 (1978) 314–28; and for the practice of Euripides see Dodds on *Bacch.* 246–7.

220–1 οὐ γὰρ ἄν . . . : the γάρ explains why he has made these slightly unexpected remarks about being a stranger to the deed and the reports of it. The correct interpretation of what follows is at least as old as Wunder: 'neque enim, nisi ignarus istius rei essem, diu ipse investigarem, quin aliquid indicii reperirem.' (For μὴ οὐ cf. 13n.) A man capable of solving the riddle of the Sphinx would not have taken long to find some vital piece of evidence, if only he had been on the case himself, when the trail was still warm.

ἔχων: usually it is the forms of ἔχω which contain σχ- that mean 'get' as opposed to 'have': e.g. *El.* 1013, 1465; *Phil.* 1420. But in Homer, *Od.* 10.239, when Circe turns Odysseus' comrades into pigs, the phrase οἱ δὲ συῶν μὲν ἔχον κεφαλὰς φωνήν τε τρίχας τε describes the acquisition of pigs' characteristics, not their previous possession; and in any event 'without having' would be a perfectly acceptable translation for our present passage. However, perhaps ἔχειν (Blaydes) ought to be written, consecutive infinitive, which would make it clear that the acquisition of evidence would come *after* a brief investigation.

σύμβολον: not exactly a 'clue', but anything you may συμβάλλειν with anything else, when putting two and two together; a piece of evidence contributing to a proof: cf. Aesch. *Agam.* 315 τέκμαρ τοιοῦτον σύμβολόν τε σοι λέγω; Soph. *Phil.* 403f. σύμβολον σαφὲς | λύπης 'clear evidence of hard feelings'.

222 νῦν δ᾽: but now, in the realities of the situation, not having been on the scene at the time, and not being a citizen until it was too late for me to have any *locus standi* in an investigation, I shall, as a second best, make a proclamation, consisting of the ἔπη mentioned in 216. The whole passage is thick with dramatic irony. He was not a stranger to the events or to what was said about them. On the other hand it is all too true that he would not have had to search long or far (μακράν) without having a σύμβολον – a word capable of meaning a token of identity.

εἰς ἀστοὺς τελῶ: τελῶ means 'pay taxes', and so, in the idiom of modern associations, to be a paid-up member of. The metaphor recurs at Eur. *Bacch.* 822 ἐς γυναῖκας ἐξ ἀνδρὸς τελῶ; 'Am I to be classed with the women, instead of, as formerly, as a man?' Only now that Oedipus enjoys full citizen status has he the right to initiate criminal proceedings.

222–75 The speech of Oedipus as printed in this edition embodies a transposition of verses (244–51 are switched with 269–72) which is intended primarily to restore a logical sequence of presentation which bears a resemblance to actual legal practice current in the time of Sophocles. It also eliminates certain technical problems in the Greek text. A full discussion can be found in *Studies* 1 221–5. The passages to be exchanged with each other both begin with ὑμῖν δέ and an actor may have confused them in his mind. (For an attempt to make sense of the speech without transposition, see M. Dyson, *C.Q.* n.s. 23 (1973) 202–12. Arguments directed against the transposition by H. Erbse, *Illinois Classical Studies* VI 1 (1981) 28–34 have left the present editor unpersuaded.)

In 224–32 we have an inquisitorial process. In Attic law denunciation against a person unknown could be made not only by citizens, but also by slaves or metics, or even accomplices, who might be offered immunity from prosecution. Then in 233–68 we have the criminal prosecution, which in real life was undertaken by a citizen (see 222n.), and, in the case of homicide, by a relative of the victim.

223 προφωνῶ: Oedipus is in a unique position, acting as both a relative, or as he thinks substitute for a relative, of the deceased; and as king. Three kinds of proclamation were known in ancient Athens. (See D. M. MacDowell, *The Athenian law of homicide* (1963) 24ff.) (1) A proclamation at the tomb on the occasion of the funeral, a religious ceremony with no legal significance, and perhaps not made at all on occasions when relatives could be present, and hence irrelevant for our purposes. (2) Proclamation in the *agora*, legal and not religious, commanding the killer to keep away from τῶν νομίμων. This proclamation would be made by relatives of the dead man, and would name the alleged killer if he was known – hence it was equivalent to a statement of intent to prosecute. (3) Proclamation by the *basileus* (cf. 1202: Laius had been a *basileus* too, 257), also ordering the killer to keep away from τῶν νομίμων. Until this proclamation was made, the man accused of homicide was under no legal disability.

227–9 'and if he is afraid that by taking the charge on his *own* shoulders <he will be subject to the death penalty, let me set his mind at rest: he may safely even denounce> himself as the murderer, because he will suffer no other unpleasantness beyond leaving the land unharmed'. However γῆς δ᾽ ἄπεισιν ἀσφαλής is a very euphemistic description of exile: contrast the language at 98, 100.

230 The audience is exclusively Theban, and the god has said (110) that the guilty person is resident in Thebes. Oedipus has begun by an appeal to all Theban citizens to lay information, even if it is self-incriminating. He now passes on to a different (εἰ δ᾽ αὖ) possibility, that the guilty person is a foreigner: Laius was out of the country (114) when killed. Oedipus himself fits both categories (452–3).

231–2 The article with κέρδος and with χάρις gives the sense 'the κέρδος and χάρις appropriate for such a service'. The same pairing of ideas at *Trach.* 191: see on 1004ff. below.

προσκείσεται: the προσ- may mean 'in addition to the κέρδος (cf. Ar. *Wasps* 1420 καὶ χάριν προσείσομαι and Plato, *Apol.* 20a πείθουσι . . . χρήματα διδόντας καὶ χάριν προσειδέναι), but it does not necessarily do so: cf. *Ant.* 1243, and frg. adesp. TrGF II 1b3 βραχεῖ λόγωι δὲ πολλὰ πρόσκειται σοφά.

233 εἰ δ᾽ αὖ: the break is even stronger than at 230. If requests for information fail, the next logical step is to invoke religious sanctions against the criminal.

φίλου: the safest way to construe this genitive is as one of separation, governed by ἀπώσει; similarly χαὐτοῦ. But K–G 1 365, and a number of commentators, prefer to construe the genitive as if it were governed by δείσας, the construction being by analogy with κηδόμενος.

235 ἃκ τῶνδε: the logical arrangement of this long speech is signposted by such phrases: νῦν δ᾽ 222, κεἰ μὲν 227, εἰ δ᾽ αὖ 230 and 232, ἃκ τῶνδε here, καὶ ταῦτα 269, οὐδ᾽ εἰ 255, νῦν δ᾽ 258 (not 263), ἀνθ᾽ ὧν 264, μὲν οὖν 244.

236 Compare the excommunication pronounced by Periander in Hdt. 3. 51–2.

236–8 'I pronounce his banishment from this land ... so that no one receive him or address him.' So I should like to construe the words, taking the ideas in the order in which Sophocles presents them. More cautious spirits, with one eye on ὠθεῖν 241 (see note), will prefer the traditional interpretation: ἀπαυδῶ ... μήτ᾽ = forbid ... to (indirect command), with γῆς dependent on τινα.

237 κράτη ... θρόνους: the same pair at *Ant.* 173, cf. 166. In *Oed. Col.* the pair σκῆπτρα and θρόνους are three times repeated: 425, 448–9, 1354.

238–40 Antiphon 6.36 ὁ γὰρ νόμος οὕτως ἔχει, ἐπειδάν τις ἀπογραφῆι φόνου δίκην (= is charged with homicide), εἴργεσθαι τῶν νομίμων.

239–40 Religious excommunication. χέρνιβος is a partitive genitive: 'to offer him no share in the holy water'. Demosthenes, *Lept.* 158, cites a law of Draco: χέρνιβος εἴργεσθαι τὸν ἀνδροφόνον, σπονδῶν, κρατήρων, ἱερῶν, ἀγορᾶς. The presence of such polluted persons could imperil the success of sacrifices. 'Many, standing beside sacrifices, have been proved to be impure and to be an obstacle to the performance of the rites' (Antiphon 5.82).

240 χέρνιβος: 'water into which they dipped a brand taken from the altar on which they performed the sacrifice; with this they sprinkled the bystanders and purified them', Athenaeus 9.409B. Cf. Eur. *Herc.* 928–9, Ar. *Peace* 956–61.

241 ὠθεῖν: a verb meaning 'order' is to be mentally supplied, the original ἀπαυδῶ (236) 'forbid' being by now almost forgotten.

243 ἐμοί: the oracle had actually spoken to Creon, not Oedipus. But Oedipus is the head of state, and intermediaries do not matter to one who is believed to have direct dealings with the gods (38). In a deeper sense, it is indeed to Oedipus that the god has delivered his oracle.

269 In case he receives no information, Oedipus has cursed the guilty person, by pronouncing a sentence of civil (236–8) and religious (239–240) excommunication. But such a sentence will only be effective with the co-operation of those who have already disobeyed the first instruction to lay information against the man they *ex hypothesi* know to be guilty. Oedipus therefore now proceeds to pronounce a solemn curse on any person who may disobey him by breaking the sanctions of excommunication. The contents of such a curse present Sophocles with something of a problem, because every one is already suffering from failed crops, etc., hence the intensification κἄτι τοῦδ᾽ ἐχθίονι (272).

271 A mild zeugma, since the gods do not strictly speaking ἀνιέναι γυναικῶν παῖδας in the same way as they ἀνιέναι ἀροτόν, cause the harvest to spring up. Cf. Hom. *Hymn to Demeter* 332 γῆς καρπὸν ἀνήσειν.

252 ἐπισκήπτω: this word, to lay the responsibility for something on someone, was used by the orators in homicide cases of dying persons, or persons under sentence of death, entrusting the duty of vengeance to their relatives.

253 The same idea as at 135ff.

254 κἀθέως: 'godlessly' is at first sight an odd word to use, since the plague was sent by a god, and τοῦ θεοῦ is actually mentioned in the preceding line. Just as remarkable is the occurrence at 1360. ἀθέως seems to have some more general meaning, 'terribly', here and at *El.* 1181.

257 γ': causal, as in ὅς γε, 'seeing that it was . . .'; Laius was not only a good man, or nobleman, in his own right; he was also your king.

258 νῦν δ': as at 222 and 263: 'as things are'.

ἐπεὶ κυρῶ κ.τ.ἑ.: Oedipus establishes that he has a legitimate right, even duty, to act on behalf of the murder victim. He is not (he thinks) a blood relative of the deceased, but he is almost as well qualified by reason of (*a*) succeeding Laius in his kingly office (κυρῶ . . . ἔχων as opposed to royal succession in the ordinary way); (*b*) being married to Laius' former wife; and (*c*) 'children born of one mother would have made ties betwixt him and me' (Jebb), and so Oedipus would have been *in loco parentis* to Laius' children if he had had any. If κυρῶ . . . ἔχων had casually set a distance between Oedipus and Laius in (*a*), the language of (*c*) does just the reverse. As Kamerbeek justly remarks, 'the κοινότης goes much further than the case posited by him as unreal'. MacDowell (*op. cit.* 223n.) 94ff. differs from other authorities in believing that although relatives *must* prosecute, others *might*, though clearly such interference might cast doubt on their motives. In either case Oedipus is well placed to prosecute.

The sentence does not proceed on a regular grammatical course (see 264n.), and it gets off to an unpromising start here, since τ' is irregularly placed.

261 'Sunt quibus phrasis horum versuum intricatior videri possit. Sensus est: *Si liberos reliquisset Laius, esset illis genus commune cum liberis meis; fratres essent illi liberorum meorum*' (Brunck). The diagnosis is correct, but it needs to be observed that the *liberi mei* may be purely theoretical: just as a young man might say of some strange event in his life, 'This is something I can tell my grandchildren about', so the children of Oedipus may be not actual children, but children which he might have, or might have had, with Jocasta. This may in fact be the sense of ἥν ἄν ἐκπεφυκότα; I have his γυναῖκα ὁμόσπορον from whom I might have had children who would have been brothers to Laius's children – except of course that, as we all know, Laius did not have any. The point is of some importance. Children appear in the spurious end of the play, but in the apparently genuine part there are only four *prima facie* references to them. This is one, and it is not conclusive. The others are 425, 1247–50, and 1375. As the notes will reveal, there is in every case grave cause for unease.

261–2 γένος . . . δυστύχησεν: ostensibly of childlessness, as at Eur. *Andr.* 713 ἀλλ' εἰ τὸ κείνης δυστυχεῖ παίδων πέρι. But the words fit all too well the other misfortunes in the house of Laius of which Oedipus is not yet aware. γένος can in effect mean 'son'.

263 But as things were, fate swooped on Laius' head before he could have children.

κρᾶτ': the neuter acc. form κρᾶτα occurs only in Sophocles, here and at *Ant.* 764, *Phil.* 1001, and less certainly 1457.

264 ἀνθ' ὧν: 'for those reasons . . .' Oedipus, having interrupted himself at 263, now abandons the course on which his sentence was embarked, and uses ἀνθ' ὧν as a resumptive formula.

268 Ἀγήνορος: Oedipus achieves great solemnity with this historic glance back into a remote past. Laius was son of Labdacus, son of Polydorus, son of Cadmus, son of Agenor, king of Phoenicia. What Oedipus does not know is that the generations which stemmed from Agenor have not yet died out.

244 μὲν οὖν: the usual particles to denote a transition: well then, all that being so . . .

τοιόσδε: i.e. qualified to act for Laius for the reasons given. The audience may also think that 'such' relates to the ancient lineage of Oedipus which he has just unwittingly traced for them: cf. 1084 τοιόσδε δ' ἐκφύς.

246 τὸν δεδρακότ': the word is common in the orators of one who has 'done' a murder, e.g. [Dem.] 47.69 τοῖς δεδρακόσι δὲ καὶ κτείνασι.

247 εἷς ὢν λέληθεν: the stress falls on εἷς ὤν not λέληθεν, and by continuing with πλειόνων μέτα not πλείονες, Sophocles plays down the idea that guilt might belong to several people, cf. τὸν κτανόντ' just below (277). See Introduction 7.

249 ἐπεύχομαι: either 'and I pray in addition' (sc. to the curse contained in κατεύχομαι above) or 'I call down on my own head the curse that I myself suffer . . .' Under Attic law it was normal in homicide cases for the prosecutor to utter an imprecation on the guilty party, and also on himself if he was lying. 246–8 and 249–51 correspond with those two imprecations.

251 τοῖσδ' ἀρτίως: sc. at 269–72.

273 ἄλλοισι: the great mass of the Theban populace, who were untainted by any suspicion of collusion, and who would approve of Oedipus' speech (ἀρέσκονθ 274).

274 ἥ τε σύμμαχος Δίκη: 'Justice, our ally' not 'Justice, as our ally'. A predicative adjective cannot come between article and noun.

276 Eustathius' εἷλες is discussed in *Studies* 1. 226.

278–9 'The search was a matter falling within the competence of the one who sent us this quest/oracle, Phoebus, that he should tell us this, who did the deed' – one of those numerous Sophoclean sentences which are perfectly clear in meaning, but which sound hideous when an attempt is made to render them with a close regard for the grammatical framework of the original.

280 δίκαι᾽ ἔλεξας: muted criticism of Phoebus: the same note that is struck at 789 about an earlier visit to the shrine.

281 οὐδ᾽ ἂν εἷς: not 'not one single person', but equivalent to οὐδεὶς ἄν. Similarly *Ant.* 884, *Trach.* 1072, *Oed. Col.* 1656.

282 τὰ δεύτερ᾽ ἐκ τῶνδ: the Chorus appear to have become infected by Oedipus' administrative style (cf. ἄκ τῶνδε 235), rather as Creon had been by the Delphic oracle (111 n.). Oedipus picks them up with a piece of proverbial humour: cf. Eur. *Hel.* 1417, or Nicetas Eugenianus 2.196: καὶ δευτέρας οὖν συλλαβῆς ἄκουέ μου ~ 197 μηδὲ τῆς τρίτης ἐμοὶ φθονήσῃς συλλαβῆς. δεύτερον is used as 'second best' also at *Oed. Col.* 1227. Bitter play with δίς ~ τρίς at *Ai.* 432–3.

283 τὸ μὴ οὐ: see 13n. Lit. 'do not omit it so as not to tell me', i.e. 'do not pass it over without telling me'.

286 σκοπῶν τάδ᾽, ὦναξ: σκοπῶν continues the idea begun in ὁρῶντ᾽ (284), and in the space of three lines Phoebus, Teiresias and Oedipus are all called ἄναξ.

287 ἐπραξάμην: if this line contained not ἐπραξάμην but εἰάσαμεν (M. Schmidt) there would be no problem of sense. It would mean 'well, I have not neglected this point either' (lit. I have not let it go ὥστε ἐν ἀργοῖς εἶναι, so that it is among things neglected). But ἐπραξάμην gives the meaning not of neglecting, compatible with ἐν ἀργοῖς, but of doing. If the text is sound, either Sophocles has fallen over himself in his hurry to say 'I have not neglected this either, but done it' or else ἐν ἀργοῖς is to be considered as an adverbial phrase, meaning 'negligently'. See LSJ *s.v.* ἐν ΙΙ 3, which however tends to lump together a number of disparate uses: there is nothing really parallel to the present case. A separate problem arises over the middle voice of ἐπραξάμην used for an active. *Ai.* 45 (L and some scholia lemmata) would be the only possible parallel. Wecklein's ἐταξάμην offers an attractive solution: Oedipus has not just shelved the problem.

288 Κρέοντος εἰπόντος: see Introduction 10.

289 μή: θαυμάζω εἰ is the regular construction, and μή is the regular negative in conditional sentences. Hence μή here, not οὐ.

290 'Well certainly all the rest is just vague, antiquated rumour.' The Chorus implicitly give their approval to Oedipus' decision to send for Teiresias. Their casual throwaway remark instantly excites Oedipus' detective instincts (cf. 120–1).

292 ὁδοιπόρων: previously they were described as λῃσταί. Either Sophocles uses the word 'traveller' because Oedipus was in reality a ὁδοιπόρος, not a λῃστής, and he wishes to play on this theme here; or the word ὁδοιπόρος like the English 'highwayman' could have a meaning not to be divined simply from its etymology. Compare the potentially dangerous ὁδιτάων ἀνθρώπων at Hom. *Od.* 13.123. See further 846n.

293 δρῶντ': see 246n. above.

ὁρᾶι: for the present tense see 113n.; or else 'there is no one who saw it'.

294 ἀλλ' ... μὲν δή: again at 523. 'Well, never mind the fact that no one saw the murderer. If he knows what fear is ...'

γ' ἔχει: the γ' is unconvincing. Denniston, *GP*² 142 takes it with εἰ, to mean *si quidem*. However none of the manuscripts used for the Teubner text has actually got γ'; they have τ' except for two which have nothing. Wunder's τρέφει (see 97n.) is a better solution than Hartung's δειμάτων ἔχει, notwithstanding φροντίδων μέρος at *Trach.* 149.

295 σάς: two related manuscripts have σὰς δ, and another σάς δ, where the accent points clearly to an original σάς γ'. That could be the true text. No one would stay once he had heard the curses of so great a figure as Oedipus, if he had a particle of fear in him.

μενεῖ: either 'stay in the land' or 'withstand' the curses.

296 Oedipus takes a more modest view of his prowess at cursing.

δρῶντι harks back to δρῶντ' (293).

οὐδ' ἔπος: words will not frighten either. οὐδ as in 287.

297 οὐξελέγξων αὐτὸν εἶσιν: the verb of motion seems preferable to the 'is' offered by the manuscripts. Although uncompounded εἶμι is notably rare in tragedy as a present tense, it does so occur – though some editors fight shy of it – at Aesch. *Sept.* 373, where, as here, a new character's arrival is being announced. Since *O.T.* 1458 comes in the spurious part of the play, and may possibly in any case be a future, we cannot use that example with the same confidence. Whichever verb we choose, the remark is strange, for the *identity* of αὐτόν is at issue, and until it is known, processes of ἔλεγχος, examining, cross-questioning, refuting, have no place. The person in question, Oedipus, is in reality present, and Teiresias will in fact expose him. Sophocles knows this, and his choice of word is perhaps influenced by these considerations. Yet even in the Oedipus–Teiresias scene that follows, the one who applies ἔλεγχος to the other is rather Oedipus than Teiresias; cf. 333.

299 μόνωι: Not 'alone' but 'pre-eminently', in a class of one's own. This use of μόνος is found mainly, but not exclusively, in religious contexts: thus at Hdt. 1.48 Croesus' esteem of the Delphic oracle is described in these terms: νομίσας μοῦνον εἶναι μάντηιον τὸ ἐν Δελφοῖσι ἐν ἀνθρώποισι, virtually repeated at 53. In the same book μοῦνος is applied to a pre-eminently just judge, Deioces. To other examples collected by Barrett on Eur. *Hipp.* 1280–2 we may add Leonidas of Tarentum, *Anth. Plan.* 206 Θεσπιέες τὸν Ἔρωτα μόνον θεὸν ... ἄζοντ' ('It would be neither true nor relevant here to say that he was the only god venerated there' (Gow and Page, *HE*

II p.388)). Xenophon *Kyneg.* 1.14 speaks of Antilochus, whose death to save his father led to him being called μόνος φιλοπάτωρ. Similar exaggerated use of μόνος at Heliodorus 4.2.1, and Nicet. Eugen. 8.198 δείλαιος ἀνθρώπων μόνος ('uniquely miserable'). In Sophocles the usage appears at *Oed. Col.* 261–2, and in our present play 349 is a likely candidate, and possibly also 389, in both cases, as here, with reference to Teiresias.

300 νωμῶν: observing, mentally (as here) or visually. The word lays the ground for εἰ καὶ μὴ βλέπεις in 302.

302 μέν: no responding δέ follows, since the one after φρονεῖς is the superfluous-looking δέ of the type called 'apodotic', used in main clauses following various kinds of subordinate clauses. See K–G II 275–8.

303–4 Oedipus applies to Teiresias the same language that others had addressed to him, and which can be used unaltered to a god. See the note on 46. For προστάτης used of a god, cf. 882 and *Trach.* 210. See also 411 n.

305 εἰ καί: suspiciously like εἰ καὶ μὴ βλέπεις (302), but this time not meaning 'even if' but 'if indeed you haven't *heard*': Denniston, *GP²* 303. The popular conjecture εἴ τι will mean 'if by any chance'.

310 φθονήσας: φθονέω is often combined with negatives to yield the meaning 'give freely'.

ἀπ οἰωνῶν: the οἰωνοσκοπεῖον Τειρεσίου at Thebes was seen by Pausanias (9.16.1; cf. 18.4). See also Eur. *Bacch.* 347.

313 ῥῦσαι μίασμα: obviously not 'save the pestilence', parallel to 'save yourself' in the line before, but 'keep it away'. See LSJ *s.v.* ἐρύω B3; the explanation they give at the end of their entry on ἐρύω may be disregarded. We may wonder how conscious Sophocles was that he was varying the sense of the verb between these two lines. Compare νόσωι ὑπηρετεῖν at 217.

314 ἐν σοὶ γὰρ ἐσμέν: 'we are in your hands'.

ἄνδρα κ.τ.ἑ.: 'for a man to give help . . .'.

315 The optatives appear to be in primary sequence (i.e. not following a main verb in a past tense) and to stand irregularly for ἄν + subjunctive: 'from whatever he may have at his disposal'. For this well-attested but none the less rare usage see K–G I 252. The optative at 979 is of the same type: cf. *Ai.* 521.

316–17 τέλη | λύηι: for λυσιτελῆι. The subjunctive without ἄν in general relative sentences (whoever, whenever, etc.) is frequent in classical Greek poetry. Teiresias' gloomy reflections on wisdom where wisdom confers no advantage on the one who possesses it ostensibly apply to himself. But they will also apply, with even more force, to Oedipus before the play is out.

318 εἰδὼς διώλεσ': see Introduction 8.

οὐ γὰρ ἄν: 'for otherwise', as at 82.

324 γὰρ οὐδὲ σοί: I do so because I see that in your case too (like any remarks that I might make) what you are saying will lead us into an unfortunate situation. Teiresias' language is at the moment veiled and restrained, as befits a prophet.

325 μηδ' ἐγώ = μὴ καὶ ἐγώ. Either there is a mild ellipse – 'so <I'm seeing that> for my part I don't make the same mistake', or he is interrupted by Oedipus' impassioned μή, πρὸς θεῶν, before he can finish.

326–7 γ': emphasizing the enormity of Teiresias' conduct. He knows, but he won't tell. πρὸς θεῶν, προσκυνοῦμεν, ἱκτήριοι, are all manifestations of submissive desperation.

328 γάρ: as in 324, 'I do so because …' The echoing of πάντες and φρονῶν is indicative of a sharpness creeping into Teiresias' manner.

329 Cf. 1066 καὶ μὴν φρονοῦσά γ' εὖ τὰ λῷστά σοι λέγω. Here 'I shall never declare what would be *best* (the italics represent γ), for fear of disclosing your κακά.' οὐ μή + aor. subj. is the most emphatic way Greek has of saying 'shall not'. λῷον, λῷστον, are words much favoured when the wisdom of a course of action is under discussion. There is a contrast drawn here between public good and private ill.

The text printed is speculative, τὰ λῷστά γ' being a conjecture for τἄμ' ὡς ἄν. The meaning aimed for by most critics in the past has been either 'I will never disclose your evils if it means disclosing mine' (very cynical – and what undisclosed skeletons has Teiresias in his own private cupboard?) or 'I will never disclose my evils – not to call them yours.' The second is better Greek, but again a very strangely mannered utterance, with τὰ ἐμὰ κακά still all but unintelligible. The idea that something is said here about 'mine' and 'your' is hard to eradicate from the mind, because it seems to be confirmed by 320–1 and by 332 ἐγὼ οὔτ' ἐμαυτὸν οὔτε σ' ἀλγυνῶ. However, this is a regular manner of speaking in Greek tragedy, to enumerate different categories in preference to using a comprehensive formula: e.g. above at 64, 253, 312; cf. Aesch. *Sept.* 254 (with all variants). The same tendency is even discernible in the famous verse 371.

330 ξυνειδώς: like φρονῶν γ' (326), but with the additional suggestion that Teiresias is hugging the knowledge to himself.

331 ἡμᾶς: presumably the same as πάντες: if poetic plural for ἐμέ were meant, we would have to accuse Oedipus of misrepresentation. Betraying Oedipus personally is the one thing Teiresias has expressly said he will not do. But in his reply Teiresias interprets ἡμᾶς as ἐμέ.

332 ἐγὼ οὔτ': the -ω and οὐ- coalesce to form one syllable: similarly at 1002. We saw that μὴ οὐ coalesced in the same way at 13.

333 ἄλλως: 'pointlessly', 'to no purpose' – one of its most usual meanings.

334 ὦ κακῶν κάκιστε: this sudden outburst is phrased in language of abnormal vehemence. Greek tragedy tends to conduct such quarrels in terms like 'you are

ill-advised' not 'you are an outright villain'. Oedipus immediately realizes that he
has overstepped the mark, and in self-justification says that Teiresias would try the
patience of a saint, and strikes a more pathetic note in his third line by calling him
inflexible and merciless (or something along those lines).

336 ἄτεγκτος: cf. Aesch. frg. 348, *Prom. Vinct.* 1008, Eur. *Hipp.* 303, *Herc.* 833, Ar.
Lysistr. 550, *Thesm.* 1047.

κἀτελεύτητος: The word is doubtless corrupt, imported by a Christian scribe
who would be familiar with its use in religious texts to mean 'without end'. No
one will believe Eustathius' explanation: ἀτελεύτητος παρὰ Σοφοκλεῖ καὶ τὸν μὴ
τελευτὴν ἐπάγοντα τοῖς ζητουμένοις δηλοῖ. 'With whom one cannot come to an
end', Schneidewin–Nauck: but one *does* come to an end with Teiresias, all too soon.
The right sense would be given by Sehrwald's κἀπαραίτητος, 'not to be deflected by
entreaty', but the change is bold.

337 ὀργήν: Sophocles exploits the ambiguities of the word, which normally means
'anger' – and hence leads on to ὀργίζοιτ' (339) – but can also mean 'mood' or 'dis-
position' or 'character'. A man's character could be spoken of as something separate
from himself, living with him (ὁμοῦ ναίουσαν).

ἐμέμψω: aorist tenses are often used in dialogue to allude to a remark just made a
moment before by the other speaker. English idiom would say 'you blame' not 'you
blamed'.

338 ἀλλ': the real contrast is between ἐμέμψω and κατεῖδες. ἀλλὰ ψέγεις belongs
only to the κατεῖδες half of the sentence. 'You blame my ὀργή, but have not noticed
the one that shares your life, preferring instead to blame me.' We have a long way
to go yet before there is any explicit allusion to Jocasta 'living with' Oedipus. The
language chosen here, however, seems designed to send horrific thoughts through our
minds.

340 ἅ: internal accusative, which in English will have to become 'the words with
which you dishonour . . .'

341 αὐτά: 'by themselves', i.e. of their own accord, as in the Homeric αὐτὸς γὰρ
ἐφέλκεται ἄνδρα σίδηρος, cf. Eur. *Med.* 727, 729, Theocr. 11.12, Callimachus *Hymn
to Apollo* 6,7. Soph. *Ai.* 1099 is probably a valid parallel too. Sophocles has glided
imperceptibly from ἔπη, words, to the events denoted by those words, as the subject
of ἥξει.

342 In that case (οὔκουν), if they are going to come anyway (ἅ γ' either like ἅπερ,
the very things we have been talking about, or, more likely, semi-causal, since they are
going to come), why don't you take the complementary step (καί) of telling me about
them? Cf. *Oed. Col.* 1149.

343 πρὸς τάδ': cf. 426n. So, with that in front of you, . . .

344 δι ὀργῆς: also at 807 'in anger'. But here probably with some influence from constructions with ἰέναι διά + noun of emotion. ἴθι δι' ὀργῆς would mean 'get angry'.

345 καὶ μὴν ... γ': expressing strong agreement with the proposal that he should become angry.

ὀργῆς: dependent on ὡς, as, e.g., γῆς can depend on ποῦ (108). 'So angry am I.' A similar construction below at 367 ἵν' εἶ κακοῦ. Further discussion of the idiom, distinguished into two categories, in J. Diggle, *STE* 35.

346 ἅπερ stands for τούτων ἅπερ. Analogous constructions can be found at *Trach.* 350 ἃ μὲν γὰρ ἐξείρηκας ἀγνοίᾳ μ' ἔχει and Eur. *Med.* 753 (ὄμνυμι) ἐμμενεῖν ἅ σου κλύω (sc. τούτοις ἅ). Here at *Oed. Tyr.* 346 and at *Trach.* 350 we could also take the accusative to mean 'so far as my understanding is concerned' and 'so far as what you have said is concerned'.

347 καί has nothing to do with the θ' following, but gives the tone 'you actually plotted the deed ... '.

347–8 ὅσον | μή: cf. *Trach.* 1214: except in so far as ...

349 μόνου: it is unlikely that Oedipus would, even in a hypothetical case, accuse Teiresias of being the *sole* murderer. For this use of μόνος see above on 299.

350 ἄληθες: an incredulous and often angry retort: '*What?*' as at *Ant.* 758. It is a favourite expression of Aristophanes: *Clouds* 841, *Frogs* 840, *Knights* 89, *Wasps* 1223, 1412, *Birds* 174, 1606, *Lysistr.* 433, *Ach.* 557. In Eur. at *Cyclops* 241, frg. 885. Tempers are wearing thin, and the language is becoming more robust. Note the accentuation on the first syllable in this usage.

351 ὥσπερ: to abide by the very proclamation you have made. ὥσπερ, lying between κηρύγματι and the infinitive ἐμμένειν which governs it, is attracted to the case of the antecedent, and stands for ἐκείνῳ ὅπερ. Jebb has a more complicated explanation, but why he should deny the legitimacy in Greek of κήρυγμα προειπεῖν, is unclear: it is not different in type from κήρυγμα τόδε ἀνειπών (Thuc. 4.105).

353 The datives would have been accusatives if τούσδε and ἐμέ had not intervened. To avoid ambiguity Sophocles proceeds as if he had used a different verb for 'address'. Much harder to explain is the case variation in Homer, *Od.* 17.554–5 μεταλλῆσαί τί ἑ θυμός | ἀμφὶ πόσει κέλεται, καὶ κήδεά περ πεπαθυίηι. Easier examples at Eur. *Med.* 57–8, *I.A.* 491–2.

355 καί: of indignation, as in 'And shall Trelawney die?'

ποῦ: on what grounds? Similar to πῶς, as at 390; cf. ὅπου at 448, and Eur. *Hcld.* 510, *I.A.* 406. Brunck's unaccented που will mean 'And I suppose you think you'll get away with it?' Answer, 'I *have* got away with it.'

357 γε: certainly not from your art. The position of γε is normal in such a prepositional phrase: Denniston, *GP*² 148, points out that ἐκ τῆς τέχνης γε would also be permissible, but not ἐκ τῆς γε τέχνης.

359 More than once in tragedy one character asks another to repeat what he has said, so that the audience may fully grasp some important point (e.g. Aesch. *Cho.* 767 τί πῶς; (What do you mean, 'How?'?) λέγ' αὖθις ὡς μάθω σαφέστερον), or because the demands of stichomythia require a line to be delivered but the sense really requires nothing. Here Sophocles puts new life into an old convention by making the very request for repetition the material for generating further ill-will between the two parties.

360 ἢ 'κπειρᾶι λέγων: the text is very uncertain. 'Are you trying to provoke me by your words?' The manuscripts have λέγειν, and Arndt conjectured μ' ἑλεῖν: 'Are you trying to trap me?'

362 In the interests of clarity this edition has substituted δίκας for the last word in the line, which the manuscripts give as κυρεῖν. Cf. *El.* 33–4 ὅτωι τρόπωι πατρὸς/δίκας ἀροίμην τῶν φονευσάντων πάρα. The change is less bold than it might appear. At least it has a parallel: Jebb's note on *Oed. Col.* 726 rightly sees κυρῶ as a false reading which has there displaced the ἐγώ which has survived in only a few (but good) manuscripts. The reason for the corruption will be the same in both cases: the mistaken belief that some part of the verb 'to be' has to be expressed. The traditional text is intolerable: 'I say that you are the murderer of the man whose you are looking for', and even if we make the all but impossible mental supplement 'whose <murderer>' we still end up with a sense that is ineffably vapid.

363 χαίρων: 'with impunity'. A familiar idiom: cf. *Ant.* 758–9 ἀλλ' οὐ ... χαίρων ἔτι ψόγοισι δεννάσεις ἐμέ. γεγηθώς below in 368 is a variation on the same theme. Contrast κλαίων 401, 1152.

πημονὰς ἐρεῖς: combinations of nouns and verbs of this type seem to belong more to the robuster language of comedy.

367 ἵν' εἶ κακοῦ: where <in the realm of > misfortune. The same phrase at 413. Cf. 345n.

368 ἦ καί: 'Do you really think you can go on all the time talking like this and get away with it?'

369 εἴπερ τί γ': Yes, I do, if ... The γ' gives assent, and εἴπερ, as often, means 'if, as is the case'. The περ in εἴπερ stresses the verb, and can contain either of the opposite nuances implicit in the English 'if it *does* rain tomorrow' sc. either 'as we have every reason for assuming it will' or 'which I regard as only an outside possibility'. The former usage is much the more common, but for an example of the second use cf. *El.* 604: 'I would have done it, εἴπερ ἔσθενον, if I had had the strength, which I didn't.'

371 A line famous not so much for the accusatives of respect which it enshrines as for its repeated τ sounds. These *may* be purely fortuitous, because the definite article and τε can hardly help having them. In any case the intellectual weight of such words is negligible, and any effect achieved seems to bear no relation to the underlying sense. Certainly there is nothing inherent in the letter τ to make it especially redolent of anger and contempt. Cf. *Ai.* 687–8 ὑμεῖς θ̲ ἑτ̲αῖροι, τ̲αὐτ̲ὰ τ̲ῆιδέ μοι τ̲άδε | τ̲ιμᾶτ̲ε, Τ̲εύκρωι τ̲, ἣν μόληι, σημήναˍτε, where there is no particular rhetorical point in the alliteration. Compare the accidental alliteration of πέντ' ἐπὶ πεντήκοντα πόδας πήδησε Φάϋλλος in Page, *FGE* 1496. Repeated π sounds in Sophocles at, e.g., *Ant.* 419ff., 1231–2, *El.* 210, *Oed. Col.* 739: accident may not be a sufficient explanation for all of these. An amazing mixture of π/φ sounds at Aesch. *Cho.* 363–71 (11 in 8 short lines), to say nothing of the 8 τ/θ sounds there. Hom. *Od.* 18.204 has four of its five words beginning with π or φ. Some notable sigmatism below at 425. On the whole question see I. Opelt, *Glotta* 37 (1958) 205–32.

For the various elements comprised in Oedipus' taunt cf. Theognis 1163–4 ὀφθαλμοὶ καὶ γλῶσσα καὶ οὔατα καὶ νόος ἀνδρῶν | ἐν μέσσωι στηθέων ἐν συνετοῖς φύεται, and Hom. *Od.* 20.365–6.

372 δ'...γε: yes, and you're ἄθλιος. δέ ...γε belong particularly to retorts. See Denniston, *GP²* 153.

374 μιᾶς: one continuous, unbroken darkness. No wholly satisfactory parallel exists.
τρέφηι: cf. Eur. *Hipp.* 367 ὦ πόνοι τρέφοντες βροτούς 'troubles that have mortals in their keeping' (Barrett).

377 ἱκανὸς Ἀπόλλων: at Hdt. 8.36 the Delphians in fear of the Persian invaders ask the god where they should put his treasures for safe keeping. The god tells them to move nothing, φὰς αὐτὸς ἱκανὸς εἶναι τῶν ἑαυτοῦ προκατῆσθαι.

378 Oedipus' sudden suspicions of Creon are at variance with the compliment he paid him at the conclusion of their conversation at 133, and pave the way for the Oedipus–Creon scene which will follow the next choral song. Teiresias' accusations sound insane, yet he has nothing to gain from making them. It follows that someone else must be behind them: cf. 357, already replacing the hasty and improbable accusations of 346–9. The most likely candidate is the person with the most to gain, Creon. To do justice to the Greek word-order we have to reverse it in English: 'Whose idea was this – Creon's?' (Note that 'Whose?', τοῦ, is only in a papyrus (unaccented), and there too only before correction.)

380–2 Oedipus apostrophizes his own position in life, one of wealth, political power and pre-eminence of mind.

380–1 τέχνη τέχνης | ὑπερφέρουσα: in particular the art of ruling, superior to all ordinary τέχναι, cf. *Phil.* 138ff. τέχνα γὰρ τέχνας ἑτέρας | προύχει καὶ γνώμα παρ' ὅτωι τὸ θεῖον | Διὸς σκῆπτρον ἀνάσσεται.

τῶι πολυζήλωι βίωι: locative dative. As the definite article shows, the phrase does not refer to jealousies in life in general, but to jealousies inseparable from the life lived by a king; the same point made by Clytaemestra at Aesch. *Agam.* 939.

382 φυλάσσεται may seem an unexpected verb to use with φθόνος, but cf. Eur. frg. 209 φυλάσσεσθαι φθόνον. At *Oed. Col.* 1213 σκαιοσύναν φυλάσσων means 'cherishing folly'; at Hom. *Il.* 16.30 we find χόλος ὃν σὺ φυλάσσεις. The verb can then mean much the same as τρέφω. See LSJ *s.v.* B 3. Since the envy is being fostered *against* the royal position, παρ' ὑμῖν must mean something like 'under your roof'. The article with φθόνος gives the tone 'how great is the envy which . . .' as opposed to 'how much envy . . .'

384 The adjectives are feminine, treated as if they had only two terminations: cf. *Trach.* 163, 208, 478, 533, 863; *Ant.* 392 (εὐκτός), 867; *El.* 313; *Oed. Col.* 751, 1460; frg. 718. See W. Kastner, *Die griechischen Adjektive zweier Endungen auf* -ος (Heidelberg 1967).

385 The articles express scorn, as at *Trach.* 541, *Ant.* 31, *El.* 300–2, *Oed. Col.* 992, and in a slightly different way, of ironic self-deprecation, at 397 below. 'Creon the loyal, Creon, the friend from the old days.' The expression ἐξ ἀρχῆς is used of πατρῶιοι ἕταιροι in Hom. *Od.* 1.188; 2.254; 17.69.

386 ὑπελθών: creeping up on me. ὑπο- compounds often denote underhand dealings or the insidious approach of something. The same idea recurs in ὑφείς in the next line, setting the priest on to him to undermine his position.

ἐκβαλεῖν: exile is meant, as too at 399.

386–8 Oedipus applies to Teiresias the kind of language which Cassandra says was used of her: καλουμένη δὲ φοιτὰς ὡς ἀγύρτρια | πτωχὸς τάλαινα λιμοθνὴς ἠνεσχόμην (Aesch. *Agam.* 1273–4). Cassandra was an inspired prophetess. Teiresias was essentially a priest dealing in omens. The two types are quite different, even if they incur the same kinds of obloquy. The attempt of K. G. Rigsby in *G.R.B.S.* 17 (1976) 109–14 to take μάγον not as 'impostor', 'charlatan' but as a specific allusion to 'kingmakers' (οἱ δεινοὶ μάγοι τε καὶ τυραννοποιοί Plato, *Rep.* 572e) with special reference to the stories of the eastern μάγοι in Herodotus (3.64, 88, 118, 150, 153, and 4.132) contains much of interest. 'Oedipus, expecting information and advice from the priest, finds, as he thinks, an ambitious and brazen conspirator in religious garb, attempting to overthrow him: in a rage he hurls at him a single noun that encompasses this meaning.' Unfortunately these lines contain much more abuse than the 'single noun' and the object of such a participle as ὑφείς could hardly be more than a henchman.

389 μόνον: To accuse a blind soothsayer of having sight only where there is a chance of profit, but being blind in the mantic arts, is certainly insulting, but the insult is clumsily phrased. Nauck proposed ἄκρον for μόνον, giving ideal sense and a good balance to the sentence, τὴν τέχνην δ᾽ ἔφυ τυφλός being phrased paratactically where we, in a translation, might prefer some form of subordination. The overall meaning will then be something like: 'who has got pretty sharp eyes when it comes to making a profit, blind though he may be when it comes to his profession'. But ἄκρον for μόνον is a drastic remedy and assumes that our present text is the product of an unimaginative interpolation. We may be able to achieve much the same effect by interpreting along the lines discussed in the note on 299. Groeneboom thought so, and proposed changing μόνον to μόνος: 'who is as clear-sighted as they come where money is involved …'. Compare Hom. *Od.* 8. 163–4 ἐπίσκοπος ᾖσιν ὁδαίων | κερδέων θ' ἁρπαλέων 'with an eye for quick gains to be made from trafficking'.

390 ἐπεί: like γάρ, justifying a previous remark, and especially at home in questions which are intended to expose the shortcomings of an opponent's argument or position: cf. *El.* 345 (?), 352, *Oed. Col.* 969, Ar. *Wasps* 519 (see also 73), Plato *Gorgias* 473e, 474b7, Lysias 12.39, Dem. 39.32, etc.

   ποῦ: on what grounds are you to be regarded as a true prophet? See 355n., and for σαφής 96, 846nn.

391ff. See Introduction 8.

393 καίτοι … γ': this combination 'introduces an objection … of the speaker's own, which tends to invalidate, or cast doubt upon, what he has just said, or to make it appear surprising …' (Denniston, *GP²* 556). It was surprising that Teiresias did not intervene.

   τοὐπιόντος as at *Oed. Col.* 752, any one who just happens to come along. The word colours μολών (396), used neutrally at 35 with reference to the same episode.

394 διειπεῖν: the choice of word is odder than it looks. 'Solving' riddles, or 'seeing through' them, would normally be expressed with λύω, εὑρίσκω, μανθάνω, γιγνώσκω, even οἶδα (1525). At *Trach.* 22 and *Oed. Tyr.* 854 διειπεῖν means 'tell clearly' or 'tell with precision', and it recurs nowhere else in tragedy. Perhaps Oedipus means here not 'solve' but 'give a clear exposition of it' to others: what Teiresias should have done.

395 προυφάνης: Teiresias was not conspicuous for his advice on that occasion. But this may be over-interpretation: cf. 790n.

397 ὁ μηδὲν εἰδώς: for the definite article see 385n. μηδέν, not οὐδέν, is used because Oedipus belonged to the *category* of non-mantic persons. The dramatic irony is here especially effective, since in, as he imagines, employing irony and sarcasm Oedipus is in fact voicing the essential truth.

398 ἀπ οἰωνῶν μαθών: sarcasm replaces the genuine respect for this form of divination expressed at 310.

399–405 In one form or another the verb δοκεῖν occurs four times in seven lines, with four different nuances.

400 Κρεοντείοις: Oedipus speaks not of 'the throne of Creon' but 'the Creontic throne'. Such a usage is not common. At 267 (Λαβδακείωι) lineage was in question;

similarly τὴν Εὐρυτείαν ... παρθένον (*Trach.* 1219). At *Phil.* 1131 Ἡράκλειον we are talking of a difference in generations. The nuance in Λαΐειον at 451 below is less obvious, but see 729n. Here the suspicious mind of Oedipus seems already to have manufactured a political faction of 'Creontics'. See 411 n. below, where Teiresias replies to this charge.

401 κλαίων: see 363n.

402 ἀγηλατήσειν: sarcastic: 'drive the pollution from the land'.

γέρων: since Teiresias *is* an old man, the implication may be 'senile': the word is linked with ἄνους at *Ant.* 281 and ἀνόητος at Ar. *Knights* 1349. ἀρχαῖος, ἀρχαιικός are certainly used for 'silly' – see Dover's note on Ar. *Clouds* 821. Above all, compare Eur. *Andr.* 678.

403 The linking of πάθος and μάθος words in Greek, especially in Homer and classical poetry, is very frequent. Here there is a minor variation in the substitution of ἔγνως for ἔμαθες. Oedipus means 'you would have learnt a lesson appropriate to your attitude'. οἷα κ.τ.έ. grammatically cannot be an indirect question, as the presence of περ proves, so it is to be construed with παθών, or the unified concept παθὼν ἔγνως: sc. <τοιαῦτα> οἷά περ φρονεῖς.

404 εἰκάζουσι: the metaphor reappears in modern American: 'as we try to figure it out'.

408 τυραννεῖς: in this, the first line of his speech, Teiresias evidently intends to tap the well of opprobrium which could, but did not necessarily, attach to τυραννίς: see 872n. So the chorus at Eur. *Bacch.* 775–6: ταρβῶ μὲν εἰπεῖν τοὺς λόγους ἐλευθέρους/ πρὸς τὸν τύραννον. Oedipus' speech had begun with τυραννί in its first line. Teiresias ignores the four-line choral intervention, and addresses himself directly to Oedipus. Similarly *El.* 1017 ignores 1015–16, notwithstanding the admirably deployed arguments of A. Petropoulou, *A.J.P.* 100 (1979) 480–6.

ἐξισωτέον τὸ γοῦν κ.τ.έ.: at any rate <the right of> reply at the same length *must be equalized.* The linguistic pudding is somewhat over-egged.

411 'Do not count me as one of your "Creontics"' (400) is part of the sense, but the other part is 'I am a full citizen, and my name shall not stand enscribed on the roll of Creon as the citizen who' – an allusion to the Attic law familiar to the audience – 'has to speak for people without citizen status.' This explanation correctly stands in the Byzantine lexicon of Hesychius.

412 Either 'since you *have* specifically taunted me with blindness' or 'since you have included my blindness among your insults', or 'since you have taunted me with being *blind*'. The first is best. For the position of καί see 772n.

413 καὶ δεδορκώς: cf. *Ai.* 85 καὶ δεδορκότα.

416 σοῖσιν αὐτοῦ: 'your own'. The genitive as if σοῖσιν were σοῦ. This construction, though rare, is regular, cf. *Oed. Col.* 344 τἀμὰ δυστήνου κακά, *Phil.* 1126, Eur. *Andr.* 107, *El.* 366, *Suppl.* 921–2. In third person form, τοῖς οἷσιν αὐτοῦ at 1248.

417 The text printed assumes that something has fallen out before this verse, something like 'this very day will bring the truth to light', i.e. disclose in what ways you are ἐχθρός to those in the world below (your father) and to those on earth above (your mother). If nothing is missing καί should be understood as καίτοι: Denniston, *GP*² 292.

ἀμφιπλήξ: striking from both sides, father's and mother's.

418 δεινόπους: the -πους compound suggests to the mind an identity between the Ἀρά and the Ἐρινύς, for καμψίπους (Aesch. *Sept.* 791), τανύπους (*Ai.* 837), χαλκόπους (*El.* 491) are all epithets of the latter. The two concepts are elsewhere too very closely related. It would be a piece of hideous over-interpretation to see here any allusion to Oedipus' lame feet.

420 λιμήν: any place that will receive his cries as a harbour receives a ship.

421 ποῖος; Κιθαιρών: The manuscripts give ποῖος Κιθαιρών, as odd an expression as 'What sort of Mt Everest?' would be to us. The repunctuation ποῖος; Κιθαιρών gives us a repetition like that at *Trach.* 996: οἵαν μ᾽ ἄρ᾽ ἔθου λώβαν, οἵαν. But there is an intriguing alternative solution: πάτριος Κιθαιρών. Cithaeron was the mountain where the infant Oedipus had been put out to die. Its association with Oedipus is quite specific; it will be mentioned again by name at 1026, 1089, 1134, 1391, 1452. πάτριος would be written in manuscripts as π̅ρ̅ι̅ο̅ς̅, an open invitation to corruption. The apparent enigma of 'parent' in 'Will not your parent Cithaeron soon be adding its voice to yours?' will then be resolved at 1090.

422-3 The missing line probably began with a word like ἄναγνον or ἀραῖον, and the sense will have been 'when you recognize the wedding which you contracted, a curse on the house of Labdacus, and the harbour which is no harbour into which you sailed all too easily'.

424-5 It is difficult to see what the *other* κακά might be, whatever we may do with 425. In that line Nauck's elegant solution of the barely credible 'make you equal with you' disposes of a problem of language but still leaves us with one of content, namely the mention of Oedipus' children. At 262 Oedipus may have been talking of possible, rather than actual, children that he and Jocasta might have. Apart from that line there is no allusion anywhere else in the authentic portion of the play to any children born to the current royal couple until we come to 1248–50 and 1375–6 (see the notes ad loc.). 424-5 were deleted by H. Otte in 1896. It remains to notice the sigmatism of 425, which has a counterpart in the spurious line 1507. Sigmatism is more a characteristic of Euripides than Sophocles: it is discussed by Page on Eur. *Med.* 476.

426 πρὸς ταῦτα: cf. *Ai.* 1115, 1313, *Ant.* 658, *El.* 383, 820, *Oed. Col.* 956, and πρὸς τάδε at 343 above. As Barrett notes on Eur. *Hipp.* 304–5 the meaning is 'that is the position; and now that you know what it is you must (may) . . . '. 'The imperative is often defiant, expressing the speaker's indifference to what the other may do.' See also J. Diggle, *STE* 38.

τοὐμὸν στόμα: me for what I have said. Cf. *El.* 633.

428 ἐκτριβήσεται: 'No one among men shall ever be crushed more miserably than thou', (Jebb). Cf. Hdt. 7.120.2 κάκιστα πάντων ἀνθρώπων ἐκτριβῆναι. After a similar explanation our scholia continue quite unexpectedly with something that holds the promise of better immediate relevance: 'a metaphor from the washing clean of silver, bronze, or other such vessels, which by being knocked about in the course of washing lose value'. The note confuses two things: (1) The showing up of base metal by the application of the touchstone (510n.) or general wear (cf. Aesch. *Agam.* 391). (2) The disclosure of something in its true colours by washing it clean. This second idea would fit well into a context which has just mentioned the slinging of mud (πηλός) at some one else (427), but there is no mention of anything liquid in Sophocles' text. The two ideas are however also linked at Theognis 447–52. Cf. ἐντριβής *Ant.* 177.

430 οὐκ εἰς ὄλεθρον: a phrase redolent of comedy; but there is nothing comic here, or at 1146.

430–1 αὖ πάλιν ... ἄψορρος: such highly pleonastic expressions are common in Greek tragedy. αὖ πάλιν is like our 'back again'.

434 σχολῇι: otherwise I wouldn't have been in such a hurry to send for you. σχολῇι becomes a virtual negative; cf. *Ant.* 390. The idiom is more familiar from fourth-century prose.

οἴκους: plain accusative for ἐς οἴκους; cf. 153n.

437 Oedipus ought to dismiss Teiresias' remark with summary contempt, if the main presuppositions of the play at this point are to hold. 774–5 explicitly say: 'my father was Polybus, my mother Merope' – but just after that Oedipus relates how a chance remark that he was a bastard lodged in his mind. He momentarily shows the same insecurity here. Sophocles quickly passes over this disturbing moment, having achieved a theatrical and psychological effect at a cost which none of his audience will notice.

ἐκφύει: the present tense is normal with such words as τίκτειν, γεννᾶσθαι, etc., when referring to the past.

445 δῆθ': δῆτα is the standard particle when one speaker echoes the word of another.

446 συθείς: σεύομαι often denotes speed, but not here, nor at *Oed. Col.* 119.

ἀλγύναις: since Sophocles does not elsewhere use the -αις form in the aorist optative, preferring the -ειας which predominates in Homer and early Attic, Elmsley substituted the present ἀλγύνοις, found also in a manuscript. But the -αις ending is in itself free from objection in Attic of this date: it is the only form in inscriptions (attested from 450 B.C. onward). Aristophanes makes occasional use of it (see Dover on *Clouds* 776). In Aeschylus it occurs at *Suppl.* 589, 660, 662; *Eum.* 618(?), 983, and in Euripides at *Med.* 325, *El.* 1058(?), *I.T.* 1184, *Hipp.* 469(?). There is a discussion by K. Forbes of these so-called 'Aeolic' optative forms in *Glotta* 37 (1958) 165–9.

πλέον: 'any more' = 'any further'. Cf. 1165.

447–62 ὧν οὕνεκ ἦλθον: 'what I came for' would normally imply purpose on the part of the speaker. Now Teiresias came unwillingly, summoned by Oedipus. We may either assume a slight inconsistency (probable) or insist that the strict letter of the phrase ὧν οὕνεκ does not *necessarily* imply purpose by the speaker (less probable). See Introduction 8–9.

448 πρόσωπον: since Teiresias cannot see that Oedipus has 'an eye like Mars, to threaten and command', a noun like στόμα (cf. *Ai.* 1110, *Ant.* 997) was more to be expected.

ὅπου: see 355n.

450 κἀνακηρύσσων φόνον: issuing a proclamation *enquiring into* the death: see K. J. Dover in *Miscellanea tragica in honorem F. C. Kamerbeek* (Amsterdam 1976) 49–53, who so understands καρῦξαι at *Trach.* 97. Cf. Dem. 25.56 ἃς ἐζήτουν καὶ ἐκήρυττον οἱ ἕνδεκα.

452 ξένος: the word used by Oedipus of himself at 219–20 in a different connection.

μέτοικος: not a 'resident alien' but just one who has moved his home.

εἶτα δ᾽: in opposition to λόγωι. In theory he is a stranger who has moved here, but in time he will be seen to be a native Theban.

454 ἐκ: 'after being', 'changed out of'. The two ideas are merged; cf. *Trach.* 284, 1075.

455–6 ξένην ἔπι: '*to* a foreign land' or '*over* a foreign land' – cf. Eur. *Hipp.* 897–8 ἀλώμενος | ξένην ἐπ᾽ αἶαν 'wandering over a foreign land'. γῆν is understood: cf. ξέναι at *Phil.* 135 for ξέναι γᾶι. γαῖαν in the next line is separate from this phrase, and is the object of προδεικνύς. Oedipus will travel to (or over) a strange land, pointing out to himself the ground before him with his staff.

ἐμπορεύσεται: the verb has about it a faintly contemptuous note from its associations with ἔμπορος; Electra uses it when addressing her sister in a less than sisterly fashion (*El.* 405), Chrysothemis then being on an errand. Teiresias, who has been called an ἀγύρτης at 388, hints at a future for Oedipus which would qualify the king himself for such a title.

458 αὐτός: ὁ αὐτός, 'the same man'.

460 ὁμόσπορος: active, 'sowing' not 'sown', notwithstanding the accent. One might have expected ὁμοσπόρος (Bothe): but see H. W. Chandler, *A practical introduction to Greek accentuation*[2] (Oxford 1881) §460. The accent does not vary with adjectives derived from verbs if they are compounded with a preposition or alpha privative, whether active or passive. Aesch. *Sept.* 752–6 dwells with relish on the horrendous crimes: πατροκτόνον Οἰδιπόδαν, ὅστε ματρὸς ἁγνὰν | σπείρας ἄρουραν ἵν᾽ ἐτράφη | ῥίζαν αἱματόεσσαν ἔτλα (lit. the parricide Oedipus, who went so far as to sow a root of blood in the sanctified field of his mother, in the place where he was given life).

462 φάσκειν: imperatival infinitive. Not 'say' but 'think', 'consider', 'regard'; cf. *El.* 9 and *Phil.* 1411.

To the problem of 'the apparent failure of the highly intelligent Oedipus to grasp what has been said to him' (Introduction 9) there is one extreme solution, first propounded by Theodor Kock in 1857 and fitfully advocated since (e.g. by B. M. W. Knox in *Greek, Roman, and Byzantine Studies* 21 (1980) 321–32). It is that Oedipus leaves the stage, or begins to leave it, as early as 447, so that he is quite simply not present to hear what Teiresias has to say. The evidence against such an idea is overwhelming. If Sophocles really intended οὐ τὸ σὸν δείσας πρόσωπον (447–8) and its attendant λέγω δέ σοι to be directed by a blind man at a retreating or absent figure, and if he really intended ἰών/εἴσω (460–1) to be similarly directed at a person who had left thirteen lines earlier, he is guilty of a tasteless lapse of judgement far worse than anything occasioned by the dramatic implausibility of an Oedipus who fails to react as we expect to Teiresias' clear denunciation. In this scene the stress is constantly on the likely exit not of Oedipus but of Teiresias: he has been furiously dismissed at 430–1; there is a momentary check at 437 (μεῖνον); and at 445 the original order is repeated. At 444 and 447 Teiresias twice says of himself ἄπειμι.

463–511 The second chorus (first stasimon)

In this chorus the first strophic pair deals with the message from Delphi and the life of the hunted criminal. The second pair expresses, with some uneasy reservations, continuing confidence in Oedipus.

463 τίς: the first choral song had asked τίς of the Delphic oracle's Φάτις itself in the first line. Now in the second choral song τίς is asked of the identity of the person the oracle referred to. On the nature of this question see Introduction 9.

464 Δελφὶς ... πέτρα: the same phrase in Theocritus, *Anth. Pal.* 6.336.4 (= A. S. F. Gow and D. L. Page, *HE* 3395). Delphi is above all things rocky.

ἦιδε: the variant εἶδε for εἶπε is known to one manuscript, and doubtless was in our oldest manuscript (L) before εἶπε was written in its place. The scholia have κατώπτευσεν, which fits εἶδε but not εἶπε, yet what we need is a verb of speaking, not of seeing. Hence J. Enoch Powell's suggestion ἦιδε, from ἀείδω. On the suitability of this verb see 130n., and compare Ar. *Knights* 61, Thuc. 2.8.2 and 2.21.3. (Not that εἶπε is itself unsuitable for a Pythian response: e.g. Pind. *Ol.* 7.33.)

465 ἄρρητ' ἀρρήτων: a kind of superlative: 'utterly unspeakable'. Cf. κακὰ κακῶν *Oed. Col.* 1238.

τελέσαντα: 'as having done'.

467–8 It is time for him to move his feet in flight more vigorously than horses swift as the wind of the storm. Greek, from Homer onward, seems to our taste oddly preoccupied with knees and feet; cf. 878n. φυγᾶι πόδα νωμᾶν in effect means simply 'run away fast' with the secondary sense 'go quickly into exile'.

469 ἔνοπλος: Apollo will be borrowing the armament of his father Zeus (200–1) if he comes with lightning.

470 γενέτας: 'son' as at Eur. *Ion* 916. More usually 'father' or 'ancestor'.

471 At first sight one would say this meant 'with Apollo', but the sense may be 'with the murderer'; they will dog his steps. Cf. Homer, *Il.* 9.512 τῶι (sc. the wrongdoer) Ἄτην ἅμ᾿ ἕπεσθαι.

472 Κῆρες: avenging spirits close to, or even identical with, the Erinyes. But Sophocles also uses κήρ in a quite different sense, of misfortune, calamity, or fate.

ἀναπλάκητοι: ἁ (μ) πλάκημα is the same as ἁμάρτημα. The Κῆρες do not miss.

475 φήμα: already the subject of the first strophe of the first choral ode (151–8). For ἔλαμψε ... φανεῖσα with a noun of sound see 186n.

476 πάντ᾽: acc. sing. masc., subject of ἰχνεύειν. Others (less well) construe it as acc. neut. plur. 'in all ways'.

477 ὑπ᾿ conveys the idea of going *up to* the wood where he hopes for shelter. Cf. ἄλσος ὑπὸ σκιερόν Hom. *Od.* 20.278.

478 πετραῖος ὁ ταῦρος: It will be seen from the apparatus that the MSS were as much taken aback by these words as almost every one else has been ever since. But the idiom whereby 'like' is omitted was recognised and discussed by Birt in *Rheinisches Museum* n.f. 69 (1914) 597–614; and by Kassel in the same periodical, 116 (1973) 109–12. The guilty person is directly called 'the bull', and πετραῖος means 'among rocks' (predicative) as a way of avoiding the repetitious construction ἀνὰ πέτρους.

479 μελέωι ποδί: the expression fits Oedipus with uncomfortable closeness, but the 'foot' metaphor is so common that it is unwise to attach special significance to it here: see 467–8n., 878n. 'Miserable, bereaved with a miserable foot' may strike us as an unhappy phrase, but to a Greek ear doubtless sounded no more peculiar than Jebb's translation does to us: 'wretched and forlorn on his joyless path'.

480 μεσόμφαλα: cf. 898, Aesch. *Sept.* 747, *Cho.* 1036, Pindar, *Nem.* 7.33.

ἀπονοσφίζων: putting a distance between himself and the oracles, something Oedipus had tried to do long ago: cf. 796–7.

481 τὰ δ᾽: 'but they'.

482 ζῶντα περιποτᾶται: language is applied to the oracles which would fit excellently the Κῆρες who were mentioned in the corresponding line of the strophe. For ζῶντα cf. Aesch. *Agam.* 819 Ἄτης θύελλαι ζῶσιν.

484 δεινά: internal accusative, equivalent to an adverb, 'terribly'.

μὲν οὖν: a rare use; see Denniston, *GP²* 473 (2). It recurs however in the responding place at 498, and again at 587. οὖν emphasizes the prospective μέν, and the tone is 'the wise observer of birds has certainly disturbed me, but what I am to make of it all I really don't know'. It is possible, however, that the responding δ is not the one after λέξω but the one after πέτομαι. 'I am much disturbed and don't know what to think, but I live in hopes, having no good reason to doubt Oedipus.'

485   οὔτε δοκοῦντ'... 'neither approving...', cf. *Oed. Col.* 317 καὶ φημὶ κἀπόφημι, κοὐκ ἔχω τί φῶ.

λέξω: future indicative or deliberative subjunctive? For Sophocles the question does not arise, such grammatical categories being not yet invented.

486   πέτομαι: entirely unrelated in thought to περιποτᾶται, just above.

ἐλπίσιν: either 'hopes', as translated above, or forebodings, as at 771, or both. At Pindar, *Pyth.* 8.90 the ἐλπίδος which is mentioned next to πέταται in a far from perspicuous context is unmistakably 'hope', not something sinister.

ἐνθάδ': not used of time elsewhere. There is no reason why it should, and some reason why it should not, be temporal at *Oed. Col.* 992, the only other place mentioned by LSJ under this heading. Doubtless the presence of ὀπίσω, which can be either spatial or temporal (here temporal, 'in the future') lessens the oddity. There is an interesting essay on ὀπίσω 'afterwards' by Jonas Palm, 'Lag die Zukunft der Griechen hinter ihnen?' ('Did the future of the Greeks lie behind them?') in *Annales Academiae Regiae Scientiarum Upsaliensis* 13 (1969). See also M. Treu, *Von Homer zur Lyrik* (München 1955) 133–5.

489–90   The Chorus mean any quarrel subsisting *between* the Labdacids *and* the son of Polybus. They choose to express it as any quarrel lying *either* on the side of the Labdacids *or* on the side of the son of Polybus. (Quarrel can mean 'cause for quarrel' both in Greek and in English.) Some of the complicated ways in which reciprocity can be expressed in Greek and Latin are briefly considered by J. Wackernagel, *VUS* II 96–101.

494   Our only possible clue to what stood in the undamaged text is in the scholia: ποίωι λογισμῶι, ἀντὶ τοῦ τίνος πράγματος κρίσει χρησάμενος τοῖς λεγομένοις πιστεύσω κατὰ Οἰδίποδος. It is a poor clue, since it speaks of the charges against Oedipus, whereas the poetic text speaks of Oedipus' public reputation. The scholion seems to have been fused with a different note intended to explain 504–6 (μεμφομένων καταφαίην). We cannot even be sure whether to construe πρὸς ὅτου as a separate phrase, or πρὸς ὅτου βασάνωι together. The general sense is however clear: the Chorus know of no quarrel which would form a reliable foundation for assailing Oedipus' reputation among his people. (It would be fanciful to see in ἐπίδαμον φάτιν a direct contrast with the Φήμα from Parnassus.)

496   Assailing Oedipus' public reputation is something the Chorus reject as a possible means of being an ἐπίκουρος to the Labdacids.

ἀδήλων θανάτων: the phrase suggests at a subconscious level the mysterious deaths from the plague sent by an unseen god. But the context determines that the primary meaning is the death (poetic plural for singular) that has not yet been cleared up (and so still ἀδήλων) of Laius. The genitive is of a very unusual kind, but is exactly paralleled at Eur. *El.* 137–8 πατρί θ᾽ αἱμάτων αἰσχίστων (Seidler's correction of ἐχθίστων) ἐπίκουρος, avenging your father for, or in the matter of, his horrible death. Cf. *I.A.* 1027 εὑρεῖν σὴν χέρ᾽ ἐπίκουρον κακῶν. So here 'avenging Laius in the matter of his still unsolved murder'. How exactly we should classify such a genitive is hard to say. See K–G I 371, Anm. 19.

498ff.   The sequence of thought is: it is true that Zeus and Apollo are our superiors in knowledge, but if we come down to the human level, there is no certain way of telling if the prophet takes precedence over me. It is certainly true that one man may excel another in σοφία (sc. as Teiresias doubtless does excel me in μαντική), but I do not intend to believe Oedipus' detractors until I see their words are actually proved true, since I have seen for myself how he responded to the menace of the Sphinx; and in the light of that experience he is not going to be accused of κακία by me.

499   ἀλλ᾽ ὁ μὲν οὖν: the ἀλλά and the μὲν οὖν seem to pull in opposite directions, ἀλλά meaning 'I won't attack Oedipus, yet at the same time I have to concede that Zeus and Apollo are intelligent and well-informed', whereas the μὲν οὖν gives the idea 'Zeus and Apollo are no doubt themselves highly intelligent, but it's not clear to me that their prophet, being human, has the edge on me.' It is possible that ἀλλά is not here adversative, but marks a fresh beginning. 'Well, certainly Zeus ... but the prophet ... '

500   πλέον ... φέρεται: cf. Eur. *Hec.* 307–8 ὅταν τις ἐσθλὸς καὶ πρόθυμος ὢν ἀνὴρ | μηδὲν φέρηται τῶν κακιόνων πλέον. φέρομαι is used of winning prizes in a competition.

501–2   κρίσις ... ἀληθής: there is no certain means of determining who wins the competition.

σοφίαι δ᾽ ἂν σοφίαν παραμείψειεν: there may be a faint tinge of dramatic irony here, an unconscious allusion to Oedipus who has the τέχνη τέχνης ὑπερφέρουσα (380–1) and who, we shall be told in a moment, σοφὸς ὤφθη in his encounter with the Sphinx.

δ᾽ ἂν: the general-purpose connective δ leaves us with a problem not unlike the one at 499. Does this sentence look back or forward? The Chorus' admission that one man may have the edge on another does not follow too well as a conclusion to their previous statement that there is no certain means of deciding if Teiresias is their superior. It reads better as a new beginning (see the paraphrase given above on 498ff.). The temptation to alter δ ἂν to τἂν (= τοι + ἂν) however ought, it seems, to be resisted, even though the remark is gnomic, in the light of Denniston's observation (*GP*² 538) that Sophocles does not use τοι in lyrics except when persons are addressed.

505 ὀρθόν: predicative. Before I see if their comments stand up when tested. μεμφομένων: one-word genitive absolute, 'when people criticize'. καταφαίην: 'assent'. The word otherwise not before Aristotle.

507 φανερά: the Sphinx was something you could see, unlike the ἄδηλοι θάνατοι of Laius (496) and the rest of Teiresias' accusations. The same idea continues in ὤφθη. ἐπ' αὐτῶι: the construction with the dative as at Aesch. *Agam.* 60–2 Ἀτρέως παῖδας ... ἐπ' Ἀλεξάνδρωι πέμπει ξένιος Ζεύς. Cf. *Phil.* 1138f., *Oed. Col.* 1472. Contrast ἐπ' αὐτόν (469) where the accusative better fits the physical speed of the assault.

πτερόεσσ' ... κόρα: the Sphinx is represented with great frequency in Greek art, in statues of all sizes, as every visitor to the major archaeological museums of Greece will testify. A female head, lion's body, and wings are customary attributes. See H. Demisch, *Die Sphinx: Geschichte ihrer Darstellung von den Anfängen bis zur Gegenwart* (Stuttgart 1977), esp. 98–100. Originally it was just another mythological monster; the connection with riddles is a later development.

510 βασάνωι: to be construed with σοφός even more than with ἡδύπολις, for the acid test in our minds, that of the Sphinx, was a test of intelligence, not of Oedipus' relations with the city. Cf. Mnasalces, *Anth. Pal.* 7.54 = Gow and Page, *HE* 2673–4 ἐν βασάνωι σοφίης. For this ἀπὸ κοινοῦ construction, as it is called, see G. Kiefner, *Die Versparung* (Wiesbaden 1964) 36. Many of his parallels are inexact, but *El.* 249f. looks appropriate: ἔρροι τ' ἂν αἰδὼς ἁπάντων τ' εὐσέβεια θνατῶν, where ἁπάντων θνατῶν has to be construed with αἰδώς as well as with εὐσέβεια. The βάσανος (cf. 494) that made Oedipus ἡδύπολις was of a different kind, and took place over a longer period: cf. [Simon.] 175 B. 1: οὐκ ἔστιν μείζων βάσανος χρόνου.

ἡδύπολις: see 82n. The formation of the adjective is unusual; but so is ὑψίπολις at *Ant.* 370. δικαιόπολις ... νᾶσος a 'just-citied island' at Pindar, *Pyth.* 8.22 is easier than the present compound, which means 'welcome *to* the city'.

τῶι: 'therefore'.

πρός: Elmsley's correction will do as well as anything else, since πρός + gen. meaning 'from' often puzzles scribes. Its usual replacement is παρά, which would also serve here. The ἀπ' of the manuscripts would give an impossible hiatus after τῶι. ἀπό is interpolated all too often. See the note on *El.* 433, *Studies* I 179, to which should be added Rupprecht's observation that –◡◡ in that position would be unique in Sophocles. See also the tables in Schein, *ITAS* (Leiden 1979) 82.

511 The Chorus choose their words well, φρήν being neither as purely rational as νοῦς nor as purely emotional as θυμός. As for κακία, one of its commonest meanings is 'cowardice'. In meeting the Sphinx Oedipus did not exhibit any want of courage, nor will he in the course of his investigations. But the κακία of which Teiresias has accused him is of a different kind.

513–696 Second epeisodion and first kommos

Since the last appearance of Creon, ending on a note of compliment (133) and comparative optimism (150), the tone of the play has darkened, as a result of Teiresias' hariolations. Creon now reappears, upset and indignant at what he has heard, and an angry scene follows, forming a political counterpart to the more religiously charged interchanges we have just been witnessing. It is Jocasta's well-intentioned intervention between the quarrelling parties that will make the crisis inescapable.

514 τύραννον: cf. 408n.

515 πάρειμ' ἀτλητῶν: ἀτλητῶν is unique: 'indignant'. πάρειμ' carries no stress whatever. Such verbs of arrival or being present often appear to us to be used almost superfluously; a marked example is *Phil.* 972 where ἔοικας ἥκειν carries no weight by comparison with μαθὼν ... αἰσχρά.

516 πρός τί μου: Hartung's conjecture is designed to give an object τι to πεπον-θέναι, to which the participle φέρον may attach itself. The word order may appear astonishing, and the sceptical may become more sceptical still on finding the only exact parallel to it is also the work of Hartung, ἔκ τι γᾶς, at *Phil.* 700, even though it was independently conjectured again for that passage by D. L. Page, *Proc. Camb. Phil. Soc.* n.s. 6 (1960) 52. The defence takes two forms: (1) That *if* Hartung is right, he solves in the two places together a number of technical problems with a tiny alteration to something which would certainly have puzzled scribes – and a vestige of the truth seems to remain in some manuscripts (see the *apparatus* and note the τ in the papyrus). (2) Comparably odd word order can be found in Sophocles at *Ai.* 155 κατὰ δ' ἄν τις ἐμοῦ, 906 ἐν γάρ οἱ χθονί, where οἱ is the dative of ἕ, 'to him'. Cf. Ar. *Wasps* 437 ἔν τί σοι παγήσεται, and Pindar, *Pyth.* 2.33 ἔν ποτε θαλάμοις (similarly *Nem.* 8.18, *Ol.* 1.17 (twice), 7.26. In none of these cases does the enclitic appear close to the beginning of the sentence; hence the strictures of T. C. W. Stinton, *J.H.S.* 97 (1977) 134 seem unmerited. (Later examples of ποτε between preposition and noun at Gow and Page, *HE* 2161, Page, *FGE* 2094.) Homer has a number of more extreme cases, e.g. *Od.* 6.167 οὔ πω τοῖον ἀνήλυθεν ἐκ δόρυ γαίης, 9.535 εὔροι δ' ἐν πήματα οἴκωι, 10.290 βαλέει δ' ἐν φάρμακα σίτωι, 11.115 δήεις δ' ἐν πήματα οἴκωι (like 9.535 just cited).

μου: πρὸς ἐμοῦ not πρός μου would be normal, but for enclitics after a preposition see Kühner–Blass 1 347. In any case of course here τι intervenes.

517 The first εἴτε, to be understood before λόγοισιν, is omitted by a well-established convention applicable also to οὔτε; cf. *Trach.* 236 ποῦ γῆς πατρώιας εἴτε βαρβάρου; λέγε, or Aesch. *Agam.* 532 Πάρις γὰρ οὔτε συντελὴς πόλις (neither Paris nor the contributory city).

εἰς βλάβην φέρον: cf. 991 ἐς φόβον φέρον: 'leading to' or 'tending to'.

522 πρός του καὶ φίλων: not 'by you and my friends', πρὸς σοῦ καὶ φίλων, as the manuscripts give it, but, as Kvičala saw, 'by one (or any) of my *friends*', i.e. as opposed to the more general ill-reputation to be expected ἐν πόλει.

523 ἀλλ ... μὲν δή: Denniston, *GP*² 394. The divided combination is peculiar to Sophocles, and the tone is here adversative. The μὲν δή (there is no responding δέ) perhaps sets the matter of the ὄνειδος on one side. 'Oh, but I expect it was just a momentary outburst ...'

525 τοὖπος δ᾽ ἐφάνθη: For nouns of sound with verbs of sight see 186n. There is less strain on the apparently incompatible ideas here than there: the unfortunate remark saw the light of day, cf. φανὲν τοὖπος at 848.

ταῖς ἐμαῖς γνώμαις: in this position for emphasis. It belongs in the ὅτι sentence. 'That it was by my prompting that ...'

526 ψευδεῖς: the order article, noun, adjective, shows that ψευδεῖς is predicative: 'falsified his account'.

527 γνώμηι τίνι: quite unrelated to ἐμαῖς γνώμαις, which in turn is unrelated to γνώμηι (524). For another series of non-thematic repetitions see the note on 399–405.

528 ἐξ: of accompanying conditions, to be rendered in English usually as 'with'; cf. *Phil.* 91 ἐξ ἑνὸς ποδός 'with only one foot'. If the eyes had not been ὀρθῶν but διαστρόφων (cf. *Ai.* 447, *Trach.* 794) Creon would assume that Oedipus was insane or under some great stress.

530 The Chorus do know, and did see. But they are the soul of discretion where their betters are concerned.

532 οὗτος σύ: a regular way of accosting some one abruptly. So at 1121 below, *Trach.* 402 οὗτος, βλέφ᾽ ὧδε, 'you there, look at me', *Ai.* 1047 οὗτος, σὲ φωνῶ, 'you there, yes, you I mean'.

533 πρόσωπον: the same idiom in English. 'Have you got the face to ...?'

534–5 ἐμφανῶς ... ἐναργής: it is not clarity, but certainty, that is meant. So in Eur. *Hel.* 21 εἰ σαφὴς οὗτος λόγος means 'if this story is true'; cf. *Herc.* 55 φίλων δὲ τοὺς μὲν οὐ σαφεῖς ὁρῶ φίλους (not true friends). See E. Mielert, *Ausdrücke für Wahrheit und Lüge in der alten Tragoedie* (Diss. München 1958). But in the sense of 'clear for all to see' the words φονεὺς ἐμφανής and ληιστὴς ἐναργής (cf. 122, 124) will fit the speaker himself with precision before the play is over. φονεύς may seem an extravagant charge. But see 669, and *Oed. Col.* 1361. At *Ai.* 1127 the idiom comes in for sarcastic criticism. From prose authors B. M. W. Knox, *Oedipus at Thebes* (London 1957) 228, n. 155 cites Dem. 21.106; Antiphon 4β7, 4γ1, 5.59. Add Hdt. 1. 124.1.

539 Spengel's ἢ οὐκ for κοὐκ gives more incisive logic, explaining separately the alternatives posed in δειλίαν ἢ μωρίαν, but κοὐκ makes sense if μαθών is conditional:

'that I would not notice your treachery, and would not defend myself against it if I did'.

540 μῶρον: the intellectually superior Oedipus had used the same word of abuse earlier against Teiresias (433).

541 πλούτου: πλήθους in the MSS comes by error from πλήθει immediately below. We need a word denoting another political asset besides φίλων. In what follows πλήθει refers to φίλων, so presumably χρήμασιν picks up the word now corrupted into πλήθους. The anonymous conjecture πλούτου has never been improved on. Oedipus' reflections on the acquisition of tyranny will have struck a responsive note in the audience of Athenian democrats. He acquired tyranny himself however by an entirely different route. The trio of πλοῦτος, τυραννίς, πλῆθος again at Eur. *Or.* 1156–7.

542 ὅ: 'a thing which'.

543 οἶσθ' ὡς πόησον: cf. Eur. *Hec.* 225 οἶσθ' οὖν ὃ δρᾶσον. 'You know what you should do.' This strange construction occurs more often in comedy. Easier are examples with the future indicative (which indeed most MSS have at *Hec.* 225), as Eur. *Med.* 600, where see Page's note, and *Cyc.* 131 οἶσθ' οὖν ὃ δράσεις; In both places R. Renehan, *Greek textual criticism* (Cambridge, Mass. 1969) 4–5 believes the future should be replaced by the imperative.

545–6 μανθάνειν δ' ἐγὼ κακὸς | σοῦ: the epexegetic infinitive with κακός, found also at Hdt. 6.108.3 and Thuc. 6.38.2, is all the easier to understand since δεινὸς λέγειν, which has an identical construction, is a familiar phrase. 'Bad at taking instruction from you.'

The position of σοῦ at the beginning of the line, with a pause following it, may give special emphasis, 'from *you*' (sc. though not from others). But we have already noticed (30n.) how closely Sophocles links his lines, and as Denniston says on this specific point of word end after the first syllable in the line (*C.Q.* 30 (1936) 74), 'The word carried over is sometimes of very slight importance.' If σοῦ were emphatic one might perhaps expect the following σ' to be placed earlier in its sentence: cf. 358 πρὸς σοῦ· σὺ γὰρ κ.τ.ἑ.

546 βαρύν: similarly 673, Eur. *Med.* 809, *El.* 1119.

547 τοῦτ' αὐτό: this is the very point (whether or not I am δυσμενής and βαρύς to you) on which you should hear what I have to say. Creon's turn of phrase is mockingly taken up by Oedipus. Something similar, though the text is insecure at the vital point, evidently took place at *Ai.* 1140–1. Further sarcastic repetition follows with εἴ τοι νομίζεις 549, 551, and οὐκ ὀρθῶς | εὖ φρονεῖς 550, 552. Such style of disputation is in our societies characteristic rather of children than adults. But what follows gives us a first taste of Oedipus as an expert in cross-examination. For the implications of the questions put see Introduction 10.

556 τινα: τινας was conjectured by the vigilant Elmsley, since at 288–9 Oedipus expressly said he sent two messengers. It is unlikely that the content of Creon's advice would have been to send a multiplicity of messengers to discharge such a simple function, whatever Oedipus actually did in the event.

557 Creon says that he sticks by his earlier advice. His turn of phrase almost suggests that he does not know that his advice has been followed. But if he knows of Oedipus' accusations against him, as he does (513), he must assume they result from Teiresias' 'lies' (526), which he also knows about. But his knowledge of the exact details of what was said at the Teiresias–Oedipus interview is sketchy (574).

αὐτός 'consistent' (in my advice). Cf. Eur. *Phoen.* 920 ἀνὴρ ὅδ᾽ οὐκέθ᾽ αὐτός· ἐκνεύει πάλιν. Slightly different is *Phil.* 521 αὐτὸς τοῖς λόγοις τούτοις, where αὐτός governs the dative. Compare Thuc. 2.61, 3.38; Plato, *Apol.* 33a; and, if we range further afield, the uses of τοιοῦτος of mental attitude at Aesch. *Agam.* 1360, Eur. *Hcld.* 266, *Or.* 1680.

559 Not the most brilliant line in this scene. Laius' *doing* of anything has no relevance. Creon, fresh from his consultation of oracles, must know this, and his wilful misunderstanding achieves nothing. In his οὐ γὰρ ἐννοῶ he speaks with the evasiveness of a subordinate (like the Chorus at 530), and at 569 he retreats even further.

560 χειρώματι: connected with χειρόω, χείρων, and not with χείρ. Laius was 'worsted' in a fatal encounter. So at *Oed. Col.* 698 ἀχείρωτον means 'inviolate' and at *Ant.* 126 δυσχείρωμα means something hard to overcome. See further Fraenkel on Aesch. *Agam.* 1326, and Hutchinson on *Sept.* 1022.

561 You would have to go a long way back (μακροί) and your calculations would arrive at a time far in the past (παλαιοί).

562 οὖν: 'then', i.e. in that case my next question is …

οὖτος: contemptuous. It is the word regularly used by prosecutors in the orators. cf. 568 οὖτος ὁ σοφός, and 672, of Creon in disgrace.

ἐν τῆι τέχνηι 'in the business'. The phrase does not sound over-respectful.

565 οὔκουν … γ': Denniston, *GP*[2] 423. 'Certainly not at any time that *I* was around.'

566 See 126n.

567 τί δ᾽ οὐκ ἠκούσαμεν: the MSS have been defeated by this simple 'What *didn't* we hear?', a way of saying 'We heard all sorts.' We know that rumour was rife: cf. 290, 292, 731. The Chorus' reply to Oedipus' question prompts his next one: if everyone was busy talking about it, how come this clever prophet had nothing to say on the subject? The line as emended has the same rhythm as 110.

568 οὖν: as at 562.

570 γ': 'this much at any rate you do know'.

εὖ φρονῶν: the language of menace: 'if you've got any sense'.

571 ἀρνήσομαι: Creon is very defensive. He has been asked questions of fact so far, and nothing has yet been put to him that he need 'deny', though Sophocles of course knows that Creon's own involvement will be the subject of Oedipus' next question. If we read τὸ σὸν δέ γ᾽ in 570 ('yes, but you know about your own rôle in this affair') Creon will have better reason to use ἀρνήσομαι, and it is certainly true that one expects τὸ σὸν δέ to be corrupted into τοσόνδε rather than the reverse. But Jebb is correct to say that 'the coarse and blunt τὸ σόν would destroy the edge of the sarcasm'.

572 ὀθούνεκ᾽ = ὅτι. οὕνεκα can also be so used.

572–3 τὰς ἐμὰς ... διαφθοράς: he would never have spoken of 'my assassination of Laius'. The article gives the nuance 'this assassination of mine'. An actor delivering these lines would be able to avoid the obvious pitfall of apparently having Oedipus blandly admit he had killed Laius, while the audience, with their superior knowledge, would find the choice of words strangely ominous.

575 ἅπερ: always the favourite choice of relative pronoun where there is some stress on identity: 'precisely the same things which ...' would be an over-translation of the underlying thought.

576 οὐ γὰρ δή ... γ᾽: ruling out an unlikely alternative: cf. *El.* 1020, *Phil.* 246, *Oed. Col.* 110, 265; Eur. *Ion* 954, *Tro.* 210. Whatever else Oedipus may have to divulge under Creon's questioning, he will never be found a murderer, of all things, as he had accused Creon of being at 534 (and as in reality he is).

577 γήμας ἔχεις: the periphrastic perfect, in form like the English perfect, 'you have married', perhaps used here instead of the ordinary perfect to give the sense 'you married her, and you have her now as your own'. The periphrastic perfect is used in Greek mainly by Sophocles (28 times), Euripides (24 times) and Herodotus. Aeschylus has only one example. It belongs primarily to the time before the development of the resultative perfect. All the Sophoclean examples are examined by J. Pouilloux in *Mélanges Merlier* III (Athens 1957) 117–35. His attempt to show that in every case Sophocles wishes to draw our attention to something abnormal is much over-done; e.g. here 'le γήμας ἔχεις retentit comme un avertissement du destin aux hommes qui ne savent pas deviner la vérité du monde'. Much better treatment is given by W. J. Aerts, *Periphrastica* (Amsterdam 1965), Part Two, 128ff.

579 A much emended line. γῆς could belong either to ἄρχεις or to ἴσον: either 'Do you govern the land on the same terms as her, giving her an equal share?' or 'Do you govern on the same terms as her, giving her an equal share in the land?' The second interpretation seems too geographic. (Note that κομίζεται in the reply 580 makes it less likely that νέμω is here being used in the rare sense 'rule', as opposed to 'apportion', given to it by Pindar, *Pyth.* 3.70, an otherwise attractive idea: 'Do you govern the land on the same terms as her, ruling equally?') In either case Oedipus' answer, 'Anything she wants she gets from me' presupposes a question more like 'Does she rule alongside you?' rather than 'Do you rule alongside her?' Probably the text is sound, though blurred *more Sophocleo.*

580 ἦι θέλουσα: see Aerts, loc. cit. (577n.).

581 σφῶιν: dative of the dual: 'you two'. See LSJ *s.v.* σύ 11.

582 ἐνταῦθα γὰρ δὴ καί: 'and it is precisely in that respect ...'

583 'No, not that is if you ...' Creon has evidently already given some thought to the advantages of ranking no. 3 in the state hierarchy. A similar γ in 586, 'if, that is, he is going to have the same power'.

586 ἄτρεστον εὕδοντ': contrast Oedipus' words about himself at 65.

587 μὲν οὖν: as at 484, 498, the οὖν emphasizing the forward-looking μέν. 'Certainly *I* have never been one to desire ...' The periphrasis with ἔφυν is used because Creon wishes to stress that the whole idea of becoming τύραννος is alien to his nature. Similarly ἐραστής ... ἔφυν (601).

590 φθόνου: Creon can avoid the φθόνος from others that normally accompanies the tyrant: cf. Oedipus' complaints at 382 and 624. Equally he receives from Oedipus everything ungrudgingly (καίτοι ἄνδρα γε τύραννον ἄφθονον ἔδει εἶναι, ἔχοντά γε πάντα τὰ ἀγαθά Hdt. 3.80.4). φθόνου is therefore the ideal word for two different reasons. The former sense predominates, and the next sentence develops the idea: if I were a tyrant I would be having to do a lot of things I did not like doing, i.e. for fear that otherwise my actions might provoke φθόνος, or in the knowledge that they inescapably must provoke φθόνος. φθόνου is Blaydes's correction of φόβου, itself translatable but flabby. The corruption is frequent, and φόβοισι in 585 gives it ideal conditions to germinate in. The essentially second-rate nature of Creon becomes more and more clear with each facile argument that he advances in self-exculpation. (We are prepared to be more indulgent towards Hippolytus in Eur. *Hipp.* 1017–20, a remarkably similar passage.)

594 οὔπω: see 105n. So at *El.* 403 μή πω νοῦ τοσόνδ᾽ εἴην κενή means not 'may I not yet be so vacant-minded' but 'may I never under any circumstances ...'.

596 πᾶσι χαίρω: whereas important people have to be careful in their choice of friends. In the same passage of Hdt. quoted above (590n.) it is said of the archetypal tyrant: φθονέει γὰρ τοῖσι ἀρίστοισι περιεοῦσί τε καὶ ζώουσι, χαίρει δὲ τοῖσι κακίστοισι τῶν ἀστῶν ...

597 ἐκκαλοῦσ᾽ ἐμέ: they ask Creon to step outside for a quiet word. This is just the sort of thing Creons revel in (cf. Eur. *Bacch.* 319–20); people cast in the mould of Oedipus are different. Sophocles has already illustrated this in action at 91–4.

598 Their chance of getting what they want resides wholly in such a course.

600 Three translations are theoretically possible; in descending order of probability they are: (1) No mind that is sensible can become evil. (2) No evil mind can be thinking well. (3) An evil mind that is sensible cannot exist. None of these edifying remarks immediately impresses as relevant to the context, and Wolff excised the line. In 601 τῆσδε τῆς γνώμης and in 602 μετ᾽ ἄλλου δρῶντος clearly refer specifically to a treasonable plan which has not been mentioned in our texts (κεῖν᾽ will hardly do duty for it). It follows then that the interpolation of 600 has displaced the true text. 600 may have begun life in the margin as an illustration of 614–15.

603–5 τοῦτο μὲν ... τοῦτ᾽ ἄλλ: similarly Sophocles avoids the dully obvious τοῦτο δέ at *Ai.* 670–2, *Ant.* 165–7, *Phil.* 1345–6, *Oed. Col.* 440–1.

603 ἔλεγχον: as proof of this. The accusative stands in apposition to the rest of the sentence. Cf. Eur. *Herc.* 57–9 δυσπραξία | ἧς μήποθ᾽ ὅστις καὶ μέσως εὔνους ἐμοί (who is even moderately well-disposed towards me) | τύχοι, φίλων ἔλεγχον ἀψευδέστατον. The text-book example is Eur. *Or.* 1105 Ἑλένην κτάνωμεν, Μενελέωι λύπην πικράν. 'Let us kill Helen – a bitter sorrow for Menelaus.' As Barrett points out in his note on Eur. *Hipp.* 752–7, the construction can often be much more subtly interwoven with the rest of the sentence.

603–4 Πυθώδ᾽ ... πεύθου: see 70–1 n.

604 σαφῶς 'truly'. See 534–5n.

608 γνώμηι δ᾽ ἀδήλωι: an 'unclear judgement' is a judgement made on the basis of facts not clearly established. Cf. ἀφανεῖ λόγωι (657) and δόκησις ἀγνὼς λόγων (681). *Trach.* 669–70 is fuller, προθυμίαν | ἄδηλον ἔργου.

χωρίς: separately, by yourself, in isolation from the facts.

609 μάτην: not 'in vain' but with a sense like that in μάταιος λόγος, 'without evidence', or 'falsely'. See 874, 1057nn.

610 Creon avails himself of polar expression: τοὺς κακοὺς χρηστοὺς νομίζειν is there only to set in relief the point he is making, that one should not condemn friends without adequate reason; because, he continues, the loss of a true friend is like losing one's life, the dearest thing one has. One or two critics have wished to dispense with these lines, but Sophocles seems to have associated sententiousness especially with Creon. At *Ant.* 661 ff. Creon's immense stream of γνῶμαι, badly related to each other, have been impugned by Dawe, *Studies* III 108–9, but doubtless a nucleus of them is authentic.

611–12 ἴσον ... καί: the same as. Similarly ἴσα καί at 1187.

612 παρ᾽ αὐτῶι: the life of a man can be regarded as in some way separate from himself. See 1082n., and for the use of παρά in such an expression compare Pindar, *Pyth.* 3.86–8 αἰὼν δ᾽ ἀσφαλής | οὐκ ἔγεντ᾽ οὔτ᾽ Αἰακίδαι παρὰ Πηλεῖ | οὔτε παρ᾽ ἀντιθέωι Κάδμωι.

613–15   Creon's epigram, though not so intended by Sophocles, is one among many useful points of departure for looking at the events of *Oed. Tyr.* as a whole: e.g. compare and contrast 1213–14.

616   εὐλαβουμένωι: in the judgement of any one wary of making a slip (as you should be, Oedipus). The dative is similar to the one at *Ant.* 904 καίτοι σ' ἐγώ 'τίμησα, τοῖς φρονοῦσιν, εὖ 'well, in the judgement of sensible people'. Further exemplified in K–G I 421.

618   ταχύς τις: predicative. For this use of τις with adjectives see K–G I 663. The nuance it imparts varies from context to context, but seems often to imply disparagement or contempt. Cf. [Aesch.] *Prom. Vinct.* 696 καὶ φόβου πλέα τις εἶ; Soph. *Ai.* 1226 ὡς ταχεῖά τις βροτοῖς | χάρις διαρρεῖ; Eur. *Hipp.* 424 ἄνδρα, κἂν θρασύσπλαγχνός τις ἦι.

619   ταχὺν δεῖ κἄμε: Speed is characteristic of Oedipus: cf. 142, 765, 1154, and the claim of 220–1; and after the catastrophe 1340, 1410, 1436.

622   On the choice of death or exile, cf. 100, 308, 640f., 659, 669f., and Introduction 11. At Eur. *Phoen.* 1621 (a line deleted by Kirchhoff) the poet seems to have attempted to reconcile the two: ἀποκτενεῖς γάρ, εἴ με γῆς ἔξω βαλεῖς (Oedipus speaking to Creon). In Attic law any one accused of deliberate homicide could go into exile before termination of his trial. If he stayed, and was found guilty, he could expect the death penalty.

623   The gap after this line may have been more extensive than a single row of dots indicates, for 625 is the kind of line delivered when a whole repertoire of possible arguments has been deployed in vain, a recognition of failure, as at *Ant.* 757, *El.* 1048.

624   Whatever stood in the gap between 623 and 624 an answer beginning 'yes, when ...' looks more promising than one beginning simply 'when ...'. Meineke's προδείξηις <γ'> would give that meaning.

628   ἀρκτέον: passive: one must be ruled, i.e. obey. So at 1516 πειστέον is from πείθομαι, obey, not πείθω, persuade.

629   γ': limiting a condition: not in a case where ...

ἄρχοντος: genitive by analogy with the use of πείθομαι + gen. recorded by LSJ *s.v* πείθω B I 3.

ὦ πόλις, πόλις: at *Oed. Col.* 833 ἰὼ πόλις again bursts from Oedipus' lips. Less expectedly ὦ πόλις, πόλις πατρία (or ὦ πόλις ὦ πατρία) is the cry of the marooned Philoctetes as he looks forward to death (*Phil.* 1213) on his lonely island. Ar. *Ach.* 27 parodies the expression; so does Eupolis, frg. 219. It is not necessary to assume they had the present passage in mind: see on 1515–30.

630   Creon takes Oedipus' exclamation as an expression of the 'l'état, c'est moi' philosophy, but, as the examples cited on 629 show, this is a partial view. In *Ant.* 734ff.

Creon's understanding of the relative rôles of ruler and city is much more autocratic than anything we have heard from Oedipus in this play, and the priest and the Chorus evidently regard Oedipus as a democratic ruler. 63–4 have shown the king's deeply felt solicitude for his city.

631 καιρίαν: cf. *Ai.* 34, 1168. Sophocles does not hesitate to make a virtue out of dramatic necessity.

633 εὖ θέσθαι: 'put right'. This phrase and καλῶς τιθέναι are about as common as each other: καλῶς θέσθαι only Soph. frg. 350 and Eur. *Hipp.* 709, *Or.* 512 in tragedy.

634 ὦ ταλαίπωροι: not 'unhappy' but a word of scolding, giving an effect something like 'Dear me, what is all this noise?' The uses of τάλας at *Ant.* 228 (and τλήμων in 229), *El.* 902, *Oed. Col.* 318 are worth study. New Comedy uses the idiom more extensively, cf. Men. *Epitr.* 434, and the clutch of examples at *Samia* 245, 252, 255 (δύσμορ'), 260. Here at *Oed. Tyr.* 634 the only difference is that Jocasta is apostrophizing others, not herself.

637 οὐκ εἶ: for οὐ with the future indicative phrased as a question, but equivalent to a command, cf. 676, 945–6, 1154.

κατὰ στέγας: the phrase is used of position, 'in the house', at *El.* 282, 1308 (where, as here, there is a pairing with οἶκοι), *Oed. Col.* 339, and 14 times in Eur. κατά with an accusative of motion, 'to', the meaning we require here, is otherwise found in tragedy only at Eur. *Phoen.* 1088. Also noteworthy is the evidence of possible textual disturbance; κατά is omitted by two manuscripts, and deleted by a third, which also originally had Κρέον or Κρέων wrongly placed after στέγας. κατά may be an interpolation, just as ἐς or εἰς is interpolated by all but one close-knit group of manuscripts before οἴκους. On the other hand it could be plausibly argued that those manuscripts which omit κατά do so to accommodate the presence of εἰς, giving the line οὐκ εἶ σύ τ' εἰς οἴκους, σύ τε, Κρέον, στέγας, with no normal caesura (permissible) and with τε lengthened before a mute and liquid in another word (not permissible).

638 Either to be construed as τὸ μηδὲν εἰς μέγ' ἄλγος or as τὸ μηδὲν ἄλγος εἰς μέγα τι. μηδέν used adjectivally between article and noun is said not to occur, and the στάσις is perhaps not an ἄλγος to the participants yet (in Jocasta's opinion) but in danger of becoming one. So the first interpretation is to be preferred.

639 ὅμαιμε and ὁ σὸς πόσις bring out Creon's latent thought, that his avenue to persuading Oedipus to relent lies now through family ties since reasoned appeals have failed.

640 A metrically unusual line, for δυοῖν must be uniquely scanned as a monosyllable. The metrical lengthening of ο in ἀποκρίνας is permissible, coming as it does before a mute and liquid in the *same* word (contrast what was said about τε Κρέον at the end of 637 n.), but such lengthenings of ἀπο- and ἐπι- are rare. The sense required, 'selecting for me one of two evils', is not easily arrived at in the absence of θάτερον or ἕν from the Greek. For the discrepancy between 640 and 623 see Introduction 11; 640 agrees with what at 100, 309, we were told was necessary. Dindorf eliminated all difficulties by writing δρᾶσαι δικαιοῖ, θάτερον δυοῖν κακοῖν, assuming ἀποκρίνας to be a gloss. Such a solution is clean and effective, but desperately bold.

642 δρῶντα: conative: trying to do.

643 τοὐμὸν σῶμα: possibly Creon's suspicions that Oedipus has a 'l'état, c'est moi' fixation (see on 630) receive a vestige of support here from the king's own lips. Treason against the royal person is meant.

τέχνηι κακῆι: see LSJ *s.v.* κακοτεχνία, 'malicious conspiracy… esp. subornation of perjury'.

644 νῦν: cf. 106n.
ἀραῖος: 'under my own curse'.

648 ἔπειτα: without δέ; similarly after πρῶτον μέν: Denniston, *GP*² 377.

649–96 We now desert the continuous iambic metre for something more excited. Iambic trimeters still occur, but cretics (–◡–) appear in their company, and more particularly pairs (dimeters) of dochmiacs. A dochmiac (◡̆ ◡̆◡̆ ◡̆◡̆ ◡̆ ◡̆◡̆) can appear in many guises. Thus 662 takes the form ◡ – – ◡ – ◡ – – ◡ – but 661 for all its different appearance is also a dochmiac dimeter:–◡̯◡̯ ◡̯◡̯ ◡ ◡̯◡̯ ◡ ◡̯◡̯◡̯ ◡ ◡̯◡̯.

649 The parallel aorist participles and imperative imply that a single change of decision is sought, rather than a change of attitude. Correspondingly Oedipus' reply is specific too: what concession then do you want me to make? Contrast the presents συγχώρει θέλων at *Phil.* 1343, where an entire change of attitude is sought. An aorist imperative can *only* be specific: a present *either* specific (e.g. φράζε 655) *or* general.

651 θέλεις … εἰκάθω; cf. *El.* 80–1 θέλεις μείνωμεν αὐτοῦ …; *Phil.* 761 βούλει λάβωμαι δῆτα …;

652 νήπιον: the choice of word may surprise, and indeed has confounded LSJ *s.v.* ('no child before and now full-grown (i.e. in mind)'); but cf. *El.* 145–6 νήπιος ὃς τῶν οἰκτρῶς | οἰχομένων γονέων ἐπιλάθεται where there is a strong moral tone, as there was already in Homer, *Od.* 22.370 σὲ δὲ νήπιοι οὐδὲν ἔτιον. At Pindar, *Pyth.* 3.83 νήπιοι are contrasted with ἀγαθοί; examine too the nuance at Eur. *Med.* 891. Like Electra, Creon is intelligent, and knows where his duty lies. He is now a more considerable figure (μέγαν) because of the oath he has taken (ἀραῖος 644 ∼ ἐν ὅρκωι here).

655 φράζε sometimes means no more than 'say', at other times 'explain' or 'make clear'; cf. *Phil.* 559 φράσον δ' ἅ γ' ἔργ' ἔλεξας. Oedipus wants the Chorus to spell out their request.

656–7 A prose sequence might be: <I tell> σε μήποτε σὺν ἀφανεῖ λόγωι ἐν αἰτίαι ἄτιμον βαλεῖν τὸν ἐναγῆ φίλον. 'Never, with words whose truth remains uncertain, to place under an accusation in dishonour the friend who has taken a holy oath.'

τὸν ἐναγῆ φίλον: object of ἐν αἰτίαι βαλεῖν. The friend who is ἐν ὅρκωι μέγαν.

ἐν αἰτίαι … βαλεῖν: cf. *Trach.* 940 ὡς νιν ματαίως αἰτίαι βάλοι κακῆι, where Pearson conjectured 'μβάλοι to bring the normal ἐν into the sentence. A standard phrase in prose too.

σὺν ἀφανεῖ λόγωι: cf. 608n. on γνώμηι ἀδήλωι. An ἀφανὴς λόγος is a story or version of events in which the facts are not clear. Cf. Antiphon *On the murder of Herodes* 5.59 σὺ δ' ἐμὲ ἐν ἀφανεῖ λόγωι ζητεῖς ἀπολέσαι. The rôle of σύν may not be quite what we expect it to be; one expects 'on the basis of an unproved story', giving the *cause* why Oedipus might hold Creon guilty. But the evidence for σύν given in K–G I 467, rather supports the idea that the ἀφανὴς λόγος is the unproven charge or version of events *given by Oedipus* as he condemns Creon.

σ': the position of σ' (added by Hermann) so late in the sentence in this sandwich position is not entirely convincing. The scholia do not include σ' in their paraphrase. Blaydes conjectured γ', which would underline the enormity of doing anything σὺν ἀφανεῖ λόγωι.

ἄτιμον: predicative, 'in dishonour'. The word is used too of disenfranchised citizens. Note also the use at 789.

658 νῦν: cf. 644n.: and again below at 707, 975.

659 ὄλεθρον ἢ φυγήν: see Introduction 11.

660 οὐ τὸν πάντων: the accusative of that by which the oath is sworn need not be accompanied by μά, although at times some at least of our manuscripts have μά interpolated into their texts; cf. 1088 οὐ τὸν Ὄλυμπον, *Ant.* 758 οὐ τόνδ' Ὄλυμπον, *El.* 1063 ἀλλ' οὐ τὰν Διὸς ἀστραπάν, 1239 οὐ τὰν Ἄρτεμιν.

661 ὅ τι πύματον: a powerful disclaimer: 'May I perish by the most extreme possible fate, abandoned by the gods and my friends, if I entertain the thought you speak of.'

665 The last explicit mention of the plague in this play. But see 685n.; Introduction 8.

666 †ψυχάν καί†: the responding line is 695, which scans as ∪ − − −∪− ∪−∪ −, i.e. bacchiac + cretic + iambic. If 695 is sound, it follows that we have two long syllables too many in 666. Eliminating καί, with Hermann, is desirable for reasons given below in the note on τὰ δ'; but this still leaves us with one unwanted long syllable. ψυχάν is also suspicious for another reason. An iambic metron very seldom follows a bacchiac in lyrics, and when it does, its first syllable is always short: e.g. Aesch. *Agam.* 224f. ἔτλα δ' οὖν θυτὴρ γενέσθαι θυγατρός. See T. C. W. Stinton, *B.I.C.S.* 22 (1975) 88–95 (who, as it happens does not accept *Agam.* 224 as a valid example, preferring a different colometry). *Ant.* 869f. ἰὼ δυσπότμων κασίγνητε observes the rule; the responding verse, 850, appears to begin ἰὼ δύστανος, but the severe corruption which follows may well embrace δύστανος also. We know that ψυχάν can be a gloss word (cf. *El.* 331): V interpolates it at 891 after ματάιζων. It intrudes also at Eur. *Suppl.* 1030. But to find a one-syllable synonym for it is all but impossible. κέαρ (Arndt) has been suggested with the palaeographically simple addition of αὖ after ἀλύουσαν in the responding v. 695. The metre will then run ∪–– | ∪ –∪ – | ∪–∪ –, i.e. bacchiac + two iambics. In order to confine alteration to the one indisputably corrupt line, Page prefers to accept κέαρ in the form κῆρ; a form otherwise unknown to tragedy, but one which Page may be right to introduce by conjecture at Aesch. *Cho.* 410. In that place however, but not here, κῆρ can be defended as a reminiscence of the Homeric φίλον κῆρ.

τὰ δ᾽: τρύχει has two subjects: γᾶ φθίνουσα is one, and τὰ δ᾽ εἰ 'and on the other hand if . . .' is an elegant variation for the noun subject expected as the second. τὰ δ᾽ is Kennedy's redivision of τάδ᾽. The manuscripts' καὶ τάδ᾽ εἰ 'if these too' or 'and if these' gives a less satisfactory second limb to the sentence. For τὰ δ᾽ 'on the other hand' cf. *El.* 219, 1071.

667 προσάψει: 'going to join': no certain parallel for this intransitive use exists.

669 ὁ δ᾽ οὖν ἴτω: Well, let him go. Cf. *Ai.* 961 οἱ δ᾽ οὖν γελώντων, *Trach.* 329 ἡ δ᾽ οὖν ἐάσθω, [Aesch.] *Prom. Vinct.* 935 ὁ δ᾽ οὖν ποείτω, Eur. *Herc.* 726 σὺ δ᾽ οὖν ἴθ, Ar. *Ach.* 186 οἱ δ᾽ οὖν βοώντων, *Lys.* 491 οἱ δ᾽ οὖν δρώντων.

669 παντελῶς: 'utterly'. Rhetoric overpowers logic, as Oedipus matches the extravagance of the Chorus' language (661).

672 στυγήσεται: middle futures are also passive. In fact future passives in -θήσομαι are unknown to Homer, and rare in Herodotus. They are an almost exclusively Attic development, and middle forms in passive use continue even in the fourth century. With στυγέω the -θήσομαι form seems not to exist at all.

673 βαρύς: cf. 546n.

674 θυμοῦ περάσῃς: the underlying rhetoric is 'You are every bit as unpleasant when giving way as you are odious when you go beyond all limits in your anger.' The stress is on the first half of the sentence, in spite of the paratactic form. The nature of the genitive θυμοῦ is not immediately recognizable. Presumably it takes advantage of the idea of motion in περάω, and is to be compared with such genitives as those listed in K–G I 384ff., related to locatives; cf. *Oed. Col.* 689 πεδίων ἐπινίσεται, itself modelled on a Homeric prototype. Oedipus' anger is a sort of field he has to traverse. When it (as we would say, changing the subject from Oedipus to the anger itself) has run its full course, he begins to εἴκειν. περᾶις γάρ, περᾶις appears in *Oed. Col.* 155–6 with no qualifying phrase to mean, in the metaphorical sense, 'you are going too far'.

674–5 The dangers of anger and inflexibility are the subject of a homily by Haemon at *Ant.* 710ff. Sophoclean characters are often fully aware that such charges may be brought against them, but they persist in their attitudes, true to their principles while those around them urge the merits of moderation and compromise. If Oedipus were not true to his principles, we would have no play. At the same time it has to be conceded to Creon that Oedipus' words at 669–72, even if consonant with ordinary Greek morality, are neither gracious nor admirable.

677 ἴσος: 'fair', 'just', as at *Phil.* 685. The usage is rare enough to cause the ancient scholia to interpret ἴσος (wrongly) as 'the same as I was before', which would agree with the point made by Creon at 613–15. ἴσως occurs in a number of manuscripts, and might seem to support Blaydes's conjecture ἴσων. 'I have found you incapable of discerning the truth, but in the judgement of these men here I have received a fair verdict' (sc. and they believe I am right). We would not then feel the absence of a participle like ὤν with ἴσος, which 'though not indispensable, is very desirable' – to borrow Jebb's comment on *Phil.* 685. But an unaltered ἴσως (= 'perhaps') may suggest an alternative possibility, the omission of a line, giving some such sense as 'But among these people I shall perhaps meet with a more discerning verdict (as opposed to your ἀγνώς one).'

680 γ': assentient. 'I will, when you have told me . . .'

ἥτις ἡ τύχη: = ὅτι ἔτυχεν. This use of τύχη is much rarer than might be supposed. But cf. *Trach.* 724 τὴν δ' ἐλπίδ' οὐ χρὴ τῆς τύχης κρίνειν πάρος (before the event).

681 ἀγνώς: the Chorus' choice of word supports Creon's assessment at 677, but here ἀγνώς has a word to govern, λόγων. 'An expression of opinion that has not scrutinized the evidence.' At *Trach.* 426 the limitations of δόκησιν εἰπεῖν are spelled out by the poet; cf. 656–7n.

685 προπονουμένας: the Chorus make the same point as at 665–6. The land is already in difficulties; let us not add to them by a royal dispute. προνοουμένωι and προπονουμένωι are easier but incorrect variants: it is not the function of the *Chorus* to exhibit πρόνοια or to labour on behalf of the land, and it seems impossible to separate the dative participle from ἐμοί in such a way as to give the meaning 'for one who is planning, or working, on behalf of the land'.

686 αὐτοῦ: corresponding with ἔνθ', 'where it (sc. the λόγος (684)) is'.

688 παριείς: slackening, attempting to release the tension. The word would not be easily intelligible if καταμβλύνων did not follow, and so some commentators prefer to dissociate τοὐμόν from κέαρ, and take τοὐμὸν παριείς to mean 'neglecting my interests'. But see 117n.

690 παραφρόνιμον: 'out of my mind'.

ἄπορον ἐπὶ φρόνιμα: lit. 'with no resource in the direction of what is sensible' i.e. incapable of prudent thought.

691 εἴ σε νοσφίζομαι: Sophocles 'ought' to have written what Hermann wrote, εἴ σ' ἐνοσφιζόμαν, but he breaks the normal sequence of tenses to stress the enormity of the idea. If πεφάνθαι μ' ἄν stands for not πεφασμένος ἂν ἦν (I would have appeared) but πεφασμένος ἂν εἴην (I would be shown up as) the irregularity would be considerably diminished.

695   ὅς γ᾽: causal, as at 35, 'seeing that you … '.

ἀλύουσαν: Dobree's σαλεύουσαν is attractive: cf. 22–3 πόλις … σαλεύει, and it fits well with the imagery of οὔρισας and εὔπομπος. But ἀλύουσαν is entirely compatible with Sophoclean usage at *Phil.* 174, 1194. At the first of those two places the scholia use the gloss ἀπορεῖ; the same idea, of being frantic through helplessness (ἄπορον 690) is in the poet's mind here; and at *Phil.* 1194 Sophocles does not feel obliged (though Earle did) to write σαλεύοντα for ἀλύοντα on the grounds that ἀλύοντα does not sustain the metaphor inherent in the adjacent words χειμερίωι λύπαι.

For the possibility that one or two syllables are missing in this line, see 666n.

696   †δύναιο γενοῦ†: where these words stand we require a bacchiac ⏑–⏒. Bergk's εὔπομπος εἰ γένοιο 'may you send a favourable wind' is a possible solution, but εὔπομπος ἂν γένοιο (Blaydes) more easily accounts for the manuscript reading. The scribes will have explained the potential optative as equivalent to an imperative (γενοῦ) softened by the idea 'if you can'.

697–862 Third epeisodion

Jocasta relates to Oedipus circumstances surrounding the death of Laius, and Oedipus in turn tells her of a disturbingly similar episode in which he once killed a stranger on the road. See Introduction 11–14.

698–9   ὅτου … πράγματος: words of anger keep company with genitives: e.g. ὅπλων χολωθείς 'angry over the armour' Pindar *Nem.* 7.25 or μηνίσας φόνου at *Ant.* 1177.

699   στήσας ἔχεις: periphrastic perfect: see 577n. Aerts (*loc. cit.* 577n.) notes that there is no perfect active transitive of ἵστημι until Hypereides and [Plato], *Axiochus*, when καθ- and περι-έστακα emerge. The verb ἵστημι may seem strange in combination with μῆνιν. But cf. Eur. *Held.* 656 τί γὰρ βοὴν ἔστησας, ἄγγελον φόβου (cf. 128), *Ion* 988 (μάχην) ἣν Φλέγραι Γίγαντες ἔστησαν θεοῖς. These are extensions of such Homeric phrases as ἔριν στήσαντες ἐν ὑμῖν (*Od.* 16.292) or ἵστατο νεῖκος (*Il.* 13.333).

700   Oedipus has not reacted favourably to the Chorus' sitting on the fence, and he now pointedly slights them, as he had previously (671) slighted Creon (on that occasion favouring the Chorus) by emphasizing how much more weight he attaches to the wishes of his wife, the same woman who in the end will be unable to deflect him from the awful intensity of his purpose in uncovering the truth.

701   Κρέοντος: for the genitive cf. *Trach.* 1122f. τῆς μητρὸς ἥκω τῆς ἐμῆς φράσων ἐν οἷς | νῦν ἐστίν, *El.* 317 καὶ δή σ᾽ ἐρωτῶ τοῦ κασιγνήτου τί φῃς, *Phil.* 439 ἀναξίου μὲν φωτὸς ἐξερήσομαι, *Oed. Col.* 355 and 662, and probably *Ai.* 1236 also.

βεβουλευκὼς ἔχει: here the periphrasis uses the perfect participle; the aorist, as at 699, is much commoner. But cf. *Phil.* 600 ὃν γ᾽ εἶχον ἤδη χρόνιον ἐκβεβληκότες and Xen. *Anab.* 1.3.14 ὧν πολλοὺς καί πολλά χρήματα ἔχομεν ἀνηρπακότες.

702 τὸ νεῖκος ἐγκαλῶν ἐρεῖς: 'if you are going to give a clear account of your quarrel as you formulate your accusations' is an interpretation that does not do justice to Sophocles' intentions. (For νεῖκος see 489–90n.) A more remarkable use of a noun with the same participle occurs at *Phil.* 327–8 τίνος γὰρ ὧδε τὸν μέγαν | χόλον κατ᾽ αὐτῶν ἐγκαλῶν ἐλήλυθας, where the sense is 'make these angry accusations', χόλον being an internal accusative, whereas νεῖκος here is an external object of both ἐγκαλῶν and ἐρεῖς (i.e. not 'quarrelsomely accusing'). Disentangling the words of such phrases is a tricky business, and sometimes should not be even attempted, for it is clear that often Sophocles did not intend that his noun–verb combinations should be treated as other than one concept in which the originally separate ideas are totally merged with each other. For example it would be absurd to restore the separate meanings to each word in a phrase like ποδοῖν κλοπὰν ἀρέσθαι at *Ai.* 247 ('to steal away on foot').

704 On the astounding implications of this question see Introduction 11–12.

705 μὲν οὖν: not like the μὲν οὖν at 484, 499, but here in the much more familiar use as corrective particles; though strictly speaking Oedipus is not correcting either αὐτὸς ξυνειδώς or μαθὼν ἄλλου πάρα. What he is correcting is Jocasta's perfectly reasonable assumption that Creon had made the accusation himself to Oedipus' face. Sophocles' technique in this passage is remarkable, since the vital (though quite unnatural) question at 704 could not be put at all if Oedipus had not just in 703 made a totally false statement (it was Teiresias, not Creon, who had so accused him, at 362), which he now (705–6) attempts to justify.

706 τό γ᾽ εἰς ἑαυτόν: cf. *Ant.* 1349 τά γ᾽ εἰς θεούς. The γ᾽ is limitative. For the same idiom but without γε cf. Eur. *I.T.* 691, *Herc.* 171.

ἐλευθεροῖ στόμα: he takes care not to make any self-incriminating remarks: cf. the vulgar English idiom 'he keeps his nose clean'.

707 νῦν: well now, forget all that …

709 †ἔχον†: the meaning we expect to find in this line is 'Nothing in the affairs of men depends on, or is predictable by, the arts of prophets.' The two syllables of the impossible ἔχον leave us with very little room for manoeuvre, and no plausible suggestion has been made, though we could gain the space of two more syllables by deleting τέχνης. μαντική is regular enough without the noun, as at 311, 462.

712 ὑπηρετῶν: it is worth remembering that when these lines were first delivered in the theatre of Dionysus at Athens priests of the principal deities were seated only a few feet away from the actors. Sophocles, through Jocasta, is sailing close to the wind.

715   γ': the limiting particle 'anyway, that's what they *say*' belongs more to Sophocles than to Jocasta, who has no reason to disbelieve the version of events in general circulation.

716   τριπλαῖς: if one road branches into two, the sum can be described as three roads. So Plato, *Gorgias* 524a ἐν τῆι τριόδωι ἐξ ἧς φέρετον τὼ ὁδώ, ἡ μέν εἰς μακάρων νήσους, ἡ δ' εἰς Τάρταρον; cf. 1398 ὦ τρεῖς κέλευθοι.

717   δὲ βλάστας: the βλ of βλάστας does not here cause metrical lengthening of the preceding ε. Cf. *El.* 440, *Phil.* 1311, *Oed. Col.* 972, frg. 122, Eur. frg. 429: with other words a short before βλ comes at Aesch. *Suppl.* 761, Eur. frg. 697, frg. adesp. 455.

διέσχον: commentators are largely agreed that this sentence means 'not three days separated the birth <from what happened after>'. This is a strange manner both of writing and of thinking, but no convincing alternative presents itself.

718   καί: parataxis: 'and' where we should expect 'when'.

ἄρθρα ... ποδοῖν: like ποδοῖν ἀκμάς at 1034, or ποδὸς ἄρθρον at *Phil.* 1201–2, means 'feet' not 'ankles' (and at 1270 ἄρθρα ... κύκλων = κύκλοι = eyes). The widespread idea that it was Oedipus' *ankles* that were pierced together receives no support from Sophocles, and is belied by the very name Οἰδί-πους. Not even Eur. *Phoen.* 26 supports such an idea, for σφυρά probably means 'feet' also at *Alc.* 586, *I.A.* 225.

ἐνζεύξας: the word is imprecise enough to prevent us from thinking of foot-*piercing*. Jocasta wishes to minimize the idea of parental cruelty; hence also ἄλλων χερσίν, a phrase which will turn out to be of vital importance in the development of the plot. At 1034 the anatomical details are more in place. For Oedipus' failure to fasten onto the clue of the 'yoked' feet see 1031 n.

719   ἄβατον: a one-word tribrach (‿ ‿ ‿) in this position is unusual; hence ἄβατον εἰς Musgrave. But cf. 1496, *Ai.* 459. In all three cases a pre-positive precedes: εἰς, τόν, καί.

720   ἤνυσεν: 'did not bring it about that ...' Jocasta loses sight of the real issue, which is the reliability of Apollo not as one who accomplishes, but as one who foretells. But cf. *Ant.* 1178 ὦ μάντι, τοὔπος ὡς ἄρ' ὀρθὸν ἤνυσας, which suggests that we may be drawing too rigorous a distinction, as does Hdt. 1.45 εἷς δὲ οὐ σύ μοι τοῦδε τοῦ κακοῦ αἴτιος, εἰ μὴ ὅσον (except in so far as) ἀέκων ἐξεργάσαο, ἀλλὰ θεῶν κού τις, ὅς μοι καὶ πάλαι προεσήμαινε τὰ μέλλοντα ἔσεσθαι.

723   διώρισαν: the prophecies were quite precise; and wrong.

724–5   As at 278–9 Sophocles engages in some covert criticism of the gods. χρεία is used as at 1174 and 1435 in a meaning that hovers between 'need' and 'purpose', and ἐρευνᾶι is chosen more with an eye on what the god has ordered men to do than on what the god is doing himself. 'Any necessary thing that the god is on the track of ...' Our problems are compounded if ἦν is incorrect, and the manuscripts' ὧν is sound; but 724 has one ὧν in it already, which may have helped foster the corruption.

726ff. See Introduction 11–12.

ἀρτίως: commonly used of the recent past, and sometimes of the immediate past. Oedipus is disturbed at what Jocasta has just said.

728 μερίμνης: anything that occupies the mind. At Aesch. *Eum.* 132 (κύων μέριμναν οὔποτ᾽ ἐκλείπων φόνου) we find it used of a dog on the trail of blood, as, in a sense, Oedipus is now.

ὑποστραφεὶς: cf. στραφείην *Ai.* 1117, ἐπεστρέφοντο *Phil.* 599, both as here with the genitive, 'to be concerned with' or 'bothered by'. Cf. 134n.

729 ὁ Λάιος: the article is not used at random with proper names in tragedy: thus at 711, 721 Jocasta says Λαῖωι, Λάιον, not τῶι Λαῖωι, τὸν Λάιον. Now Oedipus uses the article with Λάιος at 112, 558, here, and at 740. It may be that the article is intended to convey the nuance 'this man Laius, the subject of our murder enquiry'. If so, the distancing will be all part of the dramatic irony.

730 πρός: Jocasta had been more positive, using ἐν at 716. The vaguer πρός suits the tone of ἔδοξ᾽ ἀκοῦσαι. Oedipus is in mental turmoil (726–7).

731 γάρ: agreeing with the implications of the previous speaker's remarks.

λήξαντ᾽ ἔχει: another periphrastic tense; it has not ceased so that a stable rumour-free atmosphere should now exist. λήγω does not have a regular perfect tense unless the conjecture λέληγεν is right at Eur. *Ion* 68. At *Oed. Col.* 517 λήγω is again used of a story that will not stop circulating. Aerts (see 577n.) notes that the periphrastic perfect with intransitive verbs is a rarity, but compares *Trach.* 37, Ar. *Thesm.* 236, Plato, *Crat.* 404c.

732 πάθος: as in 730 Oedipus continues to use words which do not bring the facts into sharp focus, cf. 840n.

734 Sc. <ἀπὸ> Δελφῶν καὶ ἀπὸ Δαυλίας.

735 οὑξεληλυθώς: as the article shows, not 'what time has elapsed?' but 'what is the time that has elapsed?'. The more precise phrasing receives a less precise answer, 'just a bit before you came ...'.

741 There are two questions: (a) φύσιν τίν᾽ εἶχε and (b) τίνα δ᾽ ἀκμὴν ἥβης ἔχων; It is the second one which causes problems, since (1) it has no finite verb, (2) ἀκμὴν ἥβης begs the question: one expects Oedipus to ask 'What was his age?' not 'What was the peak of his flourishing youth?' ἥβη cannot be shown to mean simply 'life' by its uses at frg. 786 or *Trach.* 547–8. Most attempted solutions ignore this second point, and concentrate solely on reconciling the two words εἶχε ... ἔχων; e.g. Hartung's τίν᾽ ἔτυχε, φράζε, τίνα δ᾽ ἀκμὴν ἥβης ἔχων, where in effect ἔτυχε ἔχων governs both φύσιν τίνα and τίνα ἀκμήν. Wolff's proposal φράζ᾽ ἔτ᾽· ἦν δ᾽ ἀκμὴν ἥβης ἔχων; has the merit of an ἔτ᾽ which fits well with μήπω, and uses a periphrastic tense, which Sophocles seems to be favouring very much in this play. It also deals with both problems (1) and (2). But it is a poor introduction to a reply beginning μέλας, χνοάζων ἄρτι, and the double τίνα . . . τίνα sounds authentic. As for the phrase ἀκμὴν ἥβης, it may be that Oedipus uses it because part of his mind is struggling still to exclude the possibility of a πρέσβυς, like the one (805, 807) whom he knows he has killed.

742 μέλας: 'dark' as at Plato, *Rep.* 474e, Dem. *In Meid.* 71, Alexis frg. 103. 17. Similarly Shakespeare uses 'black' as shorthand for 'of dark complexion' (e.g. *Much Ado about Nothing* iii. i.63) and Thackeray (*Esmond* ii.3) can still write without fear of being misunderstood 'You are a black man. Our Esmonds are all black.' Correspondingly πυρρός is shorthand for 'with red hair' at Xenophanes B 16.2; Herodotus 4.108; Page, *FGE* 1782.) Oedipus has asked for information on Laius' physical appearance (LSJ *s.v.* φύσις. ii 2). Jocasta's reply is almost a police description: 'dark, just beginning to go grey, and not much different from your build'.

745 προβάλλων . . . οὐκ εἰδέναι: logic would require προβάλλειν . . . οὐκ εἰδώς.

747 ἀθυμῶ: construed as if a verb of fearing. ἄθυμος is what, in a more light-hearted moment, Oedipus had accused Teiresias of being (319).

ἧι: Campe's ἦν gives the sense 'I'm much afraid the prophet was right when he spoke as he did.' So at 768 fears are expressed which relate to Oedipus' past words. Cf. Hom. *Od.* 5.300 δείδω μὴ δὴ πάντα θεὰ νημερτέα εἶπεν, where most manuscripts erroneously write εἴπηι. Similarly ἥκει not ἥκηι is to be read at *Ai.* 279; scribes always expect main verbs of fear to be followed by subjunctives, since by their nature fears tend to relate to the future.

748 ἕν: we remember the ἕν at 120 of the vital clue.

749 καὶ μήν: used when one speaker falls in with the wishes of another: very well, though I tremble, when you have told me what your questions are, I will speak. ὀκνῶ μὲν . . . ἐρῶ paratactically for 'although I am afraid . . .'. There is also a quite different use of καὶ μήν which may be echoed here, the adversative use (Denniston, *GP*² 357), since καὶ μὴν ὀκνῶ, if we did not know how the sentence was going to proceed, could mean 'Your request sounds reasonable, and yet I fear to answer it.'

750 βαιός: 'travelling light': a prose author would write βαιούς, few as opposed to πολλούς. At *Ai.* 160 βαιός is the man of no consequence, opposed to μεγάλοι. Here βαιός is implicitly opposed to ἄνδρες ἀρχηγέται, in the way (οἵ') you would normally expect them to travel.

751 οἵ : see 763n.

753 κῆρυξ: the standard translation 'herald' is much too over-specialized. In the *Odyssey* κήρυκες have much to do that is non-heraldic. Whatever his function, Jocasta evidently thinks it right to give him a special mention. The other four will have been λοχῖται, the armed escort.

754 διαφανῆ: things may now be diaphanous, but we are only half way through the play, and the processes of clarification will continue for a long time yet.

756 ὅσπερ: again the περ stresses the *identity* of the person in the relative clause with the person in the main sentence. See 575n.

ἐκσωθείς: as with the French *se sauver* the idea of motion is prominent. See LSJ *s.v.* σώιζω II. Cf. Aesch. *Pers.* 450–1 ὅτ᾽ ἐκ νεῶν (or νεῶν ὅτε Page) | φθαρέντες ἐχθροὶ νῆσον ἐκσωιζοίατο – make their escape safely to the island; Eur. *I.T.* 1068 σώσω σ᾽ ἐς Ἑλλάδ᾽.

757 ἤ κἄν: not the ἤ καί meaning 'is he really …' as at 368, *Ai.* 97, but ἤ and καί separately; ἤ the interrogative particle, and καί to denote a further question in a series. So at 1045, *Ai.* 38, 44, 48, *El.* 314. The underlying thought is 'in that case my next question is …'.

758 ἀφ᾽ οὗ: 'from the moment when'; but since the main verb is ἐξικέτευσε we had better translate by 'as soon as'.

For the chronological difficulties, and the eccentric behaviour of Jocasta's employee, see Introduction 12–13.

761 ἀγρούς: probably accusative of motion towards something, but comparison with 734 shows that the preposition may go with ἀγρούς as well as νομάς.

763–4 οἶ ἀνήρ | δοῦλος: if Hermann's οἶ is right – the MSS point to an original ὅδ or ὅ γ᾽ in their common source – we shall have before us the same usage as at 751, 'as is the way with slaves', i.e. they commonly receive favours for services rendered. Similarly *Phil.* 583–4 πόλλ᾽ ἐγὼ κείνων ὕπο | δρῶν ἀντιπάσχω χρηστά θ᾽, οἶ ἀνήρ πένης 'I receive many kindnesses from them in return for the useful services I perform – as is the way with poor men.' Others prefer the sense 'he was a worthy enough fellow, for a slave, meriting even a bigger reward'. But the 'for a slave' sense, the *limiting* οἶα, described by Wedd on Eur. *Or.* 32 as 'frequent', may be non-existent. κἀγὼ μετέσχον οἶα δὴ γυνὴ φόνου comes in a bald recital of the myth of the killing of Clytaemestra. It would be charitable to ascribe to it the meaning 'I took part in the murder, so far as a woman might', but the sense could well be cruder: 'I took part in the murder, as you would expect a woman to do'; cf. *Andr.* 911–12 Ὀρ. μῶν εἰς γυναῖκ᾽ ἔρραψας οἶα δὴ γυνή; Ἑρμ. φόνον γ᾽ ἐκείνηι καὶ τέκνωι νοθαγενεῖ: 'Did you hatch plots against the woman in the way a woman might be expected to?' asks Orestes, and Hermione replies, 'Yes, death to her and her bastard child.'

765 πῶς ἂν μόλοι: a way of expressing a wish or command, delivered in the form of a question and hence capable of being answered by 'it is possible'. Cf. *Oed. Col.* 1457–8 πῶς ἄν, εἴ τις ἔντοπος, | τὸν πάντ᾽ ἄριστον δεῦρο Θησέα πόροι; cf. *Ai.* 388–91, *Phil.* 794–5. Much less peremptory is *El.* 660 πῶς ἂν εἰδείην σαφῶς 'I wonder if you could tell me…?'

766 ἐφίεσαι: 'order'. With τοῦδ, in one manuscript after correction, and conjectured by Herwerden, the sense would be 'desire'. But πρὸς τί 'for what purpose' suits 'order' better. See also 1055n.

769–70 ἄναξ may strike us as formal, but the που and the καί in κἀγώ lend a softening mildness to Jocasta's words as she expresses a wish to share her husband's burdens. The γ̓ in τά γ̓ ἐν σοί is the lightest of light brush-strokes, hinting at the idea, since they are *your* concerns they must be mine. Oedipus responds to her gentle approach with a touch of human warmth of a kind not often found in Greek tragedy, although by the standards of modern literature it might appear much under-pitched.

771 κοὐ μὴ στερηθῇς γ̓: the καί ... γ̓ shows Oedipus meeting Jocasta half-way. 'And you *shall* know. . . ' The choice of οὐ μὴ στερηθῇς as opposed to, e.g., λέξω, shows his acceptance that she has a right (ἀξία 769) to know. Cf. 323 τήνδ̓ ἀποστερῶν φάτιν.
ἐλπίδων 'forebodings'.

772 κἀμείνονι: the manuscripts give the indefensible καὶ μειζόνι, perhaps influenced by the καὶ μείζω just above at 764. The emendation printed is not to be thought of as a certain restoration of the truth, but it gives the sort of sense we expect: 'to whom *better* could I speak?' or 'to whom better *could* I speak?' (for the position of καί see Denniston, *GP²* 314). The manuscripts' καὶ μείζονι 'a more considerable figure' is alien to the tone of the context. For καὶ ἀ- crases (other than their frequent use with ἄλλος, alpha privatives, and prepositions, as at, e.g., 734 above) cf. *Ant.* 436, *Phil.* 644, 1025, *Oed. Col.* 1352; Eur. *Hcld.* 298, *Tro.* 674, *Phoen.* 916.

774ff. The following speech, beginning with the naming of Oedipus' father and mother, must, we might think, be directed at the audience by Sophocles rather than at Jocasta by Oedipus. (Aristotle's memory, *Rhet.* 1415a20, betrayed him into citing ἐμοὶ πατὴρ ἦν Πόλυβος (*sic*) as if it came from the prologue.) A modern producer might think of leaving the rest of the stage in darkness with only the figure of Oedipus illuminated. Such a procedure would be quite wrong. 800 puts it beyond doubt that Sophocles does not intend to depart far from the idea that this is indeed what it purports to be, a speech by Oedipus to his wife.

774–5 The additions 'Corinthian' and 'descended from Dorus' add precision to what are in reality untrue statements. Sophocles may have had a second motive for being so specific in this passage: as D. M. Bain (*G. & R.* 26 (1979) 141) points out, in some versions of the story Polybus is king of Sicyon, and his wife is not always Merope.

776 πρίν: the sentence, in Sophocles' manner, does not proceed on absolutely regular lines. Oedipus does not mean that he was regarded as one of the most important citizens until some drunken person called him a bastard. He means that he lived a settled life as one of the most important citizens, when suddenly one day a strange incident upset the pattern of his life. πρίν + indicative is rare in tragedy. Aeschylus has πρίν + infinitive 17 times, Sophocles 19, Euripides 68. Aeschylus never has πρίν + indicative, Sophocles only here, and Euripides 7 times: *Hec.* 131, *Med.* 1173, *Andr.* 1147, *Alc.* 128, *Rhes.* 294, *I.A.* 489, all as here marking decisive turning points; and also *Rhes.* 568. There is also one case in [Aesch.], *Prom. Vinct.* 481, again a turning point.

777 ἐπέστη: see LSJ *s.v.* ἐφίστημι B III 2 and 3, and compare παρεστάθη at 911.

779 μέθης: the genitive is usual with verbs of filling: cf. πολλῶν ὑπερπλησθῆι (874). μέθη is strong wine, as at Eur. *El.* 326 etc. The dative μέθηι is also possible (cf. Aesch. *Pers.* 132) and is well attested in our manuscripts. If it is not genuine, it may originate from the misconception that μέθη here is used in its more familiar prose sense of 'drunkenness'.

780 καλεῖ: as if νόθον were to follow; but instead of 'called me a bastard' we have 'said of me that I was an invented, fabricated, suppositious son for my father'. Eur. *Phoen.* 28–31 gives a version that fits the drunken accusation better than the story later to emerge from our play. There it says that the (unnamed) queen of Corinth received the child from some cowboys (ἱπποβουκόλοι drably interpreted as 'feeders of horses' in Pollux 7.185), who then took the risky step of persuading Polybus that Oedipus was her own child.

παρ' οἴνωι: 'over his wine'. Heimsoeth's παροινῶν is more explicit, and very suitable to the context, as a glance at LSJ *s.v.* will confirm.

782 κατέσχον: intransitive, as at Men. *Perikeir.* 824, Hdt. 5.19 'I restrained myself'. θἀτέραι: 'the next day'.

ἰὼν πέλας: 'going up to' my parents, not 'near' them. Similarly βαῖνε λευστήρων πέλας at Eur. *Tro.* 1039 cannot mean 'take a stroll near those who throw stones', but 'go and face them'.

783 ἤλεγχον: questioned them closely, cf. 333.

784 μεθέντι is used of the discharging of missiles. The parents were angry with the one who had let fly in this way.

786 ὑφεῖρπε: it got under his skin. See 386n.

πολύ: in full strength. Cf. Κύπρις γὰρ οὐ φορητὸς ἦν πολλὴ ῥυῆι Eur. *Hipp.* 443 (where Barrett prefers the οὐ φορητόν in Stobaeus, something insupportable).

788 ὁ: anaphoric, i.e. referring to a concept already mentioned, here Πυθώ, the seat of Phoebus. The underlying idea is 'Phoebus, the god of that place Pytho', rather than just 'Phoebus'.

789 ἄτιμον governs ὧν, which stands for τούτων ἅ, where ἅ would be internal accusative: 'the things for which I came', cf. 1005 τοῦτ' ἀφικόμην 'I came for this reason'. Phoebus did not accord him the honour of a response. See 280n. A similar use at *Oed. Col.* 1278.

ἀθλίωι: at best only our oldest manuscript (L) may have had this dative; all others have ἄθλια. If ἀθλίωι is right, it will stand as an interjected note of self-pity, similar to, but graver than, the uses of τάλας, ταλαίπωρος, etc., discussed in 634n. If ἄθλια is right, it is best taken as a virtual substantive, qualified by the two following adjectives, as δεινόν is by οὐκ ἀκουστὸν οὐδ' ἐπόψιμον at 1312. But to qualify ἄθλια by the epithet δύστηνα is so weak that Heimsoeth's δύσφημα becomes irresistible. It is in any case attractive in a sentence with προυφάνη λέγων in it.

790 προυφάνη λέγων The emendation προύφηνεν (Hermann and Wunder) is on the surface very attractive, and indeed the scholia of Thomas Magister gloss προυφάνη with προέδειξε as if it actually were προύφηνεν. We may note Wunder's warning 'neque diligens interpres contra me afferet huius fab. v. 395, ibi προυφάνης significare repertus es statuens' without necessarily agreeing with him. For the combination of speaking and appearing cf. 525, 848.

792 ὁρᾶν: dependent on either ἄτλητον or δηλώσοιμ᾽ or both.

793 φυτεύσαντος: not an idle addition to πατρός in this play.

795 τεκμαρούμενος: Oedipus meant to give (future participle to indicate intent). Corinth a wide berth. The language is typical of the grim humour that can appear in tragedy. 'Henceforth (τὸ λοιπόν) intending to infer the location of Corinthian territory by the stars' (like a mariner). Cf. *Phil.* 454–5 τὸ λοιπὸν ἤδη τηλόθεν τό τ᾽ Ἴλιον | καὶ τοὺς Ἀτρείδας εἰσορᾶν φυλάξομαι (look at Ilion from a distance, i.e. not look at it at all). There are a number of references in later literature to this idea: τὸ ἄστροις σημαίνεσθαι ἐπὶ τῶν μακρὰν ὁδὸν καὶ ἔρημον πορευομένων· οἱ γὰρ φεύγοντες ἀειφυγίαν τοῖς ἄστροις ἐσημειοῦντο τὴν ἑαυτῶν πατρίδα ('The expression "calculating by the stars" is used of those going on a long and lonely journey; for people going into permanent exile used to calculate the position of their home-land by the stars'), Boissonade, *Anec.* 2.238. Eustathius has a note: δηλοῖ καὶ Σοφοκλῆς καὶ παροιμία τὸ ἄστροις σημειοῦσθαι ὁδόν. See further Kamerbeek's note and the Schneidewin–Nauck edition, where numerous parallels are cited to justify τεκμαρούμενος as a correction of the manuscripts' ἐκμετρούμενος. The proverbial 'humour' (as it later became, if it was not already) from Oedipus' lips reminds us of 283 and possibly 287. Those who wish to retain the manuscripts' ἐκμετρούμενος may like to consider the merits of Seyffert's γῆν in 794, and assign to the verb the sense not of 'measuring' but of 'traversing' as at Homer *Od.* 3.179 (active voice) or Xenophon of Ephesus 1.12.3. Cf. latin *metiri*. 'A true-devoted pilgrim is not weary | To measure kingdoms with his feeble steps' – Shakespeare, *The Two Gentlemen of Verona* II. vii. 9–10.

796 ὀψοίμην: a future indicative is more usual in relative sentences of purpose even where the leading verb is in a historic tense. But future optatives are never especially common. Sophocles has just had occasion to use two in the immediate vicinity (792–3), which may have emboldened him to use another here.

797 ὀνείδη: see LSJ *s.v.* 2.

798 τοὺς χώρους: the vague plural, as Oedipus distances himself from the reality which he apprehends, as he did at 730, 732. In the following line τὸν τύραννον τοῦτον is substituted for ὁ Λάϊος as if Oedipus shrank from the name.

800 See 774n. I reproduce now the whole of Jebb's note: 'The hand which added this verse in the margin of L seems to be "as early as the beginning of the fourteenth century" (Mr E. M. Thompson, *Introd.* to Facsimile of Laur. MS.). The verse is in A (13th cent.) and all our other MSS. To eject the verse, as Dindorf and Nauck have done, is utterly unwarrantable. It has a fine dramatic force. Oedipus is now at the critical point: he will hide nothing of the truth from her who is nearest to him. It is part of his character that his earnest desire to know the *truth* never flinches: cp. 1170.'

The verse is required, for τριπλῆς is vital for the understanding of the following line. The wish to omit it had its origins in the belief fashionable at one time that L was the source of all later MSS. The successor to this theory, stating that the text of Sophocles depended primarily on *two* MSS, L and A, led naturally enough to intense study of those two MSS – yet curiously the vital observation, that it was none other than the scribe of A who wrote *Oed. Tyr.* 800 into the manuscript L, and that therefore the authority of A was not to be over-estimated merely because the corrected text of L agreed with it here, and in countless other places where A had written corrections into L, was not made until 1949, by Alexander Turyn. Unfortunately this valuable discovery was itself misapplied to deny to the manuscript A any genuine authority of its own. A more reasonable conclusion might have been that if A had been proved to have had access to the one manuscript, some three hundred years or more older than itself, to have survived to that day (other than its largely illegible twin in Leiden), it might well have had access to others too, now lost, of no less age and authority.

802–7 The following persons are named. (1) κῆρυξ, (2) ἀνὴρ ἐπὶ πωλικῆς ἀπήνης ἐμβεβώς who meets Jocasta's description of Laius (οἷον σὺ φῄς), (3) ὁ ἡγεμών, (4) αὐτὸς ὁ πρέσβυς, (5) τὸν τροχηλάτην. From Jocasta's account we know (752) that the total party numbered five. But the five here are not the five there, because (2) and (4) are obviously the same person: cf. 753. If (4) had not already been mentioned in one guise or another, αὐτὸς ὁ could not stand with πρέσβυς, 'the older man himself'. The questions remain, are (1) and (3) the same person? And who is (5)? Now the presence of the article (anaphoric) with ἡγεμών, and the fact that no further explanation is given of his presence or designation, all but prove that he is identical with the κῆρυξ. In Homer, *Il.* 24.178ff. the κῆρυξ sits in the chariot along with Priam, and drives it. Does Laius' κῆρυξ (= ἡγεμών) discharge the same function? Probably not, because (*a*) ἡγεμών is never used of a charioteer – it is essentially a guide; (*b*) the statement that the older man was in the chariot would follow oddly on the mention of the κῆρυξ if the κῆρυξ was himself also in it; (*c*) τὸν ἐκτρέποντα, τὸν τροχηλάτην, is itself an explanatory phrase, 'the one who was trying to push me aside, I mean the charioteer', and it would be very perverse to omit the vital fact that he was also the κῆρυξ if that were in reality the case.

Three persons are thus named: (1) the κῆρυξ = ἡγεμών, (2) the πρέσβυς in the chariot, (3) the chariot-driver. What remains confusing is that 806 speaks of 'the one who was pushing me aside' when we have just been told that *two* people were, and the *one* is neither of those two.

805 πρέσβυς: a senior figure, compared with the κῆρυξ, the λοχῖται, or the chariot-driver. Not necessarily an *old* man, γέρων.

807 Interpretation depends on how we punctuate. The text printed in this edition gives: 'When the older man saw (sc. what was going on), waiting for when I was passing the chariot, he came down on me with his double whip, right on the middle of my head.' Blaydes's note on μέσον κάρα deserves immortality: 'Anglice right (plump) on my head. Accusativus partis verberatae.'

809 Is this a line without a regular caesura? P. Maas, *Greek metre* (Oxford 1962) §137 compares Aesch. *Pers.* 331, *Suppl.* 467, *Cho.* 181, 193, 481, 573 (?), *Eum.* 595, in which, as here, a post-positive follows the caesura after $\times - \cup - \times - \cup$, but he cites no other Sophoclean example. Schein, *ITAS* 40 n.14 hopes that 'here the anomaly is perhaps mitigated because the enclitic μου is governed grammatically by καθίκετο'. Post-positives can certainly follow the alternative regular caesura, after $\times - \cup - \times$, as at 141 above (see note) and, e.g., at *Trach.* 1257, where σοι (Blaydes) not σοί must be right; and such words appear at places where their metrical coherence with the word they follow might appear to imperil the law of the final cretic. See 219n.

810 οὐ μὴν ... γ': a strong adversative, with force falling on the word before the γ'. With ἴσην understand <τίσιν>.

812 μέσης: the apparent safety of the middle of the chariot is contrasted with the way the πρέσβυς is pitched out of it. ἐκκυλίνδεται is drawn from the vocabulary of the *Iliad*: see LSJ *s.v.*

813 τοὺς ξύμπαντας: 'the lot of them'; cf. 752. Oedipus has been told that one person escaped from the encounter between the brigands and Laius and his entourage. As for himself, he believes that he killed *all* the persons he met at the fork in the road. He never goes on to use the argument that therefore these two events must be unrelated.

814 Λαΐωι τι συγγενές is the veiled subject of προσήκει: 'anything akin to Laius'. προσήκει, 'has any relationship with', governs the dative ξένωι. Although ξένωι and Λαΐωι do not agree grammatically with each other, the sequence τῶι ξένωι τούτωι ... Λαΐωι must produce an uncomfortable feeling in the hearer. Right at the back of his mind he may even have the memory of how Oedipus had described *himself* as a ξένος (219, 220), and he may be struck by the irony whereby Oedipus speculates on the relationship between the stranger and Laius when what is more important is whether the man in the carriage was συγγενής to and so προσήκει the man who is actually telling the story.

815–16 ἐχθροδαίμων and ἂν γένοιτο are excellently chosen if they follow hard upon mention of the Laius connection, but less appropriate if they are separated from 814 by 815 in such a way that their only function is to look forward to the theme developed in 817ff., of excommunication by *men*. ἐχθροδαίμων is a unique word, which fits Oedipus with precision, since he had been cursed by the gods at a time when his very existence was no more than a theoretical possibility. If, against all the odds, Laius was the man he killed, this is clear proof that he is ἐχθροδαίμων; no one *could be* (ἂν γένοιτο) more so.

We may therefore follow Dindorf in deleting 815 as a doublet – a kind of interpolation best known to us from *Trach*. The alternative, of retaining both 815 and 816 but in the reverse order, is unattractive because of the sequence ἀνήρ . . . τοῦδέ γ' ἀνδρός.

817 ὧι: 'for whom it is not possible that any stranger or citizen should receive him in their house'. Many scholars have demurred at the construction, fearful of the ambiguity, 'who may no longer entertain any stranger or citizen in his house'. They have written ὅν, 'whom no stranger or citizen may receive' either with τινι (possible *for* any one) or with τινα retained (possible *that* any one). The manuscripts' ὧι is however to be left unaltered; we are speaking of the closing of options *for* the person affected, and ambiguity should exist only in the minds of the malevolent or obtuse. For the ξένοι–ἀστοί pairing see the numerous other examples in E. Kemmer, *Die polare Ausdrucksweise* (Würzburg 1903) 91 f. (e.g. *Trach*. 187, *El*. 975).

819 καὶ perhaps = καίτοι: see 417n.

822 ἆρ' ἔφυν κακός: Jebb's translation, 'Say, am I vile?' may provoke undeserved merriment. ἔφυν has its full force: his whole φύσις has been κακή from the moment of his birth. κακός is a strong word in the vocabulary of tragedy. See 334n.

823 εἴ substantiates not κακός and ἄναγνος, but the whole underlying idea of his misery. ὧι fulfilled the same function at 817, without specifically developing ἐχθρο-δαίμων.

824 μῆστι: ἔστι here in the same sense as ἔξεστι 817.

825 ἐμβατεύειν: the aorist -εῦσαι is in the papyrus fragment, and the scholia in L had ἐπιβῆναι before correction to ἐπιβαίνειν. The aorist would be parallel to φυγεῖν and ἰδεῖν, and might convey the once-and-for-all idea 'set foot in'. But as ἐμβατεύειν is found in a similar context at Eur. *El*. 1251 (though ἐμβατεῦσαι at 595) we can hardly refuse the united testimony of the poetic texts of our medieval manuscripts here. The word can bear a legal sense, of entering into possession of an estate: see Wilkins on Eur. *Hcld*. 876.

825–7 Exile from Thebes cannot be ameliorated by a return to his home at Corinth, for fear of marrying his mother and killing his father. It is vital that the audience should not be confused by its own superior knowledge: hence 'father' is expanded by 'Polybus, who gave me life and brought me up'. (One scribe *was* confused by his own superior knowledge and for Πόλυβον wrote Λάϊον, with Πόλυβον as a gloss.) It is odd that the lordly Wunder should have found so many followers here: 'ego primus uncis inclusi hunc versum' (i.e. marked it as spurious). 'Neque enim nomen patris proferri hic a poeta convenit, ut cetera incommoda huius versus omittam explicare.' For Wunder's preference for anonymity see 8n.

827 ἐξέθρεψε κἀξέφυσε: The words appear in the reverse order in most of our MSS, including the oldest and best, and they may be right. It seems more prudent, however, to print the order presented by a papyrus fragment; not out of any heightened veneration for papyrus (for example at 824 above it corrupts, as some of our medieval MSS do not, μῇστι to μήτε), but because of the parallels of Eur. *El.* 969 πῶς γὰρ κτάνω νιν, ἥ μ'ἔθρεψε κᾆτεκεν; or Hom. *Od.* 12.134 τὰς μὲν ἄρα θρέψασα τεκοῦσά τε πότνια μήτηρ. (See A. C. Pearson, *C.Q* 23 (1929) 168, and K–G II 603.4.)

The two verbs compounded in ἐκ have a strongly Sophoclean ring – a mannerism appreciated by Ronald Knox, who composed a Greek iambic version of Lewis Carroll's Jabberwocky, and rendered the line 'the vorpal blade went snicker-snack' with the magnificently impressive ἔσνιξεν, ἐξέσναξεν εὐκόπνωι ξίφει (for the two verbs in asyndeton cf. 1276n.). The less frivolous may consult E. Tsitsoni, *Untersuchungen der* ἐκ-*verbal-Komposita bei Sophokles* (Kallmünz 1963); R. Carden, *The papyrus fragments of Sophocles* (Berlin – New York 1974) 65, and J. M. Bremer in *C.Q.* n.s. 22 (1972) 236–40.

831–2 ἴδοιμι . . . ἰδεῖν: hence, after the catastrophe, the self-blinding.

834 δ. . . οὖν: Denniston, *GP*² 460 notes that 'the particles are very rarely separated by an intervening word'. Comparison with other passages listed by Denniston suggests that the tone is 'Just the same, until you actually *know* . . .'

835 τοῦ παρόντος: the man who was there at the time Laius was killed. For this imperfect participle cf. 971, *Ant.* 1192, *Oed. Col.* 1587, Homer, *Od.* 8.491, Pindar, *Pyth.* 1.27, Aesch. *Pers.* 266, Eur. *Suppl.* 649, *Hyps.* frg. 757.35.

836 καὶ μὴν . . . γ': well certainly that's all I can do: cf. 290.

839–40 The question of the number of attackers, which has been before our minds since early on in the play, now looms larger. Contrast this with the potential argument neglected by Oedipus at 813.

840 πάθος: 'the euphemism of a shrinking mind' (Jebb). Cf. 732, 798nn.

841 περισσόν 'out of the ordinary'. The point which Oedipus makes now, about the number of highwaymen, is different from the point he appeared to have seized on at 726. The ξένοι ληισταί (715–16) received no prominence in Jocasta's account, and in fact it is not true that Jocasta told him that the survivor spoke of highway*men*. Her evidence was based on ἡ φάτις. The evidence of the survivor was given at 118–23. Logically, however, it is true that the φάτις must have been based solely on the evidence of the survivor.

843 μὲν οὖν: transitional. Denniston, *GP*² 471–2. 'Now if he is still going to give the same number . . .'

845 Oedipus' tragic dilemma is reduced to elementary mathematics. *One* person (γε performs the function of our italics) cannot be the same as the plurality of persons referred to already – such is the rôle played by τοῖς. But Brunck's εἷς γέ τις is attractive, keeping the sentence on the plane of pure mathematics without specific reference to Oedipus' situation, and without excluding such reference either: cf. εἷς τις 118.

846 οἰόζωνον: cf. Hdt. 1.72.3 μῆκος ὁδοῦ εὐζώνωι [ἀνδρὶ] πέντε ἡμέραι ἀναισι-μοῦνται; 1.104 τριήκοντα ἡμερέων εὐζώνωι ὁδός; 2.34.2 πέντε ἡμερέων ἰθέα ὁδὸς εὐζώνωι ἀνδρί. εὔζωνος in every case means 'travelling light' – similarly *altius praecincti* at Hor. *Sat.* 1.5.5–6. The second half of the compound in οἰό-ζωνος is therefore compatible with the idea of 'travelling', and οἰό- reinforces ἕν. But there is another possibility, that οἰόζωνος means the same as μονόζωνος, which in Josephus means a bandit. Some of our manuscripts here actually have as glosses μονόζωνον and ἔνο-πλον. Perhaps 'a man travelling alone' is another euphemism for 'highwayman' as we suspected was the case with ὁδοιπόρος (292 and note). Cf. μονοβάτας, a thief, in Hesychius.

σαφῶς: as the oracle had spoken ἐμφανῶς (96), and as we hope the survivor will φανεῖ (853) the matter in the same way that it has already appeared (φανέν 848). Everything hinges on the clear and unambiguous testimony of this survivor. Strange then that all editors from as far back as the time of the Aldine edition of 1502 have sought to separate σαφῶς from αὐδήσει by a comma, so that it may cohere with the vague and deliberately ἀσαφές expression εἰς ἐμὲ ῥέπον. Cf. 958 ἀπαγγεῖλαι σαφῶς, *Trach.* 349 σαφῶς μοι φράζε.

847 ἤδη: by that stage. ἤδη never means 'then' in a purely inferential sense. Cf. Ar. *Ach.* 315–16 τοῦτο τοὔπος δεινὸν ἤδη ... |εἰ σὺ τολμήσεις ὑπὲρ τῶν πολεμίων ἡμῖν λέγειν, 'things will have reached a pretty pass if you are going to ...'. See further Stevens on Eur. *Andr.* 1066–7.

ἐμέ: the last syllable lengthens before initial ῥ-, as almost always in tragedy. See 1289n.

ῥέπον: the familiar image of the descending scale of the balance. What makes translation difficult is that the image has the explicit τοὔργον in its midst: a sort of cross between 'the finger begins to point at me' and 'the deed begins to look as if it were mine'.

848 ὧδ': to be construed with φανέν. Cf. τοὔπος ἐφάνθη 525.

849 ἐκβαλεῖν πάλιν: we expect 'withdraw', 'retract' or 'unsay', and πάλιν fits perfectly with this idea. ἐκβαλεῖν by itself would hardly be adequate, since ἐκβαλεῖν ἔπος means not 'unsay' but 'say', as commonly in Homer; cf. Aesch. *Agam.* 1663, *Cho.* 47, *Eum.* 830; Eur. *Tro.* 1180 (with κόμπους), *Ion* 959; Pindar, *Pyth.* 2.81, Hdt. 6.69.5, etc. At Plato, *Crito* 46b we read: τοὺς δὴ λόγους οὓς ἐν τῶι ἔμπροσθεν ἔλεγον οὐ δύναμαι νῦν ἐκβαλεῖν, ἐπειδή μοι ἥδε ἡ τύχη γέγονεν, ἀλλὰ σχεδόν τι ὅμοιοι φαίνονταί μοι, καὶ τοὺς αὐτοὺς πρεσβεύω καὶ τιμῶ οὕσπερ καὶ πρότερον. No πάλιν is present, but there Socrates is talking of the total abandonment or repudiation of a life-long principle in a moment of stress, a throwing overboard of all he stands for. Such an idea will not suit *Oed. Tyr.* 849. One might be tempted to conjecture ἐκλαβεῖν 'take back', but in fact 'retract' is not one of its meanings. ἐκβαλεῖν is to be retained, and given its normal meaning of 'utter', with πάλιν meaning 'in a contrary sense'. Not greatly different is Homer, *Il.* 9.56, where πάλιν ἐρέει means 'speak against' a proposal.

851 εἰ δ οὖν: 'and anyway, if he *does* try to depart in any way from his previous version. . .' The italics represent the καί in κἀκτρέποιτο.

852 οὖτοι . . . γε: Denniston, *GP²* 547. 'At any rate he will not . . .'

853 φανεῖ δικαίως ὀρθόν: at *Trach.* 347 we find φωνεῖ δίκης ἐς ὀρθόν, and attempts have been made to standardize the phraseology. But perhaps φανεῖ δικαίως is to be taken as one phrase, meaning 'justify', and ὀρθόν as the predicate, 'as correct'. By 'the death of Laius' Jocasta really means 'the predictions about the death of Laius', the rest of the sentence ὃν γε . . . being about those predictions.

854 διεῖπε: cf. 394n. Loxias was quite specific – but wrong, thinks Jocasta. In her excitement she no longer maintains the distinction made at 712.

857-8 Lit. I wouldn't look either this way or that, for the sake of prophecy, or so far as prophecy is concerned.

859 καλῶς νομίζεις: 'he assents, almost mechanically – but his thoughts are intent on sending for the herdsman' (Jebb). For καλῶς cf. 984.

860 μηδὲ τοῦτ' ἀφῆις: 'and do not neglect the matter' is said simply to add weight to πέμψον; i.e. make quite sure you send some one to start him on his way.

862 ἄν . . . ἄν: the second occurrence (cf. 857-8) in a few lines of repeated ἄν. For other examples in this play cf. 139-40, 261-2, 339, 1053; we cannot count the spurious 1438, nor, for the reasons given in the note *ad loc.*, 1348.

ὧν οὐ σοί φίλον: one might expect μή, but cf. *Phil.* 1227 ὧν οὐ σοι πρέπον. For φίλον cf. *El.* 316 and LSJ *s.v.* 1 2 b. Jocasta's language is mild and gentle; almost the language of a mother to her son. But it is also the language of an obedient wife. 'Critics have pointed out that Jocasta, in her role as peacemaker and then as would-be comforter, acts like a mother to Oedipus; the irony of this is never expressed in ambiguous words' (G. M. Kirkwood, *A study of Sophoclean drama* (Ithaca, N.Y. 1958) 253).

863-910 The third chorus (second stasimon)

For the relevance of this ode, see Introduction 18. The structure is as follows: στρ.α An expression of reverent piety for divine laws. ἀντ.α The dangers of impiety attendant on high position in the state. στρ.β A prayer for punishment to fall on the impious. ἀντ.β A reinforcement of that prayer, with special reference to the case of Laius and Apollo.

863 May Moira be with me. Moira's rôle in Greek mythology is varied and extensive. She is Destiny, but she is also closely connected with the Erinyes. The Chorus understandably wish to keep on the right side of so formidable a figure.

φέροντι: as at *Ant.* 1090 τὸν νοῦν τ' ἀμείνω τῶν φρενῶν ὧν νῦν φέρει. Both there (where νοῦν is governed by τρέφειν in the previous line) and here τρέφω has been suggested for φέρω (cf. *Trach.* 108 τρέφουσαν Casaubon for φέρουσαν). In either case the meaning will be little more than 'have'.

τὰν εὔσεπτον ἀγνείαν: as often in poetry the second half of the compound, derived here from σέβω, is chosen for its near-synonymity with the noun it qualifies. (At 890 there will be condemnation of ἀσέπτων.) The article τὰν is picked up by ὧν: that kind of holiness in speech and action prescribed by Olympian law.

865 ὧν: ἅς, following τὰν ἀγνείαν, might have seemed more strictly logical, but νόμοι regulate ἔργα rather than holiness.

πρόκεινται: 'are prescribed'. Cf. *Ant.* 36, 481; Aesch. *Pers.* 371, Eur. *I.T.* 1189. The word is also prosaic (ζημία πρόκειται or ζημίαι πρόκεινται Thuc. 3.45) and inscriptional, but Sophocles evidently feels this no obstacle to proceeding with such poetic flights of fancy as ὑψίποδες and assigning aether and Olympus to the laws as parents.

866 †οὐρανίαν: αἰθήρ is feminine here, as always in Homer and often in Euripides; elsewhere normally masculine.

867 δι αἰθέρα†: the antistrophe, unless itself corrupt, shows that this verse should begin with ⌣‾⏞⌣. Now it is hard to see how a participle like τεκνωθέντες could ever be qualified by a διά + acc. phrase with αἰθήρ, to mean 'through' – a not particularly common use of διά at the best of times, and perhaps impossible where no sense of motion is involved; and so Enger proposed οὐρανίαι 'ν αἰθέρι. An alternative is to assume corruption in τεκνωθέντες. A quotation from Empedocles reads: ἀλλὰ τὸ μὲν πάντων νόμιμον διά τ' εὐρυμέδοντος | αἰθέρος ἠνεκέως τέταται (135 DK¹¹), and so words derived from τείνω, 'extended' or 'extending' through, have been sought: e.g. δι' αἰθέρα ταθέντες would give an initial ⌣‾⌣⏞ to correspond with ἀπότομον ὤρ- ⌣⏞⌣‾.

871 'Great is the divine power in these laws.' This extension of the use of θεός is still a long way short of that at Eur. *Hel.* 560 θεὸς γὰρ καὶ τὸ γιγνώσκειν φίλους.

873 One of the most famous lines in Sophocles, quoted in countless books of criticism, is 'Hybris begets the tyrant', ὕβρις φυτεύει τύραννον. But what Sophocles actually wrote was 'Tyranny begets Hybris', as printed in our text, and we may be sure of this for two reasons. (*a*) It is a commonplace, like Lord Acton's 'Power tends to corrupt, and absolute power corrupts absolutely.' Tyranny is the parent of crime at Dionysius trag. frg. 4 ἡ γὰρ τυραννὶς ἀδικίας μήτηρ ἔφυ, and ὕβρις is the child of success and wealth at Eur. frg. 437 ὁρῶ δὲ τοῖς πολλοῖσιν ἀνθρώποις ἐγὼ | τίκτουσαν ὕβριν τὴν πάροιθ' εὐπραξίαν and 438 ὕβριν τε τίκτει πλοῦτος. So in Solon frg. 6 West and Theognis 153 hybris is the child of koros, when ὄλβος attends one whose mind is not ἄρτιος. In the end, according to Bacchylides 15.61, after granting wealth and power, hybris ἐς βαθὺν πέμπει φθόρον its victim. (*b*) 'Hybris begets tyranny' are words of severely limited validity – very few sinners in antiquity found that hybris led to becoming a tyrant, and such a maxim has absolutely no relevance whatsoever to the case of Oedipus, who was given the tyranny of Thebes as an unsolicited gift: cf. 384. No ruler could have been less hybristic than the father of his people to whom a priest turned at the beginning of the play as one specially favoured by heaven (38). On the other hand Oedipus has now been tyrant for some considerable time, and as he himself admits (847) the finger of suspicion may soon point in his direction. In his interviews with Teiresias and Creon he has shown a certain imperiousness of demeanour. The question the Chorus are now addressing themselves to, here, close to the centre point of the play, as Oedipus' fate hangs in the balance, is whether even the admirable Oedipus may not have been corrupted along the lines laid down by Lord Acton. Compare Herodotus 3.80.3 on the dangers of monarchy: καὶ γὰρ ἂν τὸν ἄριστον ἀνδρῶν πάντων (as Oedipus was) στάντα ἐς ταύτην τὴν ἀρχὴν (as Oedipus did) ἐκτὸς τῶν ἐωθότων νοημάτων στήσειε. ἐγγίνεται μὲν γάρ οἱ ὕβρις ἀπὸ τῶν παρεόντων ἀγαθῶν ... The honest burghers of Thebes cannot conceive of the horrendous possibility that Oedipus may be guiltless in intent, and doomed by the gods before he was even born. But Sophocles can. See Introduction 3–4; as for what hybris itself is, and what it is not, see D. M. MacDowell, *G. & R.* n.s. 23 (1976) 14–31, and N. R. E. Fisher in the same journal 177–93 and n.s. 26 (1979) 32–47, and R. Lattimore, *Story patterns in Greek tragedy* (London 1964) 25–6. Valuable too is the article on Hybris and Plants by A. Michelini in *Harvard Studies in Classical Philology* 82 (1978) 34–44.

874 ὑπερπλησθῆι: the poet is thinking of κόρος, over-fullness, an idea often associated in Greek poetry with hybris. In Solon and Theognis, as we have seen, hybris results from koros, and so in Stobaeus 4.26.4–5 we learn that Pythagoras said that there often crept into states πρῶτον τρυφήν, ἔπειτα κόρον, εἶτα ὕβριν, μετὰ δὲ ταῦτα ὄλεθρον. In Pindar, *Ol.* 13.10, and the oracle cited in Herodotus 8.77, we find hybris *precedes* koros. Here in Sophocles the two concepts seem to go hand in hand, as in ὕβρι κεκορημένος Hdt. 3.80.3; or if there is any chronological priority, it is the hybris that comes first.

At 380 Oedipus himself had linked πλοῦτος with τυραννίς. Note how πλοῦτος is associated with κόρος not only in the Solon and Theognis passages, but also in Pindar, *Isth.* 3.2 and Aesch. *Agam.* 382.

μάταν: there is no simple English equivalent to some uses of this word, which poses problems of translation also at 609 and 1057 (where see note). The idea is that all the acts of κόρος will in the end prove pointless; and the word can have strong associations of imprudence. Cf. 1520, *Ant.* 1252, *El.* 1291, *Oed. Col.* 658, 1034, 1148, and frg. 929.3–4. ματαίζων is coming soon at 891. See also LSJ *s.vv.* μάτη and μάταιος.

875 'πίκαιρα: καιρός seems to have been more important in Greek ways of thinking than 'the right time' is to us: cf. *El.* 75–6 καιρὸς γὰρ ὅσπερ ἀνδράσι μέγιστος ἔργου παντός ἐστ' ἐπιστάτης, *Phil.* 837 καιρός τοι πάντων γνώμαν ἴσχων (= that determines all things). Cf. Hesiod, *W. D.* 694 καιρὸς δ' ἐπὶ πᾶσιν ἄριστος, extended at Theognis 401 (the same idea at Bacchyl. 14.17); Pindar, *Pyth.* 9.78. It is also a more natural partner to συμφέροντα than we might think: at *Phil.* 151 the Chorus promise to keep their eyes open ἐπὶ σῶι μάλιστα καιρῶι, for any opportunity that may particularly benefit you. See further J. R. Wilson *Glotta* 58 (1980) 177–204 (esp. p.191), W. H. Race, *T.A.P.A.* 3 (1981) 197–213.

876   It scales the topmost battlements, like that paragon of insolence Capaneus, who at Eur. *Phoen.* 1180 is struck by Zeus's thunderbolt ἤδη (δ) ὑπερβαίνοντα γεῖσα τειχέων. Similar imagery at *Ant.* 131, Eur. *Suppl.* 729.

877   ἀπότομον ὤρουσεν εἰς ἀνάγκαν: the verb is a gnomic aorist (see Goodwin, *Greek grammar* §1292; K–G I 158–61) from ὀρούω, to storm ahead. ἀπότομος is used of sheer cliffs and precipices. LSJ is right in thinking that the simile here is not of one falling to his ruin (ὤρουσεν would not be a suitable choice for 'falling') but of one 'who comes suddenly to the edge of a cliff'. He scales the heights, and finds nothing but a sheer fall before him. In their ode to Ἀνάγκα at Eur. *Alc.* 962ff. the Chorus ascribe to it an ἀπότομον λῆμα – a spirit of absolute harsh finality. See some of the uses of the word in later Greek catalogued in LSJ.

878   οὐ ποδὶ χρησίμωι χρῆται: 'litotes, oxymoron, figura etymologica all in one' (Kamerbeek, adding 'The phrase perhaps echoes a grim popular joke'). Confronted by a sheer drop, not even the most reckless can put his feet to any good use. There is no thematic connection with ὑψίποδες (866). The foot metaphor is so common in tragedy that at *Phil.* 1260 Sophocles can even write 'perhaps you may keep your foot clear of tears' ἴσως ἂν ἐκτὸς κλαυμάτων ἔχοις πόδα. At *El.* 455 Orestes is envisaged as *with the upper hand* trampling down his enemies *underfoot*.

879–80   The enterprise which can lead to tyranny has its good side also. The Chorus have no desire to crush the spirit of competition *per se*.

881   θεὸν οὐ λήξω . . . : the connection with the rest of the antistrophe looks at first sight tenuous, and indeed the line, like its opposite number, 871, which also mentions θεός, does not even boast a δέ to link it with what precedes. The sequence of thought is probably this: in deciding whether Oedipus falls into the category of the hybristic (872–9) or those who are virtuously energetic on behalf of the city (879–80), it is best to remit the matter to the judgement of 'the god', whom I will always regard as the protector of the city, and who would not therefore interfere with a καλῶς ἔχον πόλει πάλαισμα. For the οὐ λήξω idiom see Bond on Eur. *Heracles* 673.

882   ὑπέροπτα: the neuter plural of adjectives can be used as adverbs particularly with verbs of motion, as here πορεύεται: 'proceeds haughtily in deed or word'. Cf. *Ai.* 197–8 ὕβρις ὧδ' ἀτάρβητα ὁρμᾶται. Aristotle, *Eth. Nic.* 1124a29 speaks of ὑπερόπται καὶ ὑβρισταί. Dobree conjectured ὑπέροπλα, found in one manuscript before correction. A glance at LSJ *s.v.* will show that the word is suitable to our context, and at *Ant.* 130 ὑπεροπλίαις is required at a place where almost all manuscripts, except two, both written by a certain Zacharias Callierges, offer a word beginning with ὑπεροπτ-.

886 ἕδη: either statues, or holy places, as at Aesch. *Pers.* 404, Eur. *Hcld.* 103. It has often been surmised that Sophocles is here alluding obliquely to the mutilation of the Hermae in 415 B.C. There is no positive reason for any such supposition.

888 χλιδᾶς: χλιδή here is equivalent to the τρυφή in the Stobaeus quotation cited at 873n. In fact our scholia write ἕνεκα τῆς ἀνοσίου τρυφῆς here. χλιδή is linked with αὐθαδία at [Aesch.] *Prom. Vinct.* 436.

889 εἰ μή . . . : the main verb (ἕλοιτο) was preceded by a conditional clause. Editors assume that it is here followed by one as well, but this is not certain, since until we can be sure of the meaning of 892 we cannot be certain that a new protasis to a new sentence does not begin here. If it did, the full stop following χλιδᾶς would give the same stanza structure as the full stop following βροτοῖς in 902.

890 ἕρξεται: future middle of εἴργω: 'and keeps away from unholy deeds'.

891 θίξεται: the opposite of ἕρξεται: 'or if he touches what must not be touched'. The phrase is similar to κινήσοντά τι τῶν ἀκινήτων at Herodotus 6.134.2, to violate what must remain inviolate. ἄθικτος of holy things memorably at Aesch. *Agam.* 369–72.

μαтάιζων: see 874n. and cf. *Trach.* 565 ψαύει ματαίαις χερσίν.

892 An impossible line to understand. ἕτι ποτ᾽ ἐν τοῖσδ᾽ presumably means 'at any time thereafter in this situation' – not poetically brilliant but not obviously corrupt either. θυμῶι is quite unintelligible, and so too is βέλη unless further specified: hence θεῶν βέλη Hermann. The less well attested θυμοῦ will give the same sense as καρδίας τοξεύματα, shafts that pierce the heart, at *Ant.* 1085. The worst problem is the verb, erroneously repeated from 890. εὕξεται (Musgrave) has been a popular choice, meaning either 'boast' or 'pray', in which case it ought to govern a future infinitive: the only apparent exceptions are Aesch. *Agam.* 933, where ἕρξειν for ἕρδειν was conjectured by Headlam, and Soph. *Phil.* 1032 where Pierson's ἕξεσθ᾽ for εὕξεσθ᾽ is correct. Neither meaning dispels our difficulties. We do not even know whether we should be looking for the basic sense 'What wicked man shall ever escape the wrath of the gods?' or 'Who, in company like this, shall ever make pious prayers?' In a totally desperate place we may, *faute de mieux*, provisionally rewrite with Hermann's θεῶν βέλη and Enger's ἀρκέσει. 'What man in this situation will be strong enough thereafter to keep from his life the shafts of the gods?'

895 γάρ: I ask because if . . .

896 χορεύειν: serve the gods through the medium of the dance. At Eur. *Bacch.* 184 ποῖ δεῖ χορεύειν occurs in a context where the religious overtones of χορεύειν are plainer. ποῖ for τί would suit well here too, with various geographical alternatives about to be explored in the following antistrophe. The *syllaba anceps* would then be long in both strophe and antistrophe. 'To what place should I <go and> dance?'

ποῖ is often used with such an ellipse, not only at Eur. *Bacch.* 184 but also at *Alc.* 863 (though there ποῖ βῶ precedes), *Herc.* 74, Ar. *Eccles.* 837, and in Soph. at *Oed. Col.* 23. For a false τί where most MSS have ποῖ see *Ant.* 42 (Zf).

'To dance in a chorus was to devote oneself to a god; hence the meaning "devotee" or "pupil" which attached itself to the word χορευτής.' See J. W. Fitton, *C.Q.* n.s. 23 (1973) 254–78, who compares Plato, *Phaedr.* 252d, Julian, *Or.* 6.197D, Libanius, *Or.* 54.38. See also 1092 below.

χορεύειν is precisely what the Chorus who are acting in this play are doing, and there are some who feel that at this moment Sophocles is in a sense breaking the dramatic illusion, like Aristophanes in a *parabasis*, and saying very nearly, 'If such practices are held in honour, why should I go on writing and helping to produce tragedies for the Dionysiac festival?'

897 ἄθικτον: no special effect seems intended, although the identical word was used just above at 891.

ὀμφαλόν: cf. 480.

899 Ἀβαῖσι: in north-west Phocis. Its wealthy temple was sacked by the Persians in 480 B.C. (Herodotus 8.33).

902 ἁρμόσει: intransitive, as at *Ant.* 1318, *El.* 1293: 'fit', i.e. if the predictions and the events do not match in such a way that all men can point to them (sc. as notable examples of the infallibility of religion). It is curious that what the Chorus are really praying for, though they hardly seem conscious of it, is that Oedipus shall be exposed as a conspicuous sinner.

903 ὀρθ ἀκούεις: 'are rightly so called'. The Chorus use words reminiscent of the kind of formula that we find at Aesch. *Agam.* 160f. Ζεύς, ὅστις πότ᾿ ἐστιν, εἰ τόδ᾿ αὐτῶι φίλον κεκλημένωι 'if this name is pleasing to him'. (See Fraenkel ad loc. and contrast the more perfunctory Ζεὺς δ, ὅστις ὁ Ζεύς at Eur. *Herc.* 1263 and the more wide-ranging passage at *Tro.* 884–6.) The difference is that here in *Oed. Tyr.* the sense is 'if you *are* rightly called "ruler"'; i.e. let us see you deserve your name by making the oracles come true. The περ in εἴπερ justifies the italics. See 369n.

906–7 παλαίφατα | θέσφατ᾿: the variants recorded in the *apparatus criticus* are particularly illuminating for anyone trying to sort out the various manuscript constellations. For the emendation printed cf. Hom. *Od.* 9.507 (= 13.172) ὢ πόποι, ἦ μάλα δή με παλαίφατα θέσφαθ᾿ ἱκάνει.

907 ἐξαιροῦσιν: the subject is an unspecified 'they'. 'They' are discarding the fading oracles of Laius (i.e. *about* Laius). Some of the audience may have mentally extended the reference to include the wide-ranging collection of oracles known as 'the oracles of Laius' mentioned by Herodotus, 5.43. Such an idea may help to explain the tone of 909–10, which seem to hint at a more general decline in religious observance than the failure of one specific oracle would justify.

910 τὰ θεῖα: religious observance, as at *Oed. Col.* 1537.

The closing words of the Chorus are true but misleading. Even if Jocasta has made light of oracles, none the less every effort is being made to establish whether they are true or false in the present case. The Chorus' words however provide an excellent foil to Jocasta's immediate appearance on a mission of piety which contrasts strongly with her recent remarks 857–8. It is now not much ὕστερον (858), yet it is Jocasta herself who will make Apollo τιμαῖς ἐμφανής (909) before our eyes at this very moment.

911–1085 Fourth epeisodion

See Introduction 14–15.

911 δόξα . . . παρεστάθη: cf. τύχη . . . ἐπέστη 777.

912–13 With her στέφη and ἐπιθυμιάματα Jocasta provides a royal and private counterpart to the public acts of piety at the opening of the play, 3–4 (ἐξεστεμμένοι, θυμιαμάτων). But we are now looking for help *for* Oedipus, not *from* him.

914 ὑψοῦ γὰρ αἴρει θυμόν: in itself the phrase could mean a number of things. At Plato, *Rep.* 494d ὑψηλὸν ἐξαρεῖν αὐτόν is used of some one corrupted by power along the lines poetically laid down at *Oed. Tyr.* 872ff. But here Jocasta means that Oedipus is in a state of heightened awareness, keyed up; cf. Eur. *Hec.* 69–70 τί ποτ' αἴρομαι ἔννυχος οὕτω | δείμασι, φάσμασιν;

915 οὐδ ὁποῖ' ἀνὴρ κ.τ.ἑ. 'and it is not like a man of sense that he judges the recent, strange (καινά means both) developments in the light of the past; on the contrary, he is under the sway of any one who comes to him with a tale of fear to tell'. Oedipus *has* been comparing the present with the past, with results that he finds disturbing (726). It is therefore incorrect to translate these lines as if they meant 'and he does not do what a sensible man would do, viz. judge the present in the light of the past', though this is how they have been interpreted from the time of the scholia onward, the argument being that since the oracle given to Laius has proved false, so too may the predictions of Teiresias be false. τὰ καινά τοῖς πάλαι is phrased too generally for us to make such specific deductions. It is not Jocasta's function to talk Delphically. For the layout οὐδ. . . ἀλλ' cf. 1278–9.

917 ἔστι τοῦ λέγοντος: cf. Ar. *Knights* 860 ὦ δαιμόνιε, μὴ τοῦ λέγοντος ἴσθι.

ἦν . . . λέγηι: εἰ . . . λέγοι, in some manuscripts, can be defended, even though the sequence is primary: cf. *Ant.* 1032 (though the MSS vary), or Hom. *Od.* 1.414 οὔτ' οὖν ἀγγελίηι ἔτι πείθομαι, εἴ ποθεν ἔλθοι.

918 πλέον: not 'more'. The sense is of making headway with something, or gaining some advantage as at Aesch *Pers.* 631, Soph. *Ant.* 40, 268, *Phil.* 818, Eur. *Hcld.* 466, *Hipp.* 284, *Ion* 1255, *Hel.* 322, *I.T.* 496, *I.A.* 1373, frg. 84, Phocylides 3 (τί πλέον γένος εὐγενὲς εἶναι), Peek *GVI* 1508 ἀλλὰ πλέον θνητοῖς οὐδὲν ὀδυρομένοις, Moschion fr. 7.2; in prose e.g. Hdt. 1.89.

ποιῶ = ◡ –, so spelled ποῶ by many MSS: but see Threatte *GAI* 1 324–9.

919 ἄγχιστος: 'nearest'. Apollo is nearest in three senses: (*a*) physically, through his statue, altar or other symbol, e.g. the stone of Apollo Agyieus at the front of the house; (*b*) he is to be, hopes Jocasta, a very present help in trouble: for this usage cf. Aesch. *Agam.* 256, Pindar, *Pyth.* 9.64; and (*c*) because he is most closely connected with the oracles to be worked out within the family circle (cf. 1329).

920 κατάργμασιν: the ἐπιθυμιάματα, offerings, ἀπαρχαί. So Eur. *I.T.* 244f. χέρνι-βας δὲ καὶ κατάργματα | οὐκ ἂν φθάνοις ἂν εὐτρεπῆ ποιουμένη. Sophocles is in effect writing a stage direction into his text. τοῖσδε all but proves that some physical object is meant, so we may discard the manuscripts' κατεύγμασιν, which would in any case provide a poor antecedent to the final clause ὅπως ... πόρῃς. P. Stengel in his article on κατάρχεσθαι and ἐνάρχεσθαι in *Hermes* 43 (1908) 459 takes κατάργμασιν for granted here. It looks very much as though the same error has even occurred on an inscription, *IG* vii.235 = Dittenberger, *Syll.* 1004 = Buck no. 14. The inscription has κατεύχεσθαι δὲ τῶν ἱερῶν, and Stengel conjectured κατάρχεσθαι. A genuine κατεύχεσθαι comes on the stone three lines later.

921 εὐαγῆ: derived from εὖ + ἄγος; cf. *Ant.* 521. But there is another, more spec-ulative, possibility, that the word in question is εὐᾱγής, bright, clear, a word used of the Sun, and so appropriate to Apollo. (For the possible connection of Λύκειος with light see 203n.) The Chorus have asked that the oracles shall fit χειρόδεικτα, and have complained that Apollo is not τιμαῖς ἐμφανής. But now that Jocasta has made him τιμαῖς ἐμφανής, perhaps he will send a εὐαγὴς λύσις, corresponding to a λαμπρός oracle (see 81n.), a λύσις that will clear the air and be seen far and wide.

922–3 Jocasta means 'we are as afraid as a crew would be that sees its helms-man dashed overboard', but she has expressed herself with a little too much speed. Since the metaphor is familiar, there is no chance of her not being understood. Aristotle invokes the idea at *Physics* 195a: 'We ascribe the wreck of a ship to the absence of the pilot whose presence was the cause of its safety.' Cf. Stobaeus 3.35.7–8 ἐν μὲν τῶι πλεῖν πείθεσθαι δεῖ τῶι κυβερνήτηι, ἐν δὲ τῶι ζῆν τῶι λογίζεσθαι βέλτιον.

924 The rôle of the Corinthian messenger is curiously garbled by Aristotle, *Poetics* 1452a. He wishes to illustrate περιπέτεια according to probability or necessity, and gives as an example (with no subject expressed in our texts) ἐν τῶι Οἰδίποδι ἐλθὼν ὡς εὐφρανῶν τὸν Οἰδίπουν καὶ ἀπαλλάξων τοῦ πρὸς τὴν μητέρα φόβου, δηλώσας ὃς ἦν, τοὐναντίον ἐποίησεν. What the messenger actually comes to do is to offer Oedipus the throne of Corinth, now that Polybus is dead. Later (1002, 1016) he assures Oedipus that Polybus was not his father. The messenger did not come with the *intention* of releasing Oedipus from fears over his mother *or* father; and in any case he has much more to say about Polybus as Oedipus' non-father than about Merope as his non-mother. The present participle ἀπαλλάσσων in codex B of the *Poetics*, would be of some help in meeting the objection about intention, but leaves the point about ὁ πρὸς τὴν μητέρα φόβος untouched. See also 774n.

The arrival of the Corinthian messenger has been described as the only event in the play lacking sound human motivation. It is as though, by this coincidence, the gods were mocking Jocasta's act of piety. The messenger does indeed herald a λύσις, but it is not one that will be εὐαγής.

With the possible exception of some scenes in Homer, the next three hundred lines constitute the finest achievement in Greek poetic technique to have survived to our era. It begins on a quiet enough note, very similar to the arrival of the bogus messenger (Orestes) at *El.* 1098.

926   μάλιστα: 'better still'.

928   ἥδε is the subject, 'this lady here', and γυνή, μήτηρ τε τῶν κείνου τέκνων the predicate. The full description of Jocasta, and the juxtaposition of γυνή and μήτηρ, create an ominous effect in the minds of those who know more than the characters on stage. As the scholia say, κἀνταῦθα ἔθηκεν τὸ ἀμφίβολον ὃ τέρπει τὸν ἀκροατήν.

929–30   The messenger's blessing is a *captatio benevolentiae*, from a lower member of society to his betters, and one which finds an echo in every day and age. His third person γένοιτ᾽, if genuine (γένοι᾽ Wecklein), will be a further expression of polite deference; he does not like to accost the queen directly.

γ᾽: causal: seeing that she is …

παντελὴς δάμαρ: his wife from every point of view, the complete wife. The messenger indicates that the fullness of the description Jocasta has just been given has not been lost on him. The word τέλος is used also of the marriage rite itself. Pollux 3.38 καὶ τέλειος ὁ γάμος ἐκαλεῖτο, καὶ τέλειοι οἱ γεγαμηκότες.

933   ἀφῖξαι: another, to our taste superfluous, verb of motion or presence, where all the weight of the sentence falls on the accompanying participles. See 515n.

935   πρὸς τίνος: Jocasta asks 'Who sent you?', not expecting the messenger to reply that he has come not from an individual but from a whole city. See below 940n.

936   τὸ δ᾽ ἔπος: 'as for the message'. Accusative of respect; cf. 785 τὰ μὲν κείνοιν ἐτερπόμην.

οὑξερῶ: ὃ ἐξερῶ.

937   The messenger is now more guarded than he was at 934. His πῶς δ᾽ οὐκ ἄν self-interruption, and his balanced phraseology ἥδοιο ∼ ἀσχάλλοις, as he draws a distinction as he did at 925–6 between δώματ᾽ and αὐτόν, sound like a piece of Sophoclean character-drawing. Already, in eight lines, by processes that elude analysis, Sophocles has given his messenger a quite distinctive manner of speech. However, the remarks on joy and grief are odd, coming from a messenger. Coming from Sophocles, one could understand them – joy at the prospect of the throne of Corinth, joy (964ff.) at no longer having to fear killing his father, as Oedipus still believes Polybus to be at this stage in the play, but pain at the loss of a parent.

938   τί δ ἔστι: preceding a more specific question, as at 1144, *Trach.* 339, *Ant.* 387, *Phil.* 896.

ποίαν: ποῖον (sc. ἔπος) was taken for granted without discussion by M. L. Earle in his commentary, perhaps by accident, since no alteration was made in his text. The case for it is well argued by H. Reynen, *Gymnasium* 67 (1960) 533–6. The manuscript reading ποίαν cuts across ὧδ᾽, and the question is answered almost before it is put, lit. 'What is the double effect that it has like this?' Furthermore the messenger does not answer ποίαν δύναμιν but ποῖον (sc. ἔπος). Cf. ἔστιν δὲ ποῖον τοῦπος; (89) and ποῖον ἐρεῖς τόδ᾽ ἔπος; *Phil.* 1204.

Defenders of ποίαν may reply that the messenger is answering not ποῖον but τί δ᾽ ἔστι; and that ποίαν is not so much a genuine query as a slightly amused comment, in the form of a question, on the messenger's portentous style: cf. 89. 'What sort of double effect is this that you describe?' A formal parallel (this time anything but amused) is *Ai.* 46 ποίαισι τολμαῖς ταῖσδε. Such an interpretation is adequate, and in Sophocles we need not press for logical precision. But the merits of ποῖον remain considerable.

939–40   χθονὸς τῆς Ἰσθμίας: dependent on τύραννον. Another conspicuous case of hybris *not* being the parent of tyranny (see 872n.).

940   ὡς ηὐδᾶτ᾽ ἐκεῖ: the messenger then is not an official representative, but one hoping to earn a reward on his own account by enterprisingly informing Oedipus of local gossip. 1005–6 are an engagingly honest confession of his motives.

942   No longer ἐγκρατής, but in the power of Death. 'Said with peasant humour' think Schneidewin–Nauck. The variant δόμοις for τάφοις is stylistically superior, and it is easy to see how τάφοις could have started life as a gloss. But it is none too well attested, and the messenger may be no great stylist, to the question 'Isn't Polybus still in power?' bluntly replying 'No; he is dead and buried.'

943   The words Πόλυβος, ὦ γέρον are conjectural, and suspicion remains. The repetition of the proper name Πόλυβος from 941 is uncharacteristic – but then we may argue that Sophocles wishes to get his point across with absolute clarity. All manuscripts except two cease after Πόλυβος, and continue with the first words of the messenger's reply. The two manuscripts to have anything in the gap write the incredible and unmetrical ἤ τέθνηκέ που Πόλυβος γέρων. The note of surmise given by ἤ ... που is unsuitable after definite news has been given, and not even a proper name can create a so-called 'fifth-foot' anapaest unless it is of the metrical shape ‿‿‿¯, as, e.g., at *Ant.* 11, 1180, *Oed. Col.* 1. The presence of που, and the erroneous repetition of Πόλυβος, could be accounted for if we assumed an original ἤ τέθνηκεν Οἰδίπου πατήρ, on which Πόλυβος was a gloss (for such a phenomenon see 825–7n.). That was Nauck's conjecture of 1856, not printed by him in his edition of 1872, but accepted by Pearson. But then the messenger ought by rights to reply, 'No, not Oedipus' father, but as I have just said, Polybus' (though it is true he does not correct the same misapprehension when he replies to 955–6). This point was appreciated by Nauck, who rewrote the next line to include mention of Polybus.

The text adopted by us, Bothe's Πόλυβος, ὦ γέρον, cannot be regarded as anywhere near certain, but at least ὦ γέρον is a suitable way of addressing the messenger: cf. γέρον 1001, (ὦ) γεραιέ 990 and 1009, and πρέσβυ 1013.

944 The metrical problems caused by the deficient text of the previous line have repercussed here, as the *apparatus* shows. In itself λέγω 'γώ is not to be rejected on grounds of euphony. There is however not enough space for it, or for the εἰ δὲ μή of most manuscripts, and there is nothing to be gained by ἀντιλαβή, i.e. beginning the messenger's reply at some point late in the previous line. As printed 944 is crisp and good.

946 ὦ θεῶν μαντεύματα: In the excitement the distinction drawn at 711 f. is forgotten.

947 ἵν' ἐστέ: 'See where you lie now.' Similarly 1311 ἰὼ δαῖμον, ἵν' ἐξῆλου. The exclamatory force is not extinguished by the interrogative even at 367, 413, 687; and so 953.

950 A very formal address for a man to give his wife, but as at *Ant.* 1 (ὦ κοινὸν αὐτάδελφον Ἰσμήνης κάρα) we are at a point of much gravity.

951 ἐξεπέμψω: the middle voice, as in μεταπέμπομαι; 'sent for me to come out here'.

955 ἥκει Κορίνθου: 'He comes from Corinth' gives a better answer to the question put than 'from Corinth' (ἐκ τῆς Κορίνθου, given by the manuscripts by a false reminiscence of 936) could ever do.

957 σημάντωρ: there is a variant σημήνας, but decisive in favour of the noun are the parallels of ἐσηγητὴς γενοῦ at Hdt. 5.31.2 and διηγητὴς γενοῦ at Ach. Tat. 4.15.3. σημάντωρ is, as it happens, not used in the pre-Alexandrian period in the sense of 'informant'. But the word itself occurs in Homer, of one who gives signals, hence a commander. It is likely that Oedipus is playing on the latent self-importance that seems to be inherent in some messengers in tragedy. To be asked to be the instructor of a king is a high compliment, and that the normal roles are in this instance to be reversed is the point of αὐτός.

958 What would the messenger have mentioned second? The same as at 939–40, *viz.* the prospect of the Corinthian throne? Or would he have corrected the equation πατέρα τὸν σόν = Πόλυβον? In any event he seems nettled at the insistence of his betters that he give priority to the less attractive side of his message.

960 The experienced politician senses intrigue, as he did with Teiresias and Creon, and as he did at 124–5.

ξυναλλαγῆι: the same word as at 34, and as there clothing a matter of some solemnity with an expression whose meaning cannot be pinned down. 'Or touched by some disease' (?).

961–3   A slight tilt of the balance is all it needs to lay an aged frame to rest. The most beautiful line in Sophocles receives from the great administrator – notwithstanding the sympathetic ὁ τλήμων – the unnecessary and faintly impatient (ὡς ἔοικεν) clarification of a coroner's verdict (962) softened again by the old countryman.

ῥοπή: at Pindar, *Pyth.* 9.25 ῥέποντα is used of sleep that weighs down gently upon the eyelids. But ῥοπή is also a medical term: see B. M. W. Knox, *Oedipus at Thebes* (London 1957) n. 114 (246–7) who among other examples cites Aretaeus 3.12 βραχείης ῥοπῆς ἐς εὐνὴν θανάτου. Cf. Eur. *Hipp.* 1163 where it is said of an Hippolytus who is near death δέδορκε μέντοι φῶς ἐπὶ σμικρᾶς ῥοπῆς.

συμμετρούμενος: cf. 73.

964–72   Oedipus' sudden release of emotion, signalled by φεῦ φεῦ, begins with some disparaging remarks about the Delphic oracle and the reliability of cawing birds as guides to the probabilities of parricide. Oedipus did not think much of birds at 395, 398, either. At 967 his excitement is mirrored in a metrically most unusual line with three resolved long syllables: ∪ – ∪ – | – ⌢⌣ ∪ ⌢⌣ | ∪ ⌢⌣ ∪ –. (According to S. L. Schein's figures *ITAS* 77, in the whole play there are 82 resolutions in the 1189 trimeters.) There follows a strained attempt at humour, enshrined in a conditional clause not logically integrated with the main sentence, and the whole ends on a note of triumphant relish. The triumph will not last long.

968   δή: possibly half-temporal, approximating to ἤδη, but more likely stressing the adverb, as, e.g. δή emphasizes πέλας at Eur. *Ion* 393. Laius is actually under ground now.

968–9   ἐγὼ δ ὅδ᾽ ἐνθάδε κ.τ.ἑ: and here am I, and I haven't so much as laid hands on a sword. ἔγχους is another genitive dependent on an alpha-privative adjective. The passive use of such constructions is more frequent, but attempts to make the meaning 'untouched by sword', referring to Polybus, with ἐγὼ δ ὅδ᾽ ἐνθάδε as a parenthesis by itself, are most unattractive.

969   εἴ τι μή 'unless perhaps … '. Oedipus' humour is far-fetched; so far-fetched that such scholars as Nauck and Groeneboom have even argued that humour is not his aim at all, but the words are of a man piously seeking some way of reconciling the apparent facts with the oracular prediction. συλλαβών and ἄξι᾽ οὐδενός in the next couplet prove however that Oedipus is indeed contemptuous of oracles, at this moment.

τὠμῶι πόθωι: longing *for* me. Cf. Hom. *Od.* 11.202–3 ἀλλά με σός τε πόθος … μελιηδέα θυμὸν ἀπηύρα, and Ar. *Peace* 584 σῶι γὰρ ἐδάμην πόθωι.

970   ἂν θανὼν εἴη: the effect of the periphrasis is, '*that* would make his death my responsibility'. Cf. Antiphon 2.4.4 ὁ παιδοτρίβης ἂν ἀποκτείνας αὐτὸν εἴη.

971   δ᾽ οὖν: whatever the cause of death may have been, the important fact is …

παρόντα: imperfect participle: cf. 835n. The oracles that were before us are now παρ᾽ Ἅιδηι. παρόντα has been much emended, and certainly we know of isolated manuscripts of Sophocles writing παροῦσι for πολλοῖσι (*Ai.* 682) and παρόντας for θανόντας (*El.* 940). Pearson conjectured προδόντα, in the intransitive sense of 'having failed'; cf. *Ai.* 1267 (where 'betrayed' will not suit χάρις), probably Aesch. *Cho.* 269 notwithstanding the apparent parallel of 'betraying' at *Eum.* 64, Herodotus 7.187 (of rivers giving out). But προδόντα is an unwelcome anticipation of ἄξι' οὐδενός. Other suggestions are no better. Oedipus' dismissal of the oracles, which, he says, Polybus has taken off with him to the nether world, should be compared and contrasted with the words Teiresias had used at 460 f. in his καὶ ταῦτ' ἰὼν εἴσω λογίζου.

973 πάλαι: 'Isn't that what I've been telling you all along?' As Jocasta enjoys her moment of satisfaction over the failure of oracles, she uses of herself a word, προύλεγον, that has a particular connection with oracular predictions.

974 τῶι φόβωι: not just 'by fear', a translation which ignores the article, but 'my fear' (Jebb), or 'the element of fear', or, most probably, the specific fear attaching to the possible event that has just been under discussion.

975 ἐς θυμὸν βάληις: 'take to heart'.

976 Jocasta had inadvertently half opened the door to Oedipus' apprehensive question by using the phrase αὐτῶν μηδέν instead of τοῦτο μή.

977 τὰ τῆς τύχης: a common expression, even in prose. What Chance has to offer. τύχη τὰ θνητῶν πράγματ', οὐκ εὐβουλία Chaeremon frg. 2.

979 δύναιτο: see 315n.

980 εἰς: have no fears in that direction. Cf. φοβῇι πρός at *Trach.* 1211.

981 κἄν: the only meaning to be extracted from the Greek that is even faintly plausible for the context is 'in dreams too <as you have been warned you will do by this oracle>, plenty of men have slept with their mothers'. It is not easy to make the necessary mental supplement, for at first sight the words mean 'in dreams too <as in real life>' – as if Jocasta were casually assuring Oedipus that incest was quite an ordinary occurrence. It may be significant that in our oldest manuscript, L, κἄν is written in an erasure. But a convincing monosyllabic correction seems beyond our grasp.

983 παρ' οὐδέν: 'of no importance'. Cf. *Ant.* 35, *El.* 1327.

984 καλῶς: all very well and good; precisely similar in tone to 859. Two lines below, in κεἰ καλῶς λέγεις, καλῶς has changed to something less idiomatic: 'even if you are right'.

987 ὀφθαλμός: metaphorically this word, like ὄμμα, can mean anything highly prized: cf. Aesch. *Pers.* 168–9, *Cho.* 934, Eur. *Andr.* 406, Pindar, *Ol.* 2.10, 6.16. None of the meanings to be elicited from those passages fits easily here. The sense we expect is omen, augury, or indication. Blaydes's οἰωνός will give that sense; cf. Eur. *Or.* 788, also with μέγας. Defence of ὀφθαλμός has to rest on the fact that its synonym, ὄμμα, would yield an acceptable, though different, sense: the death of Polybus to be considered as a bright spot on the horizon (see LSJ *s.v.* ὄμμα III).

989 ποίας: more lively than τίνος (cf. ποίαν 938). The messenger wonders what description of woman it may be that causes such reactions in the royal couple. καί contributes to the same effect. '*Who* is the woman . . . ?' See Denniston, *GP*² 312.

ἐκφοβεῖσθ': The use of the plural is an interesting touch. It is not honorific; the substitution of plural forms of address for singulars (you for thou, *vous* for *tu*, etc.) only took place in Greek at a later era: see Wackernagel, *VUS* I. 101. It may be that the messenger has seen that Jocasta's words of reassurance do not stem from any genuine inner conviction.

990–4 With γεραιέ, ὦ ξένε (992) and the genial μάλιστά γ' (994), Oedipus seems to establish a closer and more relaxed *rapport* with the messenger.

990 Oedipus does not need to tell the messenger that Polybus 'lived with' Merope. Even if Sophocles wishes to remind his audience of the position once again, the reason why he has chosen this form of words, and not, e.g., called Merope, as Jebb revealingly translates the phrase, 'the consort of Polybus', is not entirely clear. See on 774–5.

991 ἐς φόβον φέρον: cf. 517n.

997–8 The language is reminiscent of 794–5, and again the phrase 'gave Corinth a wide berth' comes to mind. What we have before us is ἐγὼ μακρὰν ἀπῴκουν τῆς Κορίνθου put into the passive voice.

999 A human touch. Cf. Hom. *Od.* 9.34–6 ὡς οὐδὲν γλύκιον ἧς πατρίδος οὐδὲ τοκήων | γίγνεται, εἴ περ καί τις ἀπόπροθι πίονα οἶκον | γαίηι ἐν ἀλλοδαπῆι ναίει ἀπάνευθε τοκήων.

1002–3 A good question: he had his opportunity following 955–6, or, if Nauck was right, following 943. But to intervene then would have been merely to correct a misapprehension. Only now has the messenger a powerful reason for setting the record straight.

1004 χάριν . . . ἀξίαν: even more of a euphemism than εὖ πράξαιμί τι (1006). At 232 Oedipus had mentioned concrete reward before χάρις; and so *Trach.* 191 πρὸς σοῦ τι κερδάναιμι καὶ κτώιμην χάριν.

1005 μάλιστα τοῦτ': that is mainly what I came for . . . The messenger's καὶ μήν following Oedipus' καὶ μήν . . . γε ('well certainly') is judged by Denniston, *GP*² 354 to be 'rather impudent'. It is perhaps rather the case that the geniality of the one has its influence on the other.

1006 σοῦ πρὸς δόμους ἐλθόντος: Oedipus could perfectly well reward the messenger now, without waiting to be installed at Corinth. But the phrase opens the door to Oedipus' reply, which in turn precipitates the countryman's frightening disclosures.

1007   ἀλλ': rebutting the suggestion implied in πρός δόμους ἐλθόντος that he should return home to Corinth.

γ': underlining: not them, of all people. Since Polybus is dead, the reference is really to Merope, even though φυτεύω is used more of male parents.

ὁμοῦ: the phrase ὁμοῦ + dative is used because it can also suggest sexual association. Cf. 337n., *Trach.* 1237.

1008   ὦ παῖ: the father of his people, the κυβερνήτης (923), is now addressed as a son, or at any rate a junior, by the old countryman (cf. the corresponding ὦ γεραιέ in the next line). Aeschylus achieved a similar effect in *Seven Against Thebes* 686, when the Chorus, who had hitherto been terrified and dependent on Eteocles, mark the change in his dramatic rôle by calling him τέκνον.

καλῶς: cf. *El.* 1017, Ar. *Lys.* 510.

εἶ δῆλος: the personal construction for 'you are clearly', as at *Phil.* 1011 δῆλος δὲ καὶ νῦν ἐστιν ἀλγεινῶς φέρων or Ar. *Birds* 1407 καταγελᾶις μου, δῆλος εἶ. In combination with the καλῶς idiom Ar. *Lys.* 919 ἦ τοι γυνὴ φιλεῖ με, δήλη 'στὶν καλῶς.

1011   ταρβῶν is in the manuscripts UY, and in our earliest printed text, the Aldine edition of 1502, which was primarily based on Y. AUY normally form a very closely knit group, yet here A, like all manuscripts other than UY, has ταρβῶ. The participle is much to be preferred. It is like χρήιζων at 1001.

1014   πρὸς δίκης: cf. *El.* 1211 πρὸς δίκης γὰρ οὐ στένεις.

1018   ἀλλ' ἴσον: in itself a weak addition, but useful when exploited in Oedipus' reply.

1019   ὁ φύσας: Oedipus' choice of word for 'father' shows that the messenger's previous remark has not fully sunk in, or is at any rate not yet accepted.

τῶι μηδενί: in itself 'a mere nobody', but in the context 'someone totally unrelated', like οὐδὲν ἐν γένει (1016).

1020   οὔτ' ἐγώ: another case of parataxis where we would use some kind of subordination: 'any more than I did'.

1021   ἀντὶ τοῦ: 'Why'; or more fully, 'What consideration led him to call me his son?' The messenger does not answer Oedipus' question precisely in the terms in which it is put.

1023   ὧδ' ἀπ' ἄλλης χειρός: we might wish to understand '<me, coming from> another's hand like this'. But grammatical prudence teaches us that the phrase is to be construed with another λαβών, supplied from the previous line. ὧδ' is much better taken with this putative λαβών ('in the way you describe') than with ἔστερξεν μέγα. See also 1037n.

1025   ἐμπολήσας: did you buy me?

τυχών: all manuscripts have τεκών, which will hardly do after both sides have expressly said that the messenger is as unrelated to Oedipus as any one could possibly be. We seem to see before us the original Freudian scribal error. κιχών, from κιγχάνω, is an equally plausible emendation. εὑρών in the following line shows clearly enough what kind of participle should be opposed to ἐμπολήσας here. Cf. οὐδ' αὐτὸς τυχών at 1039.

1026 εὑρών: the messenger is not as forthcoming as he might be, especially with ἐμπολήσας in the line before, with its suggestion of things changing hands from one person to another. Not until 1038–40 shall we learn that the child was given to him by someone else. Sophocles is not the man to waste all his ammunition at once.

ναπαίαις . . . πτυχαῖς 'winding glens' (Jebb), suitably reversing the rôles of noun and adjective in translation.

1029 γάρ: you mean you were a shepherd . . . ?

θητείαι: a θής stood very low in the social order, and the messenger's reply to this description of himself contains within it the elements of a dignified reproof.

πλάνης: nominative singular, continuing the idea of travel inherent in ὡδοιπόρεις (1027). The Corinthian prefers to describe his way of life in more stationary terms (ἐπεστάτουν).

1030 σοῦ τ': σοῦ δ. . . γε which is only in one manuscript, would mean 'yes, but . . .' – too overt and spirited for the context. σοῦ γ' in the others would leave us with two occurrences of γε too close together in the same sentence: 'yes, and I *saved* you'. It is Hermann's τ' that gives the right tone, an understatement of the idea 'I was a ποιμήν and I was a θής, but to that you can add the fact that I was the one who saved your life.'

ὦ τέκνον: we have come a long way from the *pater patriae* figure of the opening lines, though the herdsman's choice of address may be influenced by his recollection of the time when Oedipus really was a child. However, τῶι τότ' ἐν χρόνωι is itself not entirely above suspicion: when the phrase was used at 564 questions of time were paramount; in the present context an allusion to the physical distress of an infant provides a more obvious opening for the τί ἄλγος of Oedipus' next question: hence Hertel's τῶι τότ' ἐν πόνωι.

1031 ἐν χεροῖν was conjectured by at least three scholars independently before being found as a variant in one or two of our manuscripts. It fits well with 1022–3. Our oldest manuscript (L) and a few others have ἐν καιροῖς, which except for the last letter is phonetically the same as ἐν χεροῖν in later Greek pronunciation – thus χερός appears as καιρός in two manuscripts at *Trach.* 517. All our other manuscripts here have the listless ἐν κακοῖς. It remains worrying that the *concept* of καιρός, the idea of arriving in time to save the child's life, as opposed to its actual unmetrical manifestation in manuscripts, is appropriate, and a number of conjectures have been made to try to restore that sense, none of them persuasive.

Oedipus' question τί δ' ἄλγος ἴσχοντ' and its sequel strongly suggest that Sophocles intended his Oedipus to know about his pierced feet. If so, he ought to have latched on to the vital clue given him by Jocasta at 717–19, even if it was wrapped up in the word ἐνζεύξας. But Sophoclean characters in other plays besides this one seem at times to suffer from dramatically convenient transitory amnesia. In *Proceedings of the Cambridge Philological Society* n.s. 12 (1966) 22 Fitton Brown used the argument from real life, that although Oedipus would be conscious of his lameness, he would not know the cause. 'A surgeon has informed me that a growing child, however intelligent, would not be able to infer, from examining his body, that his feet had been deliberately pierced three days after birth. There would be no palpable scars left.' Fitton Brown continued with the other dangerous real-life argument that Polybus and Merope could not 'have explained away the mutilation without admitting that Oedipus had once been outside their care'. It is better to accept the inconsistency (see Introduction *passim*) as typical of Sophoclean technique than to invest the author with the attributes of a paediatric (not to say podiatric) Agatha Christie.

1032 ποδῶν ... ἄρθρα: cf. 718n.

1033 τί: 'What' rather than 'Why'.

1035 γ': mildly exclamatory. Cf. *Ai.* 1127 κτείναντα; δεινόν γ' εἶπας, εἰ καὶ ζῆις θανών, *El.* 341 f. δεινόν γέ σ' οὖσαν πατρὸς οὗ σὺ παῖς ἔφυς | κείνου λελῆσθαι. Further examples in Diggle on Eur. *Phaethon* 164.

   ὄνειδος: his disfigurement.

   σπαργάνων is to be construed with the verb; as we would say, 'from my cradle' (lit. the clothes in which a baby is wrapped). Aelian, *Var. hist.* 2.7 records a Theban law by which unwanted children were not to be exposed but taken to the magistrates σὺν τοῖς σπαργάνοις.

1036–7 πρὸς μητρὸς ἢ πατρός: These words are plainly not to be construed with ὠνομάσθης, and to refer them further back to διατόρους or ἀνειλόμην is impossibly strained. For a thousand years commentators had noted that the line fits neither with what precedes nor with what follows, but editors were strangely reluctant to draw the obvious conclusion that there is a gap in our texts. It seems that Herwerden was the first to do so.

1038 λῶιον φρονεῖ: 'has got a better idea of the matter than I have'. φρονεῖ governs ταῦτα, leaving ὁ δούς deliberately bare. As with many of the effects in this play it is the apparently casual word that triggers off explosive reactions and consequences.

1039 ἦ γάρ: 'you mean you got me from someone else?'

1042 δήπου: rare in tragedy: see Denniston, *GP²* 267. 'I think he was called one of the household of Laius' (Jebb). Compare the phrasing of 1167.

1044 Note the word order as the vague memories (δήπου τις) of 1042 begin to crystallize into something more solid. 'Yes, that's the one. He was his shepherd.'

1045 ἦ κἄστ': for ἦ καί cf. 757n.

1048 ὃν ἐννέπει: the ποιμὴν ἄλλος (1040) who was called one of Laius' employees or an employee of one of his circle (1042), the unspecified βοτήρ (1044), is now brought into focus.

1049 εἶτ᾽ οὖν: see 90n.

κἀνθάδ᾽: the καί underlines the opposition of the idea of ἐνθάδε to that of ἐπ᾽ ἀγρῶν. cf., e.g., Aesch. *Agam.* 552–3 τὰ μέν τις ἂν λέξειεν εὐπετῶς ἔχειν | τὰ δ᾽ αὖτε κἀπίμομφα. See Denniston, *GP²* 305 for a more wide-ranging discussion.

1051 ἐξ ἀγρῶν: *in* the fields. Cf. Hdt. 5.34 ἐσηνείκαντο τὰ ἐκ τῶν ἀγρῶν ἐς τὸ τεῖχος. Other examples in K–G 1 546. We are talking now of the man sent to the country at his own request (761). The Chorus are remarkably well informed on matters about which Oedipus himself is ignorant.

1052 κἀμάτευες: the καί stresses the idea of identity between the subject of the main verb and the object in the relative sentence. Cf. Ar. *Peace* 240 ἆρ᾽ οὗτος ἐστ᾽ ἐκεῖνος ὃν καὶ φεύγομεν, 'Is this the same man that we were running away from?' (Olson *ad loc.* wrongly interprets). Oedipus was *also* trying to see him earlier, in a different connection. This function of καί, stressing what is identical, similar, or complementary, is much more frequent than the adversative use at 1049 above.

1053 The responsibility shifts again, now from Chorus to Jocasta, as previously (1046) from messenger to Chorus.

1055 ἐφιέμεσθα: at 766 the same word was used in the same connection. Here the royal 'desired' (in effect = ordered) to come will do very well.

1056 τί δ᾽ ὅντιν᾽: 'Why <bother about> whom he meant? Take no notice . . . ' Cf. [Aesch.] *Prom. Vinct.* 766 τί δ᾽ ὅντιν᾽; Jocasta's sentence lurches ahead jerkily as she tries to fend off disaster.

1057 If we construe μάτην with μεμνῆσθαι, which seems the obvious thing to do, the translation will be: 'As for the things that have been said, don't even think of them – it would be pointless.' And so in Pindar, *Ol.* 1.82–4 θανεῖν δ᾽ οἷσιν ἀνάγκα, τά (Doric for τί) κέ τις ἀνώνυμον | γῆρας ἐν σκότωι καθήμενος ἕψοι μάταν | ἁπάντων καλῶν ἄμμορος. 'For people who have to die, why should any one sit in the dark nursing an old age without fame, *all to no purpose*, without any share in all the fine things of life?'

Some prefer to construe μάτην with ῥηθέντα, since Sophocles is particularly fond of using μάτην with words of speech, as at *Phil.* 345, λέγοντες εἴτ᾽ ἀληθές, εἴτ᾽ ἄρ᾽ οὖν μάτην. There are two ways of achieving this aim. The first is simply to switch τὰ δέ (written as the one word τάδε) to where μάτην now stands, and *vice versa*. The second is to say that even more unexpected word order can be found; at *El.* 78–9 καὶ μὴν θυρῶν ἔδοξα προσπόλων τινὸς | ὑποστενούσης ἔνδον αἰσθέσθαι, τέκνον where the scholia construe the otherwise inexplicable genitive θυρῶν as governed by ἔνδον. We have already come across μαντείας at some distance from its governing οὕνεκα at 857–8 above. It remains only to note that the enjambement of τὰ δέ with the following line is characteristically Sophoclean.

1062 θάρσει 'Don't worry.' Sophocles is fond of the word, used in an unfriendly spirit also at *Ant.* 559. At *El.* 173 it means 'take heart', and in other places, *El.* 322,

1435, *Phil.* 667, 810, 894, 1267, *Oed. Col.* 726, 1185, the exact tone must be deduced from the context.

1062–3 τρίδουλος is not unique to Sophocles, and is used to mean 'third generation slave' in Theopompus. But here we are not intended to attach any more arithmetical precision to the τρι- prefix than we are with τριγέρων (μῦθος) at Aesch. *Cho.* 314 (see Garvie ad loc.), or with τριβάρβαρος in Plutarch *lib. educ.* 20. It seems likely that originally the τρι- prefix had nothing to do with 'three': see Kretschmer in *Glotta* 10 (1919) 38–45, and we are plainly not talking in purely mathematical terms when we read τρὶς νόθος at Eur. *Andr.* 636, or the word which should perhaps be written *divisim* at *Oed. Col.* 392, τρισαθλίοιν. But a poet could still play the numbers game when it suited him: cf. Hom. *Od.* 5. 306: τρὶς μάκαρες Δάναοι καὶ τετράκις.

If Oedipus had been an 'infimus servus' – to borrow the translation in Italie's *Index Aeschyleus* of the entry δ]οῦλον ἢ τρίδουλ[ον in Pap. Oxy. 2161, 2, 1: 5 – he would not have been a suitable subject for tragedy. He was, however, descended from a long line of kings: 268n.

1063 κακή: as opposed to the nobles, οἱ ἄριστοι. 'Of low birth.'

1064 Sophocles could have written δρᾶ, imperative, and indeed most of our manuscripts say he did. But the infinitive is more choice; cf. Aesch. *Eum.* 794 ἐμοὶ πίθεσθε μὴ βαρυστόνως φέρειν.

1065 I will not do as you say if it means not finding out for sure. See 13n.

1066 φρονοῦσά γ' εὖ: both good sense and loyalty to Oedipus are comprised in this phrase. εὔφρων regularly means 'loyal'.

1067 There is a rough edge to Oedipus' tongue. We saw it already at 1062–3. From now until the end of the scene his language will be robust and vigorous. The personality of the king of Thebes becomes submerged in that of the possible τρίδουλος who now searches wildly to find out the one thing Jocasta has warned him not to find out, namely who he is.

1070 χλίειν: Subkoff's conjecture for χαίρειν, based on the scholion's gloss τρυφᾶν καὶ ἐναβρύνεσθαι ('revel in'). A glance at LSJ *s.vv.* will show what a good contrast χλίω and χλιδάω form to the life of a slave. But if it were not for the scholion χαίρειν would have to be retained, for it is fully adequate to the context. Cf. Eur. *Ion.* 646–7 ἴση γὰρ ἡ χάρις | μεγάλοισι χαίρειν σμικρά θ' ἡδέως ἔχειν, and more especially *Suppl.* 491 χαίρει δὲ πλούτωι. See also 888n.

1075 σιωπῆς: Sophocles can only by special pleading be acquitted of the charge of using here a piece of dramatic technique not appropriate to the situation. At *Trach.* 813 τί σῖγ' ἀφέρπεις; the Chorus ask of a genuinely silent Deianeira; and silent too is the departure πρὶν εἰπεῖν ἐσθλὸν ἢ κακὸν λόγον of Eurydice at *Ant.* 1245. Here Jocasta has cried aloud ἰοὺ ἰού, and her 'silence' can only be explained in terms of the things she might have said, but has declared she will not say. Yet κακά, one might think, are less likely to *burst* (ἀναρρήξει) from this qualified kind of silence than they are from the genuine voiceless silences of Deianeira and Eurydice, indicative as they are of choked emotional strain.

Alternatively we may assume that Jocasta's last two lines are not a violent outburst, but a stage 'aside' directed, notwithstanding the σ', at the audience. The problem is left unsolved in D. M. Bain, *Actors and audience* (Oxford 1977) 75–6.

κακά: nominative plural subject of ἀναρρήξει.

1077   The same idea as with τρίδουλος (1063). Ion, in Euripides, felt very differently, but he had less at stake: εἰ γάρ με δούλη τυγχάνει τεκοῦσά τις | εὑρεῖν κάκιον μητέρ' ἢ σιγῶντ' ἐᾶν (1382–3).

βουλήσομαι: future it shall be my will. We have the same idiom in 'I *shall be* very pleased to accept your invitation.' Cf. *Oed. Col.* 1289 or ἐθελήσω at Pind. *Ol.* 7.20. *Ai.* 681 is perhaps not quite in the same category: 'from now on I shall . . .'. The usage is treated by Radt in *Mnemosyne* Suppl. 235 (2002) 310–14.

1078   ὡς γυνή: either 'considering she is only a woman' or 'just like a woman'.

1079   γ': limitative. It ought to be a matter only for Oedipus, but Jocasta is unreasonable enough to feel ashamed of it on her own account.

1080–5   The great king of Thebes blazes defiance at the world and its conventions, true to himself as he plots his course into the unknown. His few brief words 1080–5 are as characteristic of his inner motivations and beliefs as the electrifying one minute and twenty seconds of *Fin ch'han dal vino* are of Don Giovanni. It is one of the ironies of this play that Oedipus endorses the philosophy recommended by Jocasta at 977ff. at the very moment that he repudiates her more specific advice not to proceed.

1080   cf. *Anth. Pal.* 9.74.4 (of a field!) εἰμὶ δ' ὅλως οὐδενός, ἀλλὰ Τύχης. The helpless victim of a runaway horse is succinctly described by Achilles Tatius 1. xii 5 with the words: τῆς Τύχης ἦν.

1082   τῆς: demonstrative. *She* was the mother from whom I was born.

1082–3   συγγενεῖς μῆνες: a man could speak of his life as if it had in some way a separate existence, parallel to his own. So at *Ai.* 645 we hear of ἄτα being fostered by not an Aeacid, but αἰὼν Αἰακιδᾶν. At *Trach.* 34–5 Deianeira wishes to speak of Heracles' way of life in coming and going, but her words say that it is his way of life (τοιοῦτος αἰών) that sends him on his way; cf. *Phil.* 1348 where the hero addresses his own στυγνὸς αἰών. At *Oed. Col.* 7f. Oedipus speaks not of his long life, but of χὠ χρόνος ξυνών | μακρός. We have already noted the βίοτος that dwells παρ' αὐτῶι at *Oed. Tyr.* 612, and observed the parallel of Pindar, *Pyth.* 3.86–8. Similarly Pindar, *Nem.* 5.40 speaks of πότμος συγγενής, and Aesch. *Agam.* 106 of σύμφυτος αἰών. See also 1302n.

1083   διώρισαν: Oedipus speaks as if the course of his life could be charted on graph paper. The months marked out the limits of his obscurity and greatness. The same verb at 723.

1084–5   The plays of Sophocles have been rewardingly analysed in terms which place plot far above character in importance. This tendency is healthier than its reverse, but the mainspring of Sophoclean clockwork – if we may adopt an analogy decisively rejected in the Introduction – is always to be found in the character of the individual. Here Sophocles himself, in the sequence τοιόσδε δ’ ἐκφύς κ.τ.ἑ., makes Oedipus’ own character the determining force in his exposure and downfall. (Compare and contrast the τοιόσδε at 244.)

ἐξέλθοιμ: will emerge at the end of the day as a different sort of character in such a way that I do not find out the secrets of my birth.

1085   ποτ’: the very close connection between verses, commented on at 30, makes the position of ποτ’ less remarkable than it might seem. What remains remarkable is that, despite that close connection, the last syllable of ἔτι is still made long by virtue of its position at the end of the line, i.e. in metrical ‘pause’. See M. L.West, *Greek metre* (Oxford 1982) 84. ποτε does not always obey the rules for a full-blooded enclitic: it follows the feminine caesura at the Homeric *Hymn to Apollo* 53, as it does in ‘Simonides’ XLVI (Page, *FGE* 270).

1086–1109 The fourth chorus (third stasimon)

The Chorus’ baseless optimism in the ensuing ode provides a brief relaxation of tension between the two scenes of interrogation: the first with the messenger, the second with the herdsman. That their optimism *is* baseless no one will doubt who has studied the play up to this point. The introductory words with their self-confident ring (a similar note is struck, with more justification, at *El.* 472ff.) are doubtless designed as a frontal assault on our natural incredulity. In his plays Sophocles more than once uses this choral technique: e.g. *Ai.* 693ff.

1086   εἴπερ: if, as is the case . . . See 369n.

1088   οὐ τὸν Ὄλυμπον: see 66on.

1089–90   The sentence is analogous in form to 1084–5, except that μὴ οὐ replaces ὥστε μή. ‘You will not be without the experience of . . .’ ἀπείρων in the sense ἄπειρος, as opposed to ‘without limits’, ‘vast’, occurs elsewhere only in the single word ἀπείρονας, cited by the lexicographer Hesychius, who glosses it with ἀπειράτους, and attests its use by Sophocles in his *Thyestes* (= frg. 266).

1089   αὔριον: indeclinable adverb. This usage is regular: cf. *Trach.* 945 ἤ γ’ αὔριον (sc. ἡμέρα). Mention of the full moon receives its poetic justification as continuing the theme of μῆνες (1083). It may be pure coincidence that the Great Dionysia festival, at which *Oedipus Rex* was produced, was followed by the Pandia, which was held on the day of the full moon. For the accusative see 1138n.

1090–1 The text given is by no means certain. According to it Οἰδίπουν is the subject of αὔξειν. Oedipus will exalt in honour Mt Cithaeron as (a) his fellow countryman, (b) his nurse, and (c) his mother. (c) is justified because Cithaeron gave him life after his real mother consigned him to death.

1092 χορεύεσθαι: the construction now changes, Cithaeron becoming the subject: 'and you are honoured in the dance by us'. See the note on χορεύειν (896).

1094 ἐπίηρα: some editors prefer to print ἐπὶ ἦρα as two words. The Homeric phrase is ἐπὶ ἦρα φέρεν. From it the adjective ἐπίηρος 'pleasing' was coined.

1095 τυράννοις: poetic plural for singular. Here at any rate τύραννος carries no unpleasant overtones. (See 872n.)

1096 ἰήιε: as at 154. But this time the Chorus ask not for delivery from the plague, but for delivery for Oedipus.

δέ: a regular use after vocatives: to be omitted in an English translation.

1099 ἄρα: the very late position of ἄρα in its sentence is perhaps to be explained by supposing that Sophocles meant not 'Who then gave you birth?' but 'Who gave you birth – was it one of the near-immortals, then, lying with Pan?' It is as though a possible answer strikes the Chorus as they speak. By μακραιώνων Nymphs (cf. 1109) are meant. The Homeric *Hymn to Aphrodite* (260) says of the Nymphs δηρὸν μὲν ζώουσι, and the next line mentions their dancing. *Hymn* 19, to Pan, 3, associates him with the χορο<γ>ήθεσι Νύμφαις. Dancing is doubtless included in the entertainments mentioned at 1109.

1101 πατρός: predicative: Pan would become a father after the Nymph had lain with him.

πελασθεῖσ': πελάζω can be used as a euphemism for sexual intercourse; cf. Pindar, *Nem.* 10.81, Bacchyl. 17.35. Sophocles uses πελάτης of Ixion attempting rape on Hera at *Phil.* 677. With εὐνάτειρα the language becomes more explicit. Cf. [Aesch.] *Prom. Vinct.* 895–7.

σέ γ': cf. *Phil.* 1116f. πότμος σε δαιμόνων τάδ', οὐδέ σέ γε δόλος | ἔσχ' ὑπὸ χειρὸς ἐμᾶς: 'it was fate from the gods that did this to you, not any trickery at my hands that caught you.' At *Ant.* 789 σέ γ', Nauck's conjecture for ἐπ', is widely accepted: καί σ' οὔτ' ἀθανάτων φύξιμος οὐδείς, οὔθ' ἀμερίων σέ γ' ἀνθρώπων, 'and no immortal can escape you, and none of mortal men'. In all three cases the γε is used with a σε which repeats an earlier σε, as also at e.g. Hom. *Od.* 8.488, 22.197, Theognis 560, 875, Emped. 3.5. At Herodotus 7.10.θ σέ γε is used following not an earlier σε, but 'Mardonius' used in the third person in a place where 'you' could have stood instead: Μαρδόνιον . . . ὑπὸ κυνῶν τε καὶ ὀρνίθων διαφορεύμενον, ἤ κου ἐν γῆι τῆι Ἀθηναίων ἤ σέ γε ἐν τῆι Λακεδαιμονίων. It would clearly be incorrect to say that γε lays emphasis on the σε, for emphasis is the last thing required. We must simply accept the idiom for what it is. σέ γε at 1090 is not in the same category, and γε is there emphatic: *you* (of all possibilities).

εὐνάτειρά τις: this conjecture, for τις θυγάτηρ, or θυγάτηρ alone, is a brilliant restoration which satisfies every requirement of sense, style and metre. What calls for special comment is that whereas most errors are caused by confusion of sounds, the present confusion is one of letters, in uncial script. Perhaps some psychological forces were at work too, 'father' suggesting 'daughter'. The archetype will have omitted τις, and then added it after correction to the only available place, above the line. Some of our manuscripts still omit it, others have added it to the text, but before instead of after the word which now stands as θυγάτηρ.

1102 τῶι: demonstrative: 'to him'. Cf. 1082 above.

1103 ἀγρόνομοι: fields on which cattle could range. Ἀγρονόμος (active, as the accent denotes) was a title of Apollo.

1104 The 'ruler of Cyllene' was Hermes: Hom. *Hymn* 4.2. Cyllene is a mountain peak in N. E. Arcadia.

1105 ὁ Βακχεῖος θεός: not simply Βάκχος: Cf. Hdt. 4. 79 Διονύσωι Βακχείωι, and later τῶι Βακχείωι.

1108 ἑλικωπίδων: 'dark-eyed': see D. L. Page, *History and the Homeric Iliad* (Berkeley 1959) 244–5. Dionysus prefers brunettes. Similarly the Nymphs are described as κυανώπιδες in Anacreon, *PMG* 357, where συμπαίζουσι also occurs, as well as mention of ὑψηλὰς ὀρέων κορυφάς (cf. 1106) in a poem addressed to Dionysus, in Sophocles the βακχεῖος θεός.

αἷς πλεῖστα συμπαίζει: the ode ends on a sprightly note. Disaster is to follow.

1110–1185 Fifth epeisodion

See Introduction 15–16.

1110 κἀμέ: the καί is modest: 'if I too, who have never met him'. Oedipus had met the herdsman, but he was an infant at the time. Sophocles tightens the emotional screws on the audience by spinning out the arrival of the herdsman over several verses, as he did with the arrival of Creon from the Delphic oracle.

1111 πρέσβυ: the last syllable is lengthened before the στ- following. The singular is used again at 1115 and 1117, so πρέσβυ is to be preferred to πρέσβεις. The third variant, πρέσβυν, arises from scribal preoccupations with the most important old man of all, the herdsman, and can be ignored.

σταθμᾶσθαι: we expect the meaning 'guess', but σταθμᾶσθαι is 'to make calculations based on measurement' and fits here because inferences based on the man's age are to follow. The nearest parallel would be Aesch. *Agam.* 163–4 οὐκ ἔχω προσεικάσαι, πάντ' ἐπισταθμώμενος 'I can make no comparisons, taking everything into account.'

1112 πάλαι: at least since 1069, and in intent since 1047ff. In a different capacity, as sole survivor of the encounter with Laius, his appearance has been a *desideratum* ever since 118ff.

1113 ξυνᾴδει by itself would suffice, or ἔστι σύμμετρος. Sophocles has merged the two, and it is really the ages which coincide, rather than the persons being 'consonant' with each other. The metaphor in ξυνᾴδει is not some striking coinage of Sophocles' own: see LSJ *s.v.*

1114 ἄλλως τε: 'and in any case'. Oedipus uses a second argument, different in type from the first.

ὥσπερ: 'I recognize the people bringing him as my own servants' runs naturally in English, but in Greek ὥσπερ would not normally be used in such a sentence. Neither is the ellipse of ὄντας normal. Nauck therefore conjectured ἄγοντας <ὄντας>, deleting ὥσπερ.

1115–16 For all his acknowledged mental superiority, when it comes to certain vital questions of factual knowledge, Oedipus is inferior to the Chorus, as he here admits. We are concerned now with specific (hence τῆι) ἐπιστήμη, not with σοφία: contrast 501–2.

1117 γάρ: Yes, I do recognize him. In a letter to Gilbert Murray the playwright Bernard Shaw cruelly parodied this passage in his criticism of the stagecraft of *Oedipus Rex*, which he described as 'crude to rusticity'. 'By one of those fortunate accidents which seldom occur more than six times even in a play by Sophocles, I recognize that most respectable man – whom I have not seen for forty years – in the gentleman who will now enter.' Bernard Shaw, unlike Sophocles, did not work under the constraint of having no more than three actors.

Λαΐου κ.τ.ἑ.: again two ideas are merged: (*a*) he did belong to Laius; (*b*) he was a shepherd faithful to his master.

1119 A notable instance of a virtual stage direction being written into the poetic text. Without it we might suppose Oedipus was still talking to the Chorus leader.

1120 ἦ τόνδε φράζεις; 'Is this the man you mean?'

1121 οὗτος σύ: see 532n.

1123 The servant who has been so curtly addressed essays to regain some dignity by establishing that, though a slave, he was one born in the household of Laius, and as such a notch above one who had been bought in (ὠνητός). He has already been described as πιστός, by the standards appropriate to a νομεύς (1118).

1125 τὰ πλεῖστα τοῦ βίου: for the most part he earned his livelihood by tending flocks.

1126 μάλιστα: the herdsman had described how he spent *most* of his time. Oedipus in the conversation that follows will be constantly trying to narrow down the scope of the enquiry to the few vital specific facts. He has begun by establishing the man's status, his function in the household, and now he wants some geographical precision.

1127 The herdsman has to admit that Cithaeron was the area he worked in, but instantly tries to leave a loophole open by adding that 'there was the surrounding area too'.

1128 τῆιδέ που: there somewhere. The herdsman's geographical imprecision is not the protection he thought.

1129 τὸν ἄνδρα τόνδ᾽ had been very specific, and in the reply τί χρῆμα δρῶντα the herdsman obviously knows who is meant. His second question, 'and anyway what man do you *mean?*' is a desperate attempt to gain a second's respite. Again in 1131 he is doubtless playing for time rather than genuinely searching his memory. Compare 559 and note. The καί is not quite the same as the one at 989: see Denniston, *GP*² 323n.

1131 cf. 361 οὐχ ὥστε γ᾽ εἰπεῖν γνωστόν. In both places the γε stresses the idea that follows. The herdsman really cannot say, off-hand.

1134 ἦμος: an epic word, used at *Ai.* 935, *Trach.* 155, 531, and by Eur. at *Hec.* 915, otherwise never in drama. There is nothing in the rest of the herdsman's language to suggest that he is attempting any special effects (unlike the Guard in *Antigone*), rather the reverse: see on 1136–7.

τὸν Κιθαιρῶνος τόπον: τόπος is frequently joined with another word to make such a periphrasis: see the beginning of the entry in LSJ. The accusative is governed by a verb which once stood in the passage now missing after 1135.

1136–7 'Three whole seasons', or as the herdsman puts it, 'three whole six-monthly periods from spring to autumn'. Jebb has a note in his Appendix on 'The significance of Arcturus in the popular Greek calendar'. Arcturus is the brightest star in the constellation Βοώτης, the ploughman. 'In the age of Hippocrates and Sophocles (say in 430 B.C.) Arcturus began to be thus visible about a week before the autumnal equinox, which falls on Sept. 20–1; and, in the popular language of that age, "*the rising of Arcturus*" commonly meant, "shortly before the autumnal equinox".'

1138 χειμῶνα δ᾽ ἤδη: in the winter, when it was already that season. Thucydides can say χειμῶνος ἤδη, 'it being already winter', and one of our manuscripts actually has the genitive here too. Most have the dative, which is also intelligible. But the accusative is correct and not just because it helps to denote the period of time during which the flocks will be in the high country. Expressions of time and season often appear, to our minds unexpectedly, in the accusative. Thus at 1089 we have τὰν αὔριον πανσέληνον (cf. νεομηνίας πάσας at Hdt. 6.57.2). At Eur. *Hipp.* 1117 we have τὸν αὔριον χρόνον. Examples with ἡμέραν occur at *Oed. Col.* 433, Ach. Tat. 3.9.3 and 3.14.2 and with ἆμαρ at Pind. *Isthm.* III–IV 85; with ὥραν at Aesch. *Eum.* 109, Eur. *Bacch.* 723, and Hdt. 2.2.2. See further Gow's note on Theocritus 1.15, and K–G I 314 § 410 Anm. 15.

In a remarkable note in *Philologus* 34 (1876) 753–5, E. A. J. Ahrens, enlisting none other than Lord Byron as an ally, pointed out that Cithaeron, which is at its highest between Thebes and Corinth, is often under snow for eight months of the year. Hence the reading ἑκμήνους, for six months, could not be right, since only four months would be available for pasturing sheep. If one wishes to engage in these scholarly games, it may be enough to reply that we must not leave ὁ πρόσχωρος τόπος (1127) out of account.

1140 'The Corinthian has been talking at the Theban slave thus far: he now talks to him' (Earle). We can see exactly what 1140 means without difficulty, and all the words in it are simple enough. None the less to English ears the phraseology is peculiar. λέγω means 'Am I right?' (cf. 1475–6). Am I right, and did it happen as I say?

1145 ὦ τᾶν: used by Sophocles again at *Phil.* 1387, and in the extensive *Ichneutae* fragment, 314. 104. See Dodds on Eur. *Bacch.* 802.

1146 οὐκ εἰς ὄλεθρον: cf. 430n.

οὐ σιωπήσας ἔσηι: the aorist participle is appropriate to an abrupt once-and-for-all command. 'Hold your tongue, won't you?'

1147 ἆ: as at *Phil.* 1300. 'Often it expresses urgent protest' (Dodds on Eur. *Bacch.* 810–12).

κόλαζε: Oedipus uses this word to refer to the previous speaker's sharply phrased sentence 1146. Physical violence is not meant.

1149 ὦ φέριστε δεσποτῶν: δεσπότης is a word which at Eur. *Hipp.* 88 a more independent-minded servant declines to use to his master (he uses ἄναξ instead) thinking that only the gods should be addressed as 'master'. The herdsman has in reality met the adult Oedipus for far too short a time for the expression to be other than a subservient formula designed to soothe irritation. φέριστε in fifth-century tragedy elsewhere only at Aesch. *Sept.* 39, with ἄναξ.

1151 ἄλλως: = μάτην.

1152 πρὸς χάριν: a 'polar' sentence, with two halves phrased paratactically as if of equal weight, but with the main weight in reality falling on only one half, here κλαίων ἐρεῖς. i.e. 'if you won't speak πρὸς χάριν, you will speak under more painful circumstances'. The antithesis is however not quite straightforward, since the χάρις belongs primarily to Oedipus, not the herdsman. (πρὸς χάριν of gratification to oneself only *Ant.* 30, *Phil.* 1156.) So 'if you won't speak at my pleasure . . .'.

1153 τὸν γέροντά μ': to explain the article it is necessary to over-interpret: we can say it is used as the herdsman steps out of his own identity for a moment, and sees the scene as a tableau, with the Inquisitor threatening the Old Man. 'Me, the old man in this scene.' So, e.g., Io sees her own pathetic rôle as through the eyes of a third person at [Aesch.] *Prom. Vinct.* 566b χρίει τις αὖ με τὰν τάλαιναν οἶστρος. 'An old man like me' will do as a translation. Cf. 1441 τὸν πατροφόντην, τὸν ἀσεβῆ μ' ἀπολλύναι.

αἰκίσηι: αἰκίζω and αἰκία commonly include the idea of physical harm.

1154 τις: an indefinite number of persons.

ἀποστρέψει: not necessarily twisting his arm behind his back in the manoeuvre widely but incorrectly known as the half-Nelson, but drawing the arms back as a first step to tying him up ready for interrogation under torture. The same verb is used of the hands and feet of the wicked goat-herd Melanthius in the *Odyssey* (22.190) before he is hoisted upwards and left swinging. Sophocles' audience would be less taken aback by this threat of physical violence than we are, for in their society a slave could only give evidence under torture. See Gerhard Thur, *Beweisführung vor den Schwurgerichtshöfen Athens, Die Proklesis zur Basanos* (Wien 1977).

1155 δύστηνος: commentators have for 700 years normally treated this as an expression of self-pity. But with no interjection (as in ὦ δύστηνος at *Trach.* 377) or accompanying ἐγώ (as at 1307 below) the one-word change of direction is unwelcome, and δύστηνος should be construed as an address to, or rather a comment on, the misguided Oedipus. δύστηνε was what Jocasta had called him at 1071.

1158 τόδ': sc. ὀλέσθαι.

μὴ ... γε: 'if, that is, you do not ... '

1159 γε: corrective: so at *Ai.* 78, *El.* 164. We have the same idiom in English, often with a touch of schoolboy sarcasm: 'Yes, and I'm much more likely to perish if I *do* talk too.'

1160 ἐλᾷ: Pindar, *Nem.* 3.74 uses this form as a present tense, and Pearson so understood it here. So also Timotheus, *Persae* (*PMG* 791) 210.

1161 πάλαι: with εἶπον 'I have just said ... ' For πάλαι of the recent, sometimes immediate, past, see *Studies* I 208, 264, III 119. Sophocles seems particularly fond of the usage. See also 1477n.

1162 οἰκεῖον: 'of your household'. The herdsman correctly infers that Oedipus means in effect 'your own'.

1163 The herdsman recoils from the suggestion that he might have given away his own child. The practices of mighty families threatened by divine predictions are not current in the cottages of simple rustics.

1164 πολιτῶν τῶνδε: it is almost as though Oedipus felt some tie of identity was about to be established with one of those who now stand about him. But he was the child of no ordinary citizen.

1167 τοίνυν: 'Well then, if you insist on knowing.' In the extant plays of Sophocles this particle occurs only seven times, and it is rare too in Aeschylus and Euripides.

The language is still ambiguous, meaning either 'he was one of the children of Laius', or 'he was one of the children of the people belonging to Laius, of his household'. Cf. 1042. Oedipus' next question is intended to resolve the ambiguity.

1168 κείνου: genitive, because ἐγγενής is considered as equivalent to ἐν γένει ὤν, in his family.

1169 αὐτῶι ... τῶι δεινῶι: cf. *El.* 1329 ὅτ' οὐ παρ' ἄκροις (so Diggle and Dawe for αὐτοῖς: cf. Peek, *GVI* 432.4 κακῶν οὐδ' ἄκρα γευσάμενος) ἀλλ' ἐν αὐτοῖσιν κακοῖς. The herdsman is on the verge of the frightful thing itself.

λέγειν: epexegetic infinitive: so as to declare it.

1170   'And I too <am on the verge> of hearing it.' The infinitive has the same construction as λέγειν.

1171   κείνου γέ τοι δή: the γε coheres closely with κείνου, i.e. Laius, whose actual name the herdsman now prefers not to use. τοι has the effect of bringing the point home to the hearer, and δή underscores the enormity of what is being said.

ἐκλήιζεθ': he was, and was called accordingly. A regular use: cf. 1359n, and 1451n. for geographical applications of the idiom.

ἡ δ ἔσω: with no more than an ordinary adverb of place Sophocles plays on our latent fears. Why, at this critical moment in the king's life, is Jocasta 'inside'? What is she doing? May it be that the forebodings of 1073ff. are in the process of being translated into fact? Note the word order: 'The lady inside could best tell you, your wife, how things are.'

1172   κάλλιστ': an interesting choice of word, in a place where nothing that Jocasta might say could be said καλῶς.

1173–6   The change of speaker within the line (ἀντιλαβή) indicates a quickening of pace.

1175   τλήμων: both active and passive senses may be felt here, as in the English 'desperate'. After giving birth she must have been *unhappy* to *venture on* such a step.

γ': confirmation is accompanied by explanation: 'yes, in fear of . . .'.

1176   Oedipus' two next questions, ποίων here, and 1177, strip away the last vestiges of a veil over his misfortunes. In real life no one would ever ask these supplementary questions after facts of incomparably greater importance had been revealed, not even a man as remorseless in the pursuit of the truth as Oedipus. It is for the audience's benefit that Sophocles is giving the final clarification here.

1178   κατοικτίσας: aorist participle in its own right: 'as an act of compassion', rather than attracted to the tense of ἀφῆκας, though such a usage is quite normal: see Barrett on Eur. *Hipp.* 289–92.

1178–9   ἄλλην χθόνα: 'praepositionis omissio neminem morabitur' said Linwood, though in reality the construction exemplified here is normally found only with ordinary verbs of motion. K–G I 312 class our passage along with 434 (οἴκους . . . ἐστειλάμην) and Eur. *Tro.* 883 πέμψομέν νιν Ἑλλάδα.

ὡς . . . δοκῶν <σφ'>: 'in the belief that he . . .', Blaydes's <σφ'> is necessary, otherwise the sense given would be 'thinking that *I* . . .'

1180   κἀκ' εἰς μέγιστ' ἔσωσεν: cf. 1456–7 οὐ γάρ ἄν ποτε | θνήισκων ἐσώθην, μὴ 'πί τωι δεινῶι κακῶι.

αὐτός: the whole question of identity, whether Oedipus is the same man as the one in our minds all this time, is summed up in this word, restored to the text by Heimsoeth.

1181 δύσποτμος γεγώς: the phraseology is conventional, but each word will bear as much stress as we care to put on it, Oedipus' *fate* and *birth* pre-eminently deserving epithets beginning with δυσ-.

1182 ἰοὺ ἰού: it is now Oedipus' turn to utter the same cry as Jocasta (1071). Similarly Heracles, on recognizing the truth, at *Trach.* 1143.
σαφῆ: seen to be true.

1183 ὦ φῶς κ.τ.ἑ.: these words, to Greek ears, would sound like the declaration of an intention to commit suicide: compare *Ai.* 856ff. Oedipus, however, plans a different way of avoiding the light of the sun.

1184 ὅστις: causal again: 'since I . . .'.

The story of Oedipus the King is now over. But we can hardly bring the tale of calamity to an abrupt end at 1185. In what follows, Sophocles will explore the emotional, religious and philosophic aspects of what we have seen already. He is not, however, concerned to state explicitly the answer to the problem with which the play began, namely the Plague, unless, of course, he did so in the section now occupied by the compositions of the interpolator.

1186–1222 The fifth chorus (fourth stasimon)

In the ode upon which we now enter, the Chorus pessimistically draw conclusions at the very outset for the whole of the human race. If men are to be equated with τό μηδέν (1187), nothing need be said overtly about the power of the gods. As for the infallibility of oracles, the Chorus express no satisfaction at finding they still have adequate reasons for χορεύειν (896). The nearest they come to hinting at oracular certainty is 1213, where the word χρόνος is as discreet and reticent as anything could be. The prevailing tone throughout is one of shock and human sympathy, expressed in human terms.

1186 ἰὼ γενεαὶ βροτῶν: very likely a deliberate echo of Homer's famous line οἵη περ φύλλων γενεή, τοίη δέ καὶ ἀνδρῶν (*Il.* 6.146).

1187 ὡς: exclamatory.
ἴσα καί: the same construction as at 611–12, except that ἴσα is this time a neuter plural used adverbially, as at *Phil.* 317. Cf. Eur. *El.* 994 σεβίζω σ' ἴσα καὶ μάκαρας.

1187–8 τὸ μη- | δὲν ζώσας: instead of saying 'I count your lives as nothing', the Chorus say, literally, 'how I count you as living a life that is a nothingness'. Others prefer the interpretation 'how I count you as nothing while you live'.

1189 γάρ: the Chorus give their reasons. Their general exclamation was prompted by the impermanence of human happiness as exemplified by the specific case of Oedipus, once apparently the best possible example of human felicity.

1190 τᾶς: the definite article is not used in lyrics unless some special point is being made. Here the thought is 'the quality of happiness' (sc. for which we all strive).

φέρει: either just 'has' or, more likely, 'wins', like φέρεται.

1191–2 δοκεῖν | καὶ δόξαν γ' ἀποκλῖναι: the infinitives are consecutive: 'just enough to seem to exist, and then to decline'. δόξαν picks up δοκεῖν as, e.g., at 1404 φυτεύσαντες picks up ἐφύσαθ' where in English we would probably say 'and then' or 'and afterwards'. The MSS give δόξαντ' (Stobaeus δόξαν). It is perverse to argue (H. Musurillo, *A.J.P.* 82 (1961) 183) that we must mentally supply ἄνδρα τινά for δόξαντ' to agree with, when τίς ἀνήρ is explicitly given as the subject of the main verb, and could perfectly well be followed by the nominative δόξας as the unaltered subject of the infinitives. Secondly, ἀποκλῖναι is much more likely to mean 'decline', of happiness, than 'veer away from', of the person who seems happy. Happiness is like a star which makes its appearance, and having appeared, declines, or sets. καὶ ... γ' gives added importance to ἀποκλῖναι, and gives the sentence a mild progressive impetus: compare the use at *Oed. Col.* 1352: ἀξιωθεὶς ... κἀκούσας γ'.

1193 τὸν σόν: to be construed with δαίμονα. παράδειγμα is the predicate, 'as an example'. The triple τὸν σόν is a stylistic rarity, *your*. The Chorus are almost incredulous that Oedipus, of all people, should have met with such a fate. Triple σός, for pathetic effect, can be found also at Hom. *Od.* 11.202f.

1194–5 βροτῶν | οὐδέν: nothing in the life of men, like βρότειον οὐδέν (709) in Jocasta's less reverent expression.

1196–1203 Antistrophe α, beginning with a causal ὅστις, 'seeing that you ...' sketches the heights of Oedipus' career, as strophe β will sketch its depths.

1196–7 καθ' ὑπερβολὰν | τοξεύσας: Oedipus shot his (metaphorical) arrow pre-eminently well when he hit upon the answer to the Sphinx's riddle. But in the phrase καθ' ὑπερβολάν there is a note of warning, for the noun regularly denotes not merely superiority, but, as in the English 'hyperbole', excess. In Aesch. *Agam.* 365f. shooting ὑπὲρ ἄστρων is described as being just as ineffective as shooting πρὸ καιροῦ, short of the mark.

1197 ἐκράτησας ἐς: The manuscripts offer ἐκράτησας τοῦ, where the definite article is faintly suspicious on stylistic grounds (it would presumably give the nuance 'the prosperity which you did in fact enjoy'), and the metre is more than faintly suspicious. Sophocles very rarely allows the penultimate syllable of a glyconic (οο–◡◡–◡–) to be long: this so-called 'dragged' glyconic occurs in him only at *Ant.* 104 = 121, 1122 = 1133, and *Phil.* 1151. Only at *Phil.* 1151 is there responsion between dragged and normal glyconic (= 1128), and Hermann suggested an emendation (ἀκμάν) which would eliminate even this. But Euripides has several such cases in aeolic metres: *Hipp.* 741 = 751, *El.* 730 = 740, *Ion* 206 = 220, *Bacch.* 867 = 887, *I.A.* 1056 = 1078. To restore exact syllabic responsion in our present passage Hermann suggested ἐκράτησε, which has also been found in a manuscript. But scribal tendencies are to turn genuine second persons into thirds after relative pronouns. At 1200b just below, the weight of manuscript evidence favours ἀνέστας against ἀνέστα. In a similar conflict at Aesch.

Cho. 360 Page is probably right to favour Abresch's solution of ἦσθα for ἦν as against Hermann's ἕζη for ἕζης.

The text adopted in the present edition keeps the second person of the manuscripts, and takes advantage of an alternative solution proposed by Hermann, namely to read ἐς for τοῦ. This would give us an expression like the εἰς ἅπαντα of [Aesch.] *Prom. Vinct.* 736 and Soph. *Trach.* 489, Eur. *Phoen.* 1642 and frg. 44. It remains curious, however, that those examples all involve ἅπας, not πᾶς, and that where πᾶς is involved the normal usage is εἰς πᾶν, not εἰς πάντα. It is for that reason that this edition slightly modifies Hermann's proposal. With it we can retain ἐκράτησας, and the only doubts remaining are whether we should construe ἐς πᾶν with the verb ('made yourself complete master of') or with the adjective ('totally happy prosperity'); and whether we should succumb to Heimsoeth's attractive suggestion that following the τοξεύσας metaphor we should read not ἐκράτησας but ἐκύρησας (actually his proposal was couched in the third person) as at Aesch. *Agam.* 628, and, if Ahrens was right, at *Agam.* 1194. ὦ Ζεῦ does not interfere with the second person construction, for it is recognizable as a stereotyped exclamation: so at *Trach.* 995 ὦ Ζεῦ follows an address ὦ Κηναία κρηπὶς βωμῶν, and at *Phil.* 1233 ὦ Ζεῦ, τί λέξεις; the subject of λέξεις is Neoptolemus. At Eur. *El.* 137 ὦ Ζεῦ Ζεῦ occurs in a wish sentence (ἔλθοις ...) addressed to Orestes; cf. *Med.* 764–5.

1199   γαμψώνυχα: see 507n.

1200–1   θανάτων ... πύργος: a tower *against* death. The genitive is justified because he was a protection to the city *from* death.

1201   καλῆι: 'are called', parallel with ἀκούειν 1204. (For the usage there cf. ἀκούεις 903.) The conjecture κλύεις, which fits with ἀκούειν even more closely than καλῆι does, was made by Heimsoeth to avoid hiatus between καλῆι and ἐμός. However there is an exact parallel of such hiatus between one glyconic and another at *Oed. Col.* 1215–16 ἐπεὶ πολλὰ μὲν αἱ μακραὶ | ἁμέραι. And just above in our present chorus, at 1190–1, the second glyconic of its group is in hiatus with the third. The phenomenon remains highly abnormal. καλῆι τ᾽ (Blaydes) would be another way of avoiding it, taking the first καί to underline the verb, 'which is precisely the reason why you are ...'. Such a way of construing the first καί may in any case be the best.

In their words of appreciation it is doubtless no accident that the Chorus prefer to say that Oedipus was called their βασιλεύς, and avoid the possibly ambivalent τύραννος.

1205   The metrical form of this line does not respond as it should with 1214. The construction ἐν πόνοις ξύνοικος is one to be avoided, and ἐν πόνοις may be a gloss on the more poetic ἄταις, although the standard gloss word on ἄτη is βλάβη. Wilamowitz's proposal, τίς ἄταις ἀγρίοισιν ἐν πόνοις, has some merit, but is exposed to the same objection as most others, namely that it invites the translation 'Who that lives in misery with disaster can be called more wretched than Oedipus?' as if there were a whole range of miserable persons who had experienced a change of fortune in their lives (ἀλλαγᾶι βίου) and who might now be considered potential rivals of Oedipus in a sort of Most Miserable Man competition. The τίς questions require the sense, 'Who is more the companion of disaster than Oedipus?', but this requires a <μᾶλλον> or equivalent, which cannot be understood from the comparative force inherent in ἀθλιώτερος. The problem is one not likely to be persuasively solved by conjecture.

1208 The nautical imagery applied to the marriage reminds us of Teiresias' prediction at 422ff. In that speech, however, the actual word λιμήν was used by Teiresias (420) of a harbour for Oedipus' cries of woe, and it is other words of nautical imagery that are used of the marriage.

ἤρκεσεν: 'was enough'. There is a bitter edge to the word.

1209 παιδὶ καὶ πατρί: 'for the child and the father', i.e. Oedipus and Laius, not 'for you as child and as father'. Oedipus-as-father has received little enough attention in the play so far; the only possible allusions are discussed in the note on 425. We do not require any such allusion here, where it would tend to confuse the point to be made in πατρῶιαι ἄλοκες just below. At 1215 the participles are attached to γάμον rather than explicitly to the person of Oedipus; and the further mention at 1250 is quite possibly spurious.

θαλαμηπόλωι: as bridegroom. The familiar Homeric word for a lady's maid is here put to a new use. Perhaps Sophocles felt the -πολος termination especially appropriate here with ἄλοκες following. Cf. *Ant.* 341, and West's note on Hesiod, *Works and Days* 462-3.

πεσεῖν: as in the tragic parody spoken by Euripides in Ar. *Thesm.* 1122: πεσεῖν ἐς εὐνήν καί γαμήλιον λέχος.

1210 πατρῶιαι: one manuscript writes ματρῶιαι, which might seem on physiological grounds more obviously right, and which would agree with Aesch. *Sept.* 752-4 ὅστε ματρὸς ἁγνὰν σπείρας ἄρουραν ἵν᾽ ἐτράφη. The metre however will permit only a short penultimate syllable (–∪∪– ∪–∪–) and ματρῶιαι is therefore impossible. This purely technical consideration can therefore teach us something about the art of Sophocles in not writing what posterity might expect of him. He is not saying 'his mother's field' as Aeschylus did, but 'the furrows that were the property of his father'. The reverse error at *Ant.* 863 (LRZc).

1213 ἄκονθ᾽: the word provokes thought. Of all the heroes in Greek tragedy Oedipus is the last of whom it could be said that he was 'found out against his will', since his energies have been directed, in the teeth of much opposition, precisely to 'finding out' who he is and what he has done. We may say that either (*a*) the Chorus, as ordinary men, do not understand the true position, or (*b*) ἄκων is justified because no one could ever really *want* such facts to come to light, even if he was determined to discover the truth, however unpleasant. Thus at *O.C.* 987 ἄκων ἔγημα or at Eur. *Hipp.* 1433 ἄκων γὰρ ὤλεσας νιν in each case the person intended his action, but with hindsight would not so have acted, or (*c*) Sophocles is writing rather mechanically, and has not perceived that ἄκων does not fit his treatment of the myth. None of these three explanations looks attractive. The least objectionable is (*b*), and the most objectionable (*c*), since at 1230 an awareness is shown of the importance of ἑκών–ἄκων distinctions.

ὁ πάνθ' ὁρῶν χρόνος: cf. 614, *Oed. Col.* 1453–4. Frg. 301 reads πρὸς ταῦτα κρύπτε μηδέν, ὡς ὁ πάνθ' ὁρῶν | καὶ πάντ' ἀκούων πάντ' ἀναπτύσσει χρόνος. Pearson's note there refers to other close verbal parallels.

1214 δικάζει: usually 'tries', here 'brings to justice'.

πάλαι: to be construed with the two following participles, describing the marriage which sought to produce children while being itself composed of a union in which a child was one half of the wedded pair.

1216 The ὦ in this line was inserted by Erfurdt to restore the metre. The separation of epithet and noun by a repeated interjection (if that is how we regard ἰὼ ... ὦ) is foreign to English usage, but not to Greek: e.g. *Oed. Col.* 1700 ὦ πάτερ ὦ φίλος, Eur. *Ion* 112–14 ἄγ' ὦ νεηθαλὲς ὦ καλλίστας προπόλευμα δάφνας, and so we should interpret *I.T.* 983 ἀλλ' ὦ φιληθεῖσ' ὦ κασίγνητον κάρα. Further examples of ὦ (not repeated) in sandwich position, in K–G I 49.

1217 εἴθε σ' εἴθε σε: the last of the repeated phrases which are such a feature of this choral ode: others already at 1189, 1193–4, 1204–5, 1210. This mannerism, the palaeographic elegance of the restoration of σε after -θε, and the fact that the reading has now turned up in a manuscript, confirm the superiority of this conjecture by Wunder over its competitors.

1218–19 The text printed is speculative only. περίαλλα is a word recurring at frg. 245 ἔκ τε νόμων οὓς Θαμύρας περίαλλα μουσοποιεῖ; the Homeric *Hymn to Pan* 46; Pindar, *Pyth.* 11.5; Ar. *Thesm.* 1070, Ap. Rhod. 2.217; 3.529; Theocr. 12.28. It is likely to be authentic here, being especially appropriate to any sense of pre-eminently honouring Oedipus, or of his being pre-eminent in woe.

1220–2 The ode which had begun with ἰὼ γενεαὶ βροτῶν ends on a highly personal note, and the Chorus use language of an intensity that is almost erotic as they contrast the warmth of their former feelings for Oedipus with their present dismay at the discoveries that have been made. 'It was from you that I drew my breath, and in thinking of you that I closed my eyes in sleep.' The last paragraph in Thomas Hardy's *The Woodlanders* has a strangely similar sentence. 'But I – whenever I get up I'll think of 'ee, and whenever I lie down I'll think of 'ee again.' It continues in a way which, if applied to Oedipus, could be endlessly discussed: 'for you was a good man, and did good things'. Other commentators prefer to take ἀνέπνευσα and κατεκοίμησα as much more specific in their reference, ἀνέπνευσα meaning 'I drew breath again after you had put an end to the Sphinx' and κατεκοίμησα κ.τ.ἑ. as either 'it was through you that I was able to go to sleep peacefully at night' or 'and now, after your downfall, darkness has fallen on my eyes' – a very ambitious translation. The phrase τὸ δ' ὀρθὸν εἰπεῖν, 'to tell the truth' fits best with the first of the interpretations given in this note. Contrast the less personal note of civic approval with which the Chorus had concluded their ode much earlier in the play, 510–11.

1223–1296 Sixth epeisodion: the death of Jocasta and blinding of Oedipus

1223 The ἐξάγγελος, the messenger from the interior of the palace, will not be using the words 'ever most held in honour in this land' at random. He knows, as the Chorus do not, that the royal family now hardly exists. It is the ἀεὶ τιμώμενοι who will have to provide some kind of continuity. They had already been called χώρας ἄνακτες by Jocasta (911).

1225 εὐγενῶς: This is Hartung's conjecture for the MSS ἐγγενῶς, a word suggested to the scribal mind by all that has been said in this play about family connections. In uncial script the difference is hardly more than a minute stroke of the pen. At *Oed. Col.* 728 a speech begins with ἄνδρες χθονὸς τῆσδ᾽ εὐγενεῖς οἰκήτορες (ἐγγενεῖς Brunck (!)), which would seem to afford a good parallel. But there Creon is trying to curry favour with the citizens. The sort of sense we might have been expecting in our present passage is not so much 'nobly' as 'steadfastly': cf. 1322 ἔτι μόνιμος, or the phrasing of *Ant.* 169 ἔτι ... μένοντας ἐμπέδοις φρονήμασιν. The positioning of ἔτι is also favourable to the idea that it goes with the adverb rather than the verb, i.e. 'still steadfast in your concern for the royal family', not 'nobly still concerned'. Hirzel's ἐμπέδως lacks the palaeographic simplicity of Hartung's emendation, but should not be dismissed from consideration.

1227 The two remote rivers are named together also in Aesch. *Niobe* frg. 155. The Istros is the river Danube, and the Phasis, called by Aeschylus in another fragment the great boundary of the land of Europe and of Asia, is a river in Colchis beyond the Black Sea, or possibly the even more remote Tanais. (In Hesiod, *Theog.* 339–40 the naming of Phasis straight after Istros in a list of rivers seems to have no special reason for it.) The limits of the known world contrast with the narrow compass of τήνδε τὴν στέγην. The idea expressed is most familiar to us from *Macbeth*: 'Will all great Neptune's Ocean wash this blood | clean from my hand?' Aeschylus in a difficult passage, *Cho.* 72–4, seems already to have said very much the same thing.

1228 ὅσα: indirect exclamation: 'so many are the horrors which it hides'.

1229 τὰ δ᾽ αὐτίκ᾽: a mild anacolouthon, phrased as if it were an independent sentence, and not part of the ὅσα clause. If we wish to categorize, we may say that the concealed horror is the corpse of Jocasta, and the one to be revealed is the blinded Oedipus, who, as we shall learn later (1287ff.), is calling for the palace doors to be opened so that the world can see the parricide who married his mother. But we do not have to equate ὅσα κεύθει with the things the Chorus will *hear* (1224) and the blinded Oedipus with what they will *see* (εἰσόψεσθ᾽ *ibidem*). The messenger may simply be saying that the two mighty rivers could not wash clean the house of Oedipus, such are the horrors it contains, part of which will soon be visible to every eye.

1230 ἑκόντα κοὐκ ἄκοντα: 'willing' for 'willed'. 'Deliberate' will preserve the ambiguity. For the polar expression see 58–9n. No contrast is intended between voluntary blinding now and involuntary parricide etc. earlier.

1230–1 Cf. *Ai.* 260–2 τὸ γὰρ ἐσλεύσσειν οἰκεῖα πάθη κ.τ.ἑ. 'Misfortunes one can endure – they come from outside, they are accidents. But to suffer for one's own faults – ah! – there is the sting of life' (Oscar Wilde, *Lady Windermere's fan*, Act One, in a less sombre context). If this is what the messenger means, Oedipus for one would not agree with him. Some commentators think he means the Chorus, and audience, to be the object of λυποῦσι (cf. their πένθος 1225). This gives better sense in the wider context, but the absence of an expressed object gives us no help in arriving at this view, and the fact that the relative sentence is general (hence the subjunctive), and so refers to *any* πημοναί that are αὐθαίρετοι, might seem to exclude it altogether. Compare and contrast τούτων δ' αὐθαίρετον οὐδέν at *Oed. Col.* 523.

1231 Subjunctive without ἄν, as at 316–17.

1232 λείπει: intransitive active: 'falls short'. No parallel from classical poetry exists: LSJ cite *El.* 514, where ἔλειπεν is, in properly constituted texts, transitive, governs οἴκους, and ἐκ τοῦδ means 'from this time'; Eur. *Hel.* 1157, where λήξει is an easy emendation, and *Heracles* 133 τὸ δὲ κακοτυχὲς οὐ λέλοιπεν ἐκ τέκνων, which some editors delete: κακοτυχὲς must at least be corrupt since the idea will not fit with the immediately following οὐδ' ἀποίχεται χάρις.

τὸ μὴ οὐ: lit. are not deficient so as not to be βαρύστονα; i.e. fully merit lamentation.

1237–40 The messenger here draws the distinction latent in his two verbs of hearing and seeing at 1224. In his ἡ γὰρ ὄψις οὐ πάρα he speaks with the crispness of one who might almost be thought anachronistically to have read Aristotle's *Poetics*: see Lucas's note on 1449 b 33.

1239 κἄν: like the γε, the καί gives a modest turn to the phrase. Cf. κἀμέ 1110, and ὅσ' οἶδα κἀγώ *Oed. Col.* 53.

μνήμης: not 'memory'. The messenger could hardly have forgotten already the horrendous events that have just taken place. Mnemosyne was the mother of the Muses, and as the messenger approaches his epic recital he depreciates his own poetic ability to do justice to his theme. At *Oed. Col.* 508–9 τοῖς τεκοῦσι γὰρ | οὐδ' εἰ πονεῖ τις, δεῖ πόνου μνήμην ἔχειν, and Aesch. *Suppl.* 270, 'mention' or 'a taking account' of something is the meaning. Here the sense is rather the power to describe.

1241ff. This recital should be compared with the description of Deianeira's conduct and suicide, *Trach.* 900–46.

1241 ὅπως: 'when', here and at 1244.

ὀργῆι χρωμένη: 'anger' is not in point. Jebb's 'frantic' is right.

1242 θυρῶνος: it is not certain whether a hall or cloister is meant. The important thing is that it represents the point at which one goes into a place or comes out of it. Cf. *El.* 328 πρὸς θυρῶνος ἐξόδοις.

ἵετ᾽ εὐθύ: 'rushed straight'.

1243 ἀμφιδεξίοις ἀκμαῖς: high tragic style, impossible to render into any English that does not smack of parody, for 'with both hands'.

1244 ἐπιρράξασ᾽: ἐπιρρήσσει· ἐπικλείει (i.e. 'close') Hesychius. All our manuscript evidence with the exception of L above the line favours the spelling with eta, and we may be wrong to change it to the Attic form with alpha.

ἔσω: one expects ὅπως εἰσῆλθε . . . ἔσω to take us on to the next stage in the action, like ὅπως . . . παρῆλθ᾽ ἔσω in 1241. But then the tense of the participle ἐπιρράξασ᾽ cannot be explained, since the slamming of the doors must come after Jocasta's entry into the bedroom. Hence some commentators take ἔσω with the participle, as if the meaning were 'from inside': ἔσωθεν might then be expected. The layout of the sentence makes it difficult to understand as 'when she went inside, after slamming the doors shut she called on Laius'; and it is highly artificial to construe ἔσω with καλεῖ, though even this has been suggested.

The best interpretation will be to take ὅπως εἰσῆλθ᾽ . . . as subordinate to πύλας ἐπιρράξασ᾽, with mildly interlaced word order (cf. 1251 n.). 'Slamming the doors shut when she went inside, she called on Laius . . . '

1246 σπερμάτων: as the adjective παλαιῶν indicates, we must take this to mean the sowing of seed, though LSJ know only of Hesiod *WD* 781 in this sense.

1247 θάνοι: optative mood because in 'virtual indirect speech' (Moorhouse, *Syntax of Sophocles* (Leiden 1982) 235), i.e. reflecting Jocasta's thoughts.

1248 οἷσιν αὐτοῦ: see the note on 416

παιδουργίαν is an abstract noun denoting the act of procreation, and as such can hardly stand in apposition to τὴν τίκτουσαν. But if it does not, then it becomes hard to unravel the syntax. Possibly τὴν δέ is to be separated from τίκτουσαν, i.e. 'and left her giving birth . . . ', in which case we shall have to assume a lacuna after λίποι. Platt made the construction easy enough by altering to τῆι δὲ τικτούσηι, but 1248 has the air of a concluding accusative phrase in apposition to the whole sentence; which again supports the idea of a lacuna, as well as the suggestion mooted below that 1249–50 should not stand in our texts.

1249 γοᾶτο: for the absence of augment see below on 1255n.

διπλῆι only in one manuscript, with διπλᾶ above the line in another. (*Ant.* 725 διπλῆι Hermann for διπλᾶι.) We need 'in two respects', not, as most MSS have it, 'double'.

1250 τέκν᾽ ἐκ τέκνων: these words seem to prove the existence of the children (425n.). But it is possible that 1249–50 are interpolated; they do nothing but duplicate what has already been said. The use of εὐνάς when we have already had λέχη (1243) – and the use of ἔνθα proves we are still talking of a physical object – may surprise.

1251 Interlaced word order, with οὐκέτι used as described in the note on 115. We are distantly reminded of the way Aeschylus passes over the more gruesome details of the sacrifice of Iphigeneia at *Agam.* 248: τὰ δ᾽ ἔνθεν οὔτ᾽ εἶδον οὔτ᾽ ἐννέπω.

1253 ἐκθεάσασθαι: 'because of whom it was impossible to see her misfortune through to the end'. These somewhat ghoulish words are immediately justified by saying that the rampaging Oedipus claimed their full attention. The playwright has to deal successively with events which in real life would present themselves to the eye simultaneously.

1255 φοιτᾶι: the imperfect φοίτα, conjectured by Blaydes and others, is in some manuscripts. Similarly some editors like to print the imperfect κάλει at 1245, giving consistency with the suspect γοᾶτο at 1249. The use of such forms without the syllabic augment in messenger speeches in tragedy is discussed by L. Bergson in *Eranos* 51 (1953) 121–8. φοιτάω itself is particularly appropriate here, since as well as being a verb of motion it and its cognates are used in contexts where some sort of wild raving (λυσσῶντι 1258) or desperation is described. Cf. *Ai.* 59, Aesch. *Sept.* 661, Eur. *Or.* 327, *Herc.* 846. At *Phil.* 807f. a violent attack of pain is described: ἥδε μοι | ὀξεῖα φοιτᾶι.

ἔγχος: in this rapid recital we have no time to ask ourselves what Oedipus intended to do with the sword. If we do ask ourselves, we cannot avoid the answer that he intended to kill his wife/mother.

1256 γυναῖκά τ᾽ οὐ γυναῖκα: the smoothest sense would be given by mentally supplying some such word as καλῶν, 'calling his wife no true wife', along the lines discussed in 117n. But the switch from ἐξαιτῶν would be especially harsh since ἐξαιτῶν has to be understood again with only a mild change of meaning, 'ask a question' as opposed to 'request', immediately afterwards to govern the μητρώιαν ὅπου clause. It may be more prudent to assume an ordinary zeugma: the bystanders are asked to produce (*a*) a sword and (*b*) the wife that is no wife; and then, by the further zeugma already noted, allow ἐξαιτῶν to govern also the μητρώιαν ὅπου clause. Attempts by some commentators to let the phrase γυναῖκα οὐ γυναῖκα get swallowed up in the μητρώιαν ὅπου clause do not do justice to the presence of τ᾽ and δ᾽ in the sentence. In the end some of us may prefer to believe that Sophocles has chosen to represent Oedipus' fevered mind and rapid actions by using words and phrases thrown together in a way that is not susceptible to ordinary grammatical analysis.

1257 οὗ: from ἕ, 'of himself'.

1259 Not merely for polar effect. The messenger as well as stressing the supernatural also exculpates the bystanders.

1260 ὑφ᾽ ἡγητοῦ: cf. 966. At 1252 above ὑφ᾽ also discharges a weightier rôle in the sentence than is normal for a preposition. Here 'as if led by . . .'.

1261–2   The language is very vigorous. Oedipus flung himself at the folding doors, and broke them inwards (κοῖλα predicative, 'bulging inwards'), tearing them off the more solid structure they were fixed to, and burst into the room.

1262   κλῆιθρα: used here and at 1287 by itself, and accompanied by πυλῶν at 1294. In all three places the meaning is 'doors', things used to close rooms with (κλήιω). It does not mean 'bolts', 'hinges' or 'sockets'. See further Barrett's notes on Eur. *Hipp.* 577–81, 808–10, and compare Eur. *Herc.* 1029f.

1263   οὗ δή: cf. [Aesch.] *Prom. Vinct.* 814; Eur. *I.T.* 320, *I.A.* 97 (both of time), and the attractive conjecture of Kvíčala at *Phil.* 276. 'And there it was that . . .' rather over-translates the idiom.

1264   'Caught up in woven elevated-swingings' i.e. dangling from a rope. ἑώρα is for αἰώρα, which is connected with ἀείρω but has the notion of swinging as well as of raising. ἑωρήσασα was restored by Wunder for θεωρήσασα at *Oed. Col.* 1084 (exact syllabic responsion, though mol./bacch. would tolerate αἰωρήσασα, which some older editors sought to introduce, believing that ἑώρα was not a permissible form in the time of Sophocles).

1266   χαλᾶι: χαλᾶν can mean both 'loosen' and 'lower' (LSJ *s.v.* 1.2). Oedipus lowers the body to the floor, thus releasing the tension on the noose.

1267   τλήμων: sc. Jocasta.

γ': probably in its normal stressing function 'terrible indeed'. Others would take it as apodotic, i.e. standing early in the main sentence as a kind of redundant introductory signpost, following the ἐπεί clause. Most manuscripts have δ, which if correct would also be an apodotic usage. Further discussion of this unexhilarating question may be found in *Studies* 1 258. See also K–G II 276.

1270   ἄρθρα . . . κύκλων: κύκλοι = 'eyes' again in Sophocles at *Phil.* 1354, *Oed. Col.* 704, and accompanied by ὀμμάτων *Ant.* 974. Equally ἄρθρα κύκλων are simply 'eyes' (sc. which can swivel), just as ἄρθρα ποδοῖν are 'feet' (sc. which can swivel). See 718n.

1273–4   ἐν σκότωι . . . ὀψοίαθ': ἐν σκότωι discharges the same function as οὐκ with ὄψοιντο just above, but with a self-taunting savagery. Previously his eyes had looked on those they should not (οὕς μὲν οὐκ ἔδει, cf. 1184–5), while failing to recognize those he wanted to, or needed to, recognize. In the future such activities would be conducted in total darkness, i.e. the eyes would cease to function in that or any other way. The moral reasons given by Sophocles here and at 1385–90 for Oedipus' self-blinding are artistically the only correct ones for the play he has written. Self-blinding forms no part of the story in Homer (Introduction 1), but appears in Aeschylus (*Sept.* 778–85). Freudian speculations on the original significance of the theme may be found in articles by G. Devereux and R. G. A. Buxton, *J.H.S.* 93 (1973) 36–49; 100 (1980) 22–37.

ὁψοίαθ' = ὅψοιντ'. There are a number of such Ionic forms in tragedy: others in Sophocles at *El.* 211, *Oed. Col.* 44, 921, 945.

1275 ἐφυμνῶν: as if chanting some ritual refrain as he performs his dire act.

1276 ἤρασσ' ἔπειρεν: for the asyndeton cf. ἔπαιον, ἐρράχιζον at Aesch. *Pers.* 426, αὔειν, λακάζειν *Sept.* 186 and βάλλων, ἀράσσων at Eur. *Andr.* 1154, *Hec.* 1175, *I.T.* 310. All these examples, like the present passage, involve the first two words of the line, and they all involve violence. Less violent, though still excited, *Ai.* 60, *El.* 719, *Phil.* 11.

1278–9 At *Agam.* 1534 Aeschylus writes ψακὰς δὲ λήγει 'the sporadic drops (of blood) cease', implying, as the previous words there make clear, 'now for the real shower'. Sophocles points a similar contrast by a different technique, putting 'and it was not wet drops of blood that they released, but . . .' between two positively phrased sentences, both with ὁμοῦ.

1279 χαλαζῆς is an adjective, a contracted form of χαλαζήεις: cf. χαλαζάεντι φόνωι Pindar, *Isthm.* 5.50. ἐτέγγετο is a corruption fostered by the appearance of ἔτεγγον two lines earlier.

ἔρρωγεν: cf. 1075.

1280 The scribal mind or eye has been wandering here too, and κακά has been elevated from the line below. Wilamowitz's emendation μονούμενα provides a satisfactory contrast with the συμμιγῆ of the next line.

1284–5 It is difficult not to be reminded of the opening words of Sophocles' earlier play *Antigone*, spoken by Oedipus' daughter as she looks back over the woes of his time and her own.

ὀνόματ': 'name' for the thing going by that name; cf. διπλοῦν ἔπος at *Ant.* 53. To put it crudely, the messenger is saying 'You name it, they've got it.' There is another row of nouns in asyndeton at 1406f.

1287 κλῆιθρα: cf. 1262n. For the idea of disclosing the scene of horror to the local inhabitants cf. *El.* 1458–9. We are perhaps to imagine the *ekkyklema* will be rolled out, the device conventionally used to depict interior scenes in an open-air theatre. A. W. Pickard-Cambridge, *The Theatre of Dionysus in Athens* (Oxford 1946) 111, seems unduly sceptical in denying the use of the *ekkyklema* by Sophocles altogether.

1289 οὐδὲ ῥητά μοι: there are no certain examples in tragedy of a short final vowel remaining short before initial ῥ - in another word except: (*a*) τί before ῥέξεις, ῥέξων etc.; (*b*) before forms of ῥύομαι, a category which would disappear if we substituted the equivalent forms of ἐρύομαι (cf. 72); (*c*) two or three places in [Aesch.] *Prom. Vinct.*; (*d*) Eur. *Hipp.* 123 (ῥυτάν), *Herc.* 1204 (ῥέθος), *Bacch.* 128 (Ῥέας). It might therefore appear that οὐδὲ ῥητά μοι breaches the law of the final cretic (see on 219). But a number of *prima facie* violations of this law involve the word οὐδείς, οὐδέν, and this may be because οὐδείς is treated as two words, just as it is in οὐδ' ἂν εἷς (281n.). Possibly then οὐδέ is a further licence by analogy. Or we may say that it is an honorary prepositive, like ὥσπερ at *Oed. Col.* 1543 (cf. Hipponax 6.2 West, perhaps also 92.4) or ἄνευ at *Oed. Col.* 664. But the fact remains that οὐδὲ –◡–, which might have been often convenient to the ancient tragedians, is elsewhere avoided. There is a mild metrical anomaly in the next line too, which lacks the regular caesura.

1293   ἤ: for ἢ ὥστε. 'Too great to bear.' Cf. Eur. *Hec.* 1107 κρεῖσσον᾽ ἢ φέρειν κακά.

1294   δείξει: δόξει, conjectured by Reiske, and in one manuscript, would be easier, and should be resisted for that very reason. δείξει, with Oedipus as subject and with the object, the insupportable νόσημα, left unspecified, will be correct; it fits well with δηλοῦν (1287).

1295   θέαμα δ᾽ εἰσόψει: the messenger ends as he began, with a conscious allusion to the power of ὄψις.

1296   And so of another great hero, Ajax, Sophocles had written ὡς καὶ παρ᾽ ἐχθροῖς (in the house of, or among, his enemies) ἄξιος θρήνων τυχεῖν (*Ai.* 924). The infinitive ἐποικτίσαι is used after τοιοῦτος οἷος by analogy with ὥστε constructions; cf. *Trach.* 672–3 τοιοῦτον . . . οἷον . . . μαθεῖν.

1297–1530 Second kommos and final scenes (exodos)

The Chorus and Oedipus dwell on his act of blinding, and review some of the crucial moments in his life that have culminated in this deed of horror. Creon appears, and we are given a glimpse of the cheerless future that awaits the former king.

1297–1311   In these anapaests the Chorus observe the rules for so-called 'marching' anapaests: they use the same dialect as in iambics, and there is word-end separating the two halves of the dimeter ‿‿⏑⏑‿‿⏑⏑ | ‿‿⏑⏑‿‿⏑⏑. Oedipus himself uses the more highly wrought 'melic' or 'lyric' anapaests: his dialect is like that of the choral odes (δύστανος, τλάμων), and he is not bound by the word-end rule (1310). His final paroemiac ends with –––, where in marching anapaestic systems only ◡ ◡ ––would have been allowed. (A paroemiac is ‿‿ – ‿‿ – ⏒‿–––, and is normal at the end of a group or period of anapaests. In lyric anapaests, but not marching ones, it is permissible to have more than one in succession. It is worth adding that the distinction between the two kinds of anapaests is not always rigidly maintained: see A. M. Dale, *Lyric metres of Greek drama*² (Cambridge 1968) 52, and Dawe, *Dionysiaca* (Cambridge 1978) 102 n. 2.)

1298   ὅσ᾽: προσέκυρσ᾽ ought to govern a dative, and analogies with internal or quasi-internal accusatives of pronouns and adjectives, like οἷα μηδεὶς . . . τύχοι (*Phil.* 509) or οὐ γὰρ ἂν τύχοις τάδε (Eur. *Phoen.* 1666) do not entirely satisfy, for the sense in the present passage is of 'coming across' some phenomenon quite external to the speaker, not of undergoing an experience. It is probably wiser to swallow the anomaly, as if προσέκυρσ᾽ were equivalent to 'I have seen', than to emend (ὁπόσοις for ὅσ᾽ ἐγὼ

Blaydes; ὅσ' ἐμοὶ with προσέκυρσ(ε) Herwerden: neither meritorious). Or we may argue that since at *El.* 1463 and *Phil.* 552 the simple verb in προστυγχάνω overrides the preposition with which it is compounded, so that it governs a genitive, not a dative, therefore we may admit a plain accusative after προσ-κύρω (-κυρέω) since the simple verb governs one at Aesch. *Sept.* 699 (the other examples in LSJ *s.v.* 13 are less convincing). Comparable arguments are used by commentators on παιδὸς ὑπαντήσας at *Phil.* 719. Cf. ἐπιτόσσαις with the accusative at Pindar, *Pyth.* 10.33f. (genitive at 4.25!).

1301 μείζονα: sc. πηδήματα.

μακίστων: the word can be used of size: τὰ μάκιστ' ἐμῶν κακῶν Eur. *Hipp.* 818; or of length or height, which is more appropriate to the imagery here. English has as a parallel only the archetypal sergeant-major's 'falling from a great height on'. μάκιστος is one of a small number of words which tragedy only ever uses in Doric-looking forms (i.e. not μήκιστος). Doric forms can be found even in iambic trimeters: e.g. *Ai.* 37, *Ant.* 1196, *Trach.* 173.

1302 πρὸς σῆι δυσδαίμονι μοίραι: on you, in your unhappy destiny. We have already noticed the tendency to speak of a man and his destiny as half-separate, half-identical things: see 1082–3n. Here the tendency has a curiously blurring effect on the imagery, for the δαίμων and the μοῖρα have much in common, especially when μοῖρα actually has δυσδαίμων as its epithet. Others prefer to take πρός as meaning 'in addition to', and the μοῖρα to refer to the parricide and incest, in addition to which we now have the blinding.

1305 πολλά δ' ἀθρῆσαι: the last element in the concessive phrases is only with difficulty reconcilable with the main sentence οὐδ' ἐσιδεῖν δύναμαί σε. The emotion, however, of feeling compelled to look at some ghastly sight while simultaneously feeling revulsion at it is one not unknown to the human spirit, as Plato, *Rep.* 439e noted.

1310 διαπωτᾶται: LSJ's entry for this word is to be found in the revised supplement of 1996. It was conjectured by Musgrave and Seidler, and may be in the papyrus fragment. For the form with omega see Fraenkel on Aesch. *Agam.* 978.

φοράδαν continuing the idea in φέρομαι. His voice will be carried on the winds. Teiresias had already predicted where to at 420ff.

1311 ἐξήλου: the leaping idea as in πηδήσας (1300). The compound with ἐξ- not ἐν- (contrast 263) because Oedipus is speaking here not of something that has swooped down on his head, but of some extravagant departure from the norm. ἵν' of indirect exclamation (see 947n.).

1312 δεινόν is used as a singular noun here and at *Ant.* 1097. This seems to be a special licence, for even in poetry if an adjective is used substantivally in the singular it is almost invariably accompanied by the definite article. (Some exceptions: *Ai.* 1144–5 ἐν κακῶι | χειμῶνος, *Phoen.* 968 ἐν ὡραίωι ... βίου (so Reiske for βίωι); and some would so explain εἰς ἀναιδές at Soph. *Phil.* 83.) ἀκουστόν and ἐπόψιμον are adjectives qualifying δεινόν, and show the same preoccupation with the hearing–sight theme that we noted at 1224: see 1229, 1295nn.

1314 ἀπότροπον: from which one would turn away.
ἐπιπλόμενον ἄφατον: unspeakable in its onset.

1315 δυσούριστον ⟨–⟩: an οὖρος would normally be a favourable wind; the initial δυσ- gives the compound its *un*favourable sense. Jebb's 'sped by a wind too fair' is an attempt to preserve the intrinsic irony. A syllable is missing, and Jebb's δυσούριστ' ἰόν, with the neuter plural of the adjective standing for the adverb, as frequently with verbs of motion, agrees well with the style of one who has just written ἐπιπλόμενον ἄφατον. Good too is the suggestion made by Blaydes in 1859, and again by Wilamowitz in 1879, δυσεξούριστον, 'hard to banish', the οὖρος being Ionic for ὅρος: see 193n.

1317 μάλ' αὖθις: this to us rather curious qualification of an exclamation, 'I say again, "alas"', occurs most memorably in Agamemnon's death-cry at Aesch. *Agam.* 1345.

1320 διπλᾶ: either with reference to the double exclamation, or to the pairing of the οἴστρημα and the μνήμη which gave rise to it. We may even have the best of both worlds by adopting the first explanation for διπλᾶ πενθεῖν and the second for διπλᾶ φρονεῖν.

φρονεῖν: note from the *apparatus criticus* how precariously this word has survived (if 'survived' is right: see *Trach.* 965 (Zo), *Ant.* 705 (K^{ac}S)). The Chorus continue the mental theme inherent in μνήμη κακῶν. Cf. *Ai.* 940ff. where the Chorus having heard Tecmessa cry ἰώ μοί μοι comment that they are not surprised at her lamentations. She answers: σοὶ μὲν δοκεῖν ταῦτ' ἔστ', ἐμοὶ δ' ἄγαν φρονεῖν: 'it is a matter for me to feel all too deeply'.

1322 μέν: no δέ follows, and the effect is similar to γε: 'you at any rate'.
ἐπίπολος: the word is unique, and coined along the lines of ἀμφί- and πρόσ-πολος.

1323 ὑπομένεις picks up μόνιμος, in the sense of standing by him. But there is also inherent in the word the sense of standing *for*, enduring, something unpleasant.
τόν: see 1153n.

1329 Ἀπόλλων: does Oedipus gesture to, or stumble at, the altar or statue of Apollo which lies close to his own palace (919)?
τάδ ἦν: 'This was Apollo', a statement like κοὐδὲν τούτων ὅ τι μὴ Ζεύς at *Trach.* 1278. τάδε is regularly so used in apposition to a singular noun: ἆρ' οὐχ ὕβρις τάδ; *Oed. Col.* 883; οὐ τάδε Βρόμιος Eur. *Cycl.* 63 (cf. 204); οὐ γάρ ἐσθ' Ἕκτωρ τάδε *Andr.* 168. With ταῦτα at *Rhesus* 861 καὶ ταῦτ' Ὀδυσσεύς. Cf. further *Tro.* 99, Ar. *Ran.* 21, *Lys.* 658, Thuc. 6.77, Theocr. 15.8. A similar, if not identical idea, in Hdt. 3.157.4: πάντα δὴ ἦν ἐν τοῖσι Βαβυλωνίοισι Ζώπυρος. Closer still, ''Tis the Cardinal,' (i.e. Wolsey is responsible for all this), [Shakespeare] *Henry VIII* ii.1.160.

When the Chorus framed their questions πῶς ἔτλης and τίς σ' ἐπῆρε δαιμόνων, they were doubtless speaking in the conventional manner, normal from Homer onwards, whereby the same question is put under two different aspects, human and divine. When Phemius, at *Od.* 22.347, says 'I am self-taught, and a god has inspired me with all kinds of poetry' no one would accuse him of imprecise or self-contradictory thinking. But Oedipus fastens on to the Chorus' actual words, and assigns the shares of responsibility with clarity to Apollo and to himself. A similar distinction, less sharply made, appears at *Ai.* 489–90 νῦν δ' εἰμὶ δούλη· θεοῖς γὰρ ὧδ' ἔδοξέ που | καὶ σῆι μάλιστα χειρί. In naming Apollo Oedipus is right on more than one count. Apollo was the god of Delphi and the god of both healing and illumination. Teiresias' prediction at 377 has been fulfilled. *Ant.* 51–2 lays the blame solely on Oedipus himself.

1330   The repetitions are a feature of excited dochmiac verse. (A dochmiac is ⏑ ⏑⏑ ⏑ ⏑⏑: see the Appendix on metre.) The last two syllables of πάθεα pose a problem. They stand in hiatus before the next word, just as the last syllable of φόνου does in the corresponding verse 1350. That is a clear indication of metrical period end. But where a short syllable stands at the end of a period, it counts as long. That being so, πάθεα would scan as two shorts plus one long. Elmsley's πάθη is too facile a solution, and it would be in the highest degree abnormal to suppose that -εα is in synizesis; that happens only with the imperative ἔα and with otherwise intractable proper names like Ὀδυσσέα. West in his *Greek metre* (Oxford 1982) 110 writes of the dochmiac metre: 'Metra succeed each other for the most part in synapheia, but with hiatus and *brevis in longo* appearing here and there on no obvious principle.' See also Mastronarde on Eur. *Phoen.* 177.

1335   ὅτωι γ': both ὅστις and γε, as opposed to simply ὅς, impart a causal sense.

1337   δῆτ': used in repetitions, as τί δῆτ' here echoes the previous τί γάρ; but also with the sense 'why then' following the Chorus' admission that he is right.

   ἦν: imperfect, as ἔδει was, and for the same reason: they both explain the situation at the time of the self-blinding.

1338   ἢ προσήγορον: understand ⟨τί⟩ 'or what greeting'. Once again the pair of hearing and sight appears; at 1386–7 Oedipus will express the wish that he could have lost the power of hearing as well as of sight.

1340   Cf. *Ant.* 1322 ἀπάγετέ μ' ὅ τι τάχος, ἄγετέ μ' ἐκποδών.

1341   Bergk's τὸν ὄλεθρόν με γᾶς (see LSJ *s.v.* ὄλεθρος II) has the merit of keeping the epsilon short before θρ. Lengthening before mute and liquid in dochmiacs is rare: see N. C. Conomis *Hermes* 92 (1964) 38.

1347   Wretched *for* the intention he has put into effect (or perhaps for the apprehension of his fate: cf. φρονεῖν 1320), and *for* his fate. The genitives are of the type discussed by A. C. Moorhouse *The syntax of Sophocles* (Leiden 1982) 73. Others take τοῦ νοῦ to refer to Oedipus' intellectual penetration, and συμφορά as the awful consequences that stemmed from the exercise of this νοῦς.

1348 'How I could have wished never to have known you at all' – the same idea as that expressed at 1217. ἄν must stand close to its verb ἠθέλησα, as the parallels of *Ai.* 88, *Phil.* 427 and 1278 show: hence Elmsley's emendation. It is perfectly permissible to have ἄν twice in the same sentence, though we might legitimately wonder what is gained by having ποτ' ἄν rather than ποτέ at the very end of the line, as the majority of MSS do, particularly since then we would have an ἄν standing close to a verb it does *not* go with, namely γνῶναι. Rather than print a text in which ἄν appears twice, as many editors (not Jebb) do, it is better to assume that ποτ' ἄν is an anagrammatical corruption of τὸ πᾶν. This then gives us a sentence like [Aesch.] *Prom. Vinct.* 215, οὐκ ἠξίωσαν οὐδὲ προσβλέψαι τὸ πᾶν. The final syllable of μηδαμά undergoes metrical lengthening before initial γν-, as at 1068 above.

1349 'Curse the man, whoever he was that released me from the cruel fetters (ἀγρίας πέδας, genitive singular) on the pasture lands, and rescued and saved me from death.' The text is uncertain, particularly in the phrase νομάδος ἐπὶ πόας. νομάς usually means 'roaming', but here will have to mean 'roamed over' (sc. by sheep etc.). ἐπὶ πόας 'on the pasture lands', like γᾶς ἐπὶ ξένας 'on foreign soil' at *Oed. Col.* 1705 and 1713–14.

1358 ἦλθον: sc. to Thebes. Oedipus is tracing the milestones in his career of misfortune: (*a*) his rescue, (*b*) the killing of his father before arrival at Thebes, (*c*) his marriage. There is no need to embark on the uphill task of attempting to prove that ἦλθον means ἐς τοσοῦτον ἦλθον ὥστε. We have already noted (515n.) how verbs of motion are often used in tragedy where the idea of arrival seems devoid of importance.

1359 βροτοῖς: dative of the agent is more usual with the perfect or pluperfect passive, as with ἐμοὶ . . . εἰργασμένα at 1373–4. See Goodwin, *Greek grammar* §1186, K–G I 422. Sophocles uses the construction with present tenses at *Ai.* 539 and *Ant.* 1218 (more problematic *Ant.* 503–4).

ἐκλήθην: not 'was called' but 'was, and was known as': cf. 1171, 1202.

1360 ἄθεος: see 254n. The manuscripts give ἄθλιος, in which the first syllable is long, being contracted from ἀεθλ-. We need a short syllable to give the dochmiac – ⌣ – ⌣ –. ἄθεος is a good choice, giving us two alpha-privative adjectives, one in each half of the dochmiac dimeter. Such parallelism is much favoured in dochmiacs. At *El.* 124 one manuscript writes ἀθλιωτάτας where the prevailing reading is ἀθεωτάτας (and ἀθεώτατα is correct, restored by Porson).

1361 ὁμολεχής: Meineke's effective alteration of ὁμογενής. To say that Oedipus slept with his mother takes us further up the scale of horror – which is precisely where we are going, as the next line makes clear – whereas ὁμογενής is merely drab. Of course Oedipus belonged to the same family as his mother; and it requires special pleading to urge that here ὁμογενής has the meaning 'having children born of the same wife as was married to his father'.

1365 πρεσβύτερον: 'graver'. An unusual word to use of crime, since its associations are rather with things or persons to be held in veneration. But cf. Aesch. *Cho.* 631 κακῶν δὲ πρεσβεύεται τὸ Λήμνιον. Oedipus, passing a verdict on himself in the third person, stands in awe of the magnitude of the crimes he has involuntarily committed.

1367 φῶ: deliberative subjunctive.

1368 κρείσσων: 'better off', as at *Ai.* 635 κρείσσων γὰρ Ἅιδαι κεύθων ὁ νοσῶν μάταν.

ἦσθα: without ἄν, because κρείσσων ἦσθα together have the effect of ἔδει σε, and ἄν would normally only be used with ἔδει in the specialized sense 'there would have been the necessity'.

1373 οἶν . . . δυοῖν: dative of interest, or disadvantage. ἐμοί is dative of agent: see 1359n.

1374 κρείσσον' ἀγχόνης: see the end of the note on 175–7. There is no special reference intended here to the manner of Jocasta's suicide. 'Too great for hanging' (phrased like κρεῖσσον ἐκπηδήματος 'too much to jump over' at Aesch. *Agam.* 1376) is evidently an idiom. The use of ἀγχόνη is similar to that found at Ar. *Ach.* 125, Eur. *Hcld.* 246, *Bacch.* 246. At *Alc.* 228–30 Euripides develops the idea further.

1375–7 βλαστοῦσ': logic would require βλαστόντων. βλαστόνθ with the comma removed after ἔβλαστε 'for me to look on them, born in the way they were' (Hartung) restores logic by a different route, and smoothes the path for προσλεύσσειν after ὄψις. But the lines may be spurious, and the interpolator clumsy. 1377 is especially feeble: 'never with *my* eyes at any rate': 1371 had expressed that kind of idea much more effectively. The nature of the transition of 1378 'and not the city either . . . ' and the difficulty of finding a specific backward reference for the τούτους of 1385 both suggest that the reference to the children has displaced some genuine lines which would have taken us back from the speculative world of Hades to the immediate realities of life in Thebes.

1376 βλαστοῦσ' ὅπως ἔβλαστε: phrases of this kind are discussed by H. W. Johnstone in *Glotta* 58 (1980) 49–62; see also Denniston on Eur. *El.* 1141.

1378 There is a distant echo here, near the end of the play, of what the priest had said at 54–7. For οὐδ. . . γ᾽ see Denniston, *GP*² 156.

1379 τῶν: for ὧν. A frequent use *metri gratia*, and also found in our manuscripts at *Trach.* 47, *Oed. Col.* 35 where metrically unnecessary; as also in Aesch. *Suppl.* 265, *Agam.* 342 (cod. V), Eur. *Suppl.* 858, *Herc.* 252 (see also 1300), *Bacch.* 338.

1380 κάλλιστ' . . . εἷς: εἷς with a superlative adjective or adverb in the vicinity occurs at *Ai.* 1340, *Oed. Col.* 563; cf. 'oon the fairest' in Chaucer's *Franklin's Tale*; [Shakespeare] *Henry VIII* 11.4.46–7 'one the wisest'. *Trach.* 460 is of a slightly different type. Other examples in Fraenkel on Aesch. *Agam.* 1455. There is then nothing suspicious about that particular idiom. But (1) It is not true that Oedipus was brought up (τραφείς) in Thebes. He was brought up in Corinth, as ἀνὴρ | ἀστῶν μέγιστος τῶν ἐκεῖ (775–6), (and so κάλλιστα τραφείς) all too clearly states. (2) The γε discharges no recognizable function beyond making the line scan.

1382–3 We expect 'telling them to expel the guilty party'. τὸν ἀσεβῆ causes no trouble, but τὸν ἐκ θεῶν φανέντ' ἄναγνον is not quite what we expect, because the gods had not then disclosed the unholy person – at least not his identity, only his existence. But by the time we arrive at καὶ γένους τοῦ Λαΐου we have passed from the instructions given earlier about expulsion to the state of affairs as we now know it to be. When the sentence has reached its end, we realize that the underlying structure may have been intended to be 'the guilty party, the one who has <since> been shown by the gods to be unholy and a member of Laius' family'. But we may be wiser to accept this as another example of Sophocles' 'blurred-edge' style, while sympathizing with the motives which led Badham in 1855 to delete 1383 altogether, ending 1382 with τὸν ἔκθεον. (The adjective has however the demerit of not existing.) It would not occur to most of us to say that it was the gods who had disclosed Oedipus' guilt, and Oedipus himself in 1384 is just about to say that he disclosed it himself. At 1213 the disclosing was done by Time.

1384 μηνύσας: ambiguous as between 'reveal' and 'denounce'. Similarly ἐμήν is ambiguously both 'my' and predicatively 'as mine'.

1385 ὀρθοῖς: cf. 528; also 419.

1387 πηγῆς: sound goes through the ear, as water may come through a fissure in the ground.

οὐκ ἂν ἐσχόμην: 'I would not have held back from cutting myself off . . . '

1389 The words 'blind' and 'deaf' remind us of the jibe Oedipus directed at Teiresias (371) τυφλὸς τά τ' ὦτα κ.τ.ἑ., and Teiresias' *tu quoque* immediately after. Similarly ἰὼ Κιθαιρών (1391) calls to mind the prophecy of 421.

For the τὸ γάρ sentence to be rescued from the charge of irrelevant vapidity it is necessary to take ἔξω τῶν κακῶν to mean 'apart from <all perception of> misfortune'.

1395 λόγωι: with πάτρια. It was 'in theory' his father who lived in the ancient palace of Corinth.

ἄρα: the inferential particle ἄρα, which the poets may use with a long first syllable *metri gratia*: hence the change of accent.

1396 κάλλος κακῶν ὕπουλον: 'the beautiful thing that underneath is festering' we can easily understand. But the genitive κακῶν belongs to no easily recognizable category. In itself ὕπουλον should mean no more than 'under the scar', but in ancient Greek generally it means 'festering underneath'. We are presumably meant to understand κακῶν as if the full sense were 'festering underneath with sores consisting of κακά'.

1403 αὖθις: 'thereafter' or 'on a different occasion'; not 'again'. Similarly *Trach.* 270 and *Ai.* 1283. LSJ do not deal adequately with this usage, and wrongly classify the present example.

1405 ἀνεῖτε ταὐτὸν σπέρμα: for ἀνεῖτε cf. 271 n. Sophocles speaks in a highly elliptic manner. The full truth is that having produced Oedipus, the marriage <accepted the seed of its own progeny and> again brought the same seed to see the light of day (in the form of Oedipus' children). The intermediate step is omitted. Nauck's τοὐμὸν for ταὐτὸν partly meets the logical difficulty, but does not convince.

1406 αἷμ' ἐμφύλιον: in this catalogue of horror (cf. 1284) we have no leisure to evaluate grammatical niceties, but plainly these words are on a different plane from πατέρας, ἀδελφούς κ.τ.ἑ. At the same time to point out that fathers, brothers, and children, are consanguineous is to do no more than state the obvious. αἷμ' ἐμφύλιον is not then an ordinary predicate, but an additional brush-stroke in an impressionistic picture. The words themselves apply to marriage within the prohibited incestuous limits, but can also mean 'bloodshed of kin' (cf. Pi. *Pyth.* 2.32), and so the death of Laius too hovers on the edges of Oedipus' grim recital.

1407 τε can be used by itself to link the last member of an otherwise asyndetic series to what has gone before.

1408 ἔργα: one might well have expected ὀνόματα, as at 1285, but Oedipus' choice of word shows that his mind is running on the horrific things that he has *done*.

1409 μηδέ: one should not speak of things which one is not prepared also to do. μηδέ is the negative form of the pleonastic καί which would be regular in a positive sentence: αὐδᾶν καλόν ἐστιν ἃ καὶ δρᾶν καλόν.

1413 ἀξιώσατ': 'deign'. They are not to be afraid of touching Oedipus as if he could pollute them.

1414–15 Oedipus senses that he is a man apart: similarly 1455–7.

1417 τὸ πράσσειν: the best parallel for this unusual construction is *El.* 1030 μακρὸς τὸ κρῖναι ταῦτα χὠ λοιπὸς χρόνος. There 'for the purposes of deciding', here 'for the purposes of action and advice'.

1420 πίστις ἔνδικος is used as at *Oed. Col.* 1632 χερὸς σῆς πίστιν ὁρκίαν, to denote something that enables the other party to repose confidence in one. A πίστις ἔνδικος could be either a thoroughly justified guarantee, or a guarantee that the man who offers it is thoroughly δίκαιος.

1424–1530 The spurious end of the play

(What follows draws heavily, often *verbatim*, on the article published in *Rheinisches Museum* n.f. 144 (2001) 1–21.)

The original end of *Oedipus Rex* is lost. Suspicions were first raised a century and a half ago by K. Schenkl (Z.Ö.G. 8 (1857) 195), who perceived the break after 1423. Then fitfully one scholar after another made suggestions on what should be excised or transposed or defended. The argument has continued to the present day. Those who yearn for a defence of authenticity will find one given, with useful bibliographical references, by G. Serra, *Il dramma Sofocleo* (Beiträge zum antiken Drama und seiner Rezeption, Band 13 (2003) 321–39). But the case against is overwhelming.

This can be deduced from following two different strands of argument: the general, literary one, and the detailed, linguistic one. The general argument runs as follows. Everything in the play so far has led us to suppose that Oedipus, as the guilty party, will go into exile. If he does not go into exile, we shall have the unparalleled spectacle of a prophet's prediction being falsified. Exile for the guilty party is a hitherto unquestioned datum of the plot: see 96–8 (Apollo), 228–9, 236 sqq. (Oedipus), 417 sqq., 454–6 (Teiresias). It is in accordance with this requirement that at 1410–12 Oedipus himself asks to be exiled. But now Creon, who had himself brought Apollo's ruling from Delphi, declares that the sun, rain and light should be protected from the sight of Oedipus, a philosophy very different from Oedipus' own at 1451 in what looks to be a surviving fragment of the original ending. There Oedipus regards Cithaeron as the right place for him to be. It was the place where Teiresias had predicted he would soon be: τάχα 421, cf. τάχιστα 1436. Creon, however, orders that Oedipus be confined to the palace to be looked after by τοῖς ἐν γένει – though just who they may be we have as yet no idea; and how exactly piety (εὐσεβῶς 1431) is best served by locking up Oedipus with his all too closely related children also taxes the imagination.

The cause of all this confusion is the need to bring the plot of *Oedipus Rex* into conformity with the plot of the later play, *Oedipus at Colonus*, presumably on an occasion when the two plays were produced together – possibly with *Antigone* as a third.

The interpolation betrays itself almost as soon as Creon enters. The action of the play is all but over, and when Creon appears once again after his long absence we may reasonably expect him to usher things to the conclusion which has been so long and so often predicted. What ensues is a series of surprises. He does not comment on his sister's suicide, Oedipus's self-blinding, or – less important in view of 1418 – the transfer of power to himself. Suddenly we find him addressing nameless attendants without so much as a ὑμεῖς δέ to mark the transition, and he includes in that address uncalled-for censorious remarks about their apparent lack of respect for what he is pleased to call the θνητῶν γένεθλα.

1427 τό: relative pronoun, like τῶν at 1379.

μήτε: not οὔτε because the ἄγος is *of such a kind* that the land will not receive it.

1428 ὄμβρος: Empedocles uses ὄμβρος for 'water' (frg. 21.5; 73.1; 98.2; 100.12; 100.18 D–K^{11}) and it is often assumed that the author is following his example here. But more likely the trio is of earth, *rain* and sunlight, which together give healthy life to the crops and livestock, a life recently blighted by the plague which his ἄγος has caused.

1430 μάλισθ': with εὐσεβῶς ἔχει.

1432 ἐλπίδος μ' ἀπέσπασας: The verb ἀπέσπασας, 'torn away from', is oddly forcible, and does not appear to suit the context, one of appreciation of kindly condescension. It is more at home at *El.* 809 where Electra says that the death of Orestes has torn from her her only surviving hopes. And what 'hope' was Oedipus entertaining anyway? The only hope remaining to Oedipus, one now torn away from him by Creon, was the hope to be allowed to roam freely on Cithaeron. Perhaps the line was originally coined to suit some such context. Taking ἐλπίδος as 'expectation', or as Jebb puts it, 'uneasy foreboding', would still leave us with the problem of the over-vigorous verb.

1433 ἄριστος ἐλθών: if it were not that Creon's actual coming provided the reason for Oedipus' remark at 1432, i.e. 'by coming here, you, noblest of men, to one utterly worthless', we might reasonably regard ἐλθών in the phrase ἄριστος ἐλθών as another superfluous word of motion (515n.), at best a token of recognition that Creon had used ἐλήλυθα at 1422, for the adjective ἄριστος is clearly not one that would normally accompany a full-blooded verb of motion, and ἄριστος πρὸς κάκιστον can in itself mean 'a noble like you *vis-à-vis* a wretch like me'. The ideas of physical motion and moral condescension are merged.

1434 πρὸς σοῦ: 'from your standpoint' and so 'in your interests'. Similarly *Trach.* 479 τὸ πρὸς κείνου 'his side of things'.

1436 cf. 1410–11.

1437 μηδενὸς προσήγορος: the genitive μηδενός stands by analogy with alpha-private adjectival constructions. Similarly *Phil.* 1066–7 οὐδὲ σοῦ φωνῆς ἔτι | γενήσομαι προσφθεγκτός, as if ἀπροσήγορός σου, ἀπρόσφθεγκτός σου. There is no such thing as a genitive of agent without a preposition: with Page's δίδαγμα *El.* 344 is not in evidence, and at *El.* 1214 οὕτως ἄτιμός εἰμι τοῦ τεθνηκότος the usual translations are wrong. The sense is not 'dishonoured of (sc. by) the dead', but 'without rights or privileges in the dead man's concerns'.

1440 πᾶσ': Phoebus' oracle was *all for* getting rid of me.

1441 What the god had ordered (cf. 96–8) was the expulsion of 'the unholy one'. With hindsight we know that 'the unholy one' was also 'the parricide' and 'me'. Compare 1382–3n.

1444 οὕτως: better taken with the verb than with ἀθλίου.

1445 Creon's remark is unsympathetic, and not justified by anything we have seen in the play.

1446 καὶ σοί γ': the καὶ ... γε is progressive (Denniston *GP²* 157), but progressive from what? A line, or several lines, seems to have fallen out at the start of Oedipus' reply. The mixture of tenses in the two verbs, present and future, is anomalous, and cannot be covered by any conventional explanation.

1447–57 With the exception of 1454, these lines may well be survivors from the authentic end of the play as Sophocles wrote it. There is nothing against them stylistically, and they coincide with our expectations in a way that Creon's 1424 sqq. conspicuously do not. In particular the loose end of Jocasta's suicide is tied up.

1447 τῆς μὲν κατ' οἴκους: her name is unspoken.
αὐτός: with θέλεις, not with θοῦ: on which word see 545–6n.

1449–50 'Let this city of my fathers never be thought right to have me as one of its inhabitants while I live.' The sentence is awkward in English, less so in Greek, where ἐμοῦ can go directly with ἀξιωθήτω, and ζῶντος and οἰκητοῦ τυχεῖν fill out the sense epexegetically. For the usage '*A* is worthy of *B* where logic requires '*B* is worthy of *A*, cf. Eur. *El.* 252 σκαφεύς τις ἢ βουφορβὸς ἄξιος δόμων, where the real sense is that the *house* is worthy of a labourer or herdsman as occupant.

1451 ἔα: a monosyllable, as at *Ant.* 95, *Oed. Col.* 1192.
κλήιζεται: 'where the mountain called Cithaeron is situated', like Pindar, *Nem.* 9.41 ἔνθ' Ἀρείας πόρον ἄνθρωποι καλέοισι, 'where the well-known ford of Areia is situated'. Cf. 'Simonides' xvi 3–4 (=*FGE* 742–3) ὑπ' Εὐβοίαι καί Παλίωι, ἔνθα καλεῖται | ἁγνᾶς Ἀρτέμιδος τοξοφόρου τέμενος; Hom. *Il.* 11.757; Eur. *Ion* 11–13; Cratinus frg. 7; Xen. *Hell.* 5.1.10 – all these with ἔνθα.

1452 οὑμὸς ... οὗτος: this mountain of mine: cf. 1088–91, 1391–3. The presence of the definite article rules out any idea of taking οὑμός as predicative.

1453 κύριον: it is difficult to find a single English adjective which will do full justice to this word. LSJ offer 'authoritative', 'decisive', 'valid' and 'appointed' among their various translations. Since the exposure of the infant was an *ex tempore* measure, we cannot but see some bitterness in the speaker's choice of epithet.

1454 That this line is spurious is proved by the direct connection of καίτοι τοσοῦτόν γ' οἶδα in 1455 with 1453. 'Let me live on the mountains, on this famous Cithaeron of mine which my mother and father set to be my grave while I was alive – yet this much I know, that neither disease nor anything else could have destroyed me, for I would never have been saved as I was dying, unless for something terrible.' The 'something terrible' is of course what *Oedipus Rex* is all about, the μέγιστα κακά of 1180. 1454 has been inserted by an interpolator who thought he saw a chance for spicing up the text with a touch of dramatic irony, but the idea that turning out the helpless king onto Mt Cithaeron would make Laius and Jocasta his killers after all is highly artificial.

1456 ἐπί: on condition of.

1457 τωι: not τῶι.

1458–60 Interpolation had begun almost as soon as Creon entered at 1422, but some genuine Sophocles had survived to be turned to account by the interpolator. But now everything from this point on to the end of the play is spurious, and the voice of Sophocles is heard no more. We begin with the unexpected appearance of the children, important figures in *Oedipus at Colonus*, but persons whose very existence in *Oedipus Rex* has been surrounded by all sorts of problems (see on 261, 425, 1247–50, 1375–6). The male children are swiftly dealt with (1459–61). It is the girls who are paraded before us now, much as they are in the equally interpolated end of Aeschylus' *Seven Against Thebes*.

1458 ὅπηιπερ: cf. Plato, *Apol.* 19a τοῦτο μὲν ἴτω ὅπηι τῶι θεῶι φίλον.

1460 προσθῆι: take upon yourself.

1463–4 It is strange that Oedipus should stress how close he was to his daughters by pointing out that he never sat at a separate table. Two ideas seem to be confused: first, one expects either 'their table was never set apart from me', or 'my table was never set apart from them', not the unhappy amalgam 'For whom my dining table was never set apart without me'. Second, on to this contorted sentence is piled another, telling us that Oedipus never ate without giving his daughters some of the same food as himself – as if they were pets. The very word βορά is used of human bodies serving as dog-food at *Antigone* 30, fish food at [Aesch.] *Prom. Vinct.* 583, and is never used of delicacies such as princesses might expect. At Aesch. *Pers.* 490 the word is used of people starved of anything they could eat even as animals, and at Soph. *Phil.* 274 'rags and a bit of something edible' is Philoctetes' contemptuous description of the charity handed out to him by people passing through. Lastly the construction 'a table of food' is just about unknown in classical Greek.

1465 τῶνδ': the layout of 1462–6 suggests that τοῖν (the correct form of the feminine, not ταῖν as we find it in Zr) in 1466 is correct, and is resumptive of the whole long clause οἷν . . . μετειχέτην. If it were not for this, one would readily accept Schneidewin's τώδ for the lack-lustre τῶνδ here.

1465–7 'Look after them, and for preference let me touch them' is perilously close to nonsense.

1468 A bacchiac ($\smile--$) here and at 1471, 1475, interrupts the iambic sequence. Cf. *Trach.* 865 τί φημί; *Phil.* 750 ἴθ, ὦ παῖ, 785 παπαῖ φεῦ, 804 τί φήις, παῖ; and perhaps also 736 ἰὼ θεοί; *Oed. Col.* 318 τάλαινα, 1271 τί σιγᾶις. O. Taplin, *Proc. Camb. Phil. Soc.* n.s. 23 (1977) 124, lumps together with these exclamations and stereotyped phrases the quite different προσέρπει of *Phil.* 787, deleted by Dawe in 1968 as a stage direction, and omitted, as it later turned out, by two not particularly closely related manuscripts. ξύνες δέ at *Trach.* 868 is in a class of its own since it leads straight on to the next line without a break.

1469–70   γονῆι γενναῖε: probably less pleonastic than we feel it to be. At Menander, *Theophoroumene* frg. 1. 14–15 Sandbach εὐγενής is followed by σφόδρα γενναῖος. δοκοῖμ': an unusual form, but cf. *Phil.* 1044.

1472   οὐ δὴ . . . που: this, and πρὸς θεῶν, express incredulity. Surely that can't be my daughters that I hear crying? The girls had probably entered with Creon at 1422, but only now does a sob betray their presence.

1474   τὰ φίλτατ': cf. *El.* 1208, *Phil.* 434, *Oed. Col.* 1110 for this phrase used for 'dearest one(s)' or 'darling(s)'. Also Aesch. *Pers.* 851; Eur. *Med.* 16, *Herc.* 514.

ἐκγόνοιν: constituent genitive, the dear things which are my children. The prevailing manuscript spelling ἐγγόνοιν may have been what the interpolator wrote himself, in the sense ἐκγ-. Some inscriptions have this spelling, but it does not predominate: see Threatte, *GAI* 1581–3.

1475   λέγω τι 'am I right?' Cf. 1140–1.

1477   The manuscript variants make it difficult to say exactly how we are to take this sentence. Our choice lies between: (1) Recognizing (i.e. foreseeing) your present pleasure, the pleasure which came over you just now. This assumes that πάλαι refers to the immediate past (see 1161 n.), and that ἥ σ' ἔχει, conjectured by Hermann and found in one manuscript, is correct. (2) Recognizing some time ago the pleasure that occupies you now. This construes πάλαι with γνούς, and would continue the self-congratulatory note of ἐγὼ γάρ εἰμ' ὁ πορσύνας τάδε. (3) Recognizing your present pleasure, the pleasure you felt in the past. This is the version favoured by most editors. Another choice that has to be made is between ἥν εἶχες and ἥ σ' εἶχε (the metre actually requires εἶχεν). In general Greek prefers to speak of emotions holding people rather than people holding emotions.

1478   ἀλλ': the first word in the messenger's benediction at 929. Aesch. *Cho.* 1063 also begins ἀλλ' εὐτυχοίης.

τῆσδε τῆς ὁδοῦ: there are two problems here: (1) The construction of the genitive, which is supposed to be causal, cannot be explained; the alleged parallels are disposed of in the *Rheinisches Museum* article referred to in the note on 1424–30. (2) ὁδοῦ is supposed to mean 'because of this sending, or conducting, here of the children'. No such active meaning of the word is known.

1481   ἀδελφάς: for the noun used as an adjective with χείρ cf. Aesch. *Sept.* 811. Similarly παρθένους γε χεῖρας Eur. *Ion* 270; ἀδελφῆι χειρί is also read by some editors at *Suppl.* 402. ὡς = 'to' can only be justified by saying that 'my hands' is equivalent to 'me'. The supposed parallel of *Trach.* 366 has been eliminated in many reconstructions of the text. The mention that the hands that will caress will be those of a brother was described by Fräulein Eicken-Iselin, a lady who perceived the deficiencies of the end of the play with a remarkable clarity of vision, in a doctoral thesis published in Basel in 1942, as 'revolting'.

1482–4 προυξένησαν: the interpolator has availed himself of the developed use of this verb in later and more prosaic Greek, where it can mean simply 'cause' or 'bring it about that'. The original idea is of a πρόξενος who uses his good offices to achieve a particular result. One can see from *Trach.* 726 ἐλπίς, ἥτις καὶ θράσος τι προξενεῖ how the original idea might give rise to its further extension. If the line before us had been the authentic work of Sophocles, we would have the unwelcome sense 'Hands, whose good offices have brought it about that my formerly bright eyes see like this!' (i.e. do not see at all: cf. 1273–4n.). Problematic too is the grammar of the infinitive ὁρᾶν as dependent on προυξένησαν.

The fact that the eyes were formerly bright does not prevent the interpolator from continuing with οὔθ' ὁρῶν when describing Oedipus' marriage with Jocasta. He does, however, know the Sophoclean mannerism of scanning the second syllable of ὑμίν as short (cf. 39n.); indeed in his anxiety to stress the closeness of the rapport between Oedipus and the children he uses the ethic dative so scanned twice, here and just two lines earlier.

1485 ἀροτήρ: the same point is made at 1497–8. ἀροτήρ is a conjecture by Herwerden for the manuscripts' flat and obvious πατήρ. Not seeing what he was doing, and not learning of it in any other way, Oedipus, as has now been disclosed (ἐφάνθην), sowed his seed in the very place where the seed from which he sprang himself had been sown. οὔθ' ὁρῶν οὔθ' ἱστορῶν suits the *action* of sowing seed much better than the *fact* of being father to Antigone and Ismene – which no one had ever doubted. If πατήρ is to be defended, all the stress must fall on ἔνθεν αὐτὸς ἡρόθην, and ἔνθεν has to take the strain of meaning 'by the woman from whom'. The metaphor of ἀροτήρ is less unusual than we might suppose: cf. ἄλοκες at 1211 and see Sandbach on Men. *Perik.* 1014.

ἔνθεν αὐτός: but αὐτὸς ἔνθεν at 1179 (ἔνθεν αὐτός O).

1486 προσβλέπειν γὰρ οὐ σθένω: it is not clear how this short sentence fits into its context. There are few attractions in the explanation of Longo that weeping is what Oedipus' eyes are doing because their other function, of sight, is no longer operative; or of Groeneboom, that Oedipus weeps because he cannot give the children the consolation of his glance. More probably γάρ is anticipatory: I weep for you, intuitively – for I cannot actually see you – understanding what the rest of your life will be like. Such a sentence will not satisfy an implacable logician, but persons who have just pierced their eyeballs after discovering they are guilty of parricide and incest should be allowed a certain latitude of expression.

1487 νοούμενος: a unique occurrence of the middle for active participle. But Sophocles himself does the same thing with ποθουμέναι at *Trach.* 103: see further Pearson on frg. 858.2, who lists a number of comparable examples.

Arguments can be found for both τὰ λοιπὰ τοῦ πικροῦ and for τὰ πικρὰ τοῦ λοιποῦ. Since what Oedipus apprehends are the πικρά which he goes on to enumerate, the various unpleasant things which will come the girls' way in the rest of their lives, it seems better to accept that minority reading rather than τὰ λοιπὰ τοῦ πικροῦ, which would have Oedipus foreseeing the future of a life described without further argument as πικρός. πικροῦ forms a slightly easier introduction to the οἷον clause following, and it does have superior manuscript support, but there is no real objection to 'the rest of your life as you will have to live it'.

1488 βιῶναι ... πρὸς ἀνθρώπων: the extraordinary grammar is supposed to give a cross between 'living a life' and 'gaining a livelihood from'. Appeals to *Trach.* 935 ἄκουσα πρὸς τοῦ θηρὸς ἔρξειεν τάδε are of little avail, for there the change of a single letter to give ἁλοῦσα makes the construction vanish, and the line is in any case suspected of being one of the play's numerous doublets. The hand of the interpolator here at *O.T.* 1488 is betrayed by something else too: the very word βιῶναι is ill chosen (as βορά was at 1463). The verb is not found in tragedy except at Eur. *Alc.* 784: 'No mortal knows if tomorrow he will be alive' i.e. still drawing breath. See, however, *TrGF* 1 566a.

1490 κεκλαυμέναι: for the perfect participle cf. Aesch. *Cho.* 457, 687, 731, and compare Homer's δεδακρύσαι, -νται *Il.* 16.7, 22.491; *Od.* 20.204.

1491 ἀντὶ τῆς θεωρίας: the writing is clumsy: 'What festivals will you go to from which you will not come home in tears instead of seeing the festival!' Then the ἀλλά sentence immediately afterwards involves a usage which Denniston (*GP²* 241) can parallel only from prose, almost exclusively Plato and Aristotle.

1493 παραρρίψει: the dice-throwing metaphor, used several times in tragedy. 'Who will take the risk?'

1494 †ἐμοῖς†: the scholia show clearly what the expected sense is: ἃ γονεῦσιν ὑμῶν καὶ ὑμῖν ὁμοῦ. Reproaches levelled at 'my parents' = Antigone's and Ismene's grand-parents are not an obvious hazard to be expected by a potential bridegroom. Her-werden's τοῖσί τε gives the expected sense.

1498–9 τῶν ἴσων ... ὧνπερ: poetic plural, 'the same ... as'. Jocasta is meant.

1500–1 κᾆτα τίς γαμεῖ: the words sound as if they introduced a new topic, but the theme of the daughters' marriage has already been spoken of at 1492–5. In the next line δηλαδή is a word with dubious connections: at Eur. *Andr.* 856 it was deleted by Triclinius, and it finds no place in Kovacs' edition. *Iph. Aul.* 1366 has it in a ludicrous exchange in a passage all of which is thought to be spurious. The only remaining parallel is *Or.* 789, where scholars tell us it is a colloquialism – hardly the tone here.

1502 χέρσους: barren.

1503–14 All of this section, in which Oedipus entrusts his children to Creon, is ignored by the new regent.

1505 δύ' ὄντε: the pair of us. The expression is used in a perfunctory way. We may contrast the way it is effectively exploited at *Trach.* 539 καὶ νῦν δύ' οὖσαι μίμνομεν μιᾶς

ὑπὸ | χλαίνης ὑπαγκάλισμα, of two women in one man's embrace or Eur. *Ion* 518
σὺ δ' εὖ φρόνει γε, καὶ δύ ὄντ' εὖ πράξομεν, 'you behave yourself and we'll both be all right.'

The conjecture περιίδης for παρίδης is widely accepted, though περιοράω is not found in tragedy, and περι before a vowel in iambics is unknown. ἴδης by itself will give the required sense: cf. Aesch. *Suppl.* 423f.; Eur. *Or.* 746, *Hyps.* frg. 757.16; but what we are then to do with παρ- is anyone's guess. πάτερ was Jackson's (=πέρ), a piece of schmaltz from which the interpolator might not have recoiled.

1506 †ἐγγενεῖς†: we need a third predicative adjective to go with πτωχάς and ἀνάνδρους. Schneidewin's ἐκστεγεῖς is far from thrilling, but it has no good competitors. The alternative is to make ἐγγενεῖς mean 'since they are, after all, part of your family', and Meineke's addition of γ' after the adjective goes some way to providing that meaning.

1507 ἐξισώσης: the advice not to 'put the girls on the same level as my own misfortunes', as well as being less than perfectly expressed (contrast 424–5), is so unexpectedly specific that it is best explained by the assumption that the person who wrote it knew that in *Oedipus at Colonus* at least one of the girls would be on the same level of misery as her father.

1509 Cf. ἐρήμους δεσπότας τοὐμὸν μέρος 'masters left on their own so far as I am concerned' at Eur. *Hcld.* 678.

1512 εὔχεσθ' ἐμέ: this reading was intended by L. van Deventer, *De interpolationibus quibusdam in Soph. trag.* (Leiden 1851), and is supported by εὔχεσθέ με now found in the manuscripts D Xr; the rest have the dative μοι.

1513 Oedipus asks his daughters to pray that he shall live wherever the opportunities of the moment permit. καιρός has played a large part in his life.

1514 Although the subject of κυρῆσαι is the same as the subject of the leading verb εὔχεσθε, ὑμᾶς, not ὑμεῖς, is written. It would be officious to switch constructions when ἐμὲ ... ζῆν had preceded, and both limbs of the sentence expand τοῦτ'. The construction is normal when sentences contain an expressed or implied contrast between subjects of the infinitive, and one of them is also the subject of the main verb. From the examples in K–G II 30–1 we may cite Dem. 24.8 βουλοίμην δ' ἂν ἐμέ τε τυχεῖν ὧν βούλομαι, τοῦτόν τε παθεῖν ὧν ἄξιός ἐστιν.

φυτεύσαντος: the word carries no special emphasis here, but 'the father that begot you' did so in very unusual circumstances, and the interpolator does not shrink from touching the exposed nerve.

1515–30 From now until the end of the play the metre used is the trochaic tetrameter, which is not otherwise found in tragedy between 472 B.C. (Aesch. *Pers.*) and 415 B.C. (Eur. *Tro.*) if we discount, as we should, the end of *Agam.* (458 B.C.): on this see *Lexis*

22 (2004) 117–25. But 'otherwise' may be misleading, for the common assumption that *Oedipus Rex* is parodied in Aristophanes' *Acharnians* (425 B.C.) because ὦ πόλις, πόλις appears in both plays (*Oed. Tyr.* 629 and *Ach.* 27), and that therefore 425 B.C. is a *terminus ante quem* has almost nothing to commend it.

1515 ἐξήκεις: 'the point you have reached in weeping is far enough' (Kamerbeek). Cf. *Trach.* 1157–8 ἐξήκεις δ' ἵνα | φανεῖς ὁποῖος ὢν ἀνὴρ ἐμὸς καλῆι.

δακρῦων: participle.

1516 πειστέον: the verbal adjective is here used in passive sense: not 'you must persuade' but 'I must obey'. The identical use at *Phil.* 994, Ar. *Pax* 218. See also 628n. By punctuating πειστέον, κεἰ μηδὲν ἡδύ; as a question we avoid the clash whereby Oedipus gives unconditional assent here, while attempting to lay down conditions in the very next line.

καιρῶι: cf. 875, 1513nn. The dative may stand for ἐν καιρῶι, or it may be possessive: cf. καιρῶι πάντα πρόσεστι καλά, Page, *FGE* 1839.

1517 ἐφ' οἷς: the conditions on which. Creon's reply, 'you will speak, and then, on hearing you, I shall know' is abject line-filling. But worse is to come. (There is more verve behind the formally parallel Aesch. *Sept.* 261 λέγοις ἂν ὡς τάχιστα, καὶ τάχ' εἴσομαι.)

1518 μ' ὅπως πέμψεις: see that you send me away. The construction is not what the context had led us to expect, but is immediately intelligible.

τοῦ θεοῦ: emphatic position in the word order. It is for the god, not me, to grant your request. The themes of exile and of consulting the god again are broached as if they had not already been discussed at 1436–45.

1519 γ': you mention the god: but the *gods* abhor me.

ἥκω: cf. *Oed. Col.* 1177 ἔχθιστον, ὦναξ, φθέγμα τοῦδ' ἥκει πατρί. This metaphorical use of ἥκω is something like the English 'come' in such a phrase as 'this comes as a shock to me'. Cf. Ar. *Lys.* 352. LSJ's citation *s.v.* 1.5 of *Ai.* 636, *El.* 1201, 'etc.' as justifying a meaning 'to have come to be' seems fanciful.

On hearing the words τοῦ θεοῦ (sc. Apollo) μ' αἰτεῖς δόσιν, Oedipus ought to have replied 'in that case we may proceed at once with my expulsion, since Apollo's wishes in this matter have been well known to every one since you announced them yourself at 96–8, a point you have already conceded at 1442 above, though you immediately tried to fudge the issue there by lapsing into a vague and unsatisfactory bid for extra time'. Instead he begins a sentence with ἀλλά which includes the word ἔχθιστος as if he were giving a reason why Apollo should *not* give him the desired δόσις, and he unnecessarily and confusingly widens the reference from τοῦ θεοῦ to θεοῖς in general.

τοιγαροῦν τεύξηι τάχα: the logic of 'But I come very hateful to the gods' – 'That is precisely why you will soon get your wish' is altogether baffling, though it need not have been if the sentence had been better phrased. Oedipus presumably means 'But

I am hateful to all gods, of whom Apollo is one, and in that case they, and he, are sure to favour my expulsion.' But that is not what he says. Whoever composed these lines has been attracted by the possibility of engineering a neat paradox at 1519, but he has written so elliptically that all we are left with is an exercise in incompetence.

1520   φὴις τάδ' οὖν: 'You mean "yes"?'

1521   ἀφοῦ: see LSJ *s.v.* ἀφίημι B 3, where all the other examples are from prose.

1522   γ': whatever else you must take from me, at least let me keep these girls.

1522–3   At 1511–14 Oedipus had appeared to resign his children to Creon's care in a final farewell. Now he protests at having them taken from him. Creon's response is no less peculiar. First, he uses μὴ βούλου like the latin *noli*, to introduce a prohibition, something which Wackernagel, *VUS* II 261, denies ever occurs with this verb. (1057 is not an exception, even though *noli meminisse* would give the sense.) Second, 'Do not wish to (= do not) command everything *or* in everything' is an exaggerated reaction to a request made by a pitiful blind suppliant. Third, 'the exercises of your power did not accompany your life' doing duty for 'your royal power is now at an end' is so awful as to be inexplicable unless we take into account *O.C.* 839 as its model: μὴ 'πίτασσ' ἃ μὴ κρατεῖς: 'Command not where thou art not master' (Jebb).

As we look back at the interpolated portion we may be struck by the plethora of repetitions: 1421/1423 τὰ/τῶν πάρος; 1435/1443 χρείας; 1413/1444 ἀνδρὸς ἀθλίου; 1410/1432/1472 πρὸς θεῶν; 1439/1443 τί πρακτέον/ δραστέον; and κακός words end 1414, 1421, 1423, 1431, 1457, 1467, 1507.

1524–30   Scholars may have been slow to see that much of 1423 sqq. was spurious, but they were quicker to diagnose interpolation in this tailpiece, and indeed after the articles by F. Ritter in *Philologus* 17 (1861) 422–36 (esp. 424–8) and W. Teuffel in *Rh.M.* 29 (1874) 505–9 there ought to have been no further doubt on the matter. To see how they were manufactured it is only necessary to examine Eur. *Andr.* 100–2, and [Eur.] *Phoen.* 1687–9, 1758–63. Any student of the play who finds himself unable to translate the lines into rational English should draw such comfort as he may from knowing that the present commentator is in a similar plight.

'O inhabitants of the father-land of Thebes, look, this is Oedipus, who understood the famous riddles and was a very powerful man, inasmuch as not with the envy of the citizens, and looking on chances, to what a great wave of terrible disaster he has come, with the result that being a mortal one looks at that final day, looking closely one calls no man happy until he has crossed the end of his life without undergoing anything painful.'

But behind this demented balbutience we can at least discern what the moral of *Oedipus Rex* was to one aspiring if ill-starred versifier. It may seem to us that the moral drawn pays no regard to the many curious and unique features of the play before us, or indeed of the Oedipus myth in any shape or form. But we should not be too quick in our condemnation. Aeschylus, *Seven Against Thebes* 720–91, tells the story of

Laius' disobedience of the oracle, and the incest of the parricidal Oedipus. But even to Aeschylus the moral to be drawn is how even the most admired and successful of men can come crashing down in ruin. 'For who among men did the gods and those who shared his hearth and the thronging assemblies of the people hold in as much honour as they then honoured Oedipus, who took away from the land the pestilence that snatched men away?' (772–7.) Cf. *Oed. Tyr.* 1186ff., where we have the authentic verdict of Sophocles, or at least the verdict passed by an authentic Sophoclean Chorus.

It is to be assumed that in the original this play ended with a tailpiece in anapaestic metre.

APPENDIX ON LYRIC METRES

‐ = a long syllable
◡ = a short syllable
◡̆ = a short syllable standing where the metre requires a long one (*brevis in longo*)

◡̆ can only occur at the end of a metrical period. A strophe or antistrophe may contain several periods. Each period consists of one or more cola, and each colon consists of one or more metra. Another sign of the end of a period can be hiatus, or catalexis (the suppression of the final or penultimate syllable of a metron).

These principles can be subjected to much further refinement and modification. But for our immediate purposes it is enough to note that in this edition each colon is printed on a separate line (which is normal practice), and indentation is used whenever it is certain that period-end does *not* occur at the end of the previous line, e.g. if the end of a colon does not coincide with the end of a word, but the word runs on into the next colon (colon-caesura). The reason for adopting this practice is that it is much easier to determine objectively where period-end does not occur than where it does.

Glossary of metrical terms employed

Dactyl	‐◡͡◡
Spondee	‐ ‐
Anapaest	◡͡◡ ‐
Paroemiac enoplian	◡◡ ‐ ◡◡ ‐ ◡◡ ‐ ‐ or ◡ ‐ ◡◡ ‐ ◡◡ ‐ ‐
Iambic	◡̄ ‐ ◡ ‐
Cretic	‐ ◡ ‐
Bacchiac	◡ ‐ ‐
Lekythion	‐ ◡ ‐ ◡ ‐ ◡ ‐ (i.e. cretic + iambic)
Ithyphallic	‐ ◡ ‐ ◡ ‐ ‐ (i.e. cretic + bacchiac)
Trochee	‐ ◡ ‐ ◡̄
Ionic	◡ ◡ ‐ ‐

Aeolic metra: ○ ○ denotes the so-called Aeolic base, i.e. ‐ ‐, ‐◡, ◡ ‐, but not ◡◡. Responsion between different kinds of Aeolic base is permitted. The choriamb ‐ ◡ ◡ ‐ is the most distinctive feature of this metre.

Glyconic	○ ○ ‐ ◡ ◡ ‐ ◡ ‐
Pherecratean	○ ○ ‐ ◡ ◡ ‐ ‐
Telesillean	⋈ ‐ ◡ ◡ ‐ ◡ ‐
Reizianum	⋈ ‐ ◡ ◡ ‐ ‐
Dodrans A	‐ ◡ ◡ ‐ ◡ ‐
(Dodrans B	‐ ⋈ ‐ ◡ ◡ ‐ is not found in this play)

204

Choriambic dimeter A $-\cup\cup - \quad \cup-\cup-$
Choriambic dimeter B $-\times-\times \quad -\cup\cup-$

Dactylo-epitrites:

D $-\cup\cup-\cup\cup-$

e $-\cup-$ (i.e. a cretic)

E $-\cup-\times-\cup-$ (i.e. e $\times$ e)

d¹ $-\cup\cup-$ (i.e. a choriamb, regarded in this metre as a shortened form of D)

The syllable which links elements D to e can be either long or short (syllaba anceps), but long is much the more common, as it is in Pindar, about half of whose odes are written in this metre.

Dochmiac $\times \cup\cup \cup\cup \times \cup\cup$.

In Greek tragedy as a whole the most frequent manifestations of this metre are in the forms $\cup--\cup-$ and $\cup \curlywedge -\cup-$. It will be seen from the metrical schemes below that the dochmiac is often subject to resolution of its long syllables, so that it can even appear as eight short syllables in a row, i.e. $\cup \cup\cup \cup\cup \cup \cup\cup$.

The first chorus (parodos)

151–158 = 159–167: mainly dactyls, but including one iambic dimeter, and one paroemiac enoplian, which in the strophe takes the shape of that part of a dactylic hexameter which follows the third foot caesura $-\cup \mid \cup$, and in the antistrophe the shape of that part of a dactylic hexameter which follows the alternative caesura $- \mid \smile\smile$. The metrical shortening of μοι (163) and πόλει (165) before open vowels in the following verse is proof that the lines are in synaphea, i.e. regarded as continuous with no metrical pause at the end of the line. This is normal with dactylic sequences in Sophocles. Note that the punctuation following πόλει does not invalidate this metrical law.

151a/159a	$-\cup\cup \quad -\cup\cup \quad -\cup\cup \quad -\cup\cup$	}	dactylic hexameter
151b/159b	$-\cup\cup \quad --$	}	dactylic hexameter
152/160	$--\cup- \quad \cup-\cup-$		iambic dimeter
153a/161a	$-\underline{\cup\cup}-\cup\cup \quad -\cup\cup \quad -\cup\cup$	}	dactylic hexameter
153b/161b	$-\cup\cup \quad --$	}	dactylic hexameter
154/162	$\overline{\cup}-\cup\cup -\cup\cup --$		paroemiac enoplian
155/163	$-\cup\cup \quad -\cup\cup \quad -\cup\cup \quad -\cup\cup$		dactylic tetrameter
156/164	$-\cup\cup \quad -\cup\cup \quad -- \quad -\cup\cup$	}	dactylic hexameter
157/165	$-\cup\cup \quad -\cup\cup$	}	dactylic hexameter
158a/166	$-\cup\cup \quad -\cup\cup \quad -\cup\cup \quad -\cup\cup$	}	dactylic hexameter
158b/167	$-\cup\cup \quad --$	}	dactylic hexameter

168–177 = 179–189: the same elements as before, but mixed in different proportions. Notwithstanding what was said above there is metrical pause between the two dactylic lines 187 and 188, since at the end of 187 there is a short syllable standing where a long is required. In 177 θεοῦ is scanned as a monosyllable by synizesis. The word is sometimes so treated in iambic trimeters too.

168/179	–⏑⏑ ⏑ ⏑⏑ ⏑–⏑–	iambic dimeter
169/180	–⏑⏑ ⏑ ⏕ ⏑–⏑–	iambic dimeter
170/181	⏑⏑–⏑⏑–⏑⏑–⏒	paroemiac enoplian
171/182	–⏑⏑ –⏑⏑ –⏑⏑ –⏑⏑	dactylic tetrameter
172/184	⏒ –⏑⏑ –⏑⏑ –⏑⏑ –⏒	anceps + dactylic tetrameter
174/185	⏑–⏑– ⏑⏑–⏑⏑–⏑⏑–⏑̇	iambic + paroemiac enoplian
175/187	––⏑– –⏑⏑ –⏑⏑ –⏑⏑ –⏓	iambic + dactylic tetrameter
176/188	–⏑⏑ –⏑⏑ –⏑⏑ –⏑⏑	dactylic tetrameter
177/189	––⏑– ⏑––	iambic dimeter catalectic (i.e. iambic + bacchiac)

190–202 = 203–215: with the exception of another paroemiac, everything here is built around iambics, cretics, and bacchiacs, with some resolution of long syllables into two shorts. In 215 θεόν is again monosyllabic.

190/203	⏑ ⏔ ⏑– ⏑⏑⏑ –	iambic + cretic
191/204	–⏑–⏑–⏑–	lekythion
192/205	⏑ ⏕⏑ ⏔ ⏑ ⏕⏑ – ⏑––	iambic trimeter catalectic
193/206	⏑–⏑– ⏑–⏑– ⏑–⏑–	iambic trimeter
194/207	⏒⏕⏑– –⏑–	iambic + cretic
195/208	⏑⏑ ⏑ ⏕⏑––	ithyphallic
196/209	––⏑⏑–⏑⏑––	paroemiac enoplian
197/210	–⏑–⏑–⏒	ithyphallic
198/211	⏒–⏑– ⏑–⏑–	iambic dimeter
199/212	–⏑–⏑–⏑–	lekythion
200/213	⏑–– –⏑–	bacchiac + cretic
201/214	–⏑–⏑–⏑–	lekythion
202/215	––⏑ ⏑⏑ ⏑–⏑– ⏑––	iambic trimeter catalectic

The second chorus (first stasimon)

463–472 = 473–482: mainly Aeolic, but with two lines of anapaests, and a sprinkling of iambics and bacchiacs.

463/473	⏑–⏑– –⏑⏑–	iambic + choriamb
464/474	⏑–⏑– ⏑–⏓	iambic + bacchiac
465/475	–––– –⏑⏑–	choriambic dimeter B
466/476	⏑–⏑– ⏑–⏒	iambic + bacchiac
467/477	––⏑⏑–⏑–	telesillean
468a/478a	––⏑⏑–⏑–	telesillean
468b/478b	⏑–⏑⏑––	reizianum
469/479	⏑⏑– ⏑⏑– ⏑⏑– ––	anapaestic dimeter

470/480   ⏑⏑ –   ⏑⏑ –   ⏑⏑ –   ‿‿ –   anapaestic dimeter
471/481   – –⏑⏑ – –   reizianum
472/482   –⏑ ⏑⏑ ⏑– –   ithyphallic

484–496 = 498–511: choriambs and ionics, some syncopated, i.e. 'knocked together'
so that a syllable falls out, or catalectic. At 490 double syncopation has taken place:
ᴧᴧ– –   ⏑⏑ – –. It is because of the uniform surrounding metrical context that we
do not describe this line as a reizianum, or treat the – – as a spondee.

484/498   –⏑⏑–   –⏑⏑–   –⏑⏑–   –⏑⏑–   choriambic tetrameter
485/500   –⏑⏑–   –⏑⏑–   –⏑⏑–   –⏑⏑–   choriambic tetrameter
486/502   ⏑⏑– –   ⏑⏑– –   ⏑⏑– –   ⏑⏑–   ionic tetrameter catalectic
488/503   ⏑⏑– –   ⏑⏑–   ionic dimeter catalectic
490/504   – –   ⏑⏑– –   ionic dimeter syncopated
491/505   ⏑⏑– –   ⏑⏑– –   ⏑⏑– –   ⏑⏑– –   ionic tetrameter
492/507   ⏑⏑–   ⏑⏑– –   ionic dimeter syncopated
493/508   ⏑⏑– –   ⏑⏑–   ionic dimeter catalectic
494/509   ⏑⏑–   ⏑⏑– –   ionic dimeter syncopated
495/510   ⏑⏑– –   ⏑⏑– –   ⏑⏑–   ionic trimeter catalectic
496/511   ⏑⏑–   ⏑⏑– –   ⏑⏑–   ionic trimeter syncopated and
                                             catalectic

The first kommos

649–667 = 678–696: the only new element here is the dochmiac.

649–650/   ⏑–⏑–   –⏑–   –⏑–   –⏑–   iambic + cretic trimeter
  678–9
651/680   ⏑ –⏑–   ⏒–⏑–   iambic dimeter
652/681   ⏑–⏑–   –⏑–   iambic + cretic
653/682   –⏑–   –⏑–   ⏑–⏑–   cretic dimeter + iambic
655/684   – –⏑–   – –⏑–   ⏑–⏑–   iambic trimeter
656/685   ⏑ ⏑⏑–⏑–   –⏑⏑–⏑–   dochmiac dimeter
657/686   ⏒⏑⏑–⏑–   ⏑––⏑–   dochmiac dimeter
658/687   ⏒–⏑–   –⏑⏑⏑⏑–   – –⏑–   iambic trimeter
659/688   – –⏑–   ⏒–⏑–   – –⏑⏑   iambic trimeter
660/689   – –   – –⏑–   ⏑–⏑⏑   spondee + iambic dimeter
661/690   –⏑⏑ ⏑⏑ ⏑ ⏑⏑ ⏑ ⏑⏑ ⏑ ⏑⏑   dochmiac dimeter
662/692   ⏑– –⏑–   ⏑– –⏑–   dochmiac dimeter
665/694   –⏑–   –⏑–   –⏑–   cretic trimeter
666/695   ⏑– –   –⏑–   ⏑–⏑–   bacchiac + cretic + iambic
667/696   ⏑– –   –⏑–   ⏑– –   bacchiac + cretic + bacchiac

The third chorus (second stasimon)

863–871 = 873–882: no new elements

863/873	– – ∪ – – ∪ – ∪ – ∪ –	iambic trimeter syncopated
864/874	– – ∪ – – – ∪ –	iambic dimeter
865/875	⤩ – ∪ – ⤩ – ∪ – ∪ – ⤨	iambic trimeter catalectic
866/876	– ∪ ∪ ∪ – ∪ ∪ –	cretic + choriamb
867/877	∪ ∪ ∪ ∪ – – ∪ – ∪ – –	iambic + cretic + bacchiac
868/878	⌒ – ∪ ∪ – ∪ –	telesillean
869/879	– – ∪ ∪ – ∪ –	telesillean
870/880	∪ – ∪ – ∪ – ∪ ∪ – – ∪ ∪ – – –	iambic + anceps + choriambic dimeter + spondee
871/881	∪ ∪ – – – ∪ ∪ – ∪ – – –	ionic + dodrans A + spondee

883–896 = 897–910: some trochaics appear, and choriambic enoplians. The lekythia could be regarded as trochaic dimeters catalectic.

883/897	– ∪ ∪ ∪ ∪ – ∪ – ∪	trochaic dimeter
884/898	– ∪ – ∪ – ∪ –	lekythion
885/899	⌒ – ∪ ∪ – ∪ – ∪	choriambic enoplian A
886/900	– ∪ – ∪ – ∪ –	lekythion
887/901	⌒ – ∪ ∪ – ∪ – ∪	choriambic enoplian A
888/902	– ∪ – ∪ – ∪ –	lekythion.
889/903	– – ∪ – – – ∪ – ∪ – –	iambic trimeter catalectic
890/904	– – ∪ – – – ∪ –	iambic dimeter
891/905	⤩ – ∪ – – ⤪ ∪ – ∪ – –	iambic trimeter catalectic
892/906	∪ ⌒ ∪ – – ∪ – ∪ – ∪ ⤨	iambic trimeter syncopated
894/907	– ∪ – – – ∪ – –	trochaic dimeter
895/908	– ∪ – – – ∪ – – – ∪ –	trochaic trimeter catalectic
896/910	⌒ – ∪ ∪ – ⤨	reizianum

The fourth chorus (third stasimon)

1086–1097 = 1098–1109: dactylo-epitrites for the most part. The first strophic pair in *Ajax* is almost entirely in this metre, and the first strophic pair in *Trachiniae* has nothing but dactylo-epitrites.

1086/1098	– ∪ ∪ – – ∪ –	d[1] e
1087/1099	∪ – ∪ – – – ∪ ∪	∪ E
1088/1100	– ∪ ∪ – ∪ ∪ –	D
1089/1101	– – ∪ – – – ∪ – – – ∪ –	– E – e
1090/1103	– ∪ – – – ∪ ∪ – ∪ ∪ – – – ∪ –	e – D – e
1091/1104	– ∪ – – – ∪ – –	E –
1092/1105	– ∪ – – – ∪ –	E

1094/1106	– –∪∪–∪∪ –	– D
1095/1107	ⵛ–∪ – ∪ ––	iambic dimeter catalectic
1096–7/1108–9	ⵛ–∪∪–∪– ⵛ–∪– ––	telesillean + iambic + spondee

The fifth chorus (fourth stasimon)

1186–1195 = 1196–1203b: wholly aeolic

1186/1196	– –∪∪–∪–	telesillean
1187/1197	– – –∪∪–ⵛ–	glyconic
1188/1198	– – –∪∪– –	pherecratean
1189/1199a	– –∪∪ –∪–	telesillean
1190/1199b	– – –∪∪–∪–	glyconic
1191/1200a	–ⵛ–∪∪ –∪–	glyconic
1192/1200b	– – –∪∪– –	pherecratean
1193/1201	– – –∪∪ –∪–	glyconic
1194a/1202	ⵎ– –∪∪–∪–	glyconic
1194b/1203a	–ⵛ–∪∪–∪–	glyconic
1195/1203b	– –∪∪– –	reizianum

1204–1212 = 1213–1221: the only new element is the hypodochmiac, i.e a dochmiac of the commonest form ∪––∪–with the first two syllables reversed. 1209b/1218b is a difficult line to analyse. In view of what follows it is best regarded as a headless (acephalous) choriambic dimeter. The same metrical form is found next to a hypodochmiac also at Eur. *Hipp.* 125 = 135.

1204/1213	∪–∪– –∪– ∪–∪–	iambic trimeter syncopated
1205/1214	∪– – ∪∪∪– ∪–∪–	bacchiac + cretic + iambic
1206/1215	∪–∪– ∪–∪–	iambic dimeter
1207/1216	∪– –∪– ∪–∪ⵎ	dochmiac + iambic
1208a/1217a	–∪–∪ ⵎ	hypodochmiac
1208b/1217b	–∪–∪–	hypodochmiac
1209a/1218a	–∪–∪ ⵛ	hypodochmiac
1209b/1218b	∪∪– ∪–∪–	acephalous choriambic dimeter A
1210/1219	–∪∪– ∪–∪–	choriambic dimeter A
1211/1220	–∪∪– ∪–∪–	choriambic dimeter A
1212/1221	–∪∪– –∪– ∪– –	choriamb + cretic + bacchiac

The second kommos

1313/1320 = 1321–1328

1313/1321	∪–∪–	iambic
1314/1322	∪∪∪∪∪ ∪∪ ∪∪∪∪∪ ∪∪	dochmiac dimeter
1315/1323	∪∪–∪– ∪– –ⵛ–	dochmiac dimeter

1316/1324   – –   spondee
1317–20/1325–28   iambic trimeters

1329–1348 = 1349–1368

1329/1349   ⏑ – –⏑ –   ⏑ ⏑⏑–⏑ –   dochmiac dimeter
1330/1350   ⏑⏑⏑⏑⏑ –   ͝⏑⏑ ⏑⏑ ͝⏑⏑   dochmiac dimeter
1332/1352   ⏑–⏑–   ⏑–⏑–   iambic dimeter
1333/1353   ⏑–⏑–   – –   iambic + spondee
1334/1354   ⏑⏑⏑–⏑–   dochmiac
1335/1355   ͝⏑–⏑–   ⏑–⏑–   ⏑–⏑ ͡⏑   iambic trimeter
1336/1356   ⋊–⏑– – –⏑–   iambic dimeter
1337/1357   ͝⏑–⏑– –⏑–   iambic + cretic
1338/1358   –⏑ –⏑ –⏑ –   lekythion
1339/1359   ⏑–⏑– – – ⏑–⏑͝⏑   iambic + spondee + iambic
1340/1360   ͡⏑ ⏑⏑–⏑ ͡⏑⏑ ⏑⏑⏑–⏑ ͡⏑   dochmiac dimeter
1342/1362   ⏑⏑⏑–⏑– –⏑⏑–⏑–   dochmiac dimeter
1345/1365   –⏑⏑–⏑⏑⏑ ⏑⏑⏑–⏑–   dochmiac dimeter
1346/1366   –⏑⏑–⏑–   dochmiac
1347/1367 ⎱
1348/1368 ⎰   iambic trimeters

INDEXES

The reference are to line numbers, unless p. precedes, in which case the reference is to a page in the Introduction.